Young America

Young America

Land, Labor, and the Republican Community

MARK A. LAUSE

University of Illinois Press
Urbana and Chicago

Library of Congress Cataloging-in-Publication Data
Lause, Mark A.
Young America : land, labor, and the Republican community /
Mark A. Lause.
p.   cm.
Includes bibliographical references and index.
ISBN 0-252-02980-1 (cloth : alk. paper)
ISBN 0-252-07230-8 (pbk. : alk. paper)
1. United States—Politics and government—1815–1861.
2. Land reform—United States—History—19th century.
3. Working class—United States—Political activity—History—19th century.
4. Labor movement—United States—History—19th century.
5. Social movements—United States—History—19th century.
6. Radicalism—United States—History—19th century.
7. National Reform Association (U.S.)—History—19th century.
8. Republican Party (U.S. : 1854–)—History—19th century.
9. United States—Social conditions—To 1865.
I. Title.
E415.7.L37   2005
303.48′4′097309034—dc22   2004020462

CONTENTS

Illustrations follow page 46

ACKNOWLEDGMENTS

A number of other historians took time from their other demands on them to read and criticize the manuscript in earlier forms. Although I had no association with him other than my admiration for his work, Eric Foner offered detailed and wise advice about the book. A former colleague from the University of Cincinnati, Zane Miller, made very reasonable observations from the perspective of an urban historian. As well, aspects of the work were presented at conferences of the Organization of American Historians, the Mid-American Conference on History, Georgia Historians' Association, and the Ohio Academy of History, and I benefited greatly from the commentary and reactions. I am also grateful for the valuable input or feedback over many years in one form or another from Jamie Bronstein, Paul Buhle, Roger Horowitz, Reeve Huston, David Montgomery, David R. Roediger, and Franklin Rosemont. The book has drawn from their insight and thoughtfulness.

I dedicate this book to my fellow workers, the historians in the former University College: Janine Hartman, L. J. Andrew Villalon, and particularly Prof. Norman Murdoch. The senior of our quartet, Norman strove to build a faculty of scholar-teachers in an institutional subculture characterized by budget cuts, bureaucratic indifference, and professional inertia. Ignoring the usual priority accorded the "newly minted" Ph.D., he sought to recruit the most published and proven among those experienced historians otherwise struggling to keep their heads above water in the rising pool of migratory academic labor. Doing so resulted in the employment of the other three of us and likely saved my professional life. Institutional restructuring and early retirements have scattered that history faculty, but its fellowship remains unbroken.

The interlibrary loan office of Langsam Library at the University of Cincinnati performed with a skill that eased what is often the most troublesome stage of research. In addition, the staff at the state historical societies of New

York, Ohio, Missouri, and Illinois regularly opened their holdings and expertise to my use, as did the public libraries in New York City, Cincinnati, Chicago, and St. Louis.

Laurie Matheson, Angela Burton, and the editorial staff at the University of Illinois Press have performed an impressive work, patiently advising and assisting in the restoration of what amounted to an important field of work that had been left fallow for years after its initial writing. Their performance has more than lived up to the reputation of the press.

Young America

INTRODUCTION

In America, where the democratic constitution has been established, the communists must make common cause with the party that is utilizing this constitution in the interest of the proletariat and against the bourgeoisie, that is with the agrarian National Reformers.

    —Friedrich Engels, *Principles of Communism*

The Chartists of Great Britain, the Repealers of Ireland, the Republican Associationists of France, and the Communists of Germany—Noble Pioneers of the good time coming! When National Reform for a Free Soil shall be triumphant throughout the world. . . .

    —George Henry Evans, National Reform Association, 1847

    In 1854, residents of Ripon braved the bitter Wisconsin February to protest the bipartisan congressional decision to open the new Kansas Territory to slavery. Their presiding officer at these meetings, Alvan Earl Bovay, persuaded the participants—half of them women—to call for a new party of social reform and to call it "Republican." For decades, even party-sponsored histories acknowledged the humble birth and christening of the "Grand Old Party," although without clearly identifying Ripon as the former socialist community of Ceresco or Bovay as the ex-secretary of the National Reform Association (NRA), already embraced by the Communist League in Europe. Later, veterans of the NRA helped arrange the first American publication of the league's "Communist Manifesto," in which Karl Marx and Friedrich Engels again reaffirmed their affinity for Bovay's organization.[1]

    Since that time, the specter of National Reform has haunted a crucial period of American history. Scholars have dogged its footfalls through that largely unacknowledged frontier where the origins of international communism overlap with those of the Republican Party. Perhaps most fundamentally, it remains one of those very peculiar cases in which a limited number of ordinary citizens turned history by helping to politicalize the concerns of "the working classes."

Since the late eighteenth century, urban white craftsmen had formed trade unions and related associations in eastern cities such as Philadelphia, New York, and Boston. By the late 1820s, they had launched short-lived local workingmen's parties, followed in New York during the mid-1830s by an antimonopolist Equal Rights Party, the so-called Locofocos. The National Reformers of the 1840s built on this history and contributed directly to a revival of labor organizing in the 1850s. They appealed to the working classes, by which they meant the unskilled as well as skilled of the city; the landless rural laborers, slave or free; and even the small-scale farmer. As historian E. P. Thompson argued, "class" has meaning only insofar as its members consciously think of themselves as a part of a distinct class with distinct interests.[2] It is obviously significant over the long run for any part of the work force to have identified itself in such terms so early in American history.

Still, the numbers involved in an organized workers' movement hardly argue for their having played a major role at the time. Between 1830 and 1860, the numbers of free Americans of all ages grew from 11,000,000 to 27,000,000, with several million additional slaves, and the nonagricultural work force from an estimated 250,000 to 1,400,000. During the peak years of labor activity in the mid-1830s, perhaps 30,000 to 35,000 passed through labor organizations, and the figure for the early 1850s is likely 100,000 to 120,000. While the nonagricultural work force grew faster than the general population, the portion involved in labor organizations, during peak years, kept pace but rarely represented more than a tenth of that category. In ordinary times, such numbers would have made the influence of such a labor movement marginal. However, the mid-nineteenth century hardly shaped up as ordinary times.

The National Reform idea that sought to mobilize and focus thee numbers has been even more misunderstood in the scholarly literature of the past century, which has tended to be thin, superficial, and, simply, wrong. Most recently, Anthony Gronowicz took up the question. Although acknowledging the complexities and fragmentations of politics and class, he nevertheless resorted to sweeping generalizations with little foundation on this matter, writing, "Labor's concern for land hardly made workers more radical," adding that Tammany "eagerly embraced" these concerns. He also extrapolated that land reform generated an "obsessive hatred of the American Indian, not aristocrats," making the issue "reactionary." In short, the method uncritically accepts what politicians say workers wanted, and selectively accepts evidence that confirms those assumptions and excludes what does not.[3] Drawing primarily on movement sources reveals a very different process, one that better fits the turbulence of the period.

National Reformers clearly spoke in a way that fit those times. Like some founders of the United States, they held that the health of a republic depended on the broader distribution of land ownership. These working-class readers about Roman antiquity in places such as New York's Lower East Side formulated a radical American version of ancient "Agrarianism" by advocating three related measures aimed at social reconstruction through radical and democratic land redistribution. First, they urged state governments to end the seizure themselves of homesteads for debts in order to defend the small-scale family farm and to thwart concentrations of land ownership and speculation. Second, they sought a federal homestead act to permit the free settlement of the landless on the public domain, land owned by a government that claimed to belong to its citizens. Third, most radically and essentially, they wanted to limit the amount of land any individual could own, pointing out that allowing limitless ownership of a finite resource actually reduced the number of property owners, while the NRA proposal "instead of lessening, would increase the landed estates generally belonging to families."[4]

Events inspired the NRA to clarify the significance of these measures through what became a wide range of "secondary" and "auxiliary" measures. At various conventions, conferences, and congresses or through local affiliates, the NRA called for a legislated ten-hour workday and the direct election of all government officers. Conversely, it urged the abolition of practices ranging from the Electoral College to slavery. While it sought to focus its efforts on these three original measures—exemption, a homestead law, and land limitation—it had varying degrees of success in doing so. National Reformers also consistently defended newcomers to the country, urged peace, and fostered international associations. In an age when people aspired to talk with the spirit of Benjamin Franklin, they proposed remaking the social structure, eliminating slavery, and assuring the fullest liberty to each and every individual.

The NRA's flexible strategy, low dues, and loose membership standards permitted its rapid, if indistinct, expansion across the country. Indeed, the growth of the agitation was phenomenal. No general records of its formal membership survive. Clearly, though, the NRA started in 1844 with only a handful of New Yorkers, mostly craftsmen who had two newspapers to support their views. By the close of the decade, however, many thousands had voted for its measures—enough to elect candidates to Congress—and over two hundred newspapers endorsed its platform, particularly a homestead bill. Over the next decade, an estimated six hundred of the nation's two thousand newspapers took up at least that aspect of the NRA's program.[5]

Reflecting this, the NRA often convinced other groups of the compatibility of their goals with agrarian politics. These allied organizations included at various points the American Union of Associationists (the socialist followers of

Charles Fourier, the French utopian thinker), the New England Workingmen's Association (renamed the New England Labor Reform League), the Mechanics Mutual Protection Association, and the fraternal Brotherhood of the Union, together with, among the German immigrants, the Sozial Reform Association and various leagues functioning under the name of the Arbeiterbund. From 1846, representatives gathered in annual National Industrial Congresses to plan strategy and call for stronger organization, and by 1849 and 1850, various statewide industrial legislatures and citywide industrial councils and congresses also formed.

The NRA's national petition drives reached a peak in 1850–52. Those petitions did more than advocate a homestead bill; they almost always called for all of the NRA's original proposals, including land limitation. Working people in cities such as New York or Cincinnati sent the largest petitions, and of these, some of the largest came from NRA auxiliaries, Industrial Congresses, Mechanics Mutual Protection, the Brotherhood of the Union, or the German Arbeiterbund. As many as a quarter of a million Americans then called on their representatives to limit the amount of land any individual in the country could legally own.[6] The importance of such numbers is evident in the fact that only 221,000 ballots separated the leading contenders in the 1852 presidential election. Under the right circumstances, such numbers of citizens could and did have an important impact on the wider course of American history.

The scale and nature of this agitation to change the world through radical social politics touched so many aspects of antebellum American life that any single study of a specific national reform leave much unaddressed. Much of what has been asserted about the class nature of this movement, including by professional historians, has come indirectly from James Gordon Bennett of the *Herald*. A bitter partisan for the conservative Democrats and an unambiguous enemy of the labor movement, Bennett insisted that social reform zealots had manipulated the course of the New York City Industrial Congress, which he editorially advised to "limit the membership to the trades, and . . . make a clean sweep of the politicians and socialists."[7] Even scholars with no affinity for Bennett's politics often embraced his assumptions that middle-class radicals were misleading the loyally Democratic workers.

The related questions about the kind of social transformations the land reformers espoused also merit more serious discussion. Focusing on the rural upstate allies of the NRA, Reeve Huston emphasized how nineteenth-century development translated the Antirent protest into a celebration of late nineteenth-century capitalist agriculture. While this bears only indirectly on the urban workers of the NRA, it revisits an interesting set of questions about the relationship between farmers and workers in the nineteenth century. Still, Antirent not only inspired capitalism but also raised serious questions about the social order. It also contributed to the kind of postwar agrarianism, usually associated with the wheat fields of Illinois or the cornfields of Kansas. However, the discussion would also take us beyond the scope of the present work.

How the American land reformers saw themselves in their world might also be fruitfully discussed. As Jamie Bronstein comprehensively demonstrated, land reform was largely a transatlantic Anglo-American phenomenon. The National Reformers alternately embraced this internationalism and asserted that their circumstances were quite different. The NRA's generally optimistic English-born founder, George Henry Evans, mused whether "it will take longer here to convince the people of the *right* to the Soil than it will in England, because the country is larger, the people more scattered, and the oppression not yet so gross."[8]

The Brotherhood of the Union also later extended National Reform into an embrace of America's potential as a "Palestine of Redeemed Labor." In New York politics, this understanding made land reform more appealing to nativists, such as the writer August Joseph Hickey Duganne and the politician Daniel Ullman. The messianic nationalism of some of its adherents in the South actually contributed to the ruthless expansionism against which the NRA had repeatedly warned. These matters are surely worth examining at a later point.

National Reform both reflected and influenced antislavery sentiment among working people in the nonslaveholding states. In reality, plantation slavery in the South had required little comment from workers concerned exclusively with local politics or conditions, but many had expressed their hostility to the institution. Most fundamentally, the NRA's successful embedding of land reform into an emerging ideology of "free labor" thoroughly transformed the way working people in "free states" saw the question.

No less an authority than Congressman George W. Julian of Indiana ascribed Republican success to the Homestead Bill, raised by both "the Free Soil platform of 1848 and the Land Reformers of New York," the former having actually adopted the issue after the latter had demonstrated its appeal. In short, contemporaries would have given more credit to Thomas Ainge Devyr's claim that when he and other founders of the NRA had "projected *The National Reform Party*," they had helped put into motion a chain of events "that eventually led to the Great Civil War."[9] An exploration of the merits of so important a question bearing on the origins of the Second American Revolution is in order.

National Reform required national survival. At a critical point in the history of the United States, its survival owed something to the land reform vision of American possibilities. Understanding that vision more thoroughly, in turn, may offer new insights into how nineteenth-century Americans saw themselves.

1

A WORKERS' MOVEMENT

National Reform: Agrarianism and the Origins of the American Workers' Movement

> The movement of which ours may be said to be a continuation under a new name and aspect, commenced in this city in the year 1829. It was the effort of the working-man to right his own wrongs, a confused, elementary endeavor to redeem himself from the slavery of wages.
>
> —Alvan Early Bovay, National Secretary, National Reform Association, 1848

> [North Americans] have had, since 1829, their own socialist and democratic school, against which their economist [Thomas] Cooper was fighting as long ago as 1830.
>
> —Karl Marx, 1846

Three working printers launched the National Reform Association at New York City in the winter of 1843–44. George Henry Evans, the labor editor, recruited John Windt, a blacklisted union organizer, with whom he had worked for over fifteen years. By late February, the two had enlisted Thomas Ainge Devyr, a veteran of the most insurrectionary faction of the Chartist movement in Britain and an upstate newspaper advocate for the familiar plight of the tenant farmers.[1] Together, they hoped to rebuild a local political labor movement and make it national in scope.

In American history, "agrarianism" emerged among such city dwellers, persons severed from the land by industrial development. Even as economic growth transformed their lives, some postrevolutionary Americans had advocated policies that ultimately became National Reform. Significantly, the effort rose from the bottom up.

The Working-Class Political Experience

Across the eighteenth-century Western world, freethinkers assailed religious and ecclesiastical orthodoxy. Although the process was less important in largely secularized societies such as the United States, the debunking of orthodoxy included an iconoclastic stance toward social and political questions. Thomas Paine's *Agrarian Justice,* for example, warned that representative politics alone would not prevent social injustice. Such ideas appealed to those working people who believed that human beings had a vast capacity for rational decision making, and saw unaccountable power as an invitation to tyranny and wealth as a form of power.[2]

A distinct social radicalism emerged in the United States after the economic collapse in the Panic of 1819. The already famous English philanthropist Robert Owen attained a respectable hearing in the United States for his proposal to found separate, secular socialist communities. Less prominently, Americans had already formed their own Society for Promoting Communities at New York City and established such communities in the West. After Owen's arrival in America, Cincinnati stove maker Josiah Warren embraced his critique of capitalism but, as a solution, proposed innovative cooperative stores rather than physically distinct communities. Meanwhile, as various American states began eliminating the property requirement for voting, the Philadelphia shoemaker William Heighton persuaded his peers to attempt independent action through a new Workingmen's Party.[3]

At this point, Evans turned up among New York City freethinkers. Few figures in American labor history attained anything like Evans's reputation among his contemporaries as "the indefatigable and tried friend of the working men of our country." A rival labor editor described him as "one of Nature's noblemen—a man of rare foresight and talent, though of unostentatious pretensions." Another remembered his "great evenness of temper, . . . mild and courteous in his intercourse with others," a man "patient in argument," who "never allowed himself to arise to a passion." "Honest George!" recalled another, "we can still see him in our mind's eye, in his murky office in Thames street, editor, compiler, printer, &.c." He was "seldom, if ever, inconsistent," being "so naturally imbued with the spirit of democracy that he brought it to bear on every question he discussed." Still a fourth rival thought him as "persevering and disinterested a Reformer as the laboring classes ever had."[4]

Born at Bromyard in Herefordshire, England, on March 25, 1805, Evans had a respectable, if modest, formal schooling.[5] His father, George Evans, had been an officer in the Napoleonic Wars, proprietor of a brickyard and the husband of Sarah White, the daughter in a declining family of the lesser gentry. After her death, he took his sons to join his own brothers at Chenango Point (now Binghamton), New York, in 1820. A year later, George Evans had remarried and soon after moved the family to a farm on the road to Oswego.

He placed both sons, George Henry and Frederick William, in apprentice-ships at nearby Ithaca, then a town of less than a thousand residents.

Each of the early crafts had their own "art and mystery," but none as distinctively ideological as "the art preservative." The printing office called itself a "chapel," implying a faith in reason and free discourse; Horace Greeley later called it "the poor man's college." If not earlier familiar with the works of Paine, the Evans boys encountered them there, along with the idea of craft self-organization. Despite its distance from a big city, Ithaca printers, like their master Augustus P. Searing, printer-editor of the *Ithaca Journal,* had been active in early printers' unions at New York City or Albany, and a member of the typographical society in New York having earlier suggested government grants to the landless. Years later, when Democratic editor James Gordon Bennett wrote that George Henry Evans had been "indoctrinated with agrarian principles in the English radical districts," Evans replied that he had "served my time to the printing business on a *bucktail* paper in this State before Bennett *came over,* and I afterwards got my agrarian notions from a *Native American.*"[6] Certainly, ideas of land reform were in the air.

Before he turned twenty, Evans had made a reputation as an editor. In April 1824, Evans and L. B. Butler—another former member of the New York union—arranged with Searing to use his shop and equipment to publish the *Museum and Independent Corrector* while both continued to perform wage labor at Searing's shop. At least into July, they issued what one scholar described as a "chatty free thought paper" twice a week. In its columns, short, sharp philosophical and political jabs punctuated the usual matter of a small-town newspaper. An unusually long piece riddled with the puns so popular among printers reported the unionization of London tailors. Another recount-ed a "dialogue" among merchants who discussed the fine points of watering rum, putting sand into sugar, wetting tobacco for weight, adding chemicals to freshen stale beer, and ending with one businessman's suggestion: "Then let's go to prayers!"[7] The *Independent Corrector* caught the collective eye of the New York City freethinkers.

At their invitation, Evans came to New York, where he spent "about eleven months of a rather irregular bachelor's life in an attic up some half a dozen flight of stairs" while tirelessly encouraging the interest of freethinkers in social reform. Evans published the arguments of a materialist and a deist over the immortality of the soul but editorially suggested that the immediate social and political tasks should have more importance than speculative and insoluble debates. Thereafter, "George H. Evans Printing Co." published the *Corre-spondent.* By the 1828 collapse of that paper, Evans issued the *Free Enquirer* on behalf of the Owenites Frances Wright and Robert Dale Owen, the son of the British communitarian; he became one of the mainstays at their "Hall of Science" on the Bowery.[8] The following year, freethinkers sympathetic to Owen helped lead the first political labor movements in world history, and Evans launched his weekly *Workingman's Advocate.*

A workingmen's party at New York formed in 1829 around "Agrarian" concerns. That spring, employers in the building trades proposed extending the ten-hour workday (won over twenty years earlier), and the city's other organized trades rallied to their support. Thomas Skidmore, a Connecticut inventor-and-sometimes-carpenter, persuaded a citywide mass meeting to adopt his "Agrarian Resolves," warning that those with power and wealth held them at the sufferance of the community, most of which had little of either and would, in self-protection, be justified in redistributing that power and wealth. The approach won the active support of Paine's old friend Alexander Ming, whose son Alexander Ming Jr. printed Skidmore's book *The Rights of Man to Property!* Encouraged by the showing of the Philadelphia Workies, the New York Workingmen's Party and did quite well in the fall elections. However, the party soon destroyed itself in a series of major splits.[9] The pressures of the 1832 presidential election devastated the remnants, subsuming into the Democratic Party the largest surviving faction, around Evans's *Daily Sentinel.*

Thereafter, workingmen mingled trade unionism with their politics. Evans's friend John Windt—with the help of Samuel Huestis of the old Society for Promoting Communities—established a new printers' union, which called the 1833 citywide convention of the crafts that launched a new General Trades' Union (GTU). Under the presidency of another printer, Ely Moore, it grew to some twenty-one societies with over four thousand members in the city, Brooklyn, and Newark. With Moore publicly associated with the Democratic club at Tammany Hall, the hostile *Courier and Enquirer* suggested that employers dismiss workers favorable to Jackson, and Windt was one of those who lost his job. Democratic defeat in the spring 1834 municipal elections left the party's hopes dependent on its ability to mobilize working-class voters.[10]

However, trade unionists and former "Workies" had formulated a peculiarly antimonopolist version of Democratic politics. For them, Jackson's veto of the Second Bank of the United States did not merely cancel privileges granted a specific business but mandated a general opposition to all chartered monopolies, including those in New York regularly supported by Democrats. In response, Tammany ran Moore for Congress and fielded an assembly ticket pledged to oppose further monopolies if sent to Albany. In Moore's absence, leadership of the GTU fell to John Commerford, the New York–born leader of both the cabinet and chairmakers union, the Brooklyn Workies. Although Commerford claimed to be a loyal Jacksonian like Moore, his partisan loyalty depended entirely on what he perceived to be best for his labor constituency. Under Commerford, New York's GTU pursued joint action with the New England Association of Farmers, Mechanics, and Other Workingmen under freethinkers and labor reformers such as Josiah Mendum and Horace Seaver of Massachusetts, Dr. Charles Douglas of Connecticut, and Seth Luther of Rhode Island. Their short-lived National Trades' Union represented the first such venture on such a scale.[11]

Democratic success sowed discord. Democratic legislators who were pledged to oppose monopolies simply went to Albany and continued to charter them. In 1835, the radicals mobilized to block the renomination by party managers of the five most objectionable "monopoly Democrats." Before the October 29 Democratic convention, Tammany officers, as expected, slipped into the meeting hall early and occupied the platform, but they faced such overwhelming opposition from the floor that they resorted to a standard machine practice, turning off the gas and leaving the gathering to dissolve in darkness. The well-prepared antimonopolists produced candles and hundreds of the new "Lucifer" or "Locofoco" matches, and held their own Democratic nominating convention. When amused observers dubbed them Locofocos, the name stuck.[12]

Reorganized as the independent Equal Rights Party, the Locofocos won a balance of power between Tammany and Whigs. The group not only included many future National Reformers but occupied much of the same ground as the Workies, not only ideologically but literally, in that they rented the same meeting place on Broome Street and appealed to the same artisan base in the Lower East Side. Ming, their 1836 mayoral candidate, had even been Skidmore's printer, but the Locofocos hoped to avoid a repeat of how the presidential election had caused the Workies to implode. They held an ongoing country convention from May into July and a September state convention at Utica that nominated the radical Dr. Moses Jaques for lieutenant governor. However, astute Whigs endorsed two Locofoco assembly candidates, including Robert Townsend Jr., a long-term leader of the carpenters' union.[13] In 1836, as in 1832, presidential politics pulled the third-party movement to pieces.

An economic depression in 1837 devastated the entire insurgency. As the cost of living spiraled, a February protest meeting in City Hall Park detonated an old-fashioned Flour Riot and an investigation by the state assembly. When Jaques got four thousand votes for mayor anyway, the Democrats opened talks with the Locofocos. By October, only a "rump faction" of insurgents refused to rejoin the Democrats.[14]

Formulating a National Reform

As the editor of various movement newspapers, Evans had been at the center of these experiences. At different points, representatives of both parties offered him money and patronage but found him "not purchasable, although at the time he was not only poor, but considerably involved," persuading some who knew him to doubt whether there lived "a more unpretending incorruptible man." Nevertheless, after four years of constant newspaper work, he had $1,500 of pressing debts with $6,000 owed him, mostly for Democratic campaign printing. Fortunately, Evans had taken advantage of the brief but lucrative cooperation with the Democrats by investing $500 in some land along the Waycake Creek in Monmouth County, New Jersey. When the Democrats declined to pay their bill, Evans and his wife, Laura, retreated to the farm, where he "had to get my living by 'regenerating' a poor worn out soil."[15]

After the collapse of the Locofocos in the city, the yet unrepentant radicals struggled to sustain their independent efforts. On the fringe of the Democratic Party, a young Walt Whitman encountered such "Moral Philanthropists" as John Fellows and Gilbert Vale and others of Evans's old comrades. Militant leaders like Commerford turned to a new secret society, the Mechanics Mutual Protection Association, which harkened back to the old days when "mechanics" of all sorts—employer as well as worker—combined for common purposes of mutual aid.[16] Evans publicized such efforts but had long decided that serious change required political action.

As "hard times" grew worse, two new labor reform currents emerged. Through the 1830s, William Lloyd Garrison's *Liberator* and its American Anti-Slavery Society had morally repudiated the older, morally gradualist schemes of emancipation and called for the immediate abolition of slavery. While "immediatists" generally favored petitioning the authorities, Garrison had opposed any electoral bid to take power within a system that sustained slavery. In November 1839, however, abolitionists who disagreed with Garrison formed the Liberty Party around a national ticket of James G. Birney of Kentucky and Thomas Earle of Pennsylvania. After showing small and localized support in 1840, the Libertymen convened at Buffalo in August 1843 to renominate Birney.[17]

The other current embraced the French socialist idealism of Charles Fourier, the tailor whose mystical views, unlike those of Owen, reached beyond freethinkers. Albert Brisbane, the idealistic son of a merchant and landowner from Batavia, New York, encountered the ideas of Claude-Henri de Saint-Simon, the social critic who had fought as a French ally in the American Revolution but spent three years under the tutelage of Fourier and translated his ideas into "Associationism." As the Locofoco insurgency folded about them, some New Yorkers launched their own "Fourienne Society," which subsequently published Brisbane's *Social Destiny of Man,* and a weekly, *Phalanx.* Members of Boston's Transcendentalist Club, who had formed their own community at nearby Brook Farm adopted Fourierism and sought to adopt the features of a phalanx. George Ripley and other Brook Farmers launched the *Harbinger.* Other newspaper editors such as Horace Greeley and Parke Godwin helped spread the movement from Maine and Ohio to Texas and California. Their new American Union of Associationists (AUA) invited the abolitionists to their own December 1843 national convention.[18]

Fourierists faced factional problems as severe as those among abolitionists. Some, such as John Orvis and Lewis Ryckman, found Fourier's critique of capitalism compelling but wanted the movement to grow beyond the rigidity of his detailed social blueprints and reach out to other radicals. The descendant of radical Quakers in Vermont, Orvis had dropped out of Oberlin College to study mutual insurance and antislavery under Boston freethinker Elizur Wright. Ryckman, a fellow Brook Farmer, was a New York shoemaker who admired Warren's cooperatives as the most practical variant of socialism.[19]

Although sympathetic to both abolition and Fourierism, Evans kept his closest political ties to his old comrades in the city. Although he tried to sow "some seeds of reform" in rural New Jersey and served as a school trustee, he and Laura used their heavily mortgaged eight-room, two-story farmhouse as "cheaper and more eligible accommodations" not only for their family but for his research and publishing. A library of four hundred volumes claimed one first-floor room, spread through an adjacent chamber into a middle room near the stairs, and even spilled over into the kitchen and the garret, with bound newspapers and stacks of unbound printed matter elsewhere. (One wonders if their globe was one of those sold by Vale or cast by Skidmore.) Periodically, they and any visitors burned the midnight oil in the makeshift printing office in two of the downstairs rooms, though Evans turned larger printing projects over to Windt, who had opened his own office in the city. By the winter of 1840–41, Evans began using a mailing address at Rahway halfway back to the city.[20] By then, his new periodical espoused what he had come to see as the most vital issue of the age—*The Radical: Devoted to the Abolition of the Land Monopoly and Other Democratic Reforms.*

The two-party electoral system had never resolved the conflict within the American elite between those eager for the most rapid settlement and those viewing the public lands as a source of revenue.[21] The Land Ordinance of 1785 established a rectangular survey grid with six-mile-square townships, each with 36 sections, each a mile square or 144 quarter-sections of 160 acres each. It also authorized the sale of land by at least a section at $1 per acre, which restricted sales to those with at least $640, roughly two years' income for a skilled worker. The Land Act of 1796 doubled the price to $2 per acre, but the Harrison Land Act promised a more rapid settlement by reducing the minimum sale to 320 acres and requiring only half the price as down payment; in 1804, Congress further halved the minimum to 160 acres. Legislation in 1820 eliminated the credit provision but halved the minimum again to 80 acres and cut the price to $1.25 per acre, which made public land available to any purchaser with $100. These solutions satisfied few.

Proponents of a more rapid settlement from Albert Gallatin to Thomas Hart Benton had pressed for more. Unsold land with no settlers, they pointed out, generated no revenue, and none of these changes addressed the growing difficulties of settlers who needed to get to the westward-moving frontier and stay there long enough to make the land profitable. These contradictions moved Benton to advocate the free distribution of public land. The tensions over this issue within the ruling Democratic coalition made it the Achilles heel of the party system itself.

The Founding

Evans understood how "the land question" suited the times. Although admirers might describe him as "the first to break up the error" of unlimited land ownership and as one who "most prominently conceived and agitated man's natural right to soil," he himself minimized the novelty of his proposals. After borrowing the name "National Reform" from evangelical Christianity, he ascribed its essential ideas to Thomas Jefferson, Paine, and Skidmore, alongside European thinkers such as Owen, Fourier, Henri de Saint-Simon, the cooperationist John Gray, and the agrarian Thomas Spence. Reprinting Paine's *Agrarian Justice,* Evans paid tribute to Skidmore's *Rights of Man to Property!* Evans readily credited Moses Jaques's October 1835 argument for applying antimonopolist principles to land.[22]

Still, none of his predecessors had envisioned an organization around land reform agitation. As early as 1841, Evans declared himself "ready to join a Union, no matter how small may be the number to commence it" bound by the agreement "to support or vote for no man for any public office who will not pledge himself to exercise all the proper influence of his station to restore to the people, in some equitable manner, the Equal Right to Land. Who will unite with me?"[23]

Evans looked at his society through the eyes of the working people he hoped to reach and recognized the potential of land reform to radicalize

American civilization. He understood that their personal identities centered on self-sufficiency, personal liberty, and willingness to accept social responsibility. Their same concerns about home, family, personal autonomy, and economic security that fueled competitive industry also ensured that those aspirations would be thwarted in most cases. Land reform turned those very aspirations to inspire a political workers' movement around a nonpartisan strategy. It could function alongside communitarian ventures and mobilize "wage slaves" unmoved by the Liberty Party. Perhaps uniquely, Evans hoped to win veterans of other struggles to a unique movement embracing experienced and diverse activists and groups.[24]

On March 8, 1844, a handful of workingmen met in the back of Windt's print shop to launch the NRA. The founders and early members were themselves white, male, and, with a single exception, skilled workers. Most were natives of the United States or had, like Evans, arrived as children. Those whose ages can be determined were within a few years of Evans's thirty-nine, sufficient to be an elder among contemporary workers in the city. Yet they aspired to an inclusive organization that would be coherent without being doctrinaire. Over the next ten days, they shifted their meetings into Croton Hall, a temperance hotel on the corner of Bowery and Division Streets, and had a constitution by the close of the month.[25]

Not surprisingly, the project appealed most directly to veterans of earlier movements who had been deprived by "hard times" of any voice in public affairs for the previous six or seven years. Both Vale and Ming—Paine's old friend and Skidmore's ally—brought many years of experience as freethinkers to land reform, though they remained at the margins. In April, ex-president Andrew Jackson received a letter soliciting his support from NRA leaders such as John Commerford, joined by other old Workies Simon Clannon, Thomas Estebrook, and Robert Hogbin. Fitzwilliam Byrdsall, the participant-author of the *History of the Loco-Foco, or Equal Rights Party*, became an episodic National Reformer, as were Locofocos John Bowie and John H. Hunt, "one of the most ultra of democrats." Locofoco trade unionists turning up in the NRA included blacksmiths Egbert S. Manning and Ellis Smalley and the bookbinder Robert Beatty. Tailor John Delamontayne and printer Herman D. Bristol had represented their trades in the GTU, while Daniel McCracken had been in the Philadelphia Trades' Union before moving to New York. James Pyne, local agent of the *Radical*, immediately came to Evans's assistance. Windt, Manning, and Hogbin had been diehards of the "rump" Locofocos.[26]

Exceptions among the early NRA membership seem to have simply not been in New York at the time of these earlier movements. Lewis Masquerier, a forty-two-year-old Kentuckian had learned printing in the West and practiced law before launching a new career as a language reformer at St. Louis. He had taken the issue east, meeting and marrying Anna Tabor, whose family had personally known Paine. On broader social questions, Masquerier clung to "the communistic views of Owen" and had applied in 1842 for membership in the "Communist Society" sponsored by Goodwyn Barmby's London *Promethean*.[27]

Other newcomers to the city also joined the NRA. Perhaps the most prominent political refugee in the country, William Lyon Mackenzie, had tried to wrest reforms from Britain in Canada in an abortive armed revolt—the "Patriot's War"—and its defeat drove him into exile. Likely a veteran of labor activism in Britain, Henry Beeny had turned up urging an 1839 convention of New York Workingmen to form "Associations throughout the United States," and apparently saw the NRA as a means of doing so. The only professional man in the group, Alvan Earl Bovay, had recently accepted a position in the city as a teacher, and he remained interested in socialism and antislavery.[28]

Yet the organization of the NRA got off to a slow start. Evans blamed "the election excitement" for the "paucity of members" that spring, and he used the hiatus to move his household back to the city. While issuing the March numbers of his revived *Working Man's Advocate* out of Windt's shop, he placed his own press into a small building at the later site of the *Tribune* building. He frankly confessed his hope not only to promote reform but "to get better than bread and water for our families, and if it should ultimately be so prosperous as to enable us to pay off some few old debts."[29] In April, the NRA elected an interim central committee to serve until the regularly scheduled June election.

The NRA's constitution sought to establish an ongoing organization rather than an electoral coalition as had been the Workies and Locofocos. The Central Committee coordinated every major function, as well as mandates to "encourage the attendance" of females and "admit them as members" and to "provide Vocal and Instrumental Music" and publish appropriate songs, but annual elections checked this centralized power. Members not only signed the nonpartisan electoral pledge but also the NRA constitution; they also got "a Ticket and a Diploma" and attended regular Thursday meetings. Each member paid a twenty-five-cent initiation fee and monthly dues of two cents in theory but in addition made weekly contributions of "two or three cents, or whatever he could afford." The NRA never resolved what to do about the large numbers that signed the pledge without assuming membership, although Bovay, Evans, and another printer, William Haddock, floated various proposals for some kind of intermediate or provisional level of membership.[30]

As spring 1844 warmed the city, the NRA's Central Committee called "a *great mass meeting in the Park"* before City Hall, site of the old Locofoco rallies. Inspired by the public response, National Reformers carried their message directly into different parts of the city from June through October. They used a simple straw-cutter's freight cart as a stage for the first rally at Abingdon Square, returning a few days later with a wagon surmounted by a platform with a full-sized American flag. Evans, Devyr, Windt, Masquerier, Pyne, and James Maxwell took turns speaking beneath the "Republican Banner of FREE LAND." The speakers decried the growing power of the landlords and bosses, fielded questions, and fended off hecklers, while those not on the platform worked the crowd with petitions and newspapers. Given sufficient volunteers and good weather, they might even hold several such impromptu rallies during a week or even repeat the meeting that same evening at another location. By July, Laura Evans and Mary Commerford—John's wife—brought a ladies auxiliary with its own large banner: *"The only Effective Remedy for Hard Times is to make the Public Lands free to Actual Settlers."*[31] Workers unmoved by the Locofocos or Workies cheered the NRA's message.

❊ ❊ ❊

The simplicity and popularity of the NRA's message brightened its prospects but made consolidating an organization more difficult. Certainly, the rallies took their toll on the activists involved. One slated for Bayard and Division Streets in the heavily scheduled midsummer weeks never took place when none of the exhausted reformers showed. Devyr complained of "the difficulties which speakers in this cause . . . had to labor under, in comparison with the facilities enjoyed by the orators of political parties, who had books and leisure . . . previous to making a speech in the evening." Evans stopped publishing the speeches as being "in great part, a repetition of those we have already reported"; by the fall, he confessed that he had "written and spoken till I am almost tired with the repetition, and yet they must be repeated over and over again." At a business meeting, Bovay, having been assigned earlier to speak, simply declined to do so "owing to the smallness of the meeting" and the presence of "few . . . who were not convinced."[32]

Nevertheless, the NRA survived. In June, it elected a regular central committee, which issued a rousing Fourth of July manifesto. Although it failed to build a neighborhood affiliate among the Democratic immigrants of the Sixth Ward, it kept trying, and early in the summer, it established "the *first* City Auxiliary" in the old Eleventh Ward stronghold of the Locofocos and Workies. "Let the strife now be," Evans suggested, "which Ward Auxiliary shall get the greatest number of Constitutional Members?" Wisely setting aside money collected at summer rallies, the city organization entered the autumn and winter with funds to rent a permanent headquarters at Croton Hall where it remained for "several years," and to lease larger halls like the Chelsea Temperance House. When unable to hold a planned "series of Public Meetings in all the wards," the NRA rotated its citywide meetings to "various halls" around the city.[33] Success beyond survival would turn on building a political united front engaged in nonpartisan electoral action.

2 Working-Class Antimonopoly and Land Monopoly: Building a National Reform Association

No one can live without breathing, eating and drinking. Food can come only from the soil; and Nature has provided earth, air and water for our equal use. Whoever denies our right to use either of these denies our right to life itself. . . . Those who have no money stand most in need of access to the soil, . . . but government also allows those who are fortunate enough to be wealthy, to monopolize and speculate in the soil, and thus place it a vast deal further from the poor. The farther it goes from our reach the more helpless we are, and must be.

—J. E. Thompson, "Land Monopoly—Despotism," 1844

The founders of the National Reform Association knew that theirs was initially but a partial white, urban, Anglo-American perspective on the working-class experience. George Henry Evans adopted the "comprehensive phrase of a black writer" to describe the origins of a civilization in the policies of a white king who "stole the black man from his land," took land "from the red men," and apportioned "the stolen bodies and the stolen land among a few of his own color, to whom he made the remainder of the whites as dependent for the means of existence as were the blacks themselves." Alvan Bovay warned of the necessity of justly reconciling the "Spanish, Indian, Negro, and Anglo-Saxon races" in the New World. Then, too, the continual influx of the foreign-born further layered white America along fault lines of language and nationality as well as class.[1] Efforts of the NRA founders to reach beyond their limitations could only take place incrementally.

Success to any extent required reaching a much broader population. Through its first year, these working people, who had generally worked together for some time, functioned alternately as an antimonopolist force within the Democratic Party and as a focus for unionism within the various trades, particularly after the NRA adopted the call for a legislated ten-hour workday.

Functioning as a component of various coalitions demonstrated a flexibility that had eluded earlier political labor movements, but it still failed to evade the dangers of presidential politics.

The Search for Allies

The fledgling NRA early invited the support of other organizations and movements. In 1844, the city Agrarians found themselves involved with the Rhode Island suffrage reformers led by Thomas Wilson Dorr, the tenant farmers in the upstate New York "Antirent War," and a reemerging New England labor movement. Most immediately, they won the support of Spartan Band, rooted in the Irish base of New York City's Democratic Party.

The enigmatic Mike Walsh led the Spartans. The son of an Irish immigrant who had acquired his own furniture store, the talented and sociable Walsh entered the newspaper business after serving an apprenticeship with a lithographer. Also a popular volunteer fireman, he formed the Spartan Band in 1840, and while later covering Washington for New York's *Aurora,* he charmed President John Tyler who bypassed Tammany to make Walsh the unofficial dispenser of presidential patronage at New York's Custom House. With such backing, Walsh formed a partnership with George Wilkes, another ambitious son of a cabinetmaker and a law clerk seven years Walsh's junior. Although Wilkes had already delved into the lucrative sensationalism that would later inspire his *Police Gazette,* he joined Walsh in 1843 to found the *Subterranean.* Although he had grown up in the streets, Walsh believed himself to be "pretty well booked up in the rascality of the age in which we live."[2] Tough, even ruthless, Walsh and his cronies led the less-skilled immigrant Irish, who had tended to shun distinctly labor politics.

However, the Spartans had found little solace in Democratic machine politics. Walsh maneuvered nationally for an alliance with Tyler and, to some extent, John C. Calhoun's Southern wing of the party, hoping to break the power of Tammany in the city's Democratic Party. Ironically, the Spartan use of intimidation and physical force, as well as periodic bolts from the party, taught Tammany the merits of immigrant-based gangs, and its superior resources and tactical flexibility eventually prevailed over rivals like the Spartans. Through the spring and summer of 1844, the NRA and the Spartans held joint meetings, and late that summer, Evans, Windt, and Walsh merged the *People's Rights* and the *Subterranean.*[3] Such collaboration seemed to presage easily won Agrarian inroads into the Democratic Party.

Ties to the Spartans, in turn, reinforced the NRA's favorable predisposition toward the Dorr rebellion. Rhode Island's property requirement for voting excluded much of its adult, white, male population, and local radicals such as Seth Luther, a tobacco-chewing, buckskin-wearing carpenter had made it as much a class concern as the ten-hour workday. The Rhode Island Suffrage Association forced a vote on a new Jacksonian "People's Constitution," which, among other innovations, combined a suffrage unrestrained by property with one from which blacks were explicitly barred. Each side claimed victory and established rival state governments, that of the insurgents headed by Governor Dorr. Horace Greeley and Jacob Frieze joined most abolitionists in bitterly denouncing the movement as a fraud, although a few such as Elias Smith extended a kind of critical support to this method of extending popular participation in government.[4]

For many, the suppression of the Dorrites overshadowed all other points of controversy. The federal government opted for neutrality as the two competing governments tried to take charge of the state. Dorr's assembly, escorted by several thousand militia, went into session in a rented industrial site on May 3 and after two days adjourned until July. Alarmed at both the audacity of the "Foundry legislature" and news that the Dorrite militia had artillery, the conservative authorities issued warrants and prepared to act. In the pitch dark, foggy night of May 17–18, 1842, Dorr's forces attempted to bluff the Providence Arsenal into surrendering.[5] After it did not comply, the largest militia prevailed and began rounding up Luther, Dorr, and other leaders of the rebellion.

The authorities held these political prisoners incommunicado, charging them with the legally dubious crime of treason to a state. Even Frieze's damning critique of the movement denounced the "undue severity" of its repression. Without addressing the People's Constitution as such, Evans insisted, *"An injury done to the meanest citizen is an injury done to the whole people!"* Rhode Island, he charged, had placed Dorr behind bars "for doing precisely what Washington did, and . . . what the Declaration of Independence declares it to be the right of the People to do, namely to change the form of government" when it fails to assure "equality of rights to the People." "Let Dorr be liberated," thundered Evans, "peaceably if he can be, forcibly if he must be." In addition to this civil libertarian defense, the NRA sent to Rhode Island Francis Treadwell, a young New York lawyer, formerly a baker who had retained his ties to the workers' movement. Already in New England, Treadwell went to Providence and started sending reports to Evans's paper.[6]

The NRA had a more natural affinity with the upstate Antirenters, given its geographic proximity, their common posing of the broader "land question," and Devyr's previous association with the movement. Disturbances between the tenant farmers and the manors established by colonial Dutch grants had

escalated since 1839 into a widespread rural resistance, which disguised itself as "Indians." The Antirenters were headed by Dr. Smith A. Boughton,
the thirty-four-year-old son of a tenant farmer and nephew of a Continental
soldier; after attending Middlebury College in Vermont, he had participated
in Mackenzie's ill-fated Patriots' War in Canada and became a mastermind
of the tenants' confrontations with the authorities and an increasingly vocal
supporter of the NRA. Although Antirent votes helped elect Barnburner Silas
Wright for governor, his administration took military action to dissolve the
movement, and the NRA became the chief defender of the Antirent cause in
the city.[7]

Within the city, the NRA hoped to reorganize the "working classes." Its
constitution mandated correspondence "with societies of tradesmen or laborers, and with benevolent societies in the cities, as elsewhere" and efforts to
invite trade organizations to send "delegates to consult with the Central Committee." In June 1844, Henry Beeny suggested that "the different Trades" in
New York City be invited to endorse the NRA measures and "to join in bodies." He convinced his own craft, the shoemakers, to do so and to recognize
"the absolute necessity of a UNION OF TRADES" with the goal of holding
"a NATIONAL CONVENTION OF THE TRADES." When news arrived
that the mechanics of Fall River, Massachusetts, had called such a convention
for October 1844, the NRA not only endorsed the call but also urged "each
of the Trades of this city" to "send at least one delegate."[8]

Evans, Walsh, Bovay, and Devyr attended for the NRA. The organization
allocated them enough for "the best of everything," but they "roughed it" to
save the cost of seats in a lighted passenger car and spent the night "in utter
darkness" with the freight. Years later, Devyr recalled that an official of the road
recognized and extended "all hospitality" to Walsh, but the Spartan celebrity
chose to remain with his comrades. At one five-minute stop, Devyr stepped
off the train into the darkness, missed the platform, and would have fallen to
his death had he not grabbed an iron rail and pulled himself to safety.[9]

This convention repaid the risks, founding the New England Workingmen's
Association (NEWA) around land reform and the shorter workday. Lewis
Ryckman, John Orvis, and other Associationists had come to see the future
of socialism among "the working classes," which bore the burdens of the
present order, and "the land question" seemed a viable agitation. So, too,
veteran freethinkers such as Josiah P. Mendum and Horace Seaver of the
Boston Investigator turned to the NRA, the latter reporting that he had never
heard "an address from old or young, more full of genuine pathos, correct
knowledge, and forcible description than that from this young champion of
the New York Spartans." The NEWA functioned as a broadly inclusive labor

reform organization somewhat like the old New England Association of Farmers, Mechanics, and Other Workingmen a decade earlier, but its founding convention embraced the three NRA measures, adding the call for a legislated ten-hour workday. As Walsh himself observed, the long workday "makes *quiet* and *orderly* citizens of us." "Be united on the Ten Hours System as a *means*," advised Evans, "let us unite on the Freedom of Public Lands as an *end*."[10]

National Reformers early made important inroads elsewhere. Over the previous years, Philadelphia's once powerful labor movement had dissipated, and some of its individual leaders scattered. Yet the Worky leader William Heighton declared his support from rural New Jersey. John Ferral, a leader of the 1835 Philadelphia general strike, also wrote on behalf of a workers' association at Pittsburgh. One of the oldest white settlers at Peoria, Connecticut-born Jeriel Root, launched an NRA that eventually sustained its own local paper, the *Nineteenth Century.* As well, Columbus printer George W. Allen launched a one-man congressional campaign in 1844 that forced pledges from another candidate and announced the victory of pledged assembly candidates in Ohio as the first electoral victory for the "National Reform phalanx" in April 1845; the following fall at Columbus, three Democrats and a Whig pledged for land reform.[11]

National Reform distinguished itself from other antebellum movements in expressing both the political skepticism of many contemporaries and the drive toward politics as part of its faith in a disembodied "people." Although the NRA's successes in places like Columbus seems tied to its threat to nominate its own candidates, the use of nonpartisan tactics could inspire a Dorr rebel, an Antirenter, a midwestern newspaper printer, or an abolitionist, because it required none to sacrifice his earlier loyalties.

Political Bearings: The Election of 1844 and Recovery

Evans's strategy built upon the experience of the Workies and the Locofocos. The NRA extended the Locofoco solicitation of Democratic pledges to Whigs, Libertymen, and other candidates; in the absence of pledges, the NRA would, like Workies and Locofocos, turn to independent tickets. Unlike these earlier movements, they hoped for a common organization in New York, Brooklyn, Albany, Troy, Lowell, Philadelphia, Boston, and other cities. The NRA's municipal reform plans included proposals common to freethinkers since the start of the century, such as the opening of public buildings and public baths to the use of the citizens, as well as greater economy in city government and the payment of aldermen to break the monopoly on such offices by gentlemen of independent means. Its ultimate reform, as Masquerier later wrote, was "to end this crowding together of the people in the cities," "to make the whole land a city of farms."[12]

The state politics with which the NRA initially grappled were as complex in New York as any in the country. Although upstate Whig politicians had begun to shift on the Antirent issue, they remained hostile to land reform for years. One group of Democrats, headed by former president Martin Van Buren, denounced fellow Democrats who favored chartering banks and "internal improvements" as "Hunkers" (being either Dutch slang for self-seekers or referring to those wanting a "Hunk o' spoils"). Hunkers recalled the Dutch farmer who burned his barn to rid it of rats and labeled Van Buren's faction "Barnburners." (With the demise of the Equal Rights Party, critics also began calling urban Barnburners "Locofocos.") National issues impinged on state questions as well, as Barnburners felt betrayed by Southern leaders who had prevented Van Buren's renomination upon discovering his private agreement with Henry Clay to keep Texas out of the campaign. When no candidate for state office responded to questioning in September, the NRA launched its own independent campaigns for the assembly and state senate.[13]

Despite its self-description as "national," the NRA remembered that presidential politics had contributed to the demise of the Workies and the Locofocos, and any position on national politics posed a vexing set of questions around enslaved labor. James Birney of the Liberty Party declined to discuss anything other than slavery, whereas Joseph Smith, the Mormon candidate, endorsed the principle of land reform, and a self-nominated Mr. Brooks also replied. However, neither the Whig Henry Clay nor the Democrat James Knox Polk responded, but internal Democratic factionalism predisposed the NRA to a bizarre, if short-lived, match. Although the Spartan Band had ties to John Tyler, Florida-born Fitzwilliam Byrdsall acted with John C. Calhoun's wing of the party to found the Free Trade Association, with Commerford for president and involving such "intelligent workingmen" and reformers as Parke Godwin the Fourierist, Windt, Walsh, Robert Townsend, John Hecker, and others of the local workers' movement. Former National Trades' Union president-turned-congressman Ely Moore and his successor in the NTU, Commerford, shared Calhoun's free trade position. In return for launching "the only Calhoun organization that ever existed in this part of the Union," Byrdsall informed Calhoun that he would be "highly gratified" by his own appointment to the U.S. Customs House.[14] Byrdsall (as well as later historians) had reasons of their own to misread into this a much broader workingmen's mandate for slavery.

The founding of the NRA threatened all of this. Although a longstanding free trader, Evans openly mistrusted the Moore-Calhoun faction, which he called a "political weather-cock" standing "sometimes for the aristocracy, at other times for the working classes." Commerford wrote Calhoun on Moore's behalf as late as June 1844, but only a few weeks later, Moore's refusal to sign the NRA pledge moved Commerford to accept an independent Agrarian nomination to run against his old coworker.[15] Men like Walsh, Byrdsall, and Moore understandably renewed their efforts to keep the NRA from drawing the "intelligent workingmen" any direction other than to their faction of the Democratic Party.

In the end, the NRA succumbed to what may have been the worst electoral position in its history. While any endorsement would divide Antirenters and Associationists, the Spartans and free traders would remain Democratic as would the Dorrites whose prosecutions would be dropped by Democratic office seekers. Levi Slamm, a veteran Locofoco-turned-party-loyalist urged support for the party, and some associated with the NRA began going to Democratic gatherings. Unknown to the agrarians, Polk had simply filed their memorials with his scribbled identification of the authors as a "Committee in N. York Proposes to abolish private property in Lands . . . not worthy of an answer." What agrarians saw was Polk's public indifference to the question contrasted to Clay's overt hostility. Also, Walsh's "challenge" to "public controversy" promised a modification of Democratic indifference to land reform.[16]

The logic of the NRA's presidential endorsement of Polk more or less subsumed its efforts elsewhere on the ticket. Agrarians exerted little effort in their own independent campaigns, distributing ballots at "few of the 85 polls" in the city. At those few, Bovay encountered "one or two 'barnburners,' who threatened violence to the National Reformers" while "Hunker Bullies" drove NRA representatives from polls in the Fourth and Seventeenth Wards. However, the rivalries of the campaign intensified tensions between the Hunkers and Barnburners, leaving the latter temporarily in charge of the state government but facing a grim future without some alliance with independent forces. On this rather tenuous basis, Evans preferred to see a "glorious victory" for reform.[17] If so, it owed little to the NRA.

Paradoxically, any importance of the NRA to the Democrats faded almost completely with Polk's national victory. While Walsh and Evans collaborated periodically thereafter, the former clearly viewed the NRA primarily as a means for garnering more influence within the Democratic Party. Nonpartisanship had not prepared the NRA for Democratic infighting. Agrarian leaders expressed disappointment in Polk almost as soon as the national results were tallied. As the first year of agitation drew to a close, hopes for easy victory through the Democratic Party dissolved before their eyes.[18] Remarkably, though, having repeated the suicidal failures of both the Workies and the Locofocos, the NRA did not simply disintegrate.

Instead, the NRA turned to rebuilding the city's labor movement. Inspired by the NEWA, Haddock proposed NRA committees "from each trade" begin organizing within their crafts to build "a Convention of the Trades of this city" as a step toward a new national labor federation. The NRA issued a February 1845 "Circular to the Trades" calling for a city convention on March 17 but found it "impossible to find out more than half a dozen Trade Associations in the city, and some of these had probably not had time to act upon the subject." Supported by veteran unionist Commerford, Haddock urged sending "tracts and delegates among the various societies." The NRA made gains despite the chronic turnover of membership in the few unions that survived. Where unions did not survive, the NRA formed groups like the "Segar [sic] Makers' National Reform Association," which not only fostered land reform but "such other remedies for the distresses and embarrassments of the productive or working classes as appear likely to be practically useful."[19]

Where the NRA did have an important impact on the future of the workers' movement may have been its efforts to mobilize women in the workforce. By August 1844, "several ladies" had begun attending NRA meetings, and the NRA began fostering the organization of women a few months later. Later that year, as they participated in the Industrial Brotherhood, they discussed the need for a similar "Industrial Sisterhood." Over the next few years, they made a major effort to assist organizing efforts, particularly of women in the needle trades in both New York and Philadelphia and in the textile mills of New England.[20]

Developments among the Antirenters pulled the NRA even further from its Locofoco predispositions. When shooting erupted at a December Antirent rally upstate, the incoming Barnburner administration of Governor Silas Wright mobilized hundreds of militia, who arrested, shackled, and held incommunicado Boughton and others. "Troops have gone out from this city, equipped with the instruments of death," protested the NRA, "for the purpose of commencing a civil war in this State, to establish feudalism over freedom." At a January rally, the NRA debated an adjutant from the nearby arsenal who defended the state action, the climax being when Windt brought forward Devyr who gave "a brief history of the Manor difficulties." When unconstitutional and illegal searches upstate failed to unearth any real evidence, the protests escalated. Declaring themselves for tenants' rights, the Democrats still prosecuted tenants without evidence. When a state commissioner ordered bail for Boughton, Attorney General John Van Buren, the ex-president's son, removed the commissioner.[21]

Barnburner repression of the Antirenters shattered much of what remained of the old Locofoco illusions. Devyr, Evans, and Bovay attended the Antirent convention at Berne, where delegates challenged the titles of the landlords and urged the state to adopt a tax policy aimed at breaking up the great estates. A few days later, state authorities received petitions with twenty-five thousand signatures only to find their concerns ignored by the governor, the president, and the legislature. Indeed, the state authorities sent troops into Delaware, Ulster, and Schoharie Counties while Van Buren got indictments against twenty-eight political prisoners; those at Hudson eventually were acquitted, while some at Delphi got harsh terms at Sing Sing. The collaboration with the Antirenters united the NRA with men such as Erastus Root, an old upstate Jacksonian earlier associated with the Workies, but it also made strangely Whiggish allies like Ira Harris, the Albany lawyer; Horace Greeley of the *New York Tribune;* and former Whig governor William H. Seward. As all factions maneuvered, the state assembly actually passed some moderate land reform resolutions. When Boughton emerged from jail, he toured the area with Devyr and Bovay, who, in turn, experienced the extent to which politics went beyond the ballot box.[22]

The NRA, in turn, learned a great deal from Antirenters about how to extend politics beyond the ballot box. An astonished Bovay wrote Evans of "one of those things so curious in this part of the State, a Sheriff's sale." He wrote:

> The people came in great numbers, the Sheriff came, but the horses, the cows and the sheep did not come. In short, it was a sale whereat nothing was sold. No obstruction, no indignity of any kind was offered to the officers: they patrolled the fields for two hours or so in search of the horses, &c., aforesaid, which were advertised for sale . . . The fates were adverse, the fun was spoiled, the Sheriff drove away his own team and nothing more, the crowd slowly closed up the passage after him, and all was still.

As "a silent spectator of the scene," Bovay "had witnessed the passive resistance of the people, like that which the atmosphere offers to the cannon ball, giving way when it is pushed aside and closing immediately after, and was glad that it was so."[23] The NRA, then, early employed the modern usage of the term "passive resistance" and favorably so.

National Reform-Socialist Relations

Evans actively encouraged comradely relations between communitarians and Agrarians, but the latter themselves represented the fruits of the older

Owenite agitation. The followers of Robert Owen had been in disarray since the collapse of the New Harmony community. Many well wishers had become involved with the Workies, the trade unions, the Locofocos, and now the NRA. In addition to Evans himself, Lewis Masquerier, Benjamin Warden, and William Gregory had long ties to the Owenites. Even a rather isolated Agrarian like William Tomlinson wrote from Brady's Bend, Pennsylvania, to describe himself as "a Socialist by profession, and schooled for many years in Owenism" before joining the campaign for land reform. Former Owenites like Masquerier naturally tried to involve their old comrades like Thomas and Marie Varney of Cincinnati. Indeed, the NRA courted Robert Owen himself when the aging reformer returned to the United States. In July, Evans reprinted from Owen's *New Moral World* a letter "to exhibit the mature views of a man . . . in the advocacy of a favorite project for the benefit of mankind." In March 1845, he publicized Owen's New York lectures, advising "no one can hear him without being wiser for it. Go." NRA leaders called the old man "the Columbus of the New Moral World."[24]

Both *Working Man's Advocate* and its successor, *Young America,* provided "a hearing to the plans of other reformers, especially those who have no papers of their own." NRA papers covered in some depth the efforts of Nathan C. Meeker, Orson S. Murray, Valentine Nicholson, Mary Loomis, and Miranda B. Randall. With "ladies" accounting for "about one third" of the number, a movement advocating "one mind" on the need for a new urban socialism united under Warden and Jonas Humbert Jr., a Worky of the Skidmore persuasion; these became the "One-Mentiens," some branches even meeting jointly with the NRA.[25]

Socialists, in turn, concluded that their plans should include land reform politics. Participants in the Hopedale community agreed that land reform deserved to "be put in practical operation as soon as possible." John A. Collins and others formed the Skaneateles Laboring Man's Political Reform Association as an NRA auxiliary in May 1845. At Richmond, Virginia, an informal circle of thirty-seven radicals (including eighteen Fourierists and seven Owenites) saw National Reform as "the first step for their different plans" and declared themselves "unflinching for free soil." Veteran Ohio socialist John Harmon declared reformers "too contracted in their efforts, directing them but to a single partial object as Temperance, Anti-Slavery &c." and hoped the NRA might provide a common political stance for the Ohio, Stark, and Trumbull Fourierist phalanstries; the Zoar community; and the North Union Shakers near Cleveland, as well as other supporters of Owen, Fourier, and "the 'Equal Exchange of Labor' plan of my friend Josiah Warren," the Cincinnati cooperationist. "A Revolutionist" in the *Social Reformer* called land reform a

"John-the-Baptist work" essential to a later, more complete "Social Salvation." Failing to construct new social relations, socialists increasingly appreciated the NRA's emphasis on politics for "uncreating . . . special privileges."[26]

Then, too, through the medium of Old World émigrés, the movement established important international associations. The NRA established some relations with the British Chartists. More immediately, the émigré veterans of the German communist movement expressed their support for land reform through both Hermann Kriege's Sozial Reform Association, launched in 1845, and Wilhelm Weitling's Arbeiterbund.[27]

Socialist goals, in turn, received higher praise from NRA leaders, including those with no real record of appreciation for, interest in, or understanding of the communitarian impulse. Evans hailed the appearance in Horace Greeley's *New York Tribune* of Brisbane's letter from Europe, as a "lucid and unanswerable argument" on the land question. Before long, Bovay described the "visions of the future" offered by Owen and Fourier as "beautiful in theory," and even the hard-headed and pragmatic Devyr later spoke of the latter as "that splendid dreamer."[28]

Among the most organized of the communitarians, the failure of Fourierist truth to remake American civilization created something of a crisis within the American Union of Associationists (AUA). Drawing on the response of the lower orders to "hard times" in the Panic of 1837, small cooperatives spread across New England but concentrated in New Hampshire and especially Vermont. Horace Seaver, the veteran Worky and freethinker, published a new exchange with Warren on the importance of cooperation as a practical step toward socialism. By summer 1844, the *Fall River Mechanic* took up the call in earnest, joined shortly by Lynn cordwainers and others. In Boston, John G. Kaulback and other Fourierists organized the first "Protective Union," a cooperative store to introduce and demonstrate socialist concepts to a broader, more working-class audience. In January 1845, the New England Fourier Society formally adopted what Warren B. Chase called "that simple, safe, and practicable system of combination among consumers of merchandise." Within a few years, these regionally federated cooperatives spread across most of the North.[29]

These more innovative Associationists tended to see political action for land reform as another intermediate stage toward socialism. Their collaboration with the NRA in the NEWA deepened this sense. By November 1844, prominent AUA leaders such as Parke Godwin began regularly attending NRA meetings, and the New England Fourier Society invited the NRA to its January convention in Boston; the NRA sent J. D. Pearson, formerly of the Sylvanian Association. At Brook Farm, Orvis and John Allen decided that the lack of land left workers helpless to form communities, and shoemaker Ryck-man concluded that any "extensive reform" required land reform. Together, they argued within the AUA that NRA politics—such as protective unions or the ten-hour workday—could hasten the American realization of Fourier's social vision. While not disputing the merits of NRA measures at that January convention, Brisbane, Godwin, and George Ripley pleaded the need to invest time in the cooperative experiments. Yet within a few weeks, each of these Fourierist leaders reversed his position, and Ryckman started an NRA tour of upstate New York. In February 1845, Brisbane returned from Paris with material from "the unpublished manuscript of Fourier" describing access to the land as a "primary right" and joined the NRA himself. The New York City election on April 8, 1845, arguably marked one of the first concerted socialist interventions into electoral politics. When none of the major candidates for mayor deigned to formal questioning, the NRA ran Ransom Smith, a clock maker and old Locofoco. Official returns on over 20,000 votes credited Smith with only 117, less than the NRA's membership. Evans charged that Agrarian ballots had been destroyed or miscategorized simply as "scattering." Never-theless, Brisbane had cast "his first vote."[30]

NRA-socialist collaboration inspired several 1845 conferences, beginning with what became the annually held National Industrial Congress (the NIC). The two groups worked together in building the March NEWA conference at Lowell, Massachusetts, which, in turn, scheduled a May assembly at Boston to prepare for a national convention. Ryckman headed the New York delega-tion of Bovay, Manning, and Pearson to Boston where they met representa-tives of the new NRA affiliates at Lynn and Boston. Given the few National Reformers present, NEWA and Fourierist votes defeated a motion to table the land question and passed a resolution for national unity around "the two great fundamental Rights of Man—the Right of Labor and the Right to the Soil."[31] The NEWA reflected an emerging consensus.

Certainly, the NRA seized on the NEWA call for a national industrial con-gress. New York Agrarians not only endorsed it "with enthusiasm and without a dissenting voice" but also sponsored their own preparatory convention on May 5. Among "about thirty persons" who gathered at Croton Hall were Fourierists such as Ryckman, Antirent leaders, and even old Robert Owen himself. Evans urged "the necessity of National Organization" projected by New England's "Industrial Convention" and an ongoing, "Annual INDUS-TRIAL CONGRESS" uniting "all associations having the same political aim." His argument at least secured a consensus for still another preliminary meet-ing—also called an "Industrial Convention" to be held at New York, with the NRA sponsoring a preliminary national conference in May.[32]

New England Fourierists, meanwhile, debated cooperation. Ryckman, who favored both cooperatives and land reform, debated priorities with William Field Young at the September 1845 NEWA convention. Young's emphasis on cooperation prevailed, but he agreed that it need not preclude political action for land reform. The following month, Boston's Workingmen's Protective Union took form under Horace Seaver, the pro-NRA freethinker. In calling for his "Union of Reformers," Ryckman argued that many Democrats viewed theirs as "an organization of reformers," albeit "corrupted by place and power." Temperance advocates had "done much real good" but engaged in the "merely animal education that is the lot of the mass." Ryckman suggested that the "sincere, ardent, heroic" abolitionists, advocates of peace and moral reform societies could unite with Associationists and National Reformers to reach "countless hordes of men and women, whose destiny, under the present system, is ignorance, want, vice." His vision seemed to take form when Evans, Bovay, and Ransom Smith of the NRA signed the call for a national "Industrial Congress" with Godwin, William Henry Channing, and Albert Gilbert of the NEWA.[33] Implicit was the mutual willingness of both socialists and land reformers to redefine themselves in common with radicals from without.

❆ ❆ ❆

The NRA's experience with the shortcomings of Democratic reformism nourished an interest in nonpartisan and independent alternatives in its first year. Land reformers had simultaneously collaborated with the Spartan Band, provided an urban voice for upstate Antirenters, waged a civil libertarian defense of the "free suffrage" advocates in Rhode Island, and established ties to some individuals and independent associations in the interior of the continent. Clearly, though, episodic and local outbursts would not transform the NRA into a truly "national" movement without its convergence with ongoing and broader reform concerns that transcended the land question.

Agrarians themselves debated the extent to which their focus on the land question should remain exclusive. At a special meeting on the issue, Haddock seemed to favor a broadening focus while Devyr and others urged agitation strictly confined to the land question. Between these two positions, Evans, Pyne, and Maxwell defined the organization in the terms of a broader historical movement in "opposition to the creation of Banks, other chartered Monopolies, an amendment of the Militia System, &c." They cited the NRA's constitutional mission "to take into consideration such *other* remedies for the distresses and embarrassments of the productive or working classes as may appear likely to be practically useful." The discussion created a consensus that the longer the list of reforms tacked onto the NRA pledge, the fewer might sign it. Most came to share Moses Jaques's view that "as in mechanics, so in social organization, the more simple the nearer the truth and perfection." For the present, the NRA confined its work as much as possible to the land question.[34] However, its adoption of the ten-hour workday issue demonstrated that it would not remain so.

The NRA itself created the basis for both its convergence with other reforms and its own transformation into a more generalized agrarian radicalism. Their self-description as "wages slaves" soon engaged in a running ideological battle over the nature of "free labor." More immediately, the NRA's electoral orientation would politicize a socialism that had earlier been unconcerned with the ballot.

A John-the-Baptist Work: The Agrarian Politicalization of American Socialism

National Reformers did *not* consider the Freedom of the Soil a panacea for every social and political wrong, but a *necessary step* in progress which would greatly facilitate all desirable reform, and without which *no* plan of reform could prevent the downward course of labor.

—George Henry Evans, 1846

Before 1845, socialists in the United States hoped to change the world by forming distinct communities around the philanthropic ideals of thinkers like Robert Owen or Charles Fourier. In that year, however, the leading American socialist, Albert Brisbane, not only embraced the land reform idea but also the NRA's sense that mass political action rather than philanthropy would be necessary because "from the capitalists, there is no hope." That spring's NRA ticket brought Brisbane to the polls for the first time in his life, along with many other Fourierists.[1] In a very real sense, land reform made socialism political.

The NRA assimilated entire groups of Owenites, Fourierists, and others. Coupled with initial inroads among Whigs, this influx of communitarians deeply suspicious of existing institutions drew the NRA ever farther from its free-thought and Locofoco roots. This made the NRA increasingly discussable within an often-evangelical abolitionism.

The Agrarian-Socialist Convergence

A series of 1845 gatherings virtually brought socialism into the NRA. At the May National Reform Convention, John A. Collins told his fellow socialists that land reform provided the "common ground where all philanthropists could meet." Backed by Benjamin Timms, Robert Owen himself doubted its feasibility as "no man made the land, no man could give just title to it." George

Henry Evans replied that Owen had just given the NRA's central argument and asked pointedly if the respected old man would advise the group to dissolve. "I want the society to go on," answered Owen, "for I think it of great use." Owen later called the "World's Convention" to meet at Clinton Hall from October 2 through 5. Among the almost 350 people who began working their way through various proposals, the young Locofoco Walt Whitman wondered whether the gathering represented a "humbug" or "the germs of a bold though fruitless inquiry into the wrongs and evils of the world." On October 4, Alvan Bovay presented the NRA resolutions. On their way to that day's deliberations, participants found the neighborhood posted with leaflets urging citizens to "Vote Yourself a Farm." By the close of the year, Owen's endorsement had become a talisman in some quarters, and Timms had taken his place in the NRA.[2]

On October 19, the NRA hosted its own "Industrial Convention" at Croton Hall. Evans thought the twenty-four participants included "some of the best minds and truest hearts within the broad expanse of the Republic." Their chair, William Smith Wait, was a Yankee printer who had gone to Illinois thirty years before, returning east to participate in the New England Association of Farmers, Mechanics, and other Workingmen during the 1830s, and he maintained ties with the movement in the East. The resolutions embraced the group's combination of a legislated ten-hour workday, the three original land reform planks, and added calls for cooperation and the regulation of child labor. (Some Fourierists, such as Horace Greeley—still a Whig loyalist with little interest in changing the nonpolitical socialist focus—complained that association had become a poor third to land reform and cooperation.)[3]

These gains had their own dynamics. In January 1846, Sarah Bagley wrote that Lowell's Female Labor Reform League increasingly saw land reform and shorter hours as related concerns, and John Ferral led the Pittsburgh NRA into the ten-hour movement, writing in the *Voice of Industry* that the ten-hour workday seemed "the primary step" to achieving any reform; without it, he argued there was "not, generally speaking, an inclination to read, cultivated among the toiling masses."[4] Movement around this issue, of course, provided an even broader common ground for Fourierists and Agrarians.

Most fundamentally, perhaps, adherents of both the AUA and the NRA came to understand "the land question" within a broad socialist agenda. "Get first the Freedom of the Soil," declared Brisbane, a Fourierist, "and then, I trust, we shall get all that is necessary for the elevation of the American people." In 1846, the *Harbinger* printed extracts from Fourier on the fundamental right to the soil and declared NRA measures "a partial realization" of Fourier's "permanent and conclusive reform," though it seemed so "very

simple,—so that its significance and its ulterior results are not at first perceived by the observer." Official NRA documents agreed that "uncertainty
of means, being provided against, Avarice, the main foe to Socialism, would
vanish." Although socialists generally came to see land reform as an initial step
toward cooperative settlements and acknowledged the value of a critical and
cautious use of the ballot, NRA members accepted cooperation as a measure
of temporary relief and left open the possibility of a socialist future. Later
National Industrial Congresses not only passed the three NRA measures but
explicitly recommended the formation of cooperatives.[5] American socialism
would never be the same.

Boston "workingmen," active episodically for decades, had tried to reconstitute a political movement in 1844. Elizur Wright's *Chronotype* and Horace
Seaver and Josiah Mendum's *Investigator* had long fostered a militant secularism at the edges of the cooperative movement and readily took up land
reform, as did such short-lived cooperationist papers as the *Laborer* and the
Social Reformer. As the NEWA evolved into the New England Labor Reform
League, their protective unions spread through New England and some of the
NEWA's leaders organized an NRA auxiliary. The Boston movement hosted
the first NIC, which convened on June 8, 1846. Although it left neither a
record of its proceedings nor a full list of delegates, its resolutions reflected
a far-reaching discussion of diverse concerns. In the end, it not only adopted
the NRA's three proposals but suggested "a limitation of the hours of daily
labor for wages in all public works, and in all establishments authorized by
law to ten."[6]

A "Massachusetts Auxiliary National and State Reform Association" began
as a straightforward Agrarian current in the NEWA. A Worcester, Appleton
Fay, spearheaded a local, then "a County National Reform Association Auxiliary," and planned a state convention to coincide with "the annual Cattle
Fair and Show, &c." To the land and the ten-hour workday issues, the convention added a call to adjust all wages "to an equal average compensation
of Useful and productive Labor" and nominated NEWA president David
Bryant for governor, heading a fully independent slate in Worcester County.
Lowell's Industrial Reform League had been a mainstay of the NEWA and
supported a series of newspapers, culminating in the *Voice of Industry.* A
Lynn auxiliary thrived alongside the AUA and its Protective Union. A circle
of local militants—Edward C. Darling, Hamilton J. Chenoweth, and William
A. Fraser of the shoemakers' union—also assumed a series of papers like the
Awl, culminating in Henry Clapp's *Lynn Pioneer.*[7]

The NRA also spread rapidly through New England. In Connecticut,
Dr. Charles Douglas, the former leader of the New England Association of

Farmers, Mechanics, and Other Workingmen became an advocate for land reform before his death in 1851. In Maine, Jeremiah Hacker took up the issue; orphaned and homeless as a boy, he had grown up to become the sickly, cranky, and pious pilot of Portland's *Pleasure Boat,* which urged the state to give land to the landless in return for road work. Indeed, the NRA's politics influenced the dozens of communities listed in the *Voice* directories, including the factory town of Chelmsford, which reported that it had "carried the Workingman's ticket complete in spite of all the combined power of codfish aristocracy." In another community, about a hundred land reformers established a coalition with the abolitionists that frightened the local Democrats and Whigs into forming a united conservative bloc.[8] With land reform becoming part of a broader program of social change, the NRA's distinctive emphasis on the ballot box was bearing some fruit.

Meanwhile, socialism carried land reform farther into the old Northwest. A middle-aged Christian socialist, Henry Hamlin Van Amringe, had left Pittsburgh to assist various Fourierist efforts along the Ohio River, where he embraced National Reform as the moral salvation of the republic. "Great reforms cannot be completed at once," he told his fellow Associationists, for "the *means* must be secured." Throughout the decade, his distinguished white-haired form became familiar on the midwestern lecture platforms. Others won to National Reform there included John Harmon and Peter Kaufmann, whose activities went back to the earliest Owenite agitation, although S. C. Frey, Orson S. Murray, Elijah P. Grant, John and Ethan A. Klippart, and younger socialists also turned to the politics of land reform.[9]

Originally an urban movement in the east, National Reform was able to replicate itself somewhat in Cincinnati. A veteran of twenty years of agitation, Elias Longley and his four sons—the most prominent was the famous spelling reformer Alcander—embraced a wide range of measures, including land reform. There, the local stove maker Josiah Warren had developed his "Time Store," which exchanged not money but "Labor Notes"—IOUs for set amounts of labor time—and marketed the goods from communities such as Rural and Utopia. By spring 1846, the local "True Brotherhood" of Augustus and John O. Wattles, Lucius Alonzo Hine, and others merged Hine's publication with Wattles's *Herald of Progression* to establish the monthly *Herald of Truth.* Their "brotherhood" launched two local NRA auxiliaries. Rejecting the idea of "a perfect order at once," they believed that "no change can be made in existing institutions until the public sentiment is prepared for and demands it."[10] They were convinced that the public was ready for land reform.

The New Harmony radicals introduced land reform into Indiana. In 1845, under Warren's influence, they formed a short-lived Free Land Association, and its 1848 revival established a lecture fund and pressed the state legislature for land limitation and homestead exemption. Most important, the group sent Joshua R. Giddings the petition of 471 Indianans urging the federal government to "no longer Trafic nor permit Trafic in the Public Lands." Murray, Wattles, and other National Reformers had associations with several of the other communities in Indiana.[11]

Socialists also planted the banner of the NRA in Michigan. Henry R. Schetterly of Ann Arbor had used the local Universalist press to organize Michigan's Alphadelphia Phalanx, absorbing a planned Washtenaw Phalanx in 1844 and establishing a short-lived community near Galesburg. Despite efforts to merge with the Integral Phalanx in Illinois, many participants drifted back to Ann Arbor where they followed the political lead of Dr. Samuel Denton, a former legislator. Evans could not name "a man better qualified to take the lead in the National Reform movement in Michigan" than Denton, "the author of a series of essays on the subject of Labor, Reform and Political Economy" in the *Alphadelphia Tocsin*, "among the best that have ever appeared in the United States." Schetterly, Denton, and local Fourierists had both political parties vying for Agrarian votes by late 1846.[12]

By the meeting of the first National Industrial Congress, the socialists had contributed much to making the NRA a genuinely national movement. As occurred back east, émigré German socialists in the Midwest supplemented the efforts of American communitarians politicized by the NRA.

The Transformation of National Reform

The NRA's assimilation of communitarian socialism transformed both. Admittedly, something of the earlier debate between communitarians and the original Agrarians over electoral action continued within National Reform as a matter of emphasis, though the line was not clearly based on previous affiliations. In October, Fourierist Lewis Ryckman, trade unionist John Ferral, and political labor reformer Dr. Charles Douglas collaborated toward "a proper and effective plan of organization of the industrial portion of the people to ensure united political action in the security of their rights." NRA representatives tended to argue most consistently for "a great Working Men's Party" and to ask whether "any political party has done anything, unless driven on by workingmen's parties, to advance or lighten the burdens of the oppressed?"[13]

Events upstate further pushed the NRA from its residual Locofoco assumptions. With no allies in power, the Antirenters turned to the time-honored techniques of rural resistance. Farmers, increasingly in "Indian" disguises, began using direct action to thwart foreclosures by removing assets to safety, preventing farm auctions entirely, or making bids pointless and unenforce-able. In the face of Barnburner repression, some Whigs, such as Ira Harris, courted Antirenters and briefly bankrolled Thomas Devyr's *Freeholder,* inspir-ing Democratic charges of Whig "Agrarianism." By the Fourth of July 1845, the Whigs locked Devyr out of the newspaper he had founded. He then launched an unfunded *Anti-Renter,* followed by the equally unprofitable *Albany Work-man.* Whereas sympathetic Antirenters like Smith A. Boughton assisted Devyr and Bovay in their tours through Rensselaer and Columbia Counties, most upstate farmers found Whigs with power preferable to National Reformers without, and the city workingmen noted opposition to land reform from "a quarter where we would perhaps, least expect it," from "that large and sturdy class, the farmers of the North."[14]

The NRA willingness to offer support to pledged candidates of any party horrified the old Locofoco Levi Slamm but impressed the Whig Fourierist Greeley. While Evans and Commerford defended the nonpartisan questioning of candidates, others urged independent nominations at once. When only a single Whig signed the pledge, the NRA turned to independent nominations for the rest of the ticket. For the state senate, they endorsed Antirenters up-state as well as Francis Treadwell, back in the city from Rhode Island. Bovay headed an assembly ticket that included Clannon, the former Worky leader, and Israel Peck, who would help to organize the city's workers in the 1850s, as well as William Rowe, a young craftsman who would remain an Agrarian spokesman for decades. Reflecting its growing mistrust of earlier partisan claims, the NRA distributed its ballots at all eighty-five polling places and reminded voters that a thousand National Reform ballots would secure the balance of power in the city. The returns conceded Treadwell 497 votes for the state senate, and Ransom Smith 384 for city register. Given their unnatu-rally low totals earlier, this four-fold increase likely registered an initial level of support rather than growth in the city. With primary support rooted in the artisan Thirteenth and Tenth Wards, the NRA also polled significant numbers in the Eighth and Sixteenth, and got enough across the city to revive plans for ward clubs. Soon after, new affiliates formed in Brooklyn, Williamsburg, and Bushwick, and in Middleton, New Jersey.[15]

The country began to hear about the rising agrarian "menace" in New York City. The *Courier and Enquirer* warned against any participation in the upcoming state constitutional convention by "the knot of agrarians calling themselves the National Reform Association." Such fears were not allayed that spring, as Commerford rebuilt bridges to discontented Democrats, defending Mike Walsh against his libel conviction, and Brisbane announced Greeley's unreserved endorsement of the NRA. Although opting to play no direct role in the NRA, Greeley virtually displaced Fourierism with land reform—including the radical demand for land limitation—in the columns of his *New York Tribune*. Already the movement had contacted every member of Congress, which as a body started getting memorials and petitions from the electorate. After Bovay gained admission to the bar in July, the Albany NRA suggested sending him as "an official agent at the seat of government," but the New York City group had already dispatched its perennial candidate, Ransom Smith, to Washington to buttonhole national figures. (Later in the year, Bovay married Smith's daughter, Caroline Elizabeth, a land reform propagandist in her own right.) That year, U.S. senators Sam Houston of Texas and Andrew Johnson of Tennessee proposed legislation to encourage moving the landless onto the public domain, and Congress began what became the annual ritual of referring the proposals to committee, where they were tabled.[16]

The NRA decided to enter Ransom Smith, then in Washington, as its candidate in the April 14 mayoral elections. It also planned to participate in the upcoming constitutional convention, Evans suggesting a joint National Reform–Antirent caucus elected around the NRA's land measures and supplementary reforms drawn largely from the earlier Workies and Locofocos. Although the spring elections became particularly partisan, mobilizing enough marginal voters for an easy Democratic victory, the NRA candidates for delegate for the constitutional convention won an impressive seven hundred votes.[17]

When the state constitutional convention met from June 1 to October 26, the NRA had some voice if little else. On June 29, Horace K. Willard, a thirty-nine-year-old physician from Albany County asked pointedly "whether the character and permanency of our institutions would not be increased by multiplying the number of freeholders—and the expediency of forbidding all future accumulation of the soil to exceed 320 acres per man—and to provide some equitable mode for the gradual reduction of the present landed monopolies as they now exist." On July 10 and September 26, John H. Hunt, the forty-two-year-old New York printer, presented NRA petitions for land limitation with resolutions to encourage "a more general distribution of landed property, and for the perpetuation of a landed democracy."[18] However, the convention shuttled aside the speeches and petitions.

On the other hand, newly mobilized land reformers did not share this central commitment to electoral politics. John O. Wattles thought it "above and overtop all other causes now in the *political* world" but opposed electoral efforts to replace "the self-constituted 'powers that be.'" Valentine Nicholson thought it "not in the *nature*, not in the power of governments to *reform* the people," and a writer from the Hopedale community opposed efforts "to cast out Devils by the Prince of Devils." Brisbane still called politics "the great prostitute" of the century, and the *Voice of Industry* balked at making endorsements only to "barter them away to one class of demagogues," arguing "that political supremacy is not the *primary* object of the workingmen's Reform," which aimed at change that "can never be overthrown by political commotions, or sectarian whirlwinds—even a *free soil*, with a *free and virtuous people*." In the NRA itself, Walter Van Dusen—"a no-human government man"—declared voting of any sort to be "an oppressive, forcible business" and urged "voluntary" land reform through the abolitionist strategy of moral suasion.[19] Such thinkers feared that the means used by reformers would determine the ends of reform.

Indeed, the NRA provided the touchstone of social radicalism not only for Wattles, Nicholson, and Van Dusen but also for James Arrington Clay, Lyman W. Case, Stephen Pearl Andrews, and Joshua King Ingalls. At Gardiner, Maine, Clay used *David's Sling* to strike the Goliath obstacles to perfection, including land monopoly, though his militant opposition to church and state would be dangerous enough, and his radical feminism made him notorious before he later came to New York. Case, a Harvard graduate, reported Connecticut's 1847 legislation of exemption as "a bright oasis in Legislation" in "a desert to Humanity," and subsequently moved to New York, where he and his wife, Marie Stevens Case (later Howland), formulated their critique of marriage as an oppressive institution. Driven from Texas for his antislavery activities, the Massachusetts-born Andrews never compromised his hostility to traditional marriage nor his advocacy of woman's rights. Ingalls rejected "the sacredness of form, the necessity of a creed" in religion, and disbelieved in "the present office-holding government among mankind."[20]

By 1847, the *Voice of Industry* urged building "the superstructure of Pure Democraty whereever [*sic*] our *Republican rubbish* can be removed." At that year's NIC, Fay proposed a detailed constitutional model for a "free state" based on regular, town-meeting democracies, woman's suffrage, and cooperative industry. Dr. Edward Newberry urged victory through individual self-improvement and cooperative self-organization. Fannie Lee Townsend, the poet and Dorr rebel, "did not see how reform was to be affected by the representative form of government." Masquerier proposed settling a colony wherein "the people would legislate without delegating their sovereignty." Several speakers agreed, including William West, a transplanted Yankee abolitionist and Fourierist who urged "*a government of* ALL *for the benefit of* EACH, in itself the PERFECTION OF SELF-GOVERNMENT." Only a slim majority defeated the movement's adoption of "direct legislation" as a means to legitimize an agrarian seizure of the land.[21]

Land Reform and Abolitionism

The NRA in 1847 stood at a neglected turning point in the relations of working-class radicalism and abolitionism. However complex that relationship had been, the NRA had always sought abolitionist endorsement. Within weeks of its founding, Evans had begun his correspondence with Gerrit Smith and James Birney. He continued to ask abolitionists how they expected to persuade landless workers to "form a political party to abolish Southern slavery, unless at the same time they could free themselves?" Then, too, despite an official NRA endorsement of James Knox Polk in 1844, at least one prominent Agrarian leader, John H. Keyser, actually voted for Birney, receiving from Democratic thugs a "severe beating for daring to insult the American voters of the period."[22] In short, some land reformers aimed to transform rather than to supersede abolitionism.

New England's *Voice of Industry* saw land reform as part of "a new party." The Yankees thought it had already begun to function with or without labeling it "the Workingmen's Party. Some call it the National Reform Party. We call it the Humanitarian party, which represents the tendency of this age to Mutual Guaranties." As its platform, the *Voice* proposed supplementing the three original NRA demands with the ten-hour workday; cooperative protective unions; "a general Lien law for the protection of laborers"; "all manufacturing, mechanical and industrial corporation" with wages "remunerated directly from the dividends"; and "methods for the organization of Industry among small capitalists."[23]

Such a platform was broad enough to include abolition. Lowell's "Industrial Reform Lyceum" provided abolitionists like Garrison with a platform and denounced slavery in Garrisonian terms as "a crime against Humanity" that "ought to be abolished immediately." "Do our anti-slavery friends ever discuss the merits of the Labor question? the Peace question? or the abolition of capital punishment?" asked one, adding that "we discuss all of these, and Slavery, South and North, besides; and are 'National Reformers.'" Increasingly, NRA members described themselves as "true abolitionists," struggling "to abolish all Slavery, North, South, East and West." Masquerier proposed a "mighty Abolition national Reform," and Ryckman saw antislavery as part of his proposed "Union of All Reformers, For One Great Reform."[24]

The possibilities for joint action increased as these movements tested both their successes and the limitations of their successes. By early 1846, the Maine NRA ascribed its gains to "the help of the Abolitionists" who were "rather friendly." That same year in Ohio, Salmon P. Chase acknowledged the NRA's goal as "an object of great importance in a republican government" but doubted "the practicality of effecting and permanently establishing these and kindred reforms, until freedom for all laborers, and just wages for all labor, shall have been secured by an impartial and resolute application of the fundamental maxims of genuine democracy—which demand equal and exact justice and equal rights for all men."[25] Usually ignored by Democratic and Whig candidates, the NRA found itself endorsing antislavery candidates pledged to land reform goals.

War with Mexico drew these currents still closer. National Reformers noted that Americans had no less a permanent excuse for war and enslavement than had the ancient Romans who also faced potentially hostile tribal peoples on their borders. Horace Greeley's pro-NRA *New York Tribune* wondered, "Do Americans ever ask themselves how and why we are visited with so many more Indian Wars than our neighbors?" Certainly, "those who provoke or begin a war can always make out a colorable pretext for it." Nevertheless, Americans "habitually crowd the Indian, bully them, rob them, mistreat them" from a belief in "the 'Manifest Destiny' of our race to take whatever they may want or fancy." "Unless those who are called to foot the bills set their faces like flint against the whole business," warned the *Tribune,* "we shall never more be rid of the villainy and waste of these atrocious speculations."[26]

From its inception, the NRA faced issues relating to Texas. Before the group had come to any conclusions, Commerford offered the Democrats' "Great Texas Meeting" in City Hall Park and support on the condition that annexation "be effected without increasing black and white slavery." Evans, on the other hand, never hesitated in opposing the admission of "Tax-us." After an internal debate in the winter of 1844–45, the NRA officially adopted both Evans's opposition and Commerford's preconditions for support. (At that point, only one member resigned, protesting that the stand introduced an antislavery dimension into the movement.)[27]

With Texas, the United States acquired a vexing boundary dispute with Mexico. Polk ordered troops under Zachary Taylor into the disputed territory already garrisoned by the Mexicans. After the predictable clashes, Polk reported to Congress in May 1846 that "invaders" had shed "American blood on American soil" and got a declaration of war. In June, prewarned allies of the administration seized California allegedly to prevent its occupation by the British, and the president got additional congressional authorization in August to "purchase" additional territory from Mexico. Pressed by Southern proponents of a "Caribbean empire" for slavery, the war—and the subsequent "filibustering" against Cuba and Central America—terrified not only abolitionists but also the NRA, which denounced warfare "waged at the instigation and behoof of Southern slavery and Northern Capital." Evans warned Mexico that a U.S.-imposed "land-grabbing system would soon turn this paradise into a purgatory."[28]

These events led National Reformers and abolitionists to the same conclusions. The NIC urged that American soldiers should no longer be sent abroad "but should only be fixed on to the watch towards of defense, as the faithful sentinels" of a self-governing republic. Evans urged Polk to "stop the war at once, on the easiest terms you can, or even to back out. You are in the wrong!" "Defeat would be more profitable to us. Retreat would be more honorable," declared Elizur Wright Jr. in his *Chronotype*.[29]

The same war that shaped this Agrarian-abolitionist convergence compromised the viability of the entire national political party system. Initial Whig opposition dissipated with rapid military success; the realization that the partisan associations of the two greatest heroes, Generals Zachary Taylor and Winfield Scott, assured the party a winning candidate in 1848, and the nagging memory of the Federalist Party's collapse after opposing the War of 1812 troubled them. In August 1846, Pennsylvania Democrat Rep. David Wilmot tried to amend a military appropriations bill to bar slavery from any lands acquired by its funds. In March 1847, Southern leaders blocked its Senate passage and denied any government authority to regulate slavery, even as Northern Democrats Lewis Cass and Stephen A. Douglas proposed "popular sovereignty," allowing regulation by the territories. The results seemed to confirm the radicals' "Modern Dictionary" that satirically defined "democracy," "liberty," and "republic" in practical terms; adding that "Northern troops" made "Glorious War" on Indians to capture a handful of free and equal, "liberty loving, runaway democrats."[30]

✲ ✲ ✲

From the start, the NRA had hoped to organize "such persons as may subscribe to the principles recommended as leading measures" into a broad coalition. They welcomed "Christians, Mormons, Infidels," as well as "anti-Slavery men, Associationists, Communitists, Temperance men, Peace men, Free Trade men, and Free Land men." Ingalls hoped the issue could unite "friends of Equality, Liberty and Justice, male and female" and "Friends of Universal Freedom, Universal Education, Universal Homes, Universal Plenty, Universal Labor and Universal Happiness" to "rally in the name of God and Humanity." Brisbane thought "the Movement Party of this country must effect an organization as complete as that of the Legions against which they have to contend."[31]

Adherents of all sorts seemed to formulate a common understanding. Socialism anticipated the realities of 1900, while National Reform focused on the more immediate possibilities for radical change. Nothing inherent in the socialist vision debarred proponents from an involvement in politics, and nothing in National Reform precluded anticipation in the emergence of socialism. Easy distinctions between Lewis Ryckman, a Fourierist who joined the NRA, and Alvan Bovay, a National Reformer interested in Fourierism, had become irrelevant. Neither category could adequately define new associates like Lucius A. Hine. If there seemed little doubt whether antislavery would fit, how and where it could do so awaited the impact of events on the ideology of this emergent land reform movement.

George Henry Evans (Mar.
25, 1805–Feb. 2, 1856). From
Lewis Masquerier, *Appendix
to Sociology.* New York: By
the author, 1884.

Lucius Alonzo Hine (Feb.
22, 1819–July 8, 1906).
From William H. Venable,
"Ohio Valley Historical and
Literary Memorials (Thir-
teenth Paper)," *Commercial
Gazette,* Feb. 20, 1887, 14.

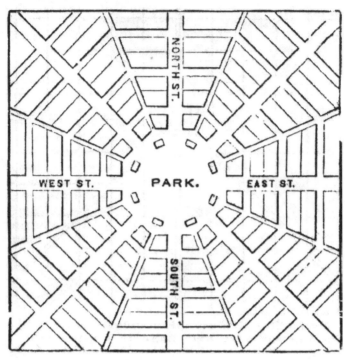

NORTH ST.

WEST ST.   PARK.   EAST ST.

SOUTH ST.

a

TOWNSHIP DIAGRAM.

Square Mile
for Park and
Public
Edifices.

b

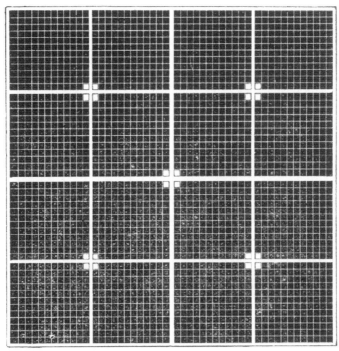

c

National Reform Village: a) village; b) village in township; c) four
villages in township. From Lewis Masquerier, *Appendix to Sociology.*
New York: By the author, 1884.

Group portrait of NRA founders. From *Documentary History of American Industrial Society.* Ed. John R. Commons, Ulrich B. Phillips, Eugene A. Gilmore, Helen
L. Sumner, and John B. Andrews. Cleveland: A. H. Clark Co., 1910.

Lewis Masquerier (Mar. 14, 1802–Jan. 7, 1888). From Lewis Masquerier, *Appendix to Sociology.* New York: By the author, 1884.

National Reform logo. From Lewis Masquerier, *Appendix to Sociology.* New York: By the author, 1884.

Alvan E. Bovay (July 12, 1818–Jan. 29, 1903). From *The History of Fond du Lac County, Wisconsin.* Chicago: Western Historical Company, 1880.

2

THE AGRARIAN PERSUASION

The Social Critique: Individual Liberty in a Class Society

The fact is . . . all men in *good society,* are endowed with certain inalienable rights, except *poor* men. All men who do not pay their honest debts are great scamps, except those who cheat on a large scale. All men are born free and equal except negroes, Indians, and foreigners. All men are great sinners except those who belong to the church. All men are allowed to think and speak freely except those who are not orthodox. All men are gentlemen, except those who work for a living. All well dressed and accomplished women are ladies, except factory and servant girls.

—*Chester Reveille and Homestead Advocate,* 1849

Ideas of class identity and interests defined National Reform. "We are poor ourselves, and have always been so; we have nothing to lose but our energies and our labor," declared George Henry Evans, who "identified with the working classes both by interest and by principle." A sympathetic observer noted that most NRA activists "have a handicraft and consequently a deep interest in the rights of labor," whereas the hostile Democratic *New York Herald* dismissed them as "a limited number of working men" without "a single name of high note in public affairs" or "a single man of wealth." National Reformers, acting "in the name . . . of the pauperized producers of the earth," sought "an avenue of escape from degrading and unrequited labor." Opening public lands would make many landowners of some and improve conditions for the rest by "relieving the labor market" and "creating a greater demand for his industry."[1] With their feet planted in American conditions, they offered an open-eyed commentary about the world that was nothing if not "the bottom up."

The NRA believed the ideals of independence, liberty, and republicanism so widely professed in America were incompatible with the unlimited "right" to accumulate unlimited wealth. The concerns of the rich and well born had built Old World hierarchies in the New. Here, too, a coercive state protected and served the ruling elite while subjugating the workers.

The Promise of a New World

National Reformers grounded their claims in the American Revolution: "The blood of our workingmen redeemed those lands from European bondage—the sweat of our workingmen paid every penny that they cost—what can give fertility to those lands, but the labor of the Workingmen?" They battled for "Our country—as yet but in name." The equality "declared by the great Charter of our Independence, to be the birthright of all is not realized." Urging "a revival of the Spirit of '76," the NRA described its activities under headings such as "The Revolution to be fought again!" and "The work of '76 to be finished!" "The American Revolution is yet in progress," insisted one NRA spokesman, and his organization regularly held its own Fourth of July celebrations in many communities. Land reformers cited Thomas Jefferson, who had corresponded with Fanny Wright, Cornelius Blatchley, Thomas Skidmore, and other social critics whose views anticipated National Reform. More accurately, perhaps, radicals also celebrated the memory of Thomas Paine, who had written, among other works, *Agrarian Justice*.[2]

NRA leaders celebrated their association with the few survivors of that revolutionary generation. They noted that National Reformer Moses Jaques had ridden with the Continental Army while a boy. Later, "a Patriarch 99 years old, strong in health, clear in intellect" was "now proud to come before the Young Americans," and declared himself a National Reformer to help restore man's "natural relation to his kind Mother Earth." Another, "a revolutionary soldier aged 80" declared his agreement with the NRA, adding "some of us wanted that as soon as the war was over; and that was the time it ought to have been done." Yet another persuaded Thomas Devyr "that neither Land Monopoly nor Bank Monopoly was ever contemplated by the heroes of the Revolution." After watching another old veteran denied a seat on the coach, Devyr quipped, "the stage manager knows little about Revolutions and cares less." (It is worth noting that the local Veterans Corps of the War of 1812 endorsed the NRA's petition drive.)[3]

These affinities for the American revolutionary tradition reached beyond rhetoric, most directly in National Reformers' urging an independent course for the nation's development. Like their transatlantic predecessors and contemporaries, they identified the idea of an unlimited private ownership of land with "the Norman yoke" of conquest and coercion. Commercial and industrial development created new hierarchies standing on the old foundations. However, they asserted that American independence posed a unique opportunity for Western civilization, "a new, a stainless, and untrodden world . . . a vast, an unpolluted continent," which might create a unique, "INDIG-ENOUS CIVILIZATION . . . better, purer, higher than ever yet appeared in the world." They quoted Thomas Jefferson on the inapplicability and injustice of the old standards in what William S. Wait called a "remote situation from the arbitrary constitutions of Europe."[4]

However, the nominal independence of the United States begged the question: "Why does our American Republicanism produce the same bitter fruit as the rotten Despotism of the Old World?" The "greedy profit-mongers of America" sustained "the British legacy to us—Landlordism." American radicals spoke of "our Egyptian bondage of British principles," which had been "imported to this country from Europe" and "grew out of robbery and murder, accomplished by the sword." Earlier, an anonymous revolutionary pamphleteer warned that independence would fail should the nation fall "into domestic slavery, when we have risked everything which is valuable in repelling a foreign one?" Almost seventy years later, Evans asked, "When shall we be able to capsize that British coat of arms?"[5]

Independence required American republicans not to replicate British, Roman, and Egyptian hierarchies. "Wealth is power," proclaimed John H. Klippart, "even under the wings of American liberty, and the all engrossing topic, is the money market, in other words, means and method of 'getting rich.' Happiness does not really enter human calculations." Here, as elsewhere, "those who have a monopoly of the land" gained "a monopoly of the money also." This gave rise to a "monstrous combination of king, temporal and spiritual lords, pensioners, professional crafts, and large and small dealers of all kinds, who are united by one common interest to crush and plunder an unresisting people." This new aristocracy could be "as fatal to liberty as the worst form of despotism." Its elimination, they believed, would be in "the rich as well as the poor man's interest," for "even the monopolizers of rights" faced insecurities. A professed mission to build a genuinely New World based on institutions representative of the producers contrasted sharply with its historical predispositions to replicate in a geographically new location the standards of the Old World with its historical cycles of inequality, hierarchy, expansion, and collapse. As elsewhere, Americans faced "singular anomalies in a Republican form of Government."[6]

Certainly, National Reformers shared the belief of the eighteenth-century founders that republics tended to be ultimately unstable and transitory. National Reformers cited Jefferson's belief that "from the conclusion of the [revolutionary] war we shall be going down hill." A Philadelphia adherent John

Sheddon reminded his audience that proportionately "fewer men in Pennsylvania at this day . . . owned land than at the time of the Revolution." Despite the growing prosperity of the nation as a whole, the workers experienced the relative, "uniformly accelerated downward tendency of the Laboring classes," and land reformers feared a time "not far off, when . . . every rod of soil will be under the claim of some of earth's multiplied sovereigns, and at the same time there will be a large class—a great majority of the whole, who will be landless—at the mercy of the more avaricious and fortunate ones."[7]

Contemporary political discourse did not assuage their fears for the republic. William Heighton, the veteran Worky, protested when the courts—eager to rationalize black slavery—relegated "the great moral and political truths" of the Declaration of Independence to "'mere lifeless forms,' 'indefinite abstractions,' intended by their Great Author for show, humbug—anything but practice." Another noted that legal authorities described the Declaration as merely "Jefferson's dogma," or "a self-evident lie" believed to be practical by "no sane man." American rulers chose "setting the fox to guard the geese" because they increasingly regarded politics as "too sacred to be handled by the rough hands of the people." NRA leader Joshua K. Ingalls warned that what existed of democratic standards and procedures in the United States "could be reversed to morrow."[8]

Unlike the patrician founders, however, National Reformers hoped that representative government might yield to citizen self-government—a modern version of classical "democracy"—as desirable, viable, and immediately possible. The American Revolution, whatever its shortcomings, had located the source of legitimate political power in the people, which, argued Henry Van Amringe, disproved any argument "that the lands belong to the government and not to the people." The policy of commercializing public lands enshrined "the injustice of compelling men to buy or pay money for that which is already their own."[9]

The NRA sought answers in the Declaration of Independence, issuing several of their own versions of this "concise exposition of Human Rights." Van Amringe called it a "folly and delusion" to discuss a right to life without recognizing an implicit right to air, earth, and water. Another NRA proponent asked, "how the poor are to enjoy the rights of 'life, liberty, and pursuit of happiness,' if capital and avarice are to be allowed to stretch forth their long arms, and monopolize the means from which those blessings flow?" "Believing all men are Created Equal; Trust[ing] that they are endowed by Nature with certain inalienable rights; among which are the Right to Such portion of the Earth as shall be sufficient to provide each with the means of subsistence and comfort," the New Harmony NRA thought "no man can by natural right possess more than a limited portion of it." Bovay thought the Declaration also attacked all "property in man" and all forms of slavery by asserting what Jeriel Root called "the divine rights of universal man."[10]

In short, faithfulness to the American principles of 1776 mandated the seizure of power by the working majority. Heighton, too, asked whether "the sacred sounds of LIBERTY and EQUALITY have any *actual* existence among us, or are, in reality, more than *mere empty sounds?*" "Have we fulfilled the promise and redeemed the pledge given by our fathers, when they sealed the Declaration of Independence?" asked Klippart. "Was it to crush down the sons and daughters of our country's industry under the accumulated and accumulating evils of neglect, poverty, vice, starvation, and disease that our fathers bought our independence with their blood and decreed by their charter our equality as citizens, and our liberty as men?" "If the right of self-government, of thought and of action . . . are little to effect no more than we behold," he suggested, ". . . let us hasten to Independence Hall. . . . let the same walls which echoed the first cry of 'liberty and equality' give back ere they totter to decay the last hollow murmurs of a deceiving sound."[11]

As a result, America should have moved differently. With an eye to the contemporary Chartist efforts to secure universal manhood suffrage in Britain, Evans noted that Americans had "most or all of those means of progress, for which the reformers of the old world are now chiefly contending: YOUNG AMERICA, then, must embody something more *ultimate* than they." Despite reservations, he thought that, of all the world's oppressed, Americans remained the "most favorably circumstanced for a restoration of the soil." Therefore, the NRA offered "the most truly American measure," and "the greatest idea" since the attainment of independence.[12]

The Old Realities of the New World

Americans had long acknowledged the reality of class. Since revolutionary days, artisan "leather aprons" had referred to a "silk-stocking" elite as home-grown "nobles," "gentry," and "nabobs" or simply "nobs." In 1802, James Reynolds wrote a cautionary tale about the replication of European classes that seemed relevant enough to be reprinted by radical freethinkers in the 1830s. Even without hereditary titles, America's "working bees" labored for "idle drones" under the rule of "the LAND KINGS and the MONEY KINGS." George Lippard, the Philadelphia novelist, and others discussed the "Upper Ten" as opposed to the "Lower Million." Contemporaries spoke of an "aristocracy of wealth," with increasing reference to "manufacturing capital in the North." "No matter how many parties and sects nations are divided into," insisted Lewis

Masquerier, "they are still divided into the two great classes of producers and non-producers, of property-holders and rent-racked, hireling and pauperized laborers; in short, divided into unconscious robbers and robbed." However, understandings of class ranged from Skidmore's use of simple inequalities in an undifferentiated "property" to John Pickering's complex analysis based on qualities of labor.[13]

Early Anglo-American thinkers from John Locke to David Ricardo had argued that "nothing but labor bestowed upon the natural elements and products of the earth" ownership, but the dispossession of the workers inverted the implications. "Capital is of no use to the world without labor," argued Root. "As nothing but labor can produce property," wrote Masquerier, "it is most outrageously unjust that property should be allowed to add other property to itself without creating any more of it in society."[14]

"The wealth of the country," concluded one radical, "is not in the hands of the just owners." Van Amringe argued that "the rich do not produce their own riches," which are "produced by the workers." "Those who produce the most are allowed to consume the least," protested Evans. "New *luxuries* are provided for some, by those who do not receive a sufficiency of the *necessaries* of life." Elizur Wright insisted "the poor have their rights . . . the most perfect right in the world to say to the capitalists, we consider that labor deserves so much (say one half, two thirds or nine tenths) of the produce of mutual capital and labor." The NRA declared its principal enemy to be "this *terrible power . . . that WEALTH and CAPITAL acquire over labor and life where ALL the surface of the earth is monopolized,* and consequently where there is no outlet for the laborer."[15]

National Reformers rejected anecdotal data about mobility as unrepresentative. Most of the elite, as Klippart said, "acquired wealth by hereditary descent," while "no son of toil ever has by the sweat of his brow become a millionaire" save by "commercial gambling, or *speculating,* if you like the term better, by wronging many a son of toil out of the fruits of his labor." Such practices were "in direct opposition of the *great thought* embodied in our charter which declares that all men are born 'free and equal.'" "Tempt no longer the fortunate workers, the one of a hundred who chanced to obtain a small prize in the lottery of human folly and misery," pleaded Evans and John Windt.[16]

The sophistication of any nineteenth-century social analysis probably turned on its handling of an emergent middle class, increasing specialization, and the role of farmers. Reynolds had described "idle people" as merchants, lawyers, militarists, clerics, and "various classes of men . . . licensed to commit these crimes" as a social buffer between the elite and the working people.

However, Pickering thought practitioners of "theology, medicine, law, authorship and art" were "useful in the present," even if the need for such specialists might fade. Antirenters and National Reformer Hugh Brooks insisted that "any union of the laboring classes should embrace the Agriculturalists," and the movement defended "all the small holders of land and farms," arguing that property below a certain amount should be "wrested from no one." "'Security of property,'" complained Wait, "no longer means security to the citizen in the possession of his moderate competency, but security to him who monopolizes thousands—security to a few, who may live in luxury and ease upon the blood and sweat of many."[17]

National Reformers used variants of the term *proletarian* to describe those propertyless in the means of production but used a plural form in discussing the "useful," "producing," or "working classes." They cited and gathered their own statistics on incomes, budgets, and the hours of labor, urging the federal census to do so as well. These documented "the almost universal usurpation of all property and power by a non-producing, tyrannical and aristocratic class," "a higher class" that would ever "treat with contempt and insolence, the very class upon whom they depend for their existence as well as subsistence." Control of land allowed the rulers to extort "more than four-fifths of the product of labor, and in some countries nearly all of it!" The character of the society "comes home to the bosoms and to the firesides of the lowest orders of men, who are thereby rendered mean-spirited and servile." Devyr saw "Fraud, Cruelty and Baseness of Soul" as permeating civilization, to which he pledged "my undying hostility" to "the criminal 'civilization.'" Elizur Wright described as "a grand lottery scramble" in which most participants would always lose. "As society is constituted," said a sympathetic reformer, "working men are but weapons, mechanized autonomatons, in the hands of others."[18]

However, as Mike Walsh noted, "Labor is a commodity, and its value is regulated like that of any other, by the demand which the market affords." The capitalists, wrote Devyr, naturally push productivity "up to the limit of endurance, and wages down to the lowest verge of subsistence." Not only did "the larger capitalist compete down the lesser," added Masquerier, but "all conspire to reduce wages down to the point of starvation, with no hope of ever laying up any support for old age, or of escaping the poor-house prison." To Commerford, these dynamics meant "that a fair day's wages for a fair day's work cannot be obtained." The process "reduced the producers to a point beyond which they can no further go—to a state of miserable starvation, and to the infamy of the almshouse."[19]

Long before Henry George's *Progress and Poverty*, National Reformers saw industrialization as a factor in the impoverishment of the workers. The mechanized degradation of labor reduced free-born Americans into the "toil-worn tenant-housed hireling of the great crammed cities," whose numbers weighed down wages and floated higher rents. In "fetid slums," stifled "with gasses and putrid air, breeding plague and raising puny, half-formed children to fill up the cemeteries," they ate "withered, adulterated, half-decayed provisions." Van Amringe thought such conditions created "crime, vice and folly." Evans urged readers to consider "the *cause* of the increase of suicides," for "pauperism, crime, intemperance, insanity and suicide *all* kept pace with the increasing insecurity of the means of existence." A rural National Reformer thought cities the "ulcers upon the body politic" and hoped the movement would eliminate the "overcrowded cities then propelling a poisonous blood through the body politic." Industry dissolved earlier communities of crafts-men, leaving the "poor and middling classes" whose children, wrote Skidmore, "must be, ninety-nine cases in a hundred, slaves, *and worse,* to some rich proprietor." The engine of civilization would be what William J. Young called "the blind but overpowering power of Capital, Landlordism, Electricity, Steam and Machinery."[20]

Workers' Rights in the Coercive State

Suspicion of government was endemic to early socialism and radicalism in the United States. From the turn of the century, radical freethinkers had urged a "simplified" legal system to "bring law and justice into union." Skidmore had disparaged law as "a little parchment, inscribed with a little ink, as is now the paper I write on," and spoke of "the duty" of the dispossessed "to destroy their own governments" to establish a just world.[21]

NRA adherents advocated a variety of political reforms aimed at making government increasingly more democratic. They urged a district system of elections and adoption of the secret ballot. More than this, they criticized major features of the U.S. Constitution, arguing for the direct election or the abolition of its unelected judiciary and its indirectly elected U.S. Senate and presidency. Evans had long urged the election of all public offices, and the 1854 NIC discussed and tabled a motion taking this position.[22]

All of this aimed at a smaller and more decentralized political order. From its earliest campaign, the NRA asked candidates to pledge not only to reform land policy but also to "reduce as much as practicable, the expense of the government and to prevent, if possible, the creation or assumption of a govern-ment debt." NRA members wanted "a *cheap* government by few and simple laws." Government, they argued, should legislate "for the protection of *rights,* leaving the *interests* of the people to their own management." They expected "little legislation" in a just society. Adherents said they wanted to "do away with the now necessary evil of law and lawyers." They wanted government "nearer the people" as part of their effort "to simplify and condense the laws, so that justice may be as accessible to the poor as the rich."[23]

National Reformers knew that large-scale governments rooted in social realities would not be socially neutral. When approached about a homestead bill, a ten-hour workday law, or the regulation of child labor, American officeholders claimed constitutional and laissez-faire mandates not to "meddle" with private property. However, the same officials chartered and subsidized "companies, such as Banks, Railroads, and large Factory Establishments," and Wisconsin land reformers recalled property taxes, eminent domain, and other acts of legislation that does "meddle with the rights of property."[24] The issue, they argued, was not whether government should "meddle" with private property but whether it might sometimes do so on behalf of the citizens in general.

Big government, in turn, attracted the self-interested rather than the disinterested citizen. Choosing men "from among property-holders, and who knowingly, and even unconsciously legislate for property and class—not for the pauperized and starving people" made them not "tenants, and hirelings, but the lords and masters of the people." While republican forms permitted some "civilization or progress" and some "of true genius and philanthropy" to exercise power, "there will never be but two or three found in a legislature." Devyr saw them among "the most false, criminal and execrable that ever afflicted any nation of God's Earth, or any party of God's Family." Elected as "a temporary two-year old Steward," those in Congress made decisions that would shape the future for generations. Root thought the nature of politics meant that practitioners as a group had "neither truth nor righteousness in them, neither love to God nor man." Masquerier thought specialized decision makers were bound to exploit a people "educated to believe that they are a necessary institution instead of being only a nuisance and usurpation of power which the people can exercise so much more in our township organizations in proper person with scarcely any expense." Government allowed "a mere change of tyrants, that still leaves the laws of alienation and monopoly in force."[25]

On its most basic level, National Reformers believed governments tend "to assume to themselves powers that the present people cannot delegate without trampling upon the rights of those that are after them." Root saw law "only in its perverted state," as "robbery in the name of law and order." Official NRA documents declared that ultimately "all legislation only operates as general deeds of conveyance, conveying away rights and property from the many to the few." Even politicians sometimes allied to the NRA—such as John

Cochrane—conceded of the monopolist, that, "though sanctioned by the law, his is not the true right."[26]

The NRA also saw the emergence of a specialized state as carrying its own logic. Root shrewdly pointed out that "to establish truth and righteousness in the earth, requires but little legislation and but short sessions of courts, with but very little expense." Masquerier and other National Reformers described a hierarchy of power based on "the erroneous institutions of general and hired soldier, of master and chattel slave, also of polygamist and concubine, of boss and hired laborer, of offices and vassal voter, of landlord and tenant, and of creditor and borrower" with "a graduated scale of superior and inferior offices, nobility, landlords and capitalists." "Our State, our Church, our orders and societies of whatever kind," wrote Ingalls, "exist for the sole purpose of Glorifying their organization and perpetuating power." Agrarians thought that those who wielded government authority, like all the professions, tended to "do all they can to perpetuate the necessity for their services." Devyr noted that law "lifts the personal odium of cruelty in all its forms—rackrenting, seizing, selling out and evicting out—entirely off the shoulders of the Blasphemers, and rests it upon that intangible and morally unapproachable thing called 'Law.'"[27]

Such logic moved society into ever more centralized and, ultimately, authoritarian politics. Wait early pointed out that patronage had become "enormous, and totally subversive" of democratic accountability. Masquerier feared that centralization and growth of government "demoralizes" the people, leaving the governing "a mere incorporated company . . . assuming exclusive privileges and honors." A Pembroke meeting urged "an Abridgement of Executive Patronage"; John Sheddon proposed curbing presidential appointment; and William J. Young condemned "the growing tendency of political parties to create new offices." Although a major proponent of politics within the NRA, Bovay "wished to have not a physical government, but a *moral* government to give out recommendations to the rest of the earth for them to follow" with "no penal laws whatever." "The art of law and the art of government," added Root, "must be done away, the earth has been cursed by them long enough." Masquerier spoke of attaining land reform without government by the people "signing a statute making it inalienable."[28]

✻ ✻ ✻

National Reform was a political movement that ultimately disliked the methods of politics and distrusted the centralized state. National Reformers like Van Amringe did not think they were asking of government "that homes should be *given* to them," but "that homes should not be *withheld* from them. Let not government *withhold* from them the homes which the Deity has already given," he argued. "Labor is the poor man's only property;" insisted Brisbane, "but while the laws have fenced in the right of all other kinds of property—the sacredness of ownership in real estate, in chattels and all kinds of goods—the property of the poor man—his labor—is mercilessly taken from him by every species of fraudulent contrivance, and yet the laws have no pity, no security for him."[29]

The contrast between the promise and the practice of America inspired the NRA and later nationwide political movements. Masquerier and others believed that delegating power seemed "an absurd dogma" as "not a single distinct thing in the Universe . . . represents another." From their critique of "the present liberty-destroying institutions of mankind" grew their vision of a new democratic social order shaped by the working citizen unfettered by class and making political decisions "by a direct vote of the people in townships."[30]

Means and Ends: Pure Democracy,
      Self-Organization, and the Revolution

> [U]se the government to destroy itself—use it to abolish despotism, to
> break down all distinctions founded on color, or sex, to overthrow Land
> Monopoly and Slavery, to destroy all mammoth companies that exist by
> virtue of chartered privileges; to abolish all tariffs and unnatural banking.
> . . . But this is a gradual work.
>   —Lucius A. Hine, 1853

Lucius Alonzo Hine and his comrades believed, with the founders
of their nation, that even good governments were, at their best, "a necessary
evil to counteract greater evils" in the chaos that would take place without
government. Unlike the American founders, they also thought that a better
civilization could mitigate the magnitude of those evils and cultivate a citizenry
capable of self-rule as the ultimate check on an ever-threatening state power.
National Reform saw itself as a vital part of a "constant improvement until the
nation shall be consummated in a genuine Democracy" and "the destruction
of all government."[1]

Antebellum land reform sought to be a step toward a "pure democracy."
To reach that goal, the NRA formulated a "transitional" program, in which the
agitation for land reform represented a political bridge to a radical social transformation. A concept of workers' revolution loomed large in this process.

Conceptions and Misconceptions of National Reform

National Reform represented more than an attempt to influence legislation
through political action. Although some NRA leaders believed the constitution denied the people "their capacity of self-government," others declared
themselves satisfied with constitutional structures "as a base work." Moreover,
some of the former thought "something of the checks, and balances needful,
even in a free government" and did not necessarily favor the direct popular

election of all offices. Most hoped, as Lucius A. Hine said, that "public sentiment liberalizes all documents and all books in proportion as it becomes itself
liberal," which allowed land reformers to "use the organic law to assist in working out the destiny of the Republic."[2] What they sought was so fundamental
that it involved far-reaching means to attain their aims.

The major documents of National Reform share the idea that a more
egalitarian distribution of land would diffuse wealth and democratize power,
allowing the working classes to shape a more rational world. The reformers'
goal was not the greatest good for the greatest number, but *the entire good
of the whole.* Although "modified by the circumstances naturally connected
with their existence," natural rights remained inalienable. John Allen described
"The Mission of the United States" as "The emancipation of the slave from the
bondage of the master, the redemption of labor from the tyranny of capital, the
freedom of the soil from the grasp of monopoly, the deliverance of the mind
from the power of superstition, the salvation of the race from the thralldom
of false society."[3]

That destiny, National Reformers believed, involved a "total change in the
relation of employers and employed." It would mean "no slavish obedience
to a boss," "no means of subsistence but the labor and skill of their hands,"
"no hireage of others" and "none of the present evils of want of employment,
glut of labor or production, taking the degrading refuge in a poor-house."
J. K. Ingalls saw it as "a great industrial reform," without which "no great
and truly valuable reforms are possible in any other sphere of society." Caleb
Pink, a Brooklyn advocate, described NRA measures as "only the wedge" for
the complete emancipation of labor. A Wheeling petitioner, Joshua Redman,
described it as "only an embryo of a probable future."[4]

Once land reform had democratized property ownership, the self-interest of the majority would move toward a cooperative society. Workers would
then control "ware-houses, foundries, ship-yards, etc., at the great sea and
river ports." With water-powered machines, factories could be "embellished
and beautified," as well as humanized. "Steamboats and Rail Roads would
be taken possession of the people, and the whole population might have access to the beauties of Nature, which are now as a sealed book, except to a
favored few." There would be "No Land or Mine Monopoly. No public debts.
Railroads made and operated by the people." "Earth's tyrants of the scepter,
of the chain, and the purse" would, after the victory of the people, become
indolent "or welcomed to the ranks of labor and of Brotherhood." In their
libertarian socialist future, "those who prefer to go out and battle for life in
the competing world" would be "at liberty so to do."[5]

This context also defined the NRA's "National Reform Village," so easily

misunderstood as simply another blueprint of utopia. Its authors, Lewis Masquerier and George Henry Evans, not only drew on the models of Robert
Owen and Charles Fourier but also the "parish" of British land reformer
Thomas Spence, the "ward republic" of Thomas Jefferson, and the township of Thomas Skidmore, as well as to the environmental technologies of
Johann Adolphus Etzler. These ideas were popularized by Masquerier and
published by Evans's friend Peter Eckler. However, the NRA talked of this
"rural city"—or "city farm"—not as a blueprint for the future society but as
an illustration of the kind of decentralized polis that the reform proposals of
the day would make possible. It centered physically on a civic square because
it would be politically focused on building and maintaining roads, bridges,
and "a phonetic newspaper" with proposed laws, banquets, mortgages, dona-
tions, and vital statistics. Citizens needed only the shadow of government to
"execute a particular business" and would cast "a free-will vote," "directly in
proper person for their laws."[6]

Clearly, the "Agrarians" did not advocate a world of family farms. H. H.
Van Amringe explicitly disclaimed any desire "to make all men farmers. On
the contrary, as Nature is more varied than Art, so a natural society would be
more varied in occupations than an artificial state of society." The National Reformers centered their ideal society around "the right and duty of man to earn
his bread by the sweat of his face, or, in other words, by some kind of useful
labor" from which would come "the independent power of self-employment
and self-government of a landed democracy." This, they argued, would allow
individuals to be rewarded for working long hours on labor-intensive projects,
or only on projects requiring less labor, for the economic relations of citizens
would rest upon "voluntary contracts to be adjusted between themselves."
Access to land would leave each citizen "at full liberty . . . to turn his attention
to agriculture, manufactures, trade or science" and to blend intellectual with
"agricultural and mechanical labor."[7]

In part, National Reformers rejected schemas for the future society as
elitist. They believed it should be "not the men of genius, the poets, the phi-
losophers, the orators, the legislators, the statesmen, who originate reforms
for the good of the mass. They come from the workmen at the bench, who
muse as they labor on the ideas which animate the efforts of the statesmen,
and strike out the spark of immortal truth." Their own organizations were but
the seeds of a future, a broadly based popular movement that would convince
"the working classes" of the necessity "for the weak to be combined for mutual
support, rather than divided for mutual destruction," as one National Reformer
argued. In the interim, Agrarians engaged in what Hine called "the rationale
of reform—contact of mind with mind, opinion with opinion assured that the

true will gradually supersede the false, the virtuous displace the vicious."[8] The solutions demanded a mass movement rather than a mere political association for political reform.

This marked an important distinction between National Reformers and the contemporary moral critics of institutional power. Adherents of the NRA proposed open-ended "transitional measures" as "a preparatory step" toward "an intermediate process . . . before the people can be brought to harmonize in community."[9] As the NRA's history reflected, the evolution of such a program became inseparable from the ideas of mobilizing the "working classes."

Transitional Program: The Dynamics of Class Organization

Radicals long ascribed injustice to superstition and ignorance and made public arguments that turned on the enlightening rationale of the written word. After reading *Vote Yourself a Farm*, one New Yorker said simply "sure enough, sure enough . . . I never thought of it before." Root described the appearance of Evans's paper at Peoria "like the rising of the morning Star in a long dark night." When Ingalls encountered it in 1848, he left the pulpit for a workshop and spent the rest of the century a proponent of the cause in his own right. Partly to support such publications, Agrarians urged workers to "form libraries, and acquire the necessary knowledge to take charge of their own business, so that they might not be dependent on a few speakers whom they would feel called upon to applaud as if they were gods."[10]

Spreading the arguments also employed speakers, "migratory, tramping from village to village, and from State to State, without any definitive abiding place." In additional to Van Amringe, a squad of lecturers assumed regional importance. Even as George "Land Bill" Allen toured from his base in Columbus, Lucius A. Hine worked out of Cincinnati, speaking almost two hundred times a year for ten years. "After reaching a town or village, and tramping around to give notice and see to other preliminaries, I commenced writing, stopping even in wagon-maker shops and in blacksmith shops, to write without table or chair." "My only financial resources during the lecture period," he recalled, "were derived from the sale of my books at the end of a lecture."[11]

The NRA urged all adherents "to become missionaries when and where there is opportunity among all men, and inform them of the leading features of National Reform." One Yankee member reported that after "ten hours on the shoemaker's bench, without eating any dinner," he and a friend braved their employers' threats and a New England snowstorm to carry *Young America* and its message to a town eight miles away—part of the local NRA's campaign to reach "all the neighboring towns." So an unknown activist on the Maine waterfront took the issue to local day laborers who borrowed his pencil stub to sign the NRA's petition.[12] Such widespread dedication and activism transformed what was intended to be primarily an electoral association into an important political movement.

The NRA—like freethinkers, vegetarians, spiritualists, abolitionists, and other social reformers—encouraged activities beyond electoral politics. From the freethinkers, National Reformers took the practice of holding large "balls"—a banquet followed by short speeches, punctuated by toasts volunteered by participants, and capped with music and dancing. The NRA constitution mandated arrangements to have music at meetings, and was followed by the publication of "Songs and Ballads, having a bearing on the condition of the working classes, and encouraging them to unite for an effectual remedy." Herman Bristol issued *The Agrarian Songster,* while Haddock and John Windt collaborated on another songbook. Producing by far the best, Haddock and Windt used the traditional tune of "Rosin the Beau" to advise its listeners to "Roll on the Agrarian Ball"—echoing the Hutchinsons' "Liberty Ball," later refurbished as "Lincoln and Liberty, Too!"[13]

The NRA assailed the ephemeral cultural self-deception that obscured the economic and social realities of hierarchy. National Reformers complained not only about the apathy of their fellow workers but also about the willingness of those workers to hide their poverty, sacrifice for "the pretended welfare and security of capital," and internalize an "idea of the inferiority of Labor." Citing "a sort of holy reverence" for the bar and bench, NRA spokesman Ransom Smith urged workers to "reverence and respect the Crow Bar and the Work Bench," and to "respect themselves and each other."[14]

Any solution rooted in "the working classes" required fostering class sentiment. William S. Wait, for example, questioned "the moral character and health of the possessor" of either wages or chattel slaves, asserting that "every one knows that the poorer is the most virtuous." Another Yankee Agrarian contrasted "one class thieving Land Monopolizers, the other cheated unfortunates, the last by far the most honorable class of the two." NRA members mocked the "monopolist, with his white kid gloves and silk stockings" who sought "to satisfy the mechanic that they *were* getting full compensation" for their work. "Do we think there will be John Jacob Astors, Van Renselaers, or Dukes of Richmond in heaven?" asked Elizur Wright. "In short, will there be human swine in heaven? Every man who says no, ought to be a land reformer here."[15]

Perhaps for this reason, some NRA militants suspected the presence of professionals like Alvan E. Bovay. Although few wanted a simple ban, some attributed the destruction of Locofocos, trades' unions, and the Workingmen's Party to "middle-class" and professional "friends." "When we should become

strong," ran a newspaper account of Evans's characteristically pragmatic remarks, "then he would narrowly watch all converts from the professional ranks,
for it was then they would be likely to deceive," but Bovay had proven himself
individually "a thorough and devoted friend of the movement."[16] Although the
NRA distinguished between genuinely radical professionals such as Bovay,
ideologically drawn to a small association, and the personally ambitious attracted to a potentially powerful base, what National Reformers most clearly
meant by the "working classes" were their own urban crafts.

Cooperatives among working people provided an essential counterweight
to the cooperation of elites implicit in capitalism. Although some questioned
this value without political action, the Agrarian agitation involved an ongoing
discussion about Josiah Warren's Labor Exchanges, and Masquerier early
proposed "Labor Exchange Marts, in connection with the Land movement,"
a cause soon taken up by the Albany radical Calvin Pepper. "Protective
Unions"—the cooperative stores advocated by the *Voice of Industry* and the
New England Fourierists—had the particular support of Greeley's *New York
Tribune*, Seaver and Mendum's *Boston Investigator*, Elizur Wright's *Chronotype*, and New York's *Spirit of the Age* (the result of the merger between
the Fourierist *Harbinger* and the spiritualist *Univercoelum*). From 1847 to
1860, National Industrial Congresses endorsed them, and Van Amringe and
Hine and other agitators urged strikers to cooperate "for the purpose of self-
employment." During these years, striking printers established cooperative
newspapers such as Boston's *Protective Union* and Cincinnati's *Nonpareil*.
Wright extended cooperation into insurance, while Ingalls and William B.
Greene applied it to banking to abolish interest and rent.[17]

Agrarians believed cooperation could get land to the landless on a modest scale. Inspired by prospects in Oregon, they discussed the cooperative
colonization of the West, and not merely through subscriptions among the
settlers. If a thousand carpenters vied for 950 jobs in the city, they argued, it
made practical sense to raise the money needed to send fifty workers and their
families to the West, which would give the migrants unavailed opportunities
and allow those who remained the chance to organize, reduce the length of the
workday, and secure "full employment at fair prices." "Whenever the price of
labor is so far depreciated as not to afford to him who exercises it the means
of living," declared another, "let him be free to go to the land and there from
it to yield that sustenance which artificial contrivances have denied." As Van
Amringe explained, such a law need not "invade *what are called* vested rights
in land," for he saw no "need in the country, to invalidate existing vested titles
to land."[18] The NRA structured its program to win widespread popular support
and to minimize the grounds for opposition.

Others pointed out that cooperation could raise political issues. Lewis Ryckman defined *"a Union of the Producers"* as the key to the direct involvement of the masses necessary for "emancipating Labor through our political power." Cooperationists also pointed out that the officials refused to incorporate their associations; without such a step, the authorities "would not recognize their society, but treat it as an outlaw." Devyr deplored the "great error" of Louis Blanc and other French socialists in emphasizing National Workshops rather than land reform, but as early as 1845, Albert Brisbane advocated "using the credit of the State (so long used to favor monopolies) in favor of the organization of Labor." By 1847, Van Amringe, as well as Young and Davis of New York's Protective Union, urged the NIC to call for the government incorporation and insurance of cooperative projects. Cooperatives provided a means to some form of "Social Guaranty." "All are liable to accident, to sickness and death," declared Ingalls, which in the present organization of society creates "a feverish anxiety to protect self." William Henry Channing seemed to address such concerns by urging Associationists to establish "mutual assurance and life insurance" as well as labor exchanges and protective unions. Elizur Wright—the multifaceted editor of Boston's *Chronotype*—would eventually be remembered primarily as a pioneer of the insurance industry.[19]

National Reformers defended and fostered trade unionism and citywide labor organizations. Although even National Reformers with the strongest unionist credentials—men such as Commerford—questioned the ultimate value of workers' organizations not explicitly involved in politics, the NRA began with favorable notices of strikes and unrest among sailors, printers, and "the men that dig out the soil and form the cellars for new buildings." Evans asked readers to consider what made strikes necessary and what circumstances made them "a necessary evil" under the present social order. Notice of the numerous strikes throughout the country moved Hine to suggest to "all who live under the trials and privation of a 'strike'" and "all who are liable as a reduction of wages, to the 'striking,' or the starving point" to address the monopolist roots of the problem and support "the most effectual" remedies, the NRA measures. National Reformers did advise caution, given glutted labor markets and the resulting intensity of competition among workers, which created both the preconditions for strikes and their defeat.[20]

Although National Reformers argued that workers had every constitutional right to organize, they mistrusted the commitment of the authorities to respect those rights. From the beginning of the century, employers had used the courts to prosecute labor organizations as "criminal conspiracies" and, much more widely, blacklisted radical workers for all sorts of activities. Workers participated in the New England–based Industrial Brotherhood, a secret society of "actual working men (not employers)" with "a plan of mutual insurance similar to the Odd Fellows" with separate "funds for political and beneficial purposes." The NRA also projected the allied Industrial Sisterhood and, "in accordance with constitutional rights and duties," uniformed Industrial Guards. Evans expected these to function as well as "Auxiliaries to the National Reform movement," as they were "not intended in any way to supersede the National Reform Association." However, the NRA insisted that "Associations of 'Young America,'" would be needed for farmers and self-employed artisans, proposing the name of contemporary underground revolutionary societies in Europe. Young America organized "bowers" rather than "lodges," and had "first" or "parent" central bodies rather than the "grand" lodges. Although rarely mentioned in print, Young America organized in New York and Ohio and survived well into 1847 and probably beyond.[21] A few years later, the fraternal Brotherhood of the Union performed much the same function.

Reform and Revolution

Scholars have often misread NRA statements disclaiming any desire to foster class hostility or threaten property relations and warning of a "Red Republicanism" (or even a leveling "Agrarianism") born of desperation. However, Warren Chase's sentiment for "Labor and Capital—twins sisters" urged the united economic functions of capital and labor in cooperatives rather than a political harmony of capitalists and laborers. Ingalls explicitly declared it as "idle to preach cooperation to capital, as it would be to preach peace to the Czar of Russia," but he could also urge cooperation within "the only union at all desirable," the "just and beneficial" foundations of *Freedom of labor and conservation of wealth.*" Oddly, Devyr urged the workers to avoid class war as they would seize all lands "stolen and given to the railroads" as well as "the mines of gold, silver, copper, iron, coal."[22] Without the wider context, the meaning is easily misunderstood as simply utopian.

Antebellum radicals rightly feared that sections of the ruling class might be unwilling to permit a peaceful social transformation. John A. Collins, the prominent abolitionist and "utopian" warned with a most nonutopian finality that "these lands could only be got hold of by a physical force revolution." So, too, men like Devyr warned of "the murderous instincts which the accursed race of enslavers have shown in all countries and in all times." Root reminded his comrades that the same officials who rejected land reform chartered banks and monopolies, levied new tariffs, granted vast tracts of land to railroads, "and at the same time, extending chattel slavery." Just as their European peers had repressed the 1848 workers' uprisings, American rulers "would, if it were possible, annihilate heaven and earth to rule the hand of labor." Anticipating a course "marked with blood" required the NRA to prepare "the military power" needed to triumph.[23]

The Americans seized on the British Chartist project of a "Grand National Holiday," the idea of a general strike to enforce the popular will on recalcitrant elites and institutions. The NRA included former leaders of the Philadelphia general strike of 1835 for a ten-hour workday. Evans suggested that one could attain that goal nationally if workers decided on "a day . . . after which no work shall be done in the factories except on the Ten Hour system" and pledged the NRA to assist "if a strike should be necessary for the purpose." An optimistic *Voice of Industry* echoed his call, suggesting July 4, 1846, as an appropriate date for ending the debate over a ten-hour day quite satisfactorily. Ingalls thought strikes over wages as "justifiable as a war measure" but called "a strike against wage work . . . intelligent and morally justifiable." Wright asserted the workers' "right to rise in one universal Strike." "Prepare beforehand," advised Devyr, "and proclaim a General Strike from work on the week ending election day."[24]

The fact that ruling classes had historically responded to such threats by suspending any constitutional mechanisms raised the matter of armed self-defense. William West had, like Elizur Wright, been a religious skeptic among the largely evangelical abolitionists and become a similarly iconoclastic Fourierist and land reformer. Becoming active in the New York NRA in 1845, West became an outspoken critic of electoral politics, warning against accepting the legitimacy of fundamentally unjust constitutions and laws. "If force is used to execute such laws," he argued, "force is justifiable to resist their execution." Justice must be had, and "if it cannot be done by the ballot box, there is a last resort, and that is the *bullet* box, and it was his honest opinion that it would come to that and that we ought to be prepared for it." When Ryckman replied that they were "not yet in such necessity," West declared that the powers-that-be "must be compelled by the force which lies in our own strong arms. We must have an organization, so that if those who are elected do not do their duty, a new government shall be already organized to spring into existence." "Is it not necessary, then, that we should consider the means to remove this monopoly, either by the ballot or the bullet?" West continued to ask. "Is it not worthwhile, then, to consider the might that exists in our arms, as well as the potency of the ballot?"[25]

However reluctantly National Reformers entered into such speculations, NRA leaders essentially shared West's conclusions. Masquerier reechoed the old slogan of the Workies that social reconstruction must become "the paramount law of the land—peaceably if they can, forcibly if they must." Evans saw the interests of "every landless man . . . *at war with society,*" and insisted that "the people have their rights, peaceably, of course, *by all means peaceably,* if they can be got that way; but in some way or other *let them be had.*" The NRA's founder urged victory "by political action, or, in failure of that, by revolution," and Devyr suggested that "the gentlest means possible ought to be used. But, that failing, use the gentlest means that may be necessary." "We have the right to bear arms," declared Wait, "we have the right of revolution—all of us and every man alike."[26]

The 1845 Industrial Convention recommended "Military Organization . . . to the several Associations of Industrial Brotherhood throughout the United States." Its uniform would "consist of a plain citizen's dress which may be worn with propriety on the Sabbath." To eliminate differences of "pecuniary ability," there would be "no difference in dress between commissioned officers and rank and file . . . beyond what is indispensable to be kept at all times in good order, and the discipline rendered perfect and efficient." While formed as independent militia companies "in strict conformity with the constitution and laws of the land," these Industrial Guards would bring power of a different kind to the movement. In the wake of this convention, Evans particularly concerned himself with "the Republican plan of Military Organization recommended by the Industrial Convention" whereby those who give the orders would be precisely those who carried them into practice. "The just order of things on this subject," noted Evans, "is now completely reversed."[27]

In a very fundamental way, Agrarians questioned the legitimacy of the governing institutions. Although heavily involved in Ohio politics, National Reformer John H. Klippart declared, "No government can, or even could produce a charter from Heaven, giving them privilege to traffick in one of the most essential supports of life, namely: *Land.*" Agrarians appealed beyond government to the people as "the fountain of power" who are "dependent on Government for no right" for it had "no rights to bestow." Another NRA proponent celebrated a sentiment: "The Will of the Majority fairly expressed—The only government we recognize, so long as they rule in justice."[28]

Agrarians such as Hine scorned "half way steps." Van Amringe accepted "no remedy which stops short of securing to man his inalienable birthright in the soil." Masquerier recalled the assertion of the Declaration of Independence "that all the sovereign power of the government resides in the whole people; that they cannot be bound by a law which has not received their consent; that they can at all times alter or abolish any law, government or alliance which has become oppressive, and substitute others." He concluded that the people should "ignore them entirely" with an aim to "abolish them and establish liberty-guaranteeing ones." He thought that when the time came, they could "supercede [*sic*] all the institutions of society" simply "by signing names" even on the state level to a new constitution legitimately establishing "the new form of society and government." In the end, he concluded, the present system would have to be "neutralized" and the social order "reformed from without."[29]

The strategy changed the nature of that movement itself. As Van Amringe argued, "before we pull down old institutions, we may build up new and better, and our reform will thus be pacific and promotive of the immediate welfare of each." "Will it not be a tribunal," Thomas Skidmore asked, "small and of few members at first, but constantly increasing" until "the entire community of the citizens of this State shall all have taken a share of duty in these investigations"? The NRA described its "tribunals"—the Industrial "Congress"—as "the proposed Industrial Government" or an "incipient Legislature." Evans called it an "Industrial Revolutionary Government, based upon the model of the Confederation of the States in 1776" and hoped it would "be permanent until the principles of the Declaration of Independence are fully carried into practice" throughout the country. Indeed, the Industrial Congress largely superseded the role of the NRA in urging the formation of auxiliaries "at least in every Representative Election District of the Union," as well as each state. These would promote land reform by "public meetings, lectures, debates, newspaper, or tracts, or by all of these means." The goal was organization "in every village and township of the country, and in every ward of the city." That of 1850 suggested the organization of a "County Reform Association," which might send representatives to a statewide "Industrial Legislature."[30] By then, citywide bodies allied to the NRA had provided a kind of shadow government at that level.

As "mankind congregated into Society do not possess any Rights not possessed in their individual capacities," Agrarians anticipated a society in which "the Constitutional legislators and Electors" would be the citizens themselves. In a process "open and free to any voter in the State," annual meetings could propose legislation, publish and debate bills, and fill any necessary offices. The people would "exercise the Legislative Power individually and directly." Further, they proclaimed that any laws "subversive of, or destructive to, the rights of the minority, or of the individual, or in any way infringing upon them, are null and void."[31] The NRA anticipated practical self-government to supersede the existing institutions of power.

Evans and other NRA leaders expected the state to become less relevant with the organization of workers and the attainment of their social program. "No power should be delegated farther than can be beneficially exercised by the family, township, county, or State." From the onset, the NRA had proposed that its measures be "discussed, adopted, or rejected by a direct vote of the people in townships, or that size of district which will contain the proportionate number of agriculturalists and mechanics needful to produce an assortment of the necessaries of life." As early as 1844, Evans suggested, "Self government will be followed by *less* government; less government, perhaps, by none at all," adding that "the time for *less* government has arrived." Privately, he told Masquerier, that calling for the abolition of the state might "frighten and repulse public sentiment to feed it with more new doctrine than it could digest at one time."[32]

     ✵ ✵ ✵

The course of the 1847 National Industrial Congress gauged the extent to which these indisputably radical views characterized the movement in general. Appleton Fay urged the body to declare the abolition of the State to be the movement's goal. Masquerier argued that "the people would legislate without delegating their sovereignty." Several speakers agreed, including West who thought that "the representative form of government must be changed" with the goal of attaining "the Perfection of Self-government."[33] In fact, only a majority of one vote defeated formal adoption of "direct legislation" to legitimize an agrarian seizure of the land.

Decades later, Ohio radical Joel Brown discussed the views he had held since the late 1820s. The emergence of municipal police forces, private detective agencies, and other mechanisms of social control had polarized the political workers' movement into reformist and revolutionary wings, but Brown still clung to his hope and determination to see justice done: "I think there will be a forcible revolution sooner or later, but I hope without bloodshed, but that I do not expect." Acknowledging that the term had not been in use, the old man frankly declared their views to have been broadly "anarchist."[34] By then, surviving National Reformers occupied a spectrum that included the most revolutionary anarchist and socialist currents in American life.

6　Race and Solidarity: The Test of Rhetoric and Ideology

> I desire no fellowship with Slavery, black or white; no annexation or disan-
> nexation by violence or bloodshed, with booms or big guns: no intoxication
> of clear heads and pure hearts.
>
> —Ransom Smith, NRA New York mayoral candidate, 1845

In 1848 Joshua King Ingalls, a self-defrocked minister-turned-agi-
tator toured upstate New York on behalf of the NRA. One Sunday, he delivered
his address at Little Falls on behalf of "land and freedom." By then, NRA
leaders urged political action to ensure access to land and Nature's bounty
for the nation's "lacklanders." Ingalls opened and closed his argument with an
invitation for his listeners to join with others in the campaign, to sign a petition, to take the NRA pledge, and to devote time convincing other citizens.
In recalling this speech, he hinted at no variation, although Ingalls gave this
"altar call" before an entirely black congregation.[1] The event underscores
the need to reexamine overconfident generalizations about antebellum labor
politics, abolitionism, and race relations.

As a group, National Reformers opposed slavery, but without the evangelical
zeal of the abolitionists, who tended to seek a Christian righting of social wrongs
done others through moral suasion. Agrarians favored freedom because of the
real impact of slavery on the political and social health of the entire body politic
as well as the inhumanity of the system. Further, evidence exists that the core
of the NRA challenged the assumptions of white supremacy. They deliberately
defied the color bar to solicit black involvement in a common movement.

Working-Class Antislavery

National Reformers thought it "a peculiar kind" of freedom that "leaves man
to perish in the midst of surrounding wealth." Its principal founder, George

Henry Evans, explicitly identified wage labor as one of "different grades of slavery" in a system of coerced American labor modified "in a thousand ways" into "different forms and degrees of servitude, but in all forms and degrees it is servitude still." "The Slaveholder," wrote Evans of the planters, "has inherited other people's *bodies,* and the Landholder has inherited other people's *land;* and thereby *holds* their bodies."[2] Read from the inside out, the evidence indicates an underlying sense of solidarity.

Initially, the NRA chose to give no "peculiar prominence" to abolition in the South, but it later voted to "give expression to its feelings against Slavery," sentiments rooted in agrarian concerns from the days of Tom Paine. Artisan-based freethinkers repudiated the hypocrisy of the "Christian slavery," and the first organized socialists indicted the civilization for African slavery. Thomas Skidmore left no room for doubt as to his hatred of slavery, and Evans had denounced the institution decades before founding the NRA. When local Democrats mobbed abolitionists and free blacks, Evans defended the moral and constitutional right of citizens to agitate on any issue with "what zeal they please," and described the abolitionists particularly as "honest in their principles" in asking for "mere justice." Slavery appeared in "its most baneful form in the United States" where workers and reformers faced a "complex form of work and whip," which had "never been combined to such a degree as in this Government is manifest." "Making a man's body a chattel is the most heinous crime to that of murder," insisted NRA founder Lewis Masquerier. Alvan E. Bovay insisted that "every National Reformer will admit, that Negro-Slavery is a great, an enormous, and a growing evil" in the nation.[3]

Nevertheless, as working-class freethinkers, the NRA suspected the abolitionists' evangelical insistence on the conscious, individual rejection of sin, spread by the massive religious revivals of the Second Great Awakening. NRA members resisted "any thing like intolerance, whether it proceeds from orthodoxy or heterodoxy, the believer or the unbeliever, from the Presbyterian or skeptic." As secularists, they viewed the political influence of organized religion as reactionary. Evans, in particular, noted with dissatisfaction that evangelical antislavery leaders usually advocated not only abolitionism but also "measures tending to a union of Church and State." "If they had been educated to believe that it was right to traffic in human flesh as well as in the material of Nature necessary to sustain existence," wrote Evans of the slaveholders, "we could not blame them from doing so *till informed of their error,* and till the owners of the bodies in which they were trafficking had claimed their rights."[4] An ever more enlightened understanding and a shifting consensus would, they believed, somehow find reflection in government policies incompatible with all forms of slavery.

Conversely, early abolitionists insisted on an antislavery rooted in disinterested philanthropy rather than on enlightened self-interest. Whereas NRA affiliates sponsored talks by William Lloyd Garrison, he scorned class self-interest as morally inadequate, and like-minded abolitionists distinguished between the views of Dr. J. E. Snodgrass, who acted on "my humanity, my sympathy with the wronged," and the views of Cassius Clay, whose antislavery was "no longer a question about Africans." Under headlines like "Not to Be Trusted," Garrison's *Liberator* denounced the NRA as "destitute of principle, and animated by a vulgar and selfish spirit" unworthy of "the respect or confidence of the true friends of down-trodden humanity." When Rev. Beriah Green chided the NRA's William V. Barr about the indifference of Northern white workingmen to slavery, Barr ascribed workers' "notions of moral, and social duties" to the influence of "the educated fraternity of law, medicine and divinity" or business. Often sharp verbal skirmishes took place between, respectively, Garrison, Wendell Phillips, and Frederick Douglass with William West, Evans, and Ingalls. After Ingalls told an abolitionist meeting in 1848 that land-reform concerns "complemented" their antislavery work, Douglass had attacked the agitation as a distraction from its rightful focus; recalling how Phillips had similarly denounced Evans, Ingalls later wrote with some satisfaction: "Mr. Evans did not live to see Mr. Phillips come to his position, on the land question, as I lived to see Mr. Douglass come to mine; but he came to it, quite as soon."[5]

More substantively, abolitionists (and, later, historians) resented the Northern working-class discussion of its "wages slavery." "The capitalist does not need a manacle upon the limb of his fellow men; he can do better without it, and exert more force on hireling labor by the vacuum, than by attaching a chain to the laborer as a slave," explained an NRA leader. Some described their lot as worse than that of Southern slaves, the more astute discussing the wage system as more deeply rooted and central to American development. Abolitionists described this as a disinterest in justice as a ploy to placate Southern slaveholders, eliciting NRA countercharges that abolitionist indifference to "wages slavery" courted Northern business interests. When abolitionists cited the separation of families, brutality, rape, and other atrocities incidental to chattel slavery, NRA leaders recited similar experiences among "wage slaves." In any event, as Evans explained, the structure of government made their views on slavery unimportant, for "the white slave states have no more to do with the black slave states on this question, than they have with England."[6]

The flap over the uses of "wages slavery" confused a well-reasoned analysis with rhetorical flourishes. Although some in the NRA described the lot of chattel slaves as better than theirs as wage slaves, most did not, and they likely shared the views of Horace Greeley that "Hireling Labor . . . in spite of the evils" would, in the long run, be more "progressive," leading "more rapidly and surely toward a better condition," whereas chattel slavery "tends towards decline, bankruptcy, dissolution." Also, some of the same NRA leaders who declared wages slavery a greater evil elsewhere described the chattel system in the South as "the worst degree of Slavery that exists," disclaiming "any desire whatever to represent Southern Slavery in any other light than that in which our Anti-Slavery friends have placed it." Indeed, Masquerier, Ingalls, Thomas Devyr, Lewis Ryckman, and others sometimes argued that nineteenth-century life represented worse oppression than feudalism, and Albert Brisbane claimed he saw less aristocracy in Germany than in the United States.[7]

Exaggerated rhetoric also reflected NRA frustration with an early abolitionist tendency to idealize the lot of "free" labor. In defining liberty simply as the absence of physical enslavement, abolitionists "appear as anxious to rivet their [the wage slaves'] chains as the Southern slaveholders are to bind their colored victims." Garrison's knee-jerk defense of Northern labor relations required "the same stereotyped arguments against 'the National Reformers' that his Pro Slavery enemies brought against him." J. E. Thompson shrewdly noted in the Northampton *Democrat* that it was "much safer and pleasanter for one to lift up his voice against evils which lie at a distance than against those immediately around him, especially when the latter are sanctioned by the customs of society."[8]

Unused to being criticized on moral grounds, abolitionists rarely responded convincingly, with some notable exceptions. A New York Liberty Party candidate pointed out that the Agrarians wanted a limit on land ownership but seemed to accept "unlimited property in human flesh," "in the bodies and souls of millions of your countrymen." So, too, D. S. Grandin, an abolitionist supporter of both land reform and the cooperative Protective Unions, used an often-repeated anecdote to make the essential point. In reply to the *Ohio Homestead Journal,* he recounted the visit of a runaway chattel slave to a meeting of Northern white wage slaves who questioned him about his decision to escape. Under questioning, the fugitive confessed to having had no personal complaint about his former condition other than being a slave. Further pressed, the black man simply announced that his old position was now vacant, should any present wish to apply.[9] None ever did.

Simply put, the NRA hoped to focus attention on land reform as "the great step stone of universal freedom." "Could Slavery, in any form exist," asked John Pickering, "if all men had the equal use of the elements?" For Jeriel Root, land monopoly anchored slavery, law making, and alcohol abuse. Lewis Masquerier described it as the key to the broader struggle to secure the "right to your *Domain, Person, Labor, Life,* and *Sovereignty*" against a system run by "profit-mongering," "tax-consuming," "capital-punishing," "war-aggressing," "office-hunting," "earth-usurping, lending and rent-extorting," "non-producing, body-selling, whip-driving, and labor-robbing masters and bosses." In contrast to struggles over "quarter, half or one-idea fragmentary reforms, such as abolition of capital punishment or slavery," the NRA literally grounded social injustices of all sort in the land question.[10] What mobilized this implicitly antislavery sentiment was a realization that the institution represented less a residue of ancient injustice than a dynamic threat to the survival and progress of the American republic.

Republicanism and Equality

The NRA called itself "Young America" (and Evans changed the name of his *Workingman's Advocate* to *Young America*) to reecho the concerns of "Young Europe" and its midcentury national affiliates. This has caused some confusion among scholars because the label is also applied to an expansionist literary circle around the *Democratic Review.* Participants in the agrarian "Young America" and the expansionist "Young America" shared an earlier proclivity for the party of Andrew Jackson and romantic vision of American destiny, but what they advocated was not only different but mutually exclusive.

Working-class radicals feared that imperial ambitions threatened the well-being of the American republic. John Cluer, a recent immigrant, warned of the effects of empire on the British people. "The debasement of a people," declared Commerford, starts with "an unjust principle in trampling the rights of every nation" to slake a "Roman thirst for the land of others," whereby a "principle of rapacity" "marched with the common soldier as well as the general." Elizur Wright denounced introducing Americans to "military lying." Although an atheist, Wright published an antiwar sermon and called the conflict "a war not only against Mexico, but against justice, climate, and God-Almighty." That American soldiers were "suffering more terrible than those of 'Valley Forge' in the cause of human oppression is too horrible to be thought of." Reprinting this piece, the *Voice* asked, "How long shall nations steal the name of Christians in which to practice the arts of war, devastation and heathenism."[11] As in antiquity, radicals warned, war linked land monopoly and the expansion of slavery.

The NRA made a clear contribution to an increasingly widespread Northern perception of a "Slave Power Conspiracy." The perspective of the land reformers owed less to their own "paranoid style" than to the moral high ground of classical republicanism. Thompson thought it "remains to be seen" whether wages slavery or chattel slavery would be first abolished. William West, with characteristic tact, labeled the entire debate over priorities "ridiculous." "We would not apologize for Slavery in any form," insisted an Ohio Agrarian, "but would be glad to strike the manacles from every slave whether white or black." Root wisely suggested that "if we saw the magnitude and power of these evils, we could not stand isolated, contending about the greatest, for all of them are deadly enemies to Christianity and Liberty" and "either of them if left alive, will consume our Republic." "Bring not my brother in bonds to me and say that I shall not investigate the question of Slavery here," declared Bovay to an 1845 conference. "I will introduce the question of Slavery here."[12]

Most directly, the NRA concluded that slavery and the imperative of waging war on its behalf had subverted the Democratic Party. Agrarians traced the Democratic view of slavery as a regrettable evil imposed by a colonial past and the evolution of that view into a morally laudable and politically defensible labor system. "A monopolized soil must produce an enslaved people," argued H. H. Van Amringe. Southern sympathizers of the NRA warned that the market forces shaped by John C. Calhoun's followers "would make the laboring freemen of this country slaves to slaves." Bovay noted of Calhoun that it had become "part of his philosophy that the laboring masses must be enslaved" for the sake of order.[13]

The term *Free Soil* emerged from a state convention at Albany in October 1846. To its questioning, Henry Bradley, Liberty candidate for governor, declared support for all NRA measures but land limitation on which, he wrote frankly, that "had I thought as much as you have done . . . I should perhaps agree with you fully." Another abolitionist candidate agreed that land reform "would produce an amazing change in the business and order of society, yet I must conclude it would be for the better, and if any evils resulted it would be because of the wrong so long indulged!" In the end, the overlapping Free Soil ticket battled against a heavy rain that kept voter turnout in the city low, Tammany's adoption of land reform resolutions, and the usual amount of fraud. Nevertheless, two Democratic assembly candidates endorsed by the NRA won (including Mike Walsh). John Ross, Commerford, Ryckman, and John Delamontayne—the exclusively NRA congressional candidates in the Third, Fourth, Fifth and Sixth Districts—won a total of 579 votes, comparable to the gubernatorial vote in these districts, 550 for Masquerier and 60 for Bradley. Statewide, the Whigs won by approximately ten thousand votes, "all Anti-Rent voters." Complaining that voters had also rejected black suffrage, Evans still took heart. They had sought not a majority but a balance of power; insurgents in the Fourth Congressional District, for example, did not aim at the 4,749 votes to win but the 712 that separated the major parties, and Commerford with the two other independents got almost 1,500 votes.[14] Clearly, the 1846 fall elections showed that, if united, third-party forces could wield the balance of power.

As Agrarians became more forthcoming on black slavery, some abolitionists addressed the NRA's broader view of slavery. Agrarians described their concerns as those of "the serfs of Russia, the Ryots of India, the Peons of Mexico, the Chattel Slaves of Brasil and of our Southern States, and the landless Wage Slaves of Great Britain and of the United States," and pro-NRA papers eagerly reprinted a similar declaration by Wendell Phillips "that the rights of the peasants of Ireland, the operatives of New England, and laborers of South America will not be lost sight of in sympathy for the Southern slave." When Phillips repudiated the statement, advising wage workers to reform themselves through thrift, self-discipline, and sobriety, abolitionists as well as Agrarians expressed disappointment in his paternalism. Liberty Party member George Bradburn angrily wrote Gerrit Smith, complaining of fellow abolitionists who thought "that it is purely the fault of the masses themselves, if every thing is not right with them, in this glorious country of ours!" "Ought our fellow citizens to regard *class legislation* with complacency?" asked Beriah Green. "Our enslaved countrymen are *especially* entitled to the benefit of our One Idea, but by no means *exclusively*."[15]

By the close of the 1846 campaign, Smith spoke for many radical abolitionists when he declared National Reform "the greatest of all Anti-Slavery measures. Abolish Slavery to-morrow, and Land Monopoly would pave the way for its re-establishment. But abolish Land Monopoly—make every American citizen the owner of a farm adequate to his necessity—and there will be no room for the return of slavery." Liberty adherents in Smith's district reorganized as the "Poor Man's Party." Evans promoted common Free Soil politics so thoroughly within the NRA that even Devyr, a cantankerous Irish Democrat mistrustful of abolitionists, came to see Smith "as politically pure as Greeley was politically villainous." In meeting with the Liberty members, Ingalls and others discovered that "when the merely political issues were not involved, the discussions were profitable, spirited and harmonious."[16]

Perhaps no aspect of National Reform has been more oversimplified and misrepresented as its views on race. Decades before Lewis Henry Morgan's influential work on the Iroquois, Lewis Masquerier, Joseph R. Buchanan, and Evans studied Indians, as did John Greig, the Rochester Fourierist to whom the young Morgan carried a letter of introduction. Evans placed the words of Black Hawk alongside those of Jefferson in his publications, which included such pieces as "Which Is the Best, the Life of the Indian Savage, or the White Operative?" in which an immigrant tailor living among the Seminole said, "There's a great deal of talk about liberty, equality, and such great things among white people, but the divil a bit of liberty or equality did I ever find till I came amongst the Indians." The Agrarian press protested Indian removal at home and U.S. involvement in suppressing a Mayan rising in the Yucatan. A New York City NRA meeting gave "loud applause" to Bovay's declaration that "the Indians have a right somewhere, and it was certainly time now that their oppression should cease." On the Wisconsin frontier, Andrew E. Elmore became known for his friendship with the Indians and his advocacy of "all rights for all men."[17]

This is not to say that the NRA remained untarnished by white racism. Fitzwilliam Byrdsall, a native Floridian and the chief historian of the Loco-focos tried to ally the Northern Agrarians to Senator Calhoun's wing of the Democratic Party. Then, too, immigrant radical John Campbell compiled a volume of pseudoscientific racial arguments, published as a warning against the *Negromania* that threatened to disrupt the American politics. Even the iconoclastic Devyr emphasized race as "a distinction fixed by the Creator of us all." However, Byrdsall's planter-labor alliance not only failed but was also to center on a common belief in free trade rather than slavery, and Campbell openly embraced white supremacism after his very brief involvement with the land reformers. Indeed, both turned up so rarely in or around land reform meetings, that by the mid-1840s, they were really less Agrarians supporting Democrats than partisans seeking movement votes. Then, too, Devyr's faith in immutable racial barriers did not preclude his admiring Gerrit Smith for his dealing on "terms of equality to any honest man, in whatever coat or of whatever color."[18]

Indeed, the idea of interracial labor solidarity grew directly from the experience of an ethnically diverse work force. NRA leaders asserted "that Labor on the Soil, in the workshop of factory, is, and of right, ought to be free, without reference to sex, color or condition." Evans complained of the "unreasonable prejudice against color," and Masquerier, John H. Keyser, Lucius A. Hine, Henry Beeny, William West, and Appleton Fay made similarly explicit egalitarian statements about race. Hine pointed out that proponents of racial exclusion were "enemies of liberty, even the liberty of white men." The "National Reform Club" at Rosendale, Wisconsin, required a pledge from candidates not only to promote land reform and to oppose slavery but also to end discrimination "on account of birth-place or color." Philadelphia's Association of the Daughters and Sons of Toil listed among their regularly published grievances the failure of the authorities "to pass laws for the accommodation of large districts of laboring people, because they were so unfortunate as to be born of Black Mothers, and Black, White, and Indian fathers."[19]

Forty Acres and More

A generation before the Reconstruction agitation for "Forty Acres and a Mule," some white and black Americans linked radical land redistribution with abolition. The prospect of mere emancipation concerned the slaves with whom Skidmore had spoken, "as they would have no property," and he proposed that they get "lands, and other property also" to give substance to their freedom. Evans wrote Smith that not only did "the slaves have a natural and moral right to take possession of themselves, but of land enough to live upon." Masquerier argued that the only justification for the U.S. seizure of Mexican territories in 1848 would have been a national commitment to "invite every landless American, Mexican, Indian, White or Black Slave throughout the earth to claim his right to an equal, individual and inalienable homestead" there. West, too, described the goals of the NRA as "a free soil for humanity, the whole of it, without regard to sex or color."[20] Genuine personal liberty and independence for blacks, as for whites, required economic and social rights.

National lecturer Van Amringe stumped Wisconsin on that platform. "I am an abolitionist, as well as a National Reformer," he declared. "I advocate a free soil as well as personal freedom to all, to a free soil for all people, whether God has painted them white, red, or black." "We do not say free to native citizens only," he explained. "For red men, all persons of African descent, although domesticated among us, and born on our soil, are not, under our national laws, recognized as citizens." Land "should be free to each one of either sex, and of all complexions of skin," he insisted. It should be given "free without money or price, to any landless actual settler, man or woman, a native of the United States or Territories, and to all foreigners who under the laws of our country may become naturalized."[21]

Even in the shadow of "the peculiar institution," the NRA linked "free homes for the people" to "freedom from the curse of chattel slavery." The association dramatically sounded the theme at the National Reform banquet on May 1, 1848, at Cincinnati, a city separated from slavery only by the Ohio River and torn by recent racial strife. There, "not less than a thousand persons" heard Hine's praise of the general movement for social change and the complaint of John Allen, a Fourierist-Agrarian, that "Working men, as Reformers, had not always been just to labor. The cause of labor was one. The time had come when the laborers of the North must make common cause with the laborers of the South; and the prejudices of color be done away with. Land reformers were especially called on at this juncture to give the weight of their influence on the side of freedom." Allen then saluted: "Universal freedom and homes for all—for the colored man no less than the white!" (Reportedly, participants offered, "applause, mingled with some slight sounds of displeasure.")[22]

Indeed, the Cincinnati movement had already begun to involve blacks. Thomas and Marie Varney, former Owenites operating a printing business in the city, corresponded with Masquerier, Greeley, and Josiah Warren. They almost certainly participated in that 1848 National Reform banquet that heard Allen's call for abolition, equal rights, and land reform. That year, they took into training eighteen-year-old Peter Humphries Clark. Their young black apprentice became particularly close friends with the southern-born William Haller of the local NRA. Years later, Clark left the Republican Party to rejoin Hine and Haller in a statewide workingmen's party and the socialist movement.[23]

At times, NRA spokesmen explicitly defended black rights to resistance. By enslaving people, charged Hine, the slaveholder had declared a "state of war, and must meet the consequences." Masquerier's father had actually gone to Santo Domingo to aid the slave rebellion there. Even the exaggerated accounts of how Nat Turner and his fellow slave rebels of 1831 had massacred white Virginians did not deter Evans from his unique defense of the right of slaves to revolt; the tactics of Turner and his followers may have been "deluded, but their cause was just," he argued, for "they expected to emancipate themselves, and they no doubt thought that their only hope of doing so was to put to death indiscriminately, the whole race of those who held them in bondage." By 1848, the NRA included such figures in the Underground Railroad as James H. Collins and Charles V. Dyer in Illinois, while their Milwaukee cothinker, Sherman M. Booth, organized a mass protest, which ended by physically storming the jail and liberating a black prisoner; another National Reformer, Byron Paine served as Booth's attorney in the years of litigation that followed to test the constitutionality of the federal law. Later, in the Kansas Territory, John Brown, another abolitionist supporter of land reform defied government and law that sustained slavery. Among his comrades in the West were such transplanted eastern Agrarians as William A. Phillips and the Wattles brothers, Augustus and John. Brown's later plans for a final general slave revolt had the active collaboration of Gerrit Smith and others with Agrarian connections.[24]

Evans's egalitarian and democratic faith in people's capacities for self-government shaped his own speculations about the future of black America. "I harbor no prejudice against color; still there is a prejudice against color," he wrote Smith. Race riots and lynching attested to a prejudice quite capable of stifling the efforts of free blacks to live among whites. Leading National Reformers suggested that a radically transformed United States would permit all peoples to choose their own destinies, and Evans applied such goals in arguing that some lands "be set apart" for those blacks wishing to live unfettered by the "prejudice against color." Just as Agrarians argued that a democratized America should permit and respect the formation of an autonomous Indian state, they discussed the idea of "an independent Negro State." Evans envisioned one alternative for the nation twenty years after the adoption of NRA measures: "In the Southern States chattel slavery is gradually dying out. . . . The emancipated Negroes have formed a settlement on the Public Lands almost large enough for a State and are debating whether they shall follow their brethren to Liberia or ask to be recognized as an independent State."[25]

Taking the "Negro state" from the context of Evans's documented views on race, some scholars have incorrectly described an NRA vision of an America with "no place for the emancipated blacks." No less an authority than Frederick Douglass warned against confusing the white colonization of blacks with the libertarian position of some NRA leaders. Perhaps most fundamentally, Evans's stance reflects the usual NRA effort to accommodate other radical concerns within Agrarianism. To them, it seemed reasonable and fair that a radically transformed America would offer its resources for the use of such contemporary black leaders as Martin R. Delany, who already advocated the physical separation of blacks from the suffocating prejudices of white American society. NRA leaders never advocated that blacks "be separated from the rest of society" or make irreversible choices about their future, for black settlers could reenter the framework of the United States individually or as a group.[26] Rather, the Agrarian discussion centered on a very rare consideration for antebellum whites: the right of blacks to make their own decisions—what would in a later day be called black self-determination.

Beyond this, land reform became a multiracial movement through the direct and deliberate efforts of NRA leaders. Philadelphia Agrarians voted to consult Mexican nationalist José Maria Jesus Carbajal and the Seminole leader Wild Cat, both of whom had resisted the U.S. military and the slave power. Growing collaboration with abolitionists was essential to this process. It naturally brought NRA leaders into direct political contact with "the colored people who are endeavoring to emancipate their brethren in the Southern States from slavery and themselves from the degraded condition in which slavery has left them." While John Murray Spear encountered what he called "colorphobia" in some reform circles, it is significant that NRA leaders decidedly and deliberately rejected racial supremacism.[27]

As seen earlier, free blacks themselves had shared less confusion about the implications of early labor agitation. During 1829–30, black voters in New York City seem to have shifted briefly from their usual Whig preferences to the local

Workingmen's Party; some likely responded to the unusually egalitarian views
of leaders such as Skidmore and Evans. When the NRA began to make strides
in New England, Evans specifically noted the participation of "a colored man
who had been a slave" in a workingmen's meeting at Milford, Massachusetts,
as a hopeful sign of a growing interest in land reform activism among blacks.
So it was that Ingalls's interracial gathering on "land and freedom" at Little
Falls was likely not exceptional. Then, too, black leaders such as William Wells
Brown "wished success to the Land Reform movement." Describing abolition
as "the first step towards ensuring their [the land reformers'] ultimate success.
Labour is degraded by Slavery. Its abolition will elevate labour, and secure
to men their manhood." Despite earlier clashes with the NRA, Frederick
Douglass by 1851 praised Rochester's *National Reformer* and its "great cause,"
which had "engaged some of the noblest heads, and most philanthropic hearts
of their age."[28]

By then, experience, as well as ideological predispositions, drew the NRA
toward standards rare in early American history. Masquerier well expressed
where they ended.

> Then rouse "ye mudsills," white and black,
>   The time has come to strike,
> Strike for God-given equal rights—
>   Your causes are alike.[29]

❀ ❀ ❀

Historians and social scientists have rightly emphasized the peculiarly American long coexistence of wage labor and chattel slavery. The most recent of
these notes that free workers often embraced standards of "whiteness" that
elevated them over other workers. However, the evidence cautions against
both a static view of working-class hostility to abolition and of a "wholesale
rejection" of labor concerns by abolitionists. Both groups held much more
complex and diverse views about each other, and their attitudes to slave labor
clearly converged. White wage workers called their lot "wages slavery" and
protested against measures tending to reduce them to "slavery" in such a
way as to persuade some scholars that they supported slavery for others. In
fact, National Reformer William West addressed other National Reformers as
"Fellow Slaves," and workers in convention described runaway black slaves as
"our fellow workingmen."[30] Extrapolated into evidence of racism, such a use
of the term actually demonstrated a sense of solidarity no less profound that
moved radicals more than at any other point in American history.

At the time, however, antislavery land reformers like William West expected that both chattel and wage slavery might be "peaceably abolished only

by the political action of the legally qualified voters of the states in which it exists and to secure this action, the cause of the chattel slave should be united with that of the wage slave." Moreover, as Hine pointed out, the agitation for land reform would "bring more skillful anti-slavery players to the board" and to so sway "public sentiment that they [slaveholders] will soon be unable to make any thing out of it."[31] On these positions, events would vindicate Hine but discredit the optimism of West.

3

THE IMPACT OF
NATIONAL REFORM

7   *Free Labor: The Coalition with*
     the Abolitionists

> From the earliest to the latest times, the whole history of republican
> communities will be found to consist in the struggle between these two
> classes—on the part of the industrious, producing citizens a struggle to
> retain control of the society which they themselves have created and which
> owes all its prosperity and all its greatness to them; a struggle on the part
> of the aristocratic class to gain the administration of affairs, to reduce the
> laboring citizens to an inferior position, finally to deprive them of their
> political rights, and to quarter themselves in the shape of office holders,
> civil or military, on the community for support.
>
> —*New York Tribune*, 1856

The NRA's national lecturer H. H. Van Amringe minced no words
in discussing slavery by 1847. He still regularly disassociated his antislavery
stance from that of "Factory lords, Land lords, Banks, Speculators and usurers
in the North" but described himself "an abolitionist and will go for no national
reformer unless he is an abolitionist."[1] Having outlived the longevity of earlier
working-class political associations, the NRA now faced an issue that now had
to be met directly.

Just as the NRA had largely subsumed the political concerns of preexist-
ing radical currents, it found itself drawn into antislavery politics. By 1848, it
concluded a national electoral alliance with the most radical wing of political
abolitionism. Thereafter, as land reform itself became a vital consideration
as an independent electoral force, the future of the NRA as an independent
force came into doubt.

The Electoral Experiments of 1847

The electoral core of the NRA in New York City once more tested its nonpartisan practice of questioning the candidates prior to the April 13 municipal election. Four thousand New Yorkers had signed NRA petitions to the

U.S. Congress, and the movement's challenge was to translate those numbers into ballots. The NRA nominated Dennis Lyons for mayor, but an eleventh-hour change of heart from Whig mayoral candidate, William V. Brady, led to his withdrawal. Between 1,600 and 2,000 voters, who had not heard of the withdrawal voted NRA, and land-reformer ballots supplied much of Brady's 1,500–vote margin of victory. Moreover, despite the Whig mayoral victory, the NRA-pledged Democrat running for almshouse commissioner ran far ahead of his ticket and won by almost 2,100 votes. Not even the postelection repudiation of the pledge by Mayor-elect Brady entirely squelched the NRA achievement, the mobilization of most of those who had signed their petitions.[2] The campaign in spring 1847 demonstrated the electoral potential of reform as an independent force capable of tipping the balance of power, and it confirmed the duplicity of the established parties, showing the necessity of concerted independent action by the reformers.

The need for such action framed the second National Industrial Congress. After assembling at New York's Military Hall on the Bowery—the old meeting place of the old Workies—it accepted the invitation of Dr. Edward Newberry to meet gratis in his Chatham Street lecture room. The gathering added both ten-hour legislation and cooperation to the land-reform pledges required of candidates. When Owenite émigré, Benjamin Timms described "the inutility" of trade unions, others wanted the NIC to endorse their "propriety . . . for temporary relief." Sensitivity to potential allies now outweighed the predisposition of National Reformers to anticlericalism, informing their defeat of Fannie Lee Townsend's resolution to condemn the clergy for dereliction of duty. William West, the anticlerical Yankee abolitionist, agreed that the clergy were "tools of the capitalists" and "instruments of the slave owners" and proposed "a government and church of our own." Still a Universalist minister, Ingalls objected, and no less a veteran infidel than George Henry Evans argued for a movement open to all regardless of their religious belief or disbelief.[3]

The war with Mexico dominated the session. Upon assembling, the body appointed a committee to draft a formal "Address of the Industrial Congress to the Citizens of the United States." It declared that "the whole organization of society, as at present existing, is a *State* of War," but particularly denounced "National acts, and schemes of aggrandizement and War, emanating from the highest councils known to our law and constitutions." The NIC urged means "of preventing all war, of disbanding the army and navy." It denounced this particular conflict with Mexico as one "waged at the insistence and behalf of Southern Slavery and Northern Capital," through "a direct tax upon the property of the country" with an army raised from among those Masquerier called "the standing army of the landless." Others denounced "aggressive wars, in which the Taylors and Scotts reaped all the 'honor,'" while "few of its so-called honors" went to "the class who bears all the burthens of War." "Working men," advised the NIC, "Resolve, Never to fight for despots who enslave you, for territory which without a change in our governmental policy, you will only be permitted to occupy as serfs or slaves."[4]

Finally, the NIC took steps toward a new third party, though it was an insufficiently radical stance for some participants. From its inception, the NRA had questioned candidates of major parties before nominating its own, but it now urged making independent nominations first while offering to support nominees of other parties willing to make a written pledge. This policy became quite obvious in discussing a presidential endorsement. Evans initially favored New Hampshire senator John P. Hale, who had won reelection as an abolitionist after being purged by the Democrats "on a strong suspicion of being favorable to Human Rights." However, Appleton Fay of Massachusetts reminded the NIC that a national Liberty convention was meeting simultaneously upstate at Macedon Lock. Hoping to be more than "a political combination for mere party purposes," the NIC opted to function "as an independent party" with the abolitionists, and sent Hugh T. Brooks, a former liaison to the upstate Antirenters, to propose concerted action with the Libertymen. The NIC failed by a single vote to adopt Fay's proposal for "Pure Democracy" as an expression of the movement's ultimate goal and the substitution of "direct legislation" for ongoing government. West and others saw this as providing an even greater basis for unity with the abolitionists.[5] The disagreement within the NIC was less over the abolition of government than an explicit public statement on the subject.

The Massachusetts 1847 fall elections provided a crucial test of both the new coalition and Fay's philosophical anarchism. Hoping to strengthen the statewide NRA, Fay and his Worcester group called a convention on October 13 to nominate candidates pledged not only to land reform and antislavery but to an "adjustment of the Salaries of all Public Officers to the average amount of wages paid to useful productive Laborers" and to "the necessity and importance of the immediate Abolition (in due form) of the Representative system of Legislation, and the benefits and *practicability* of establishing a pure Democracy in its stead, by the peaceful adoption of a Constitution by the People that shall secure *to them* the opportunity and means of enacting, by direct vote, *all the Laws* by which they shall be governed!" Fay anticipated "the Union of all The Friends of Humanity of every political party and of every religious caste, and of *no* party and of no caste, who can conscientiously co-operate with their fellow beings to establish a *Righteous Government* by 'political action' upon the broad platform of Human Equality and Humanity's Rights."[6] However, the Worcester NRA lacked the resources.

Evans's Boston allies from the free thought movement, Horace Seaver and Josiah Mendum of the *Investigator*, seized the initiative to keep the state NRA on a more electoral course. On Saturday, October 23, Seaver convened a citywide NRA meeting at the Division No. 9 Working Men's Protective Union assembly room "and appointed Mendum secretary. Participants included former Chartist John Cluer, abolitionist D. S. Grandin, Fourierist Henry P. Trask, and ten-hour activist E. W. Parkman, who urged common measures "beneficial to the working classes." If capitalists received incorporation and bankruptcy laws, workers should cooperate to gain the same benefits.[7]

On October 30, 1847, the Massachusetts NRA held its second state convention. It expanded the platform of land reform and the ten-hour workday to call for "a *Lien Law* for the protection of productive laborers,—and Direct Taxation for all Government expenses." Most important, it declared slavery "a crime against Humanity . . . to be abolished immediately" and urged "our anti-slavery and 'no voting' friends" to "adopt the Measures and Political Action that shall secure to every disenthralled slave, whatever their complexion . . . the peaceable and immediate possession of a sufficient quantity of Land to enable them to procure the necessary means of subsistence whenever their liberation is achieved." Fay joined Seaver and Parkman in issuing the Address of the Massachusetts National Reform Convention. "If some solicit your aid in the protection of the rights of the *white* man—if others ask your assistance in alleviating the oppressions of the *colored* man—we entreat you to co-operate with US in the protection and security of *all men* in the full possession and free exercise of every *natural* Right."[8]

In the end, though, Massachusetts National Reformers, like those in New York earlier, simply merged into the antislavery party. Delegates "unanimously and enthusiastically" endorsed Samuel E. Sewall, the Liberty gubernatorial candidate pledged for land reform. Although similar acclaim greeted the independent NRA nomination of Amasa Walker for lieutenant governor, the very same issue of the *Voice of Industry* that reported the convention promoted a "Liberty Ticket" that substituted John M. Brewster, the abolitionist nominee, for Walker. The results indicated only limited possibilities for a third party in Massachusetts.[9]

That same year, the New York City NRA repeated its previous "Free Soil" experiment of making common state nominations with the abolitionists. Statewide, the exclusively NRA candidates won nearly 2,000 voters; outpolling the Whigs in places, their totals fell in the city to between 343 and 423, partly because the NRA found it difficult moving its old Locofoco periphery into the alliance with the abolitionists. Most important, the official count acknowledged over 15,000 votes for independent Liberty, Antirent, and National Reform tickets, sufficient to deny either major party a majority in some races.[10] The realization that insurgents, if united, might wield a balance of power in the state was unavoidable.

The National Industrial Congress and Presidential Politics

As VanBuren's Barnburners began to break from the Democrats, the NRA chose to stand by the "friends of Impartial Freedom and Comprehensive Reform" who had met at Macedon Lock, who remained insistent on both radical land reform and immediate action on slavery—not merely in its extension to the territories but everywhere. Under Gerrit Smith, these Liberty League members held a mid-January national convention at Auburn to adopt a "broad platform" embracing NRA and other measures. Brooks and William Elder of Philadelphia attended the convention where Smith, Samuel R. Ward, and Henry Bradley helped add land reform planks to the abolitionist platform. On behalf of the NRA, Bovay wrote that "the paths of the Liberty League . . . and of the National Reformers converge" and "must soon meet."[11]

The abolitionists did not entirely share the visceral NRA response to proposals for the government subsidy of business ventures, particularly the new railroads. From its perspective, such policies amounted to making the nation pay for a restructuring of its economic life and social structure that would be entirely in the hands of private interests. It attacked particularly the ambitious plans of Asa Whitney to finance a transcontinental railroad through unprecedented land grants. In spring 1848, Whitney and his backers called a meeting "of the Bankers and Capitalists" at the Broadway Tabernacle, and the NRA turned to direct action. Ingalls recalled that Whitney "had not learned before that there were Land Reformers; but he heard from them, that evening." From the floor, the Agrarians elected Lewis Ryckman to the chair and cheered his proposal to drive from office anyone "betraying a trust" by supporting Whitney's measure, even as the entrepreneurs "left by the rear entrance, giving up the meeting to the control of the Reformers."[12]

This new militancy framed the third NIC at Philadelphia. Although the NRA had won the support of many local veterans of the earlier labor movement such as John Greig, John Ashton, Theophilus Fisk, William Heighton, John Ferral, J. Sidney Jones, and Fannie Lee Townsend, as well as local organizations of Fourierists, the German Sozial Reform Association, and a loose circle of British émigrés that included Thomas Phillips, John Mills and John Sheddon, the local movement now focused on the meteoric career of George

Lippard, a consumptive young novelist who had dabbled at the edges of the ministry, medicine, and law before turning to journalism, then fiction. His stark depictions of Philadelphia society in his book *Quaker City* made him a hero to the "laborers, the mechanics, the great body of the people," particularly when the city fathers kept the story from the stage.[13]

Suspicion of government, if not outright hostility, motivated the NIC. Although it urged the government to collect labor statistics, it criticized the government debt as imposing "the hobbies and follies of the present generation" upon the future. It opposed laws for the collection of debt; recommended an unofficial industrial legislature in each state; endorsed cooperatives; and discussed direct taxation, free trade, and township education. Although the NIC did not agree to the proposals of Townsend and others to bypass the questioning of major parties and go directly to independent political action, it did recommend making independent nominations before questioning the major parties, with an offer to withdraw from the race for a pledge. As well, the body chose to *"memorialize"* the authorities for land reform and the ten-hour day "on all public works and in all corporations chartered by law."[14]

Most notably, the NIC called for "a general law, securing to the people the means and opportunity to vote *directly"* for or against proposed laws. West envisioned abolitionist-NRA unity around *"a government of* ALL for *the benefit of* EACH, in itself the PERFECTION OF SELF-GOVERNMENT" by which he meant the abolition of special governing bodies. This marked a major shift toward an antielectoral radicalism like that of William Lloyd Garrison, whose followers had disparaged not only land reform politics but also politics in general. Whereas West had earlier appealed for the American Anti-Slavery Society to join with the NRA based in a joint opposition to slavery and land monopoly, he now urged a common nonresistance critique of American politics as indicated in the "direct legislation" approach to reform. When Evans quietly "disclaimed the remarks of Mr. West," denying that the NIC had called for the abolition of government, West admitted that although land reformers "do not differ" on slavery, they had been "nearly equally divided" on calling for the abolition of government.[15]

Indeed, the presidential race had the most immediate claim on the NIC, which, wrote Ingalls, "resolved itself into a nominating convention." Some favored running a "practical working man" for president, and others urged "a clean-ticket" of William S. Wait, Sen. Isaac P. Walker, or even Sen. Andrew Johnson, but Evans, Van Amringe, John Windt and "several of the Pennsylvania, Western and other delegates" as "true abolitionists" urged joint action with the Liberty Leaguers who had nominated Gerrit Smith and Elihu Burritt. In the end, the NIC named Smith but substituted Wait for vice president.

Van Amringe, Ingalls, Greig, and George H. Sprague spoke at the public ratification meeting, alongside local Agrarians such as Sheddon and Lippard. Later, the Liberty national convention adopted a platform with NRA planks and confirmed Smith's nomination, but acknowledged that both Wait and Burritt had declined by naming Charles C. Foote, a Michigan abolitionist for vice president. In essence, wrote Ingalls, the NRA "endorsed the Abolition ticket."[16]

The old parties, meanwhile, pressed hard. Lippard turned to Gen. Zachary Taylor and spun flights of fancy about the coming transformation of the Whig "American System" into a vast crusading "Army of Industry" to build that "Palestine of Redeemed Labor" in the New World. Indeed, the venerable Whig statesman Daniel Webster even declared support for the principle of more egalitarian land distribution. However, Democratic office seekers made an even stronger effort. Even before the congress dissolved, Evans spoke before a rally of factory operatives on the southwest side of the city who had sent delegates to the NIC, only to find himself on a platform with Lippard's Democratic friends such as "Colonels" John W. Forney and Thomas B. Florence, as well as John Campbell, Edward Powers, and others; the local Democratic press even reported the resolutions as those of the NIC. Attendance had imposed no inconvenience on Campbell, a resident of Philadelphia who "bolted outright" to Lewis Cass's campaign, and excreted his *Negromania.*[17]

Nevertheless, defections to the Martin Van Buren campaign dwarfed those of the Democrats and Whigs. Starting in late 1847, New York's Barnburners broke with the Democratic Party and denounced land speculation. Already suspicious of Van Buren and professional Democratic politicians, the core New York City NRA group bristled when the professionals appropriated the name Free Soil. The group remained unimpressed when Barnburners began discussing land reform in the legislature, and Gov. John Young endorsed the general principle in his New Year's address. Nationally, other disaffected Northern Democrats opted for a new third party opposed to the spread of slavery into the western territories, and those Liberty Party members who had not been at Macedon Lock nominated Hale and negotiated their way into the new national coalition. The NRA at Boston, Philadelphia, and Baltimore joined the project and, in smaller communities like Worcester, actually dominated the Free Soil Party.[18]

In the end, representatives of the intransigent Liberty Leaguers and the NRA did attend the August 1848 national Free Soil convention. They arrived to find that the dissident Whigs, the Barnburners who had nominated Van Buren, and the pro-Hale Liberty Leaguers had met the day before the convention to form a provisional committee that agreed to admit one of each of their number to form delegations from each congressional district. In this way, charged Van Amringe, the politicians excluded Smith's Liberty Leaguers and National Reformers, exhibiting "a spirit of disregard of Free Soil, Free Speech, Free Labor and Free Men." Even so, National Reformers were members of the delegations of Massachusetts, New York, New Jersey, Ohio, Illinois, Indiana, Vermont, Wisconsin, and Pennsylvania, the last including William E. Stevenson who would soon attempt a free-soil colonization of Virginia.[19] As a political organization—and as a movement—National Reform survived but came very near to being entirely swallowed by the Free Soil Party.

The process owed little to Van Buren, who made himself as unsupportable as possible. He made no official response to Bovay until late July when his eighteen-page reply rambled past any clear definition of what he thought "Free Soil" actually meant, convincing Evans that the candidate hoped to avoid having a coherent radical bloc in the party. More eager to support the Free Soil Party, the Rochester NRA wrote Van Buren toward the end of July and began weeks of badgering those around him for a reply. After the convention, the candidate wrote an unprecedented second reply, reiterating his old position that selling public lands constituted an important source of future revenue and insisting on the confidentiality of his letter.[20] The disappointed Rochester NRA respected his wishes but flatly refused to support his candidacy.

Despite the NRA's scorn for Van Buren, the Free Soil Party had gained roughly five times the largest earlier vote of the Liberty Party by mobilizing voters who had no doubt that "Free Soil" meant land reform and antislavery. The Free Soilers had denied Democratic victory in New York and Whig success in Ohio. As in New York, Vermont Free Soilers won majorities as well as pluralities in different communities and placed second in the state. The Worcester NRA helped push local Free Soil totals beyond those of both Whigs and Democrats. The party had pockets of great strength in the "burned-over district" of upstate New York, the "western reserve" of northern Ohio, southeastern Wisconsin, and Illinois, where NRA leader Jeriel Root acknowledged "the effect of the free soil movement." Evans decried "how many land reformers voted for Van Buren," and Thomas Devyr estimated that "nineteen-twentieths of our men" had supported Van Buren. Ingalls thought only "a few" had supported Smith.[21]

The Demise of National Reform

However narrow support for the Smith-Foote ticket became, its adherents remained adamant. Evans attacked Van Buren's emphasis on eliminating slavery in the District of Columbia as a typically cosmetic measure that would only relocate the district's slaves into Maryland and Virginia. Martha Holling-sworth denounced the "cloven hoof" of professional politicians, and Treadwell indignantly corrected the *National Reformer* report that he had embraced the Van Buren campaign and declared his continued support for the NRA's course in *Young America*. Yankee Agrarians around Boston's *Investigator* and Lynn's *Free Soil Pickaxe* held fast. From Chicago, Daniel S. Curtiss wrote that midwestern stalwarts, too, were "not willing to abandon our old and tried candidates—whose acts and sentiments are unequivocal deep, broad and firm—yes, *ultra* as truth—GERRIT SMITH." In the end, returns trickled into the Smith-Foote column to total officially 5,239 votes, of which New Hampshire and Iowa contributed about a thousand votes each, with 2,545 from New York. Official returns ceded three NRA congressional candidates in New York City with 3,800 votes but gave Smith only 159 in the entire city.[22]

The pressures of their common isolation pushed the NRA still closer to the most iconoclastic abolitionists. The New York NRA participated in the September state convention of the Liberty League at Canastota, and the Rochester and Williamsburgh affiliates participated in the ongoing radical abolitionist campaign. Gerrit Smith brought Ingalls upstate where the latter hoped to campaign for Smith "but as a Land Reformer, for they had a Land Reform plank in their platform." That summer found Smith, Ingalls, Van Amringe, Evans, and William V. Barr at a Free Church convention where they exchanged their views about working-class responsibilities for Southern slavery with Beriah Green, William Goodell, and James C. Jackson. Perhaps to the chagrin of his fellow abolitionists, Smith declared, "Consistency required Christians who exclude from fellowship those who held people as property to treat likewise the holder of other people's homes and means of living." NRA issues, sometimes under regular "Land Reform" columns began appearing in abolitionist papers such as the *Aurora* in Centre, Indiana; Nathaniel P. Rogers's *Herald of Freedom* in New Hampshire; William L. Chaplin's *Albany Patriot;* and Sherman Miller Booth's *Wisconsin Freeman*. The *Anti-Slavery Bugle* of Aaron Hinchman and George W. Keen wrote, "We wish that every Land Reformer were an Abolitionist and every Abolitionist a Land Reformer." In November 1848, the Philadelphia NRA introduced land reform resolutions into the Pennsylvania Anti-Slavery Society, which discussed them until a general consensus emerged both as to their value and the inappropriateness of their formal adoption, after which the NRA withdrew its proposals. By 1849, Elijah M. K. Glenn, the lecturer for the New York Antislavery Society also spoke on behalf of land reform as well as abolitionism.[23]

Cincinnati Agrarian Lucius A. Hine spoke for those National Reformers who still balked at West's nonresistance. Declaring that he found Garrison "the most pleasant" when "the most denunciatory" of injustice, Hine frankly admired him for both his enemies and his followers, the latter "among the best friends of all the reforms," and confidently predicted that "the poor, the oppressed, the ignorant and the slave will be under greater obligation . . . than to any other class of philanthropists." Nevertheless, Hine's *Garrisonian Politics* took them to task for their refusal to participate in elections and to use the possibilities of the Constitution. He found nonvoting abolitionists "generally in favor of Land Reform," but their refusal to participate in elections ignored an otherwise valuable opportunity to confront proslavery and monopolist power. Civilization in general, not just politics, argued Hine, is "made up of compromises with evil," and it was "absurd to talk of absolution from the sin and curse of slavery."[24]

However, the NRA was virtually spent as an independent political force. In the winter of 1848–49, Ingalls returned to a "completely disorganized" New York City NRA. It mounted a spring mayoral campaign for David Marsh, but he withdrew four days before the April 10 election, when the Democratic candidate, already endorsed by municipal reformers, gave his pledge to the NRA. However, Whig candidate Caleb S. Woodhull won, though limited managerial skills and a weak mandate left his administration unable to prevent the Astor Place Riot on May 10. Even as the radical possibilities of 1848–49 yielded to reaction across the Atlantic, the Barnburners and "Conscience Whigs" began abandoning the Free Soil coalition. Quipping that he "would keep the *Landmark* going, but it could no longer keep me going," Ingalls turned it over to William Haddock who "kept it running for several months." After losing his Antirent paper at Albany, Devyr had taught school to raise enough money to bring his press back to Williamsburgh, where he managed a landfill project on the river and tried repeatedly to launch a paper there. Then, too, the Fourierist *Harbinger* and the spiritualist *Univercoelum* merged into the *Spirit of the Age,* which "succumbed after a short life." Even the *Voice of Industry,* reborn as the *New Era of Industry* folded.[25]

By summer 1849, Evans announced that the press that had launched the NRA faced insurmountable problems. In addition to financial difficulties, years of almost constant newspaper work in the city had taken its toll on his health, and his wife, Laura, had apparently become seriously ill; she died the following year. Horace Seaver warned that if the workers "know their own interest and desire to promote it, they will never again suffer *Young America* to suspend its operations," but by the end of the year, Evans's paper fell silent, and he again retreated to his Granville farm. Without his day-to-day presence, Commerford, Ingalls, Devyr, and John H. Keyser "kept up an organization for purposes of propagandism" but "abandoned the idea of political organization."[26] Thereafter, the NRA as a "national" force opted to meet only periodically, as the broader movement seemed to need a shove toward land reform.

Through 1848–49, new organizations attempted to fill the void, the most important being Lippard's strangely mystical Brotherhood of the Union. He called the project "the child of his earliest thoughts and ambition, and the object of his constant solicitude." The Brotherhood did not become public until Elizur Wright discussed its growth in November 1849 and Greeley reported its spread through New York in 1850. Evans praised it, and Commerford, Ingalls, Keyser, William J. Young, and Egbert Manning became prominent New York leaders. Ohio leader John Klippart explained that the order sought to tend a "Holy Flame" of social justice that had initially flared with "momentary brightness in the ancient Egyptian order of Therapeuta" and left "mysterious symbols . . . alike in the pyramids of Egypt, and in the monuments of Mexico," before persisting through the Illuminati, Freemasons, Rosicrucians and Druids to when "a Great order of Brotherhood . . . extended its mysterious circle over the entire globe." In the Brotherhood, "nothing of a sectarian or political character, can be introduced" to divert the order form its struggle against "the degradation of Labor, whether manifested in the form of Wages, Slavery, Land Monopoly, or Machine Monopoly, as the great Evil which tramples into the dust the holiest Rights of Humanity" through a cooperative "Union of Capital" and the promotion of NRA measures.[27] The movement had transcended the secularism of the movement's foundations.

Notwithstanding their Locofoco background, the NRA's founders had reached a point in which they were willing to take the most boldly radical positions and let the chips fall where they may. In the course of the 1848 election campaign, the hopes and dreams of land reformers, abolitionists, and other social reformers mingled. At Gerrit Smith's home in upstate New York, abolitionists expressed their political as well as musical satisfaction with Joshua K. Ingalls's rendition of August J. H. Duganne's NRA song, "Acres & Hands." National Reformers met antislavery leaders such as Theodore Weld and Angelina and Sarah Grimké; and Weld introduced Francis Green, Llewellyn Haskell, and John H. Hunt to Ingalls, who recalled them all as "progressive people" concerned "for the wrongs of the industrious poor."[28]

✳ ✳ ✳

Association with the Grimké sisters and the active involvement of Fannie Lee Townsend, Sarah Bagley, and Martha Hollingsworth are noteworthy measures of the extent of the movement's radicalism. Just as organization of an Industrial Brotherhood had posed the need for an "Industrial Sisterhood," the emergence of the pro-NRA Brotherhood of the Union inspired talk of launching a "Sisterhood of the Union." Martha Hollingsworth embraced National Reform because it "would not only elevate the condition of man but woman also," but she sought only to be a "helpmate" and declined appointment to a national office, which she feared would be resented by male members. The need to address the specific needs of female activists inspired a woman's rights convention at Seneca Falls in July 1848, but among the handful of men present was Eliab W. Capron, a land reformer, Fourierist, and soon-to-be promoter of spiritualism.[29]

Moreover, the NRA offered an ideological prism that enlightened the broad spectrum of antebellum social reform. The 1848 National Industrial Congress had agreed to "recommend such other collateral measures as shall appear to be dictated by wisdom and experience, for the immediate relief of the toiling millions." The next two annual gatherings at Cincinnati and Chicago built these "collateral," "cognate," "secondary, subsidiary or auxiliary principles" into a broad radical platform for social change.[30] The thoroughness and radicalism of their social critique and their proposed solutions reveal neglected dimensions of the early American experience.

8   *Free Soil and Cheap Land: National Reform and the Struggle for Radical Agrarianism*

> This despotism prevails through the entire nation. It knows no North, no South—for every where is humanity robbed, depressed, degraded and brutalized. Every where are children's rights to education, men and women's rights to natural bounties and to moral freedom, to the produce of their industry, and the comforts of home, violated with impunity and without reproach from the majority of our people.
>
> —Lucius A. Hine, 1853

Making National Reform "national" turned largely on the Midwest. After his initial appointment in June 1847, H. H. Van Amringe—the national lecturer of the National Industrial Congress—turned steadfastly toward Ohio and worked his way west, entering Wisconsin at Mineral Point in October and giving daily talks on land limitation and woman's rights at Dodgeville, Madison, Ceresco (presently Ripon), Waukesha, Milwaukee, Racine, Rochester, Southport (presently Kenosha) and other towns. In March 1848, he returned to Illinois, organized an auxiliary at Chicago, attended the May Day rally at Cincinnati, got his mandate renewed at the 1848 NIC, and returned to Wisconsin. Joshua K. Ingalls thought all sorts of reforms gained a better hearing in the less formed society on the West.[1]

Midwestern successes used NRA ideas to transform national politics, albeit in an unexpected fashion. The emergence of Free Soil and Free Democratic politics allowed the NRA and its closest allies to elaborate their own ever more expansive and radical program for the social reconstruction of American civilization. The process culminated in a final, definitive repudiation of the entire second-party system centered on the two-party rivalry of Democrats and Whigs.

Midwestern Land Reform

As it spread to the West, the NRA gained important support from the same social base that had founded it in the eastern cities. Urban craftsmen built auxiliaries at Cincinnati, Chicago, and Milwaukee, although these were often subsumed into a broader Free Soil coalition that drew leadership from elsewhere. For example, Chicago's group formed in May 1848, but the Free Soil preoccupation of its leaders dissipated the group by September, leaving it to be reorganized almost two years later.[2] The NRA in the other cities seemed to have had a similarly episodic existence.

The case of Warren B. Chase and the Wisconsin Phalanx demonstrate the vital role of socialists and their communities in spreading the NRA ideas in the less-settled west. Despite a disadvantaged past, New Hampshire–born Chase had worked his way west as a farmhand, settling at Southport (later Kenosha) in the Wisconsin Territory. By 1844, he and other local readers of Greeley's *Tribune* founded the Wisconsin Phalanx at Ceresco, optimistically named for the Roman goddess of grain. Fond Du Lac County voters sent him to the 1846 constitutional convention, where he opposed a militia, capital punishment, imprisonment for debt, gender and racial barriers on the suffrage, and private ownership of unoccupied lands. Elected to the state senate in 1848, Chase continued to agitate for radical social measures, including the introduction of protective unions into the new state.[3]

The NRA had also won support among local iconoclasts such as Jeriel Root, George W. Allen, and Aaron Hinchman. Hinchman's *Self-Examiner* sought to "eradicate prejudice and selfishness from among mankind, and institute in their place a spirit of liberality, forebearance, tolerance, and brotherly love"; and, "zealously oppose all combinations of power which has a tendency to injure or abridge the rights and privileges of others." Like Allen, who ran for the U.S. Congress at Columbus, Root ran for the legislature in 1846 "against both political parties" at Peoria, contenting himself with no more than a trickle of votes. William B. Camden's mayoral campaign at Portsmouth, Ohio, in spring 1848, netted only 15 votes (the winner got over 370).[4]

As in the east, western land reformers also found abolitionist support. Sherman Miller Booth—the Yale-educated former coeditor of the eastern *Charter Oak*—took issue with the *Oak*'s characterization of the NRA as a "silly crusade against land tenure." Another old *Oak* man, Ichabod Codding, then with the *American Freeman,* covered much of the debate. Like the *Oak,* the Boston *Emancipator* opposed unity with the NRA, but the *Freeman* quickly established a regular column on land reform and printed Van Amringe's lectures. By spring 1848, Codding turned responsibility for the *Freeman* to Booth, whose pages mingled the activities of Fourierists, National Reformers, and abolitionists. His cothinkers, Morris S. Barrett and Dana Lamb, formed the National Reform Club at Rosendale, requiring pledges from candidates not only to promote land reform and the ten-hour workday but also to abolish slavery and all discrimination "on account of birth-place or color."[5]

Developments in Illinois lagged somewhat behind those in Wisconsin. Seth Paine complained that even as abolitionists elsewhere moved toward a "broad platform," the 1847 convention of the Illinois Liberty Party stuck to the "one idea," following Owen Lovejoy's *Western Citizen,* which, argued Paine, espoused a sectarian self-righteousness, "a creed . . . equally obnox- ious with any other creed system." By 1848, however, Lovejoy decided that "White oppression must receive our attention as well as black" and urged a Liberty Party platform that included "free trade, direct taxation as a conse- quence, the abolition of the army, the dismantling of the navy and the 'Murder School at West Point' and a dozen other things as further consequences." The NRA also won Dr. Charles V. Dyer, the acknowledged leader of the state's Underground Railroad, and James H. Collins, who had won court cases for runaway slaves fifteen years before the Dred Scott decision declared such rulings unconstitutional.[6]

However, the land question in the Midwest also moved to speculative landowners with a vested interest in increasing the value of their own holdings as quickly as possible. Indeed, many claims associations of self-labeled "squat- ters" or "settlers" actually represented what amounted to real estate lobbies for whom federal homestead law would shift public lands to the private sector, where competition would erode any equality of ownership. Also, lead mine owners in communities like Galena, Illinois, or Mineral Point, Wisconsin, saw land reform as a means of extricating the issue of mineral rights from legislation formulated for agriculture. The upshot meant that town leaders in the Midwest were as likely as any underclass to embrace land reform. Of the five founders of Bloomfield, Iowa, at least two were known members of the Brotherhood of the Union. A respected Ohio freemason, Samuel J. Peters, organized a circle of the Brotherhood of the Union at South Charleston, helped form two other circles at Springfield, and participated in a fourth at Vienna Crossroads under the leadership of Dr. Jacob Lingle, the justice of the peace, county treasurer, and owner of "a considerable amount of land and personal property." Men of similar local prominence took up the issue at Portsmouth, Fairfield, Norwalk, Dayton, and other communities. Calls for land reform by the *Lancaster Eagle* appeared in what was "one of the best, largest, and most creditably executed weeklies of the State."[7]

The nature of such interests became even more evident in more invested markets like Chicago. There, sometimes–congressman and mayor John Went-worth of the *Chicago Daily Democrat* and his NRA comrade William B. Ogden could simultaneously urge reform and speculate so heavily in real estate that their names still grace two of the city's most prominent avenues. The two brokered the 1848 electoral coalition around Dyer's gubernatorial campaign and got the *Chicago Times* into the hands of Chauncey T. Gaston, the British-born former employee of Wentworth's *Democrat* and the record-ing secretary of the local NRA. Gaston's former partner on the *Gem of the Prairie,* John Locke Scripps, called himself a "Free Soiler with Democratic proclivities" even after becoming editor of the Whig *Chicago Tribune.* Mean-while, émigré German socialists also shared Free Soil politics with Democratic predispositions, as voiced by another NRA founder, Dr. Carl A. Helmuth of the *Illinois Staats-Zeitung.*[8]

Land reform loomed large enough elsewhere to shape congressional poli-tics. Jesse W. Fell, a Pennsylvania cabinetmaker transplanted to Bloomington, Illinois—and a close adviser to former congressman Abraham Lincoln—began to advocate the kind of NRA measures that weakened the Democratic coali-tion downstate. Conversely, when Lyman Trumbull edged out incumbent Democratic congressman Robert Smith for the nomination in 1846, the latter financed Sparta's *Randolph County Record,* which became the *Chester Rev-eille and Homestead Advocate,* and spent some years living up to that name under the pens of Benjamin F. J. Hanna and William A. Phillips. An Ohio printer, Joseph Cable, had published papers at Steubenville and New Lisbon before building a local movement at Carrolton strong enough to elect him to Congress as a Democrat.[9]

Nowhere did the radicals attain greater success than in Wisconsin. Both the abolitionist Sherman Booth and the Fourierist Warren Chase attained statewide political influence, as did Andrew E. Elmore, the Waukesha County leader of the Democratic faction for land reform. The potential constituency for reform beyond the Liberty Party became obvious in 1846, when the party got only 973 voters statewide, while nearly 7,700 voters—over a third of the total—favored black suffrage. Milwaukee workers and labor reformers, includ-ing the German émigrés, groped toward an antislavery alliance through the 1848 Free Soil Convention called by Charles Durkee and Samuel D. Hastings. The timely arrival of Van Amringe helped unite these divergent components into a common party. The Democratic schism in New York, reported by Booth, drew Elmore's faction from the Democrats to the new party. In fall 1848, the NRA and circles of the Brotherhood of the Union helped to win 10,500 Wisconsin votes.[10]

Persistent internal tensions strained at the Free Soil coalitions across the

Midwest. The NRA endorsed Milwaukee Democratic congressional candidate William Pitt Lynde after his last-minute pledge, and Elmore dispatched riders across the district with news of the movement's support, but the abolitionists noted that Lynde "gave them very little satisfaction." The abolitionists also criticized Rep. Moses M. Strong, a Democrat, of the mining district around Mineral Point and took umbrage at the contrast between the NRA's warmth toward Elmore and its alleged coolness toward Durkee. Then, too, Milwaukee Germans such as Dr. Frank Huebschman and Frederick Fratney of the *Volksfreund* battled their ethnic loyalties to the Democrats. The Democrats interested in reform, like Rep. Robert Smith, responded by urging the states parties to adopt measures aimed a luring the prodigal Free Soilers back, the Wisconsin party going so far as to adopt the insurgent platform. Particularly after Martin Van Buren's organization in the East began returning to the Democrats, those midwestern Free Soilers led by Wentworth and Elmore urged "One Line in one grand party of progress."[11]

The more radical insurgents—National Reformers as well as abolitionists—balked at abandoning the third-party effort. Charles Clement, the pro-NRA abolitionist editor of the *Kenosha Telegraph* brought matters to a head in Wisconsin, offering to support the 1849 Democratic gubernatorial candidate if he accepted the nomination of a united "Free Democratic" convention. When the candidate refused to accept any insurgent nomination and demanded the dissolution of the third party, Elmore led his Democratic Free Soilers back to the party, with the remainder standing fast as Free Democrats behind the candidacy of Warren Chase, the socialist. Chase's campaign rallied about 3,800 of the insurgents.[12]

Back east, as well, those Free Soilers of Democratic proclivities abandoned the third-party movement to its most ideologically radical adherents. The Worcester Free Soil convention, dominated by the NRA, expanded its platform to demand the free distribution to the landless of "reasonable portions" of land. So, too, the remaining Vermont Free Soilers actively promoted homestead exemption, what Elizur Wright Jr. called "this important first installment" of land reform.[13] That broader Free Soil Party of 1848 left a significant radical residue in its wake.

The Radicalization of National Reform

The course of the midwestern insurgency permitted the NRA to move in new directions. As early as 1845, George Henry Evans warned against translating National Reform into a moderate and administrative scheme for lower land costs to hasten privatization as desired by the western land speculators. He did so because the process had already begun to take place in Illinois, Ohio, and other midwestern states.[14]

The emergence of electoral Free Soil politics liberated the NRA and its industrial congresses from electoral concerns, allowing its militants to explore the radical implications of their program. The Cincinnati 1849 NRA clearly saw itself as part of a wider struggle against corruption, slavery, and war and for "the whole of progress." It addressed a spectrum of social reforms before being scattered by the year's visitation of cholera. Newspaper reporters felt "amply repaid . . . for a lengthy visit" to its "pretty numerously attended" sessions. There, representatives from "five or six different States of the Union" engaged in "able and interesting" discussions. These covered "all subjects bearing upon the prominent reforms of the age; for the establishment of principles by which Reformers are to be guided in the furtherance of such questions as Anti-Slavery, Temperance, Land Reform—the Rights of Labor, the abuses of Capital—abolition of capital punishment, etc., etc." Speakers at public meetings in the evening included Lucius A. Hine, a Mrs. Burns lecturing on "phonography," and Fannie Lee Townsend, "a woman of clear mind, and much information." When William McDiarmid, a Wheeling Fourierist, moved for a draft document to discuss the relationship of all the various reform proposals, the congress approved and assigned the laborious task to John Pickering, the local author of *Working Man's Political Economy*.[15]

When the NIC reassembled at Chicago's City Hall on June 5, 1850, the only participants not from Illinois or Wisconsin were Ingalls and Hine, who brought Pickering's draft from Cincinnati. Under Chase's presidency, it declared, "All truth whether social, religious, political, physiological, and psychological constitutes unity, and no fragmentary reform can be carried out without going hand in hand with all other reforms." After declaring for woman's equality, it explicitly and unanimously condemned "the further extension of Slavery" and declared the institution "a moral, social and political evil, repugnant to the law of God written in the constitution of man, to the law of love revealed in the gospel of Christ, and to the declaration of rights proclaimed in the American Declaration of Independence." Anticipating Lincoln's argument about "the house divided," the National Reformers insisted that slavery "cannot exist without inevitably producing the destruction of a nation which permits it." They found it "an absurd and impious mockery of Jehovah to flatter ourselves that we can perpetuate the joint existence of Slavery and Freedom." While hoping that the slaveholding states "would offer no special opposition to the system of free lands," the Congress appealed to "inherent" and "universal" rights to insist that "no person nor class of persons can justly be deprived of these rights by birth or descent from their parents." Other resolutions touched upon free blacks, complaining of the "abridgment of the liberties of free American citizens."[16]

Hine presented the social critique by John (also referred to as "Solon") Pickering, but it faced the same fate as Fay's model of a "Free State" of three years before. The NIC listened to this sweeping declaration of primary human rights coupled to a series of related "secondary or auxiliary principles" and an impressive list of reforms. Although the congress did not understand how it would be "of any service to the cause" to endorse it, delegates voted to print it with the proceedings, and it did adopt Hine's report on auxiliary and affiliated associations. It's "Appeal to Reformers" urged the "Friends of Universal Freedom" to establish Industrial Reform Associations with county, state and national associations. Those concerned about placing their "indispensable" priorities on land reform did not oppose these "universal measures," but sought only to postpone their adoption, "except for the purposes of discussion."[17] Almost irrepressibly, though, "National Reform" began to redefine itself as "Industrial Reform."

Elsewhere, emergent labor organizations reconstituted citywide bodies and engaged the remnants of the NRA. In 1849, a Boston printers' strike galvanized a general movement of the city's trades; fourteen Pittsburgh crafts united to resist the efforts of local ironmongers to reduce wages, even as the city government of Mayor Alexander Hay declared for land reform. At Philadelphia, the Brotherhood of the Union fostered various cooperative enterprises, most notably the Industrial Association of John Mills, John Sheddon, and Isaac Rehm among the women of the needle trades. Various sources indicate similar activities at Baltimore, Albany, Auburn, Buffalo, Trenton, Chicago, Cleveland, Cincinnati, and elsewhere. To an extent, wrote one historian, "scarcely an industrial centre" escaped the movement "as far west as Illinois."[18]

In New York City, National Reformers provided the vital active nuclei within the crafts that crystallized the movement. In May 1850, after five years of trying to get a trades' convention, they launched what became the New York City Industrial Congress (NYCIC), although Evans pointed out that the name might cause some confusion with the annual national assemblies and preferred Industrial Council to suggest the municipal character. According to Elizur Wright, prime movers had been John H. Keyser, back in the city from California and Florida, and Donald C. Henderson of the *Tribune*. The hostile Democratic *Herald* also blamed K. Arthur Bailey, a printer in the Brotherhood of the Union, Henry J. Crate of the Typographical Union, and others around Greeley and his *Tribune*, "the organ of free soil whiggery and socialism." Like the NRA, the NYCIC provided what one historian called "a forum for virtually every labor, land, sanitary and political reform in vogue on either side of the Atlantic."[19] Scholars have generally followed the *Herald*'s assertion, misascribing the political course of the NYCIC to the National Reformers.

In reality, the reformist hopes of the NYCIC came to the fore because of the general Democratic effort to draw Free Soilers to the party, and from local discontent with the Whig municipal administration. Through the summer and fall, the NYCIC placed a series of proposals before the government, including lien laws, debt reform, and legislation establishing a ten- and, ultimately, an eight-hour day, as well as an extensive platform of municipal reforms including public works to employ the unemployed at a minimum wage set by law, the election of ward rent inspectors with the power to deny rents to landlords with substandard housing, and capping all rents at 10 percent of one's income. By August, the authorities granted the NYCIC use of a courtroom in the annex behind City Hall. That October, Fernando Wood, mayoral candidate of the Mozart Hall Democrats, gave the NYCIC his unreserved pledge for its endorsement. Associates of Tammany such as John Cochrane, Sanford E. Church, Theodore E. Tomlinson, and the Tenth Ward boss Elijah Purdy also courted the movement. By the fall, Ira B. Davis and William V. Barr formed "Assembly Committees" to act within the Democratic Party.[20]

With reformist rhetoric commonplace among officeholders, the land reformers as a group focused less on electoral politics than on their unprecedented national petition campaign. The NIC had discussed "the great petitions of the Massachusetts freemen and the English Chartists," and the fitfully revitalized NRA orchestrated the circulation and delivery of at least a hundred petitions on the land question to the Thirty-first Congress, most ending in its Committee on Public Lands. Of these, 43 came from New England and the Mid-Atlantic, 37 from the Midwest, and 17 from slaveholding states, with one from California. Almost all of these employed the language of the NRA, calling for exemptions and land limitations as well as a homestead bill.[21] Officeholders—and, later, historians—tended to distill these petitions for a sweeping and radical land reform into a simple call for a homestead bill, just as they had earlier appropriated the language of "free soil."

The dynamic became markedly clear after 1848 in Wisconsin, where Democrats embraced the old Free Soil platform, and Whigs protested the Fugitive Slave Law and assisted in the 1850 reelection of Free Democratic congressman James Duane Doty. Under the leadership of Chase, Booth, Durkee, and "General" J. H. Paine—recently arrived from Ohio with his abolitionist and NRA record—the Free Democrats seemed to win success upon success. Largely elected on such pledges, the Wisconsin legislature heard the governor's call for action on the land question in the winter of 1850–51. It actually passed a bill limiting individual ownership of land to four city lots or 640 rural acres, but the constitution required multiple votes, allowing for enough time for real estate interests, investors, and manufacturers to call in obligations of greater importance to the politicians. Claiming that they had fulfilled their obligations by the first vote, many pledged legislators broke ranks and voted against land limitation.[22] Radical land reform sentiment simmered angrily in the state.

The Fading of an Independent Land-Reform Movement

A crucial turning point came that June at Albany at the first NIC in three years held east of the Alleghenies. Apparently encouraged by abolitionist allies, "a colored gentleman from Philadelphia," John C. Bowers, presented credentials from what was alternately called the Philadelphia Land Association and the Truth Association, which Hine described as a "Building Society of colored men." The Democratic *New York Herald* gleefully reported the noisy protests even to accepting his papers for referral to the Credentials Committee. Hine wrote of his confusion when another delegate announced "that he would not sit with a 'nigger'," as that "the colored man in question possesses great fluency and accuracy of speech, a high intellectual and moral endowment." Apparently, he was not alone in his inability to comprehend "why any one should object to sit with one whose genius can command respect," because Evans and other supporters of Bowers's admission organized to respond decisively.[23]

On the second day of the NIC, for the only time on record, Evans lost his temper as matters came to a head. The body added members favorable to Bowers to the Credentials Committee, and these filed a minority report for seating Bowers passed by twenty-two of the twenty-eight delegates on the floor. Bowers then strolled prominently to the front, taking a seat his supporters made vacant "in the most conspicuous place" before the presiding officer, Evans. Thereafter, as Evans read the correspondence into the record, he encountered John Campbell's letter protesting the admission: "mulattoes, sambos, quadroons, mestizos, *et hoc genus omne* from a light buff or yellow, to sable dark, in fine all those with the taint of inferior blood in them." As Evans began to set it aside, a clamor arose for him to finish it, which he did, then requesting for a motion to purge it from the minutes, in effect asking the entire NIC to refuse to accept the letter. Thereafter erupted "most violent, abusive, and intolerant harangues," leading nearly to "an altercation of fisticuffs" between Bowers and Edward Powers, but the body voted to strike Campbell's letter. The integrationists then insistently nailed down an indisputable precedent by ratifying Bowers's credentials again as "a test question." In the debate, an "extremely ardent and impulsive land reformer" spoke for

Evans and others at the core of the old NRA when he declared for the "dissolution" of the existing movement and its thorough reorganization rather
than to permit the inconsistency of excluding blacks. In the end, only six voted
against integrating the movement, although a number of others voted with
their feet.[24]

The precedent's importance should not be understated. With the announcement of the next year's NIC, Greeley goaded "our sensitive friends
at New York and elsewhere" who still felt an "apprehensiveness and not a
littler Hunkerishness" over "the admission of colored Delegates," although
none had yet requested credentials to go to Washington, a slaveholding city.
Yet the selection of the 1852 NIC of veteran abolitionist U.S. Rep. Durkee
to preside over their deliberations hardly dissuaded critics who later charged
that National Reform was "resolving itself into an Abolition Society, under a
nice name." When the tenth NIC convened at Cleveland, it not only ignored
the color bar but also elected as a secretary black journalist William Howard
Day, then fighting to repeal Ohio's black codes and later involved in John
Brown's plan for a slave uprising.[25]

Briefly, the impending presidential election stirred the last embers of Locofoco hopes. Urging a strictly "progressive candidate," Evans had proposed re-
nominating Gerrit Smith into 1850, and the 1851 NIC even discussed running
black abolitionist Samuel R. Ward. Pragmatic hopes focused on Wisconsin's
senator Isaac P. Walker, who strongly favored land reform, had a moderately
antislavery record, and a seemingly realistic shot at the Democratic nomination. Before the NYCIC, John Commerford praised Walker's speech for the
Homestead Bill, and that body asked local Democratic officials to address
Walker's concerns, even as Evans went with Barr in an effort to persuade
Greeley's *Tribune* to publish it. Democrats realized that many of the most
readily identifiable trade unionists remained inclined to their party even with
no reformist frills and made an active push for a June 3 meeting of "all true
Democrats" for "Land and other Industrial reforms." That meeting installed
Barr among its officers and adopted Cochrane's resolutions urging the national
party to adopt "the land question" and nominate Walker for president.[26] The
NYCIC's Democratic inclinations, though, outlasted the Walker boom.

Across the country, the old Jacksonian coalition between the South and the
West crumbled as more petitions poured into the Thirty-second Congress. The
numbers ran to roughly 250 petitions, including the documents supporting
a massive land grant in Iowa for William Rees's NRA colonization plan (the
Western Farm and Village Association). With Ohio passing New York in the
number of petitions submitted, the expression of public will helped push the
Homestead Bill through the House of Representatives on May 12, 1852, by

a vote of 107 to 56. However, Southern leaders in the Senate sent it to committee and blocked the efforts of Sen. Salmon P. Chase, Walker, and others
to bring it to the floor. Within two weeks of the House action, the bill and its
petitions began gathering dust in the Committee on Public Lands.[27]

Within days, on June 2, 1852, the most geographically representative NIC
to date gathered at Washington, D.C. The Brotherhood of the Union and allied
German socialists there hosted delegates from New York City, Philadelphia,
and Lowell, as well as some state delegations from Delaware, Rhode Island,
New Jersey, and Wisconsin. After selecting the notorious Durkee to preside,
the NIC adopted the "Circular to the Land Reformers of the United States"
reported by Eliab W. Capron, the abolitionist, Fourierist, and spiritualist.
After denouncing the pointless rivalry of Democrats and Whigs, it declared:
"The party of masses, the Labor Party, is a third party. Organized or disjointed,
unanimous or divided, conscious or unconscious of its own existence, *it is.*"[28]
It explicitly favored an independent presidential nomination if candidates of
the major parties would not give written pledges to promote the movement's
measures.

With his nomination, Democratic candidate Franklin Pierce heard more
than he wanted from the land reformers. Capron, Thomas Devyr, Ben Price
George Gordon, and August G. H. Duganne wrote him on behalf of the
movement. The Democratic tactician Cochrane pointedly informed Pierce
that some 6,000 votes in New York turned on his response, noting Whig gains
in "a large and secret state organization of Mechanics" associated with the
NRA, likely referring to the Mechanics Mutual Protection Association of the
Brotherhood of the Union.[29]

After Pierce had repeatedly ducked the question, the NRA turned to mass
meetings. On August 4, at the Military Hall on Bowery and Spring, Commerford convened a gathering with little of the old naïveté about the Democratic Party, although E. P. Day of Brooklyn's *Democratic Free Press* urged
patience. Two days later, National Reformers attended the city convention
of the "Independent Democrats"—the local Free Democratic Party—which
passed William West's resolutions on land reform and elected a delegation
to the national convention that included him, Masquerier, and Dr. William
J. Young under the chairmanship of Abraham Levy, a dissenting Democrat
sympathetic to the NRA. On August 10, the NRA reassembled, after news
had reached New York from the U.S. Senate that sixteen Democrats and
twelve Whigs had blocked Walker's effort to get the Homestead Bill to the
floor. Day began the meeting with a recantation, and Democratic prospects
declined from there to a point where the only debate was whether the movement should support the Whigs to inflict damage on Pierce's party or await

the outcome of the Free Democratic national convention at Pittsburgh.[30] The latter course prevailed.

National Reform triumphed at the Free Democratic convention. Gerrit Smith returned a minority report from its platform committee, embracing both Agrarian and abolitionist demands. In the end, the convention declared: "all men have a natural right to a portion of the soil"; "as the use of the soil is indispensible to life, the right of all men to the soil is as sacred as their right of life itself"; the public lands "belong to the people and should not be sold to individuals, nor granted to corporations, but should be held as a sacred trust for the benefit of the people, and should be granted in limited quantities, free of cost, to landless settlers." Three members of the New York delegation—Masquerier, Young, and probably Arnold Buffum—voted to nominate Smith for president, and for vice president, none other than George Henry Evans.[31] In the end, the nomination went to John P. Hale, among those Evans had suggested as a good candidate four years earlier.

By all contemporary indications, the movement in the East as well as the Midwest generally backed the Free Democrats. At New York, Evans, Ingalls, and others clearly favored Hale. At Philadelphia, land reformers such as George Lippard, Charles Goepp, A. J. H. Duganne, and John Sheddon spoke on behalf of the insurgents offering a standard stump speech linking fate of working people, North, and South to the triumph of free-soil principles.[32]

Nevertheless, hostility to Pierce may have pushed some to the Whigs. On August 17, K. Arthur Bailey and William West particularly urged punishing the Democrats by following Greeley, Seward, Harris, and other reform-minded Whigs into supporting General Scott. Temporarily back in New York, former NRA national secretary Bovay consulted with Greeley before he "came home to Wisconsin, worked hard for Scott, but felt defeat in the air every day."[33] Other reformers must have shared that sense whether they supported Scott or Hale.

❊ ❊ ❊

The following June, the core NRA group at New York City did not participate in the NIC at Wilmington in what had earlier been proclaimed as "Delaware—A Model Agrarian Republic." The local Brotherhood of the Union and Democratic legislator Robert B. McDonell hosted representatives from Dover, Philadelphia, and Wheatland, Pennsylvania. Reversing the trend toward escalating radicalism established by the midwestern sessions, the 1853 NIC kept their deliberations "confined to the consideration of the subject of Land Reform."[34] However, the time for a Democratic faction in an eastern city to define the discussion of land reform and republican values had long passed.

Events would not permit "the land question" to be posed either unanswered or disassociated from other proposals, particularly antislavery concerns. The National Reform agitation had contributed directly to rise of a Free Soil response to the proposed expansion of slavery into conquered territories. Its plan for a thorough social transformation had intellectually challenged the alternatives of both Asa Whitney and John C. Calhoun. Even as the organized NRA faltered, a victim in a sense of its own successes, its ideas—sustained by local affiliates—seemed to take on a life of their own.

The Republican Revolution:
Victories beyond and by the Ballot

There are but two things of which the historian will speak when the lapse
of centuries summons him to his task. He will say that . . . the people of
the country held within their own hands a sufficiency of territory . . . which
would have out-stripped in magnitude of extent and capability for the
means of population almost any separate or civilized contemporary. . . . He
will say, too, that although we had the experience of the policy of preceding
nations, depicted in the sad calamities with which they were overtaken, by
the absorption within the hands of the few the lands of the many, . . . we
stood with folded arms, and useless tongues, and allowed the capitalists and
forestallers to walk on to the titled privilege of inflicting upon our children's
children the deep curse and blight of land monopoly.
    —Benjamin F. Price, 1852

In fall 1853, the the wage earners in the NRA helped to launch a
new trades assembly more strictly focused on trade union concerns. As committed as ever to land reform, Benjamin F. Price signed the call to found the
assembly and participated in it, as did his comrades K. A. Bailey and Julian
A. Magagnos. They knew that the stronger unions might win the kinds of
immediate concessions that the quest for political power had failed to attain.
Realizing that such a move would have included the immigrant workers,
they adopted the program of the new Allgemeine Arbeiterbund, or American Workers' League, launched in March by the Proletarierbund of Joseph
Weydemeyer, the émigré communist.[1] Unable to recenter national politics
quickly on their own terms, workers acknowledged a community of interests
among themselves.

The nation's crisis changed National Reform in various interdependent
ways. Although limited, NRA involvement in the settlement of the western
territories contributed a social reform dimension to the tensions over Kansas.
Meanwhile, the electoral defeat elsewhere in the country seemed briefly to
push radicals into increasingly nonelectoral efforts. However, NRA veterans

played no minor role in the emergence of the third-party movement that did make "free labor" a national issue.

Urban Workers and Western Settlement

Discouragement with politics drove men like William Haddock to seek other alternatives such as colonizing the West. Early on, Alvan E. Bovay and the New York group discussed "an emigration to Oregon, on the National Reform plan." After serving as the NRA national secretary, Bovay went west himself in hopes of joining the Wisconsin Phalanx at Ceresco under Warren B. Chase, who presided over the 1850 NIC at Chicago. At that gathering, Joshua K. Ingalls reported great prospects in the West. Back in New York, his old friends, John Commerford and printer Haddock—along with Henry B. Waterman, a veteran Worky and upstate member of the Brotherhood of the Union—headed the Western Farm and Village Association that sent Bovay's father-in-law, Ransom Smith, on a scouting mission in the winter of 1851–52; the following May, several hundred urban workers reached "Minnesota City," what became the town of Rollingstone on the Mississippi River near Winona. Badly located and funded, the effort eventually dissolved, with Haddock and others making their way south into Iowa where, at Keokuk, William Rees, the Pittsburgh Fourierist, began requesting a massive congressional land grant covering most of southeastern Iowa.[2]

In and of itself, the West proved to be no escape from politics. Those NRA adherents drawn to California by the Gold Rush found that U.S. recognition of earlier "Spanish" land grants left newcomers confronted with a western version of "land monopoly." Veteran member of the Industrial Congress and *Tribune* writer James McClatchy, Charles Robinson, and others launched a series of newspapers arguing that, regardless of the law, the landless had a fundamental right to unused land superfluous for the needs of the often-absentee owner. After armed squatters confronted the authorities in the streets of Sacramento, McClatchy and other radicals from the East launched the new Settlers' League, which used the NRA strategy of electoral nonpartisanship and persisted in its efforts for many years on a local or statewide scale.[3]

Kansas soon loomed as a more accessible potential utopia. "My right to a choice lot, though I am poor," insisted Thomas Jefferson Sutherland, "is surely as good by nature as any other person, however rich he may be." Something of a speculator and promoter, he consolidated organizations along the Ohio, such as the Cannelton Reform Association, urged colonization through a "Nebraska Emigration Association," as early as 1851. In February 1854, a year and a half after Sutherland's death, the U.S. Congress passed the Kansas-Nebraska

Act opening the territory to slavery. Among the protests across the country, "working men of New York met *en masse*" on February 18 under a call by "the Mechanics of the City" to defend "free labor" under officers like old George Bruce, the freethinking printer, and John Delamontayne of the NRA.[4] While the initial movement in New York remained in the hands of the elite, radicals played an important role elsewhere.

Nowhere did this become more apparent than in Wisconsin, where NRA measures were part of the Democratic and the reform Whig platforms, as well as keystones of the successive Liberty, Free Soil, and Free Democratic parties. The radicals not only sustained an urban base in Milwaukee but also attained such strength in the adjacent counties of Walworth, Racine, and Waukesha that voters in the 1850 congressional campaign were able to choose between two land reformers, Andrew E. Elmore and Charles Durkee. Elsewhere, the old Wisconsin Phalanx in Fond Du Lac County provided a base, although the community had dissolved. A short-lived "People's" ticket had sought to build a coalition representing neither slavery nor land reform but the prohibition of alcohol, and the Whig regulars argued that "the mission of the Free Democracy as an independent party is nearly fulfilled."[5] Reviving the insurgency, then, fell to Sherman Miller Booth and the radicals elsewhere in the state.

The following winter, news of the Kansas-Nebraska Act horrified Bovay and the Wisconsin Phalanx at Ceresco, recently renamed Ripon. Through February, Bovay chaired protests "by persons of both sexes" at the Congregationalist church and the schoolhouse. Bipartisan policies on slavery in the territories, they resolved, had absolved them of old allegiances to the Democrats and Whigs, and they called for a new party with "a cherished name with our foreign population of every nationality. They call themselves *Republicans, Republicains, Republikaner, Republicanos*—or by some modification of it in all European countries, and this name meets them here like an old friend." They understood the name without the explanation of the classically educated—Lucius A. Hine's "*re,* affairs, *publico,* by the public" or Bovay's: "*Res Publica*—the common weal." While a broad spectrum of motives inspired the new party, for the many thousands of petitioners for a federal homestead bill, the Kansas-Nebraska Act embodied their worse fears for the future imperial degeneration of the American republic.[6]

By June, the sectional conflict preoccupied the three days of the National Industrial Congress. For the next presidential elections, it urged, "Free Homes, Land Limitation, Free Schools, Free Speech, a Free Soil for Free Men, an Elective Judiciary, Elective Functionaries, and Religious Liberty." When Saxe Gotha Laws of Delaware suggested scheduling an Industrial Congress "in a Southern State," other delegates quipped that "accustomed as they were to free speech, they could not think of doing anything in the

South," or that the degradation of labor there left "no trade societies to send delegates." The gathering declared its hostility to "the infamous Nebraska Bill" and denounced institutions "inimical to all rights of free labor." Thomas J. Braidwood's proposals warned that slavery's "triumphant march threatens the annihilation of American Freedom," and he extended the NRA pledge to require opposition to "the Southern Slave power." The NIC spent its closing hours discussing how to defy the Fugitive Slave Act, as Laws resigned on the grounds that land reform was "resolving itself into an Abolition Society, under a nice name."[7]

Spokesmen for land reform did actively sabotage the Fugitive Slave Act from Massachusetts to Wisconsin. In 1850, Appleton Fay presided over a statewide workingmen's convention apparently dominated ideologically by Bernard S. Treanor, Wooster Sprague, Henry P. Trask, and other Fourierists won to land reform. Almost unanimously, they declared that "giving up our fellow-workingmen to the Slave Hunters, at the South, dispensing with the trial by Jury, and making it criminal to do good to our fellow-workingmen, is an *infamous act, fit only to be trampled under the feet of every lover of Liberty and Justice.*" Over the next few years, Elizur Wright and John C. Cluer of that state faced prosecution for their open defiance of federal law.[8]

Most famously, perhaps, the 1854 Milwaukee arrest of Joshua Glover as a runaway slave sparked a mass protest meeting that ended in an assault upon the jail that released Glover and spirited him off to Canada. The authorities chose to prosecute NRA-abolitionist Sherman Miller Booth, a major figure in the meeting. Byron Paine, another member of the local NRA, defended Booth in a case that became a national *cause célèbre* as it dragged through the courts for the next five years. They fought the prosecution along predictably radical lines, arguing that the Fugitive Slave Law violated the constitutional protection of state self-government.[9] The defensive advocacy of "states' rights," then, became a sectional argument against the expansion of slavery's legality into the North.

Such conflict spilled easily into violence beyond the courtroom. William V. Barr, Erastus D. Ladd, and Edward Lynde became Free Staters in Kansas. There, too, William A. Phillips and Augustus and John O. Wattles rode with John Brown, who expressed an interest in social reform beyond abolitionism and collaborated with William H. Day, Gerrit Smith, and Thaddeus Hyatt, Ingalls's partner in the new street-lighting business.

Radicalism beyond Politics

Other than colonization of the West, radicals explored several other alternatives to the quest for electoral triumph. For years, self-induced trances had provided means for spirit communications by Shakers such as Frederick W. Evans—George Henry's brother—or rural mystics such as Andrew Jackson Davis. In the latter's "Harmonial" faith, every human psyche regardless of race, sex, wealth, or education had access to cosmological verities. In 1849, land reformers Henry D. Barron and Eliab W. Capron, the abolitionist, woman suffragist, and veteran of the Fourierist community at Sodus Bay, encountered the three Fox sisters, who managed physical "manifestations" of the spirits through telegraphic "Rochester rappings." In short order, "spiritualism" swept the old Free Soil districts of upstate New York, New England, and the upper Midwest. Although Evans and Elizur Wright remained skeptical, Lewis Masquerier battled to reconcile spiritualism with his iconoclastic rationalism. Ingalls, with Fourierist George Ripley and NRA Yankee Woodbury M. Fernald, helped staff the *Univercoelum and Spiritual Philosopher.* As well, spiritualism inspired some land reformers such as Stephen P. Andrews, Nathan H. Bolles, Albert Brisbane, Joseph R. Buchanan, Warren B. Chase, J. C. Cluer, William T. Coggeshall, John A. Collins, Ira B. Eddy, John H. Keyser, Henry Morford, John Orvis, Seth Paine, Isaac Rehn, John M. Spear, Maria L. Varney, and many more.[10]

So, too, the goals of socialist communities had shifted from the demomstration of social perfection to the more immediate protection of greater personal freedom in the here and now. The new colony Modern Times on Long Island represented the convergence of Josiah Warren's Time Stores with Andrews's philosophical "Pantarchy." In addition to veterans of both the North American Phalanx and Brook Farm, it drew land reformers such as Edward Newberry and James A. Clay, as well as Edward N. Kellogg, the currency reformer. Sharing a commitment to land reform, they agreed to limited real-estate ownership in the projected town but explicitly rejected any doctrinaire blueprint, becoming a haven for experiments in self-transformation through vegetarianism, hydropathy, and total abstinence from tobacco and liquor. Most famously, however, Modern Times translated an intellectual critique of marriage often implicit in radical free thought into the public advocacy and practice of "free love."[11]

Just as earlier communities sought to influence life in the cities through cooperation, some of these new radicals sought to reshape cultural standards in this regard. In 1853, Ingalls, Andrews, spiritualist editor S. B. Brittan, and veteran Fourierist Henry Clapp established a Free Love League that advocated "great latitude to the 'freedom of the affections.'" For two years, it waged an uphill battle against the mores and standards of the age with twice-weekly lectures, music, and dancing upstairs at Taylor's Hotel at 555 Broadway, drawing audiences large enough to claim membership of around a thousand. Greeley's *New York Tribune* published a sensational exposé both to disassociate Fourierism from it and to discredit Fernando Wood's administration for its failure to act against it. No sooner had Brisbane and Clapp started the October 1855 meeting than the police descended on the hall. Angry "free lovers" challenged repression by the city government, contributing to the Republican justification to reorganize the police system.[12]

Some sought to introduce this new iconoclastic radicalism to the city more subtly. After years abroad, Clapp had become enamored with life in the Parisian neighborhoods on the Left Bank of the Seine and began drawing similarly alienated souls to a unique social life centered at Charles Pfaff's restaurant and saloon just up Broadway from Taylor's Hotel. Fourierist and former-Fourierist visitors to Pfaff's included Brisbane; William H. Fry; and George Arnold, the son of a New Jersey phalanx leader; they mingled alongside future socialists such as John Swinton and Albert L. Rawson. Practitioners of the arts, music, and theater, as well as writers, created this bohemian subculture, which provided a vital introduction to the city for writers from the outside, for example, William Dean Howells, or the yet-unrecognized genius of Walt Whitman.[13]

Bohemianism framed the rise of the American literati. Radical organizer George Lippard not only penned appropriately Gothic fiction but also filled an early grave, as did England's Percy Shelley, France's Henri Murger, and Germany's Georg Buechner. Conversely, Whitman remained aloof from specific radical options but repeatedly expressed his alienation from the prevailing standards of society. Lippard's friend, Edgar Allen Poe—even more concerned with self-exploration than Whitman—scorned empathy with what he saw as a faceless and dehumanized culture or popular aspirations that seemed merely manufactured opinions, but he admired the visions of both Charles Fourier and John C. Symmes, and he was personally associated with Dr. J. E. Snodgrass, Mary Gove Nichols, and other radicals. Samuel L. Clemens, as an itinerant printer at Cincinnati, met most of the people mentioned in Moncure Conway's *Autobiography,* reveled in Tom Paine's criticisms of religion, found at Philadelphia that Lippard's work "has rendered the Wissahickon sacred in my eyes," and reechoed Lippardian views that "if Christ came here now, there is one thing he would *not* be—a Christian." Reechoing land reform concerns, Ambrose Bierce defined *land* in *The Devil's Dictionary* as an excuse for robbery.[14]

Some, particularly in the printing trades, colonized language itself, abolishing the irrationalities of spelling, punctuation, and grammar. Language, as well as land reform, had inspired Masquerier, Andrews, Hine, and Elias Longley and his sons. Alcander Longley's *Fonetic Advokat* offered arguments for land reform and other radical causes to any who could read his new alphabet. Andrews, meanwhile, promoted his own "Alwato" as a corollary of phonographic and stenographic plans for a rational world order, but the adoption of a variant as shorthand later provided "monopoly" rather than "the people" with the new language of power. (One might also note the fate of Elizur Wright's actuary tables.)

Other radicals staked out pastoral reserves within the new metropolis. A relative of Booth, Frederick Law Olmsted had been a Fourierist sympathizer with ties to Horace Greeley's circle at the *Tribune* and a visitor at the London home of Karl Marx where they exchanged gossip about émigré and reform circles. In his work on New York City's Central Park, Olmsted heard reminders from Masquerier to set aside space for the public discourse as essential to any "agrarianizing" of the city; there, too, he employed Karl Marx's friend Joseph Weydemeyer as a surveyor. As well, those who sought to establish more utopian and pastoral communities sometimes found themselves planning the modern urban necropolis, like Olmsted's Spring Grove Cemetery at Cincinnati. So, too, William Saunders—founder of the Grange and cooperative ventures—would later design the national cemetery at Gettysburg.[15]

Other parks provided more specialized recreational purposes. From its inception, "the national pastime" assumed its ambiguous character as both an allegory of capitalist competition and a public celebration of cooperative teamwork, which attracted workers as much as the changing workplace tended to alienate them. John Commerford's son—possibly Thomas A. Devyr's as well—left the crafts for a new kind of career then opening up to working-class youth in "Base-Ball." Charles Commerford—an active agrarian in his own right—became one of several claimants to developing the box scoring of the game.[16] The United States would need such diversions with the future rising before it.

From National Reform to Working-Class Republicanism

At least in New York City, the absence of some of the guiding hands of the political movement slowed the realignment of the NRA remnants with the Republican Party. Not only had Barr, Haddock, and Bovay gone west, but their primary leader, George Henry Evans had died. Although on his New Jersey farm since 1849, he had been continually drawn back to the city. Through the winter of 1855–56, he—along with William Heighton—battled to keep land reform before the emergent New Jersey Republicans. An unexpected snowstorm soaked Evans on his way home from a speaking engagement, and he succumbed to "a nervous fever" on February 2, 1856. The *New York Tribune* gave only a few lines to the passing of "a prominent advocate of Land Reform and other humanitarian movements." Thereafter, leadership was shared between Ingalls, then a homeowner in distant Yates County, and Commerford, who persisted in calling himself a Jackson man.[17]

So, too, New York Republicans seemed less insurgent in New York than elsewhere. NRA veteran and Free Democrat Calvin Pepper called to order the August 1854 statewide protest meeting that launched the party, but he could not dissuade it from simply fusing with the Whigs. A September convention at Auburn launched a statewide Whig-dominated Anti-Nebraska coalition, but it neither mentioned the land question nor affiliated with the new Republican Party, sparking a walkout led by Leonard Gibbs of the old NRA and other radicals. When a Republican state convention did take place a year later, a well-established leadership of former Whigs and Americans dominated the party. Still, Jacob Seaman and William H. Fry participated in Republican meetings on the Lower East Side, while John H. Tobitt, Freeman Hunt, and Watson G. Haynes helped start the party in Brooklyn.[18]

Meanwhile, what now called itself the National Land Reform Association established ties to the developing international workers' movement. When British Chartists planned reorganization in 1850, the NYCIC suggested that it become international, and the British invited an American "mission of brotherhood" to a "World's Industrial Congress." In February 1851, Parsons E. Day, a descendent of Joseph Warren of Bunker Hill fame mingled with the Chartists and radicals from the continent exiled by the 1851 Napoleonic coup in France. A few years later, in February 1855, left-wing Chartists formed a fraternal order of European revolutionaries in a loose federation. Ira B. Davis, William West, and William Arbuthnot of the "Universal Democratic Republicans" at New York established an affiliate of what later became the International Association, a precursor of the International Workingmen's Association—the "First International." At their mass meeting on March 6, they approved a new report on the conditions of the laboring classes and urged join action with "the Workingmen's Association," most likely the local German socialist Arbeiterbund.[19]

Adherents of "Land and other cognate reforms" gathered at Cleveland's Sons of Temperance Hall for the 1855 NIC, which revived the ecumenical radicalism of the earlier midwestern gatherings, but with eastern radicals participating. Of the three secretaries, Ohioan John Hancock Klippart and Philadelphian John Sheddon were already prominent Republicans, and the third was William H. Day, the most prominent black leader in Ohio openly defying the assumptions on slavery and race.[20] Their resolutions reaffirmed the old NRA measures with an emphasis on land limitation and denounced "the purchase of lands by churches, railroads, or individuals, for speculative purposes."

With the reemergence of a nativist party in the city, that very internationalism pushed some land reformers back towards the Democratic Party of
Fernando Wood. Reform Democrats such as John Cochrane, J. W. Forney,
and Thomas B. Florence again courted radicals for another unification meeting at Tammany. However, NRA veterans Davis, West, and Arbuthnot, D. C.
Henderson, William Rowe, and Price reorganized as "Practical Democrats,"
building what even the hostile *Herald* acknowledged to be "an organization of
some importance." That fall, they launched an "American Democratic" party
that shared neither the nativism of the American Party nor the Democratic
partisanship of Tammany or Mozart Hall. In September, joined by George
Adams and K. Arthur Bailey, it battled nativist rowdies to maintain control
of its second mass meeting and provided a platform to German émigrés
opposed to prohibiting alcohol, private contracts for public works projects,
and changes in the naturalization law. It also favored municipal autonomy,
frugality in city government, and cooperative protective unions, criminal-
izing practices "to defraud working people out of their just wages for labor
performed," and the city construction of its own buildings to rent cheaply to
the landless. Devyr, Tobitt, James A. Pyne, and abolitionist George Stearns
made a similar initiative across the East River at Williamsburgh through their
Tax Payers Association.[21]

Probably in hopes of refocusing the original cadres of the movement,
the previous year's NIC had scheduled the 1856 gathering at New York City.
There, Commerford and Ingalls sought to hold together the remnants of the
original group with Price becoming national secretary and Arbuthnot, Bailey,
and John Windt among the diehard participants. On May 24, the New Yorkers scheduled a National Land Reform Convention for the Fourth of July at
Albany, along with radical abolitionists such as William Goodell and Gerrit
Smith, reflecting the survival of the old NRA-Liberty alliance within the Republican Party.[22]

A handful of of anti-electoral radicals and diehard Democratic reformers
ignored the new scheduling to convene their own Industrial Congress during
the time-honored first week of June. The gathering at Convention Hall on
Wooster Street united Robert McDonell, the Delaware Democrat, with the
Philadelphian J. Sidney Jones and his wife, Fanny Townsend, with "her usual
quota of jewelry and curls," and men sporting "that exuberance of beard for
which the pioneers and disciples of the beard and land reform school should
be noted." Long hostile to the radical but tolerant rationalism of an Evans or
Sheddon, these two groups faced a stormy first day, and only "eight persons
assembled, including two ladies" for the second, with McDonell conspicuous by his absence. On behalf of the local organization, Dr. William J. Young

urged its adjournment sine die.[23] Given that the scheduled public meeting in the park never happened, the New York City group apparently prevailed.

Moreover, the anticipated Fourth of July congress was apparently further postponed to blur into September's "Radical Abolition" convention, most likely planning to function as a caucus meeting before the 1856 Republican state convention. The national party had adopted the call for a homestead bill and nominated Gen. John Charles Frémont for president. The NRA reorganized to endorse him, and Greeley urged Devyr to edit a newspaper to be called the *Land Reformer* as a Republican campaign sheet. Visiting New York City, Frémont told the Mechanics and Workingmen's Central Republican Union that he supported land and labor reform. On the Lower East Side, Lewis Ryckman ran for the state assembly as a Republican, and the names of National Reformers like Windt, Keyser, Ingalls, Benny, Rowe, Charles A. Guinan, and Bailey appear in the campaign coverage.[24]

State by state, with varying degrees of alacrity, the new party began to raise the NRA's old "Republican banner of Free Land." In the desperate circumstances after the Panic of 1857, the Republican coupling of the tariff with land reform proved to be a formula for rapid growth. In February 1858, Galusha Grow pushed the Homestead Bill to a largely sectional and successful vote in the House of Representatives. About two weeks later, Benjamin F. Wade, Andrew Johnson, Henry Wilson, James Shields, and William H. Seward rolled the measure to victory in the Senate over Southern Democratic opposition. Then, Democratic president James Buchanan vetoed the bill, disregarding the will of tens of thousands of petitioners, abandoning much of his party's plebeian base in the North to the insurgents.[25] Events had proved right Hine's prediction that land reform would "bring more skillful anti-slavery players to the board" and so sway "public sentiment that they [slaveholders] will soon be unable to make any thing out of it."

Thereafter, even in New York City, the most skeptical land reformers repudiated the Democrats. Devyr toured the old Antirent community districts for Gerrit Smith's 1858 gubernatorial effort. So, too, John Commerford ran for the assembly as a Republican in 1859. While the old Jacksonian had resisted Frémont's appeal, he warned Andrew Johnson, that "in the next Presidential Contest, I shall have to cast my ballot for the Republican Candidate."[26]

By 1860, the matter was settled. The predispositions of West and Bovay for the Whigs or of Barr and Ira Davis for the Democrats no longer mattered. The Republicans simply assimilated the land reform movement and partially vindicated those who had consistently pressed for independent political action.

Certainly, whatever presence the new Republican Party had in the working-class quarters of lower Manhattan owed much to the former NRA. In 1858, the overwhelmingly Democratic Fourth Congressional District—including the Fourth, Sixth, Tenth, and Fourteenth wards on the Lower East Side—had sent to Congress the brother of William V. Barr, former alderman Thomas J. Barr, who declined renomination in 1860. Dominated by Tammany, the regular Democratic organization ran Michael Tuomey, and Mayor Wood's Mozart Hall faction nominated James E. Kerrigan. In early October, the small district Republican convention voted to nominate Commerford, who had earlier run for Congress as a Locofoco and as a National. Supporters of the old-line politicians briefly tried to prevent this, sparking a melee at the Fourth Ward Republican Association on October 16, but prominent figures such as Greeley, Congressman Grow, and others actively aided their veteran labor candidate and his lieutenants West, Beeny, Price, and Keyser, aided by émigrés such as Friedrich Jacobi, a Baden émigré who built the local Kommunist Klub, and the Italian "Garibaldi Wide-Awakes." On October 19, a Friday evening, three hundred torch-bearing Wide-Awakes led a large crowd through the artisan-based Tenth Ward to hear orators conjure memories of the Sons of Liberty; that same night saw two other rallies. The official tally of 12,458 gave Kerrigan a plurality of 41.3 percent; Tuomey 32 percent; and Commerford 26.7 percent, representing 3,324 votes. Commerford did worst (and both Democrats best) in the machine-dominated Sixth, and his best among the skilled workingmen of the Tenth Ward who provided half his votes.[27]

The Republican nomination of Abraham Lincoln for president suited the National Reformers. In making the case for tariffs and "internal improvements," he argued that human labor provided the only just measure of value and asserted that the worker ideally should receive "the whole product of labor"—a concept identified with "Ricardian socialism." He was confronted by what he saw as regressive innovations; he had committed what his partner called "political suicide" by opposing the Mexican War. Through the 1850s, he, like the Agrarians, listened to politicians in the North as well as the South who suggested modifying the principles of 1776; also, like the Agrarians, he thought it "endangered our republican institutions," and he made the Declaration of Independence one of the key themes of his 1858 senatorial debate with Stephen A. Douglas. He repeatedly demonstrated an affinity for the developing labor movement and its right to organize and to strike, establishing a record correctly described by one historian as "unmatched in American history" on labor. He had his own copy of Kellogg's book *Labor and Capital* advocating the government issuance and regulation of paper currency as a just means of redistributing wealth, and he corresponded with the author's son-in-law. His Illinois admirers included land reformers such as John Newlin and B. J. F. Hanna, as well as his close adviser Jesse Wilson Fell and his biographer John L. Scripps. Having repeatedly declared his support for the measure, Lincoln would, as the chief executive, preside over the passage of the Homestead Act.[28]

❋ ❋ ❋

Two weeks after the election, the last antebellum Industrial Congress gathered at the Metropolitan Hall on Sixth Avenue. Davis and others signed the call for "associations of Mechanics, Laborers, Land-reformers, Protective Unions, Progressives and Humanitarians" to send representatives. On Tuesday and Wednesday, November 20 and 21, this NIC sponsored discussions described by the *Tribune* as "generally intelligent, and not notorious." While few, if any, workers attended, the congress predictably passed land-reform resolutions and asserted the right of labor to its full product, urged an end to paper currency, advocated cooperative exchanges, and promoted woman's rights, including "the same freedom of industrial pursuits, and the same compensation enjoyed by men." Speakers at the NIC included spiritualists William White, Amanda M. Spence, Susan M. Johnson, Davis, and Andrews—the last two were also veteran radicals—with freethinker Ernestine L. Rose being "the prominent person" participating. The *Tribune* reporter promised that "while lights are cheap and words are plenty, we shall offer every quiet encouragement to movements like that at Metropolitan Hall."[29] However, in the broken world that unfolded with Lincoln's victory, Andrews's pantarchy, Rose's secularism, or Davis's municipal reformism seemed to be nothing if not naively anachronistic.

By December 22, 1860, when the *Herald of Progress* published the proposals of the Industrial Congress for the future of the nation, the government of South Carolina had already placed that future in doubt. The land reformers themselves had long hoped that reason and the ballot would prevail. Clearly, the few petitions from the slave states usually had to reach Congress through some course other than their own congressmen. While they had hoped to make land reform equally "popular in the cotton fields of the South and the cotton factories of the North," radicals had to concede that "whether we shall get any further south than Baltimore remains to be seen."[30] In the end, the secession of the political machines of the Southern states defined the real limits on progress by the ballot. In a very real sense, by making the will of the American electorate unrealizable through the ballot, secession made politics as usual "utopian" more surely than all of the radical agitation could have done.

Conclusion

I have put you in motion to offer battle to the invaders of your country.
With the resolution and disciplined valor becoming men fighting, as you
are, for all worth living or dying for, you can but march to a decisive victory
over agrarian mercenaries, sent to subjugate and despoil you of your liberties, property, and honor.
    —Confederate general Albert S. Johnston, April 3, 1862

Within days of the U.S. adoption of the Homestead Act, Albert
Sidney Johnston conjured the specter of federally sponsored expropriation
and social revolution to motivate his troops before their assault on the Union
soldiers camped along the Tennessee River. What actually inspired the blue-
clad Federals around Shiloh Meeting House reflected the complex and often
contradictory concerns that created the Republican and Unionist coalition,
but it certainly included an Agrarian component. Thirty-nine-year-old William Haddock, who had helped launch the NRA eighteen years before, had
become disgusted with the failure of the workers to respond quickly and with
overwhelming force, so he went to Minnesota with an unsuccessful colony of
city radicals and then moved on to Iowa after its dissolution. Enlisting in the
Twelfth Iowa as a sergeant, Haddock received a commission after serving in
Missouri and led his men against Forts Henry and Donelson before facing the
encircling Confederates around the "Hornet's Nest" at Shiloh.[1] If secessionist
opposition to "agrarian mercenaries" grew naturally from antebellum planter
mistrust of "the mudsills," such hostility to radical concerns did not yet prevail
among the advocates of "free labor."

In hindsight, Haddock's comrades had begun their battle long before. The
rebellion of Southern slaveholders against the standards of free labor exposed
the ultimate flaw in the NRA's hopes for a peaceful, radical social transformation. National Reformers' dedication to what had once been central to the
Union war effort and the insurgent Republican agenda did not prevent the
postwar national elite's embrace of the secession's overt hostility to National
Reform's idea of free labor. At that point, the land reformers regrouped into

a modern radical movement. However, the industrial world obscured the process and rendered National Reform all but incomprehensible.

War for Free Labor

National Reformers built their understanding on historical experience. Taking their cue from U.S. founders, they formulated a Roman model of decline and contributed it to the broader nineteenth-century Republican insurgency and, more substantively, to the workers' movement. As John Commerford warned, Americans, like the ancient Romans, had become "brokers in human flesh," and the practice of conquest tended to strengthen the very institutions that undermined "this misnamed republic."[2] Agrarians felt pressed by this history.

NRA supporters warned that citizens did not benefit equally from national conquest and expansion, which involved the access of the elite to subjugated foreign laborers and fostered the rise of large-scale agriculture that impoverished the mass of citizens. Maintaining the loyalty of these disinherited plebeian "lacklanders" required new mechanisms of repression, the use of the military as the principal mechanism for individual plebeian mobility, and a system of "bread and circuses"—a popular sense of sharing in the nation's growing wealth and the institutionalized spectacle that had replaced civic culture. As conquest led to more far-flung frontiers, the state and its repressive institutions grew larger, and as the stakes of power rose, so did the desperation of vying factions among the elite. Gradually, the authoritarian apparatus took shape beneath the old republican forms. Representative bodies increasingly became rubber stamps for the strengthened hand of the executive. War and conquest became the health of the state but the nemesis of the republic. Cheered by a populace for both their strong leadership and their ability to give a good show, officials set aside constitutional arrangements and the rule of law. Even prominent civic leaders who might be mildly independent would be murdered in broad daylight with no serious repercussions.

On this level alone, the NRA introduced a perspective that recast slavery as a threat to the future of all working Americans. Its success in making this an issue demonstrates how a relatively small number of obscure working citizens acting at the right time in the right circumstances can contribute substantially to turning the course of a nation's destiny. The popular clamor for land reform initially drowned out the message of abolitionism, but ultimately the perceived interests of the majority of free peoples in the North were pitted against the Southern Democratic aspirations for slaveholding in the settlement of the West—and of the future of the nation.

Fear that the insatiable demands of imperial administration fostered the unchecked executive authority of the Caesars seemed less apocalyptic as the 1850s progressed. Alvan Bovay feared that "it might be the destiny of this Republic to go the way of all former ones to destruction." In urging the unity of the toilers, Jeriel Root warned that "divided we may fail and the world will not be saved." Thomas A. Devyr and other Agrarians had also long warned that an "epidemic of blood took possession of heathen Rome at the close of the Republic." Benjamin F. Price thought conflicting labor systems would shape a definitive crisis "at no remote period."[3] In 1860, results at the ballot box tested the loyalty of its losers and found it wanting.

By early 1861, the wealthiest and most autocratic forces in that society sought to demolish the political mechanism by which they had ruled for a generation in order to prevent its use to ban African American slavery from places where it did not yet exist. "Landed aristocracies of the Old World may avow their affinity to the aristocracy of human flesh and blood that has so long cursed the New," wrote NRA veteran Henry Morford after donning the uniform of his country, "but now that the suicidal hand of the latter has caused the forfeit of its existence, we are the centre of the hopes, fears, and prayers of the universal brotherhood of man in the effort to blot out for ever the only foul spot upon our national escutcheon."[4] In May 1862, President Abraham Lincoln signed the Homestead Act into law, marking the achievement of Labor's first national political goal.

What National Reformers did to sustain the Union would require a volume in itself. Warren Chase spoke across the country throughout the war years. Within months of Commerford's campaign, secession closed the Southern trade, destroying his tenuous furniture business and sending him back to the workbench as a hired laborer at the age of sixty-five; he remained a vocal proponent of the Union and the war effort. John H. Tobitt revisited his native England and argued his way across Britain against any conciliation with the American secessionists. Lewis Masquerier wrote a collection of campaign songs for Lincoln's reelection, many from his own pen. In Illinois, John Newlin raised and swore recruits into service.[5]

Those in the South found themselves engaged in desperately revolutionary politics. William E. Stevenson, the Pittsburgh craftsman, sharply defended the Free State colonizers in Wood County, Virginia, and became a leader of the political movement to separate what became West Virginia from the secessionist tidewater. Indications exist that the few land reformers in the region reorganized as secret Union Leagues, a form of organization that came north with refugees and returned south on federal bayonets. There, it became the voice of the freedmen, urging radical Reconstruction of the old Confederacy, including land redistribution.

Even the youngest NRA veterans tended to be too old for military service, but many went anyway. Hamilton J. Chenoweth, the Lynn NRA shoemaker, joined hundreds of local trade unionists in the Fourteenth Massachusetts under Col. William B. Greene, the Brook Farmer and translator of French anarchist P. J. Proudhon, but Chenoweth received a medical discharge. Joshua S. Valentine of Wilmington's Brotherhood of the Union survived repeated brushes with the medical corps to command a company of the Fourth Delaware, but superiors sent him home "to prevent permanent disability." An old comrade, Solomon Shepherd of the Tenth Iowa, had charge of a convalescent camp at Kingston, Georgia, where one officer described him as "an old man being more than fifty years and physically is unable to stand the continual hardship of a soldier's life." Joel Brown, the Cincinnati radical carpenter and friend of Frances Wright, became the oldest man in the 138th Ohio.[6]

A number, in addition to Haddock, wound up with commissions. Former NRA national secretaries Bovay and Price helped officer, respectively, the Nineteenth Wisconsin and the Seventy-first New York. Peter H. Clark raised the "black brigade" to defend Cincinnati, and Col. William A. Phillips, the Illinois land reformer, wound up commanding the only integrated units of the Union Army, the brigade of Indian Home Guards. When the rebels overran the "Hornet's Nest" at Shiloh, Haddock was taken prisoner, and within weeks, Price fell into enemy hands on the Virginia Peninsula. The Confederate counteroffensive in Louisiana seized August J. H. Duganne and his 176th New York. Col. Adolphus Johnson of the Eighth New Jersey never fully recovered from his wounds at Williamsburg, and he eventually resigned. Fighting near Atlanta killed Capt. James Penn Bennett of the Twenty-fifth Indiana, formerly a member of the New Harmony Free Land Association, and twice wounded NIC participant Col. Thomas E. Champion of the Ninety-sixth Illinois. Champion was rotated back to Nashville where Col. David D. Irons, the former organizer of the Peoria NRA and commander of the Eighty-sixth Illinois, died two years before. After Price returned to the field, he was killed while leading his men in a heroic charge in Virginia.[7]

Even as the war raged, resistance to any such gains had been so desperate and intense that overcoming secession required a political and military centralization that made possible the rapid postwar monopolization of power and wealth. As the war progressed, Morford published his experiences under the title of *Red-Tape and Pigeon-Hole Generals.* Haddock became a major with an independent command in Arkansas, but he found the army ruthlessly cliquish, even when the lives of the soldiers were at stake: "I love the service, but cannot serve well when I feel that I am not wanted."[8] On the other end of that state, Phillips found himself under arrest for waging war on profiteers as well as secessionists. The meaning of the Union cause and Federal victory—"the Second American Revolution"—remained contested.

As in earlier and later revolutions, some participants attained some status and respectability. Republicans in state governments included some antebellum Agrarians, such as Bovay, most prominently; Stevenson, who became the third governor of West Virginia; Phillips who was in the U.S. Congress from Kansas; and William Turner Coggeshall, who died as the U.S. minister to Ecuador. Yet, after his time in office, Stevenson apparently gave some backhanded support to third-party movements, and Phillips could not resist writing a book denouncing land monopoly in his later years.[9]

Yet many National Reformers persisted as "true abolitionists" to assail the status quo. "Do not tell us about expediency; don't talk to us of agrarianism, radicalism, or any other ism," declared Lucius A. Hine. "Tell us, is it not right." He also transcended the old antiquarian models of republican decline by noting that the governments of Athens or Rome were, at times, representative of their citizens, but not "strictly speaking" republican because of the anomalous presence of slavery. "A *perfect* Republic cannot exist," he argued, "as long as a single individual is disenfranchised."[10]

Union victory in the Civil War failed to eradicate the racial legacy of chattel slavery, and it also failed to address the broader National Reform idea of wages slavery. Industrialization continued to subjugate every aspect of "life, liberty and the pursuit of happiness" to technological development and economic profitability, according to National Reformers, creating a social process that privatized wealth and reserved power for a relative handful of citizens. This preserved "wages slavery" or "Indirect Slavery" that left workers "free—free to STARVE."[11] For the NRA, these persistent conditions mandated unionization, the shorter workday, and other reforms, along with Agrarian measures to control industrialization and distribute its benefits more democratically.

Antebellum Agrarianism and the Postwar Radicalization

The NRA's agrarianism formed a persistent and underlying theme for the later working-class movement. Both Hine and William West participated in the annual gatherings of the new National Labor Union, which emerged from the Civil War. William V. Barr presided over the Kansas affiliate of the NLU and helped launch the Workingmen's Party of Kansas. In New York City, West, Stephen Pearl Andrews, Dr. Edward Newberry, and others reorganized the antebellum Practical Democrats into a "New Democracy" with a strong emphasis on woman suffrage. On its behalf, Commerford contacted Karl Marx and the new International Workingmen's Association (the IWA). Along with these other old National Reformers, Masquerier, Joshua K. Ingalls, and Ira B. Davis built Section No. 9 of the IWA, while West and Andrews assisted the organization of Section No. 12. When the NLU's 1872 effort to launch the National Labor Reform Party misfired, the Internationalists—now joined by William Rowe—formed the core of the renewed effort to field the Equal Rights Party ticket of Victoria Woodhull and Frederick Douglass.[12]

National Reform's explicit opposition to the unbounded growth of capitalism and the capitalist state inspired Marx and Friedrich Engels to see the movement as an early form of socialism. Later, however, they supported their émigré followers in the 1872 purge of the IWA in the United States, an often grossly misrepresented ethnic split in which German-speaking members broke with the English and French speakers. Much of the subsequent history of Marxism and socialism in America both replicated and rationalized this course, relegating the antebellum movement for land reform to insignificance or casting it as an object of polemical exorcism, in which slavery and race became a key. Smudging the National Reformer into a sort of Jacksonian "workingman" created a convenient object lesson in the dangers of Democratic politicians, utopianism, and white supremacism.

Nevertheless, NRA politics resurfaced in the Social Democratic Workingmen's Party in 1874, the Workingmen's Party of the United States in 1876, the Socialistic Labor Party (SLP) in 1878, and their successors. Members and spokespersons included Rowe; West (who signed his regular newspaper column "Precursor"); Caleb Pink in New York; Barr after moving to Chicago; William McDiarmid in Indianapolis; and William Haller, Hine, and Clark in Cincinnati. Ingalls and John Orvis maintained friendly relations with the SLP well into the 1890s, and younger party members John A. Lant and William Hanson became conscious protégés of the land reformers. Davis, Ingalls, Masquerier, Newberry, Rowe, West, Lant, Hanson, and others regularly attended conventions of Ezra Hervey Heywood's American Labor Reform League.[13]

Antebellum Agrarian ideas also helped inspire mass fraternal organizations. The Patrons of Husbandry—the Grange—which organized farmers on an unprecedented scale, numbered among its founders William Saunders and Daniel A. Robertson, an old Locofoco who had been an Ohio National Reformer before going to Minnesota. A Missouri spin-off took the name Industrial Brotherhood, recalling the old antebellum order. Upon serious examination, the Sovereigns of Industry, which grew from New England origins, drew on primarily Fourierist leadership and largely represented an extension of the old Protective Unions into a later day.[14]

Such continuities are particularly clear in the Philadelphia movement. There, Thomas Phillips, Isaac Rehm, John Sheddon, John Mills, and others connected with the Brotherhood of the Union built Section 26 of the IWA and the local affiliates of the Sovereigns of Industry. However, the cooperative work of the Brotherhood's Industrial Union in the local needle trades clearly influenced tailors such as Uriah Stephens, who went on to organize the Garment Cutter's Association and the Knights of Labor, the latter eventually mobilizing three quarters of a million Americans. So, too, Sheddon's 1878 campaign for U.S. Congress on a united Republican-Greenback-Labor nomination reflects the association to a movement that won over a million insurgent ballots in that election.[15]

The mass phenomenon of postwar Greenbackism owed much to land reform. Albert Brisbane had focused early on manipulation of the money supply as a means of adjusting the distribution of wealth. Josiah Warren, the Cincinnati stove maker and National Reformer added his own twist to the cooperative alternative whereby producers could exchange "labor for labor" through the Time Store, in which one made purchases with a "Labor Note" promising a certain amount of labor to be performed. When Warren moved east to establish the community of Modern Times, he found that Brisbane held similar views of the currency issue, and got still closer support from another resident of Modern Times, Edward N. Kellogg, the author of *Labor and Other Capital*, which he presented to Ingalls and other NRA veterans. Critical of private control of the money supply, the book urged what amounted to the national adoption of Warren's Labor Notes. Among the many thousands drawn to the idea after the war were, in addition to those mentioned above, veteran radicals such as Benjamin Urner in Ohio and Benjamin F. McAllister in New Jersey. Sherman Miller Booth turned up in the attempt to revive the Greenback Party as a National Antimonopolist Party, and Ellis V. Smalley had become a mainstay of the third-party movements around Council Grove, Kansas.[16]

Then, too, some land reformers sought to revive the NRA in a new form. John H. Keyser urged a radically progressive income tax, applying the NRA's argument for land limitation to all wealth. His new "National Limitation Association" included Rowe, Devyr, Henry Beeny, and Frank Smith.[17] It proposed to attain its goals through the familiar two-pronged strategy of petitions and political action.

Most vividly, National Reform reemerged in the movement inspired by Henry George's *Progress and Poverty*. James McClatchy and the NRA-led Settlers' League had a decisive influence on the young George, whose Single Tax idea resurrected the antebellum arguments of Dr. Joseph Rodes Buchanan of the Cincinnati NRA and Edwin Burgess, a British-born Wisconsin tailor. William Hanson wrote his own reaction to George's book, challenging the claim of originality. Masquerier thought George "a faithful disciple of old-time ideas," and Beeny made the case for the NRA's originating these ideas to the Georgist American Free Soil Society. A smaller, ideologically refined group needed the coherence of distinctive and original ideas and rarely emphasized their similarity with earlier efforts. Connecticut's representative in the Free Soil Society was John Commerford's son Charles, the ballplayer and later postmaster, who expressed his own views in *Labor and Capital* and *Strikes*. George's United Labor Party mayoral campaign in New York directly or indirectly involved Beeny, Keyser, Ingalls, Masquerier, George W. Loyd, and other very aged NRA veterans, as well as the Shaker Elder Frederick William Evans, the surviving brother of NRA founder George Henry Evans. Barr, then in Chicago, accepted an 1887 United Labor nomination. Inspired by the George movement, Timothy Thomas Fortune contributed an African American assessment of race relations in *Black and White*, which centered on the failure of land reform in the South.[18] The historic land question simply refused to fade away.

Perhaps the deaths of Davis and Warren made the NRA's aging survivors aware of the fragility of their legacy. In 1874, Commerford, Beeny, Masquerier, Ingalls, and Smith joined Rowe in New Jersey for a pilgrimage to the long-abandoned grave of George Henry Evans. For several years thereafter, they gathered on Evans's birthday, as had freethinkers once on Tom Paine's, providing a vehicle for reestablishing ties with surviving old-timers such as A. H. Wood, a coauthor of the 1835 "Ten-Hour Circular," or Thomas Davis of the prewar Western Homestead Association. Letters from Benjamin Perkins in Indiana, Smalley in Kansas, Hine in Ohio, and Wood and Chase in Massachusetts appeared episodically through the 1880s. After Devyr died in May 1887, the childless widower Masquerier hosted a June dedication of his own tomb, a version of the Statue of Liberty with a globe rather than a torch, sitting atop a marble obelisk with its carved argument for land reform, the entire gravesite agitating a slight rise overlooking potters' field in Cypress Hills Cemetery. After Masquerier died in January 1888, Lant coaxed Beeny, Frank M. Smith, Andrew J. Day, and Dr. Caleb S. Weeks to a summer rededication. The press noted that Ingalls was still living as well but that only two other NRA veterans survived, Charles A. Guinan and David Kilmer, who "are not expected to live this week out."[19] In fact, at least a dozen others still lived.

Hoping to influence the platform of the new People's Party, Lant persuaded them to reorganize the National Land Reform Association in June 1891, with Day, Kilmer, Guinan, Newberry, Ingalls, and Barr as vice presidents. Their president, Beeny, also attended the American Labor Reform League as late as May 1893. Before the end of the century, however, he, Kilmer, Newberry, and Ingalls had died, as had Orvis and Keyser. Joel Brown saw 1900. Alvan Bovay returned to Brooklyn with a comfortable nest egg from Minnesota and the Dakotas and spent several years in the city before going to California where he died in 1903. Sherman Miller Booth died the following year; Hine in 1906; and Caleb Pink, in England, toward the close of 1907. Somewhere in these years, Andrew E. Elmore and William Haddock also died.[20]

Built on the desire of the urban "working classes" for a more egalitarian land distribution, the NRA provided a crucial, political focus for otherwise non-electoral communitarian, socialist musings, and it clearly helped popularize values that ultimately mobilized public opinion strong enough to topple the slaveholders' party from office. Despite its triumphs, though, National Reform failed to remain comprehensible to those who came after it.

Agrarian Radicalism and the Modern State

Antebellum land reformers based their views on historical experience and defended their understanding of that experience. As the 1876 Centennial Exposition approached, Masquerier, Ingalls, Rowe, Devyr, and Commerford, who had wondered with Evans whether Americans would ever discard "that British coat of arms" proposed a "colossal bust of Thomas Paine." Their endorsers became a who's who of socialists, feminists, cooperationists, and prominent freethinkers from both sides of the Atlantic. When the city leaders refused to finance the project, the radicals did it themselves and sent the bust to the municipal authorities, who declined to accept the gift and never displayed it. In the end, such treatment of Paine's bust defined which historical memories would be appropriate to celebrate.[21]

Conversley, the modern industrial city and its values could manufacture the emblems of hierarchy cheaper, faster, and in greater quantity than anyone had imagined at the time the king's coat of arms insulted the colonial rebels. It had become the world the NRA had anticipated with some dread. Children "now born," warned Evans in 1844, would see a New York "as large as that of London now, which is two millions, and misery, vice, and crime in full proportion." In discussing "the destiny of New York cities in a few generations," Masquerier groped toward a poetic symbolism in discussing the way "street cleaning and sewerage are destroying the fertility of the soil. Thus not only physical but moral nature is destroyed."[22]

We have since learned to understand republican decline in terms of economic, technological, or military weakness, rather than as a function of an atomized and disintegrating civic culture. Certainly, no taxpaying citizen of merely modest means seriously expects treatment at the hands of government comparable to that received by corporate business. Given modern sensibilities, it seems strange to reflect that significant numbers of Americans in the mid-nineteenth century petitioned the authorities regularly to limit land ownership in the interest of fairness—as strange as the idea that such concerns provided a cornerstone of the Republican Party.

The brave new world of Charles Darwin and Thomas Edison established values for the social sciences that mirrored the blueprints and models useful in its manufacturing. These read into the social world the kinds of stable, exacting, scientific definitions that never really existed there, a process that befuddles an appreciation of the often diverse meanings ascribed to words and ideas by antebellum people. National Reformers espoused a "secularism" that has an affinity with "spiritualism," ideas that were simultaneously considered practical and utopian. They could think of themselves as both patriotic and internationalist, reformist and revolutionary. They could use the terms *individualist* and *socialist* almost interchangeably, but we have, in the interim, accepted a standardized, if superficial, distinction between the two. If nothing else, the confusion assists a process whereby even the most moderate social proposals to secure happiness for many individuals can, with the proper incantations, conjure images of regimentation.

NRA ideas did have some impact in the new professional history, particularly in the innovative new state universities of the Midwest. Wisconsin National Reformers had built a powerful and influential network of like-minded printers and journalists sympathetic to a homestead bill, one of whom—the editor of the local newspaper at Portage—named his son after his favorite president. Long before going to the university, Frederick Jackson Turner learned of land as a "safety valve" to relieve social conflict, the significance of the frontier to antebellum craftsmen, and the fragility of nineteenth-century republicanism.[23] Reordered and introduced by Turner at a formative stage in the development of historical scholarship, agitation became explanation, and a social critique became a social rationalization.

However, values appropriate to an age of patents and copyrights also changed the nature of social criticism. National Reformers and kindred radicals had urged an egalitarian access to land, without feeling any necessity for formulating some preliminary agreement on how that land might ultimately be owned. Some argued that land should be "never owned, bought or sold"—"an entire abandonment of the idea of property in land," and "the entire abolition and annulment of all property, value, or ownership in the soil." Others wanted land held under "the only rightful title," that is through personal occupation and labor.[24] The movement sought to win the access first, consigning such solutions ultimately to the later, more democratic considerations of the people, who would probably formulate all sorts of options for themselves.

However, later currency reformers, socialists, and Single Taxers were predisposed to claiming that they had found the philosopher's stone in the "original," "scientific" revelations of an Edward N. Kellogg, a Karl Marx, or a Henry George. Evans had freely attributed the sources of his ideas to thinkers from Tom Paine to Moses Jaques, and he reveled in the rootedness of its radicalism. In contrast, when supporters showed Henry George evidence of earlier land reformers, he feigned an ignorance we know he did not have.

The new industrialized and "scientific" radicalism required, first and foremost, a short-lived hegemony over a narrow association that had mastered the technical aspects of its social theory. In their eagerness to break with past failures and their organizational competitiveness, radicals contributed more decisively than conservatives could have to obscuring the continuity of older radical ideas and movements that had posed serious alternatives to the course of American development. Lacking the perspectives that had tended to strengthen, unite, and ground the discontent that inspired radicalism, an emergent Left, with few exceptions, generally embraced dogmas of self-dismemberment. Finally, the ruling circles translated the nineteenth-century radical hostility to all monopolies into an ascendant twentieth-century Progressive faith in government regulation of corporations, which obviously presupposes the survival, growth, prosperity, legitimacy, and hegemony of such institutions.

It is little wonder, then, that the handful of younger men who had taken up the cause of land reform in the late nineteenth century found a shrinking audience for their broadly based Agrarian-centered anticapitalism. In addition to Lant and Hanson, John William Lloyd, Horace Traubel, Charles Fowler, and others took up the land question in an increasingly hostile climate. Discouraged by the rise of U.S. imperialism in the Philippines, broken-hearted Civil War veteran Lant wrote anarchist Jo Labadie, "Is it not a disgrace to be an American citizen in 1903?"[25] In the end, the meaning of National Reform rested largely on figures destined to be more marginalized and proscribed than the National Reformers themselves.

It is not difficult to see why this was so. The aging NRA veterans, who had actually participated in the successful construction of the Republican Party, remained insistently ecumenical, despite the rise of dogmatism. In 1872, National Reformers sought to regroup radicals into a genuinely insurgent Liberal Republicanism, then into a National Labor Reform, and finally, around the "Woman's, Negroes', and Workingmen's" ticket of Victoria Woodhull and

Frederick Douglass. Events leading to the 1880 elections drove currency reformers, radical farmers, trade unionists, cooperationists, socialists, militant Southern freedmen, feminists, and other radicals groping toward a common Greenback-Labor ticket around a platform that declared, among other things: "We declare that land, air, and water are the grand gifts of nature to all mankind, and the law or custom of society that allows any person to monopolize more of these gifts of nature than he has a right to, we earnestly condemn and demand shall be abolished."[26]

Individual National Reformers sought such a coalition, even when isolated from each other. After William V. Barr returned to Illinois, he opened a storage business in Chicago and helped establish what became the SLP, but he welcomed the emergence of a broader third-party movement and ran for Congress in 1878 on the Greenback-Labor ticket. Fourteen years later, when the SLP asked the venerable John Orvis to run for governor, he agreed until he heard that that the People's Party would field a ticket, after which he withdrew and made his personal plea for radical unity behind the Populists.[27]

The most prominent national champion of the postwar insurgency, James B. Weaver, had his own ties to National Reform. At Shiloh, not far from where Haddock fought, Weaver had helped the Second Iowa cut its way to safety. In 1878, he won election to Congress on the Greenback ticket and spent years struggling to establish a succession of what he called genuinely democratic or republican parties. He ran for president as a Greenback-Labor candidate in 1880 and as a Populist in 1892. In large part, Weaver sought to ground what he hoped to be broad coalitions in "the land question."

However, these efforts—from the Greenbackers through the Populists to the Socialists—would be picked apart in a way in which the earlier Republicans were not, and in some ways, they did this themselves. The 1880s saw the successive collapse of the Greenback, Greenback-Labor, and Antimonopolist parties, the implosion of Henry George's United Labor Party, and the refusal of the Union Labor Party or the Socialist Labor Party to cooperate with other insurgents. Recalling the derailing of the antebellum Free Soilers by party politics, Ingalls asked bluntly, "Are we to have a repetition of this consummate asinine stupidity in 1888?"[28]

Based on a lifetime of experience with "a great number of societies, orders, sects and parties," Ingalls repudiated "distinctive schools of thought" and declined to wear "the badge of any party or repeat the shibboleth of any sect." Creeds ossify, and leaders "become despots and every movement seems to become the mere creature of a single mind: e.g., *Comt*ism, *Marx*ism, *Proudhon*ism, *Georg*ism." The resulting "strife among brethren . . . wastes the strength of advanced thinkers, to elevate unimportant distinctions." Masquerier found little reason to hope for a radical social transformation "by trick or stratagem . . . by little labor leagues, labor or equitable exchange notes, little communistic property and free love associations." Agrarians had urged radicals to a "perfect hospitality to the thoughts and aims of others."[29]

Simply put, the circumstances in which later radicals found themselves, particularly when framed by the social sciences paradigm, led those radicals to understand the approach used by the National Reformers—the one that had been so successful—as naive, sentimental, moralistic, and ultimately utopian, although, in fact, it represented one of the most succesful and influential social movements in American history.

✿ ✿ ✿

As represented in the NRA, the antebellum workers movement had been anything but "reactionary." The NRA increasingly urged a standard of equality essential to the genuinely democratic society its members hoped to achieve. More than most contemporaries, its leaders followed that egalitarian logic beyond asserting the equality of white men to ensure the rights of women, blacks, Indians, Hispanics, and others.

More unforgivably, perhaps, National Reformers insisted that both human rights and the old American fear of unaccountable power should have social and economic dimensions. Having rejected assertions of the innate inhumanity of the underclass, they believed the idea of a "right" to unlimited property could only be fair to all individuals if the bounty of nature could be both equally accessible and boundless. As human use of the land as a finite resource and our relationship to the natural world becomes more inescapable, a reckoning with National Reform seems all the more compelling.

In a greater sense, of course, history itself scorns the arrogance of finalities. Continuing efforts to achieve a just, democratic, and egalitarian society leave the significance of National Reform as open or as settled as we ourselves choose to keep it.

APPENDIX A: LAND REFORM, COOPERATIONIST, AND SOCIALIST ACTIVITIES, 1844–52

The following combine documentation from various sources. The movement press discussed National Reform activities (NR activities), ca. 1844–48, ranging from statements by supporters to the organization of auxiliaries. Directories survive for the local organizations of the Mechanics Mutual Protection Association (MMP), the New England Workingmen's Association (NEWA), the New England Labor Reform League (NELRL), and the Protective Unions (P.U.), the last enumerated by Edwin Rozwenc.[1] David S. Reynolds located a list of circles of the Brotherhood of the Union (BoU), 1849–1851, in the Papers of the Brotherhood of America, Historical Society of Pennsylvania, and accounts of the German groups, the Sozial Reform Association (SRA) and the Arbeiterbund (Arbnd); note where affiliates formed. I've added notes on the petitions to the Congress on behalf of the NRA's demands (NR petn) filed during the peak petitioning years from 1850 through 1852; Helene Zahler's study first noted their existence, and they are now located in various files of the Thirty-first and Thirty-second Congress in the Legislative Research Office of the National Archives in Washington, D.C.[2] It also seemed appropriate to add data from Robert S. Fogarty's directory of communities.[3] I have included very little information on any of these items, partly because of space constraints, but more because my purpose is to refer readers to these works. I have also noted the positive press mentions of the cause in the NRA press, without any attempt to discern whether the sentiment was genuine or reflected any local associations.

ALABAMA

Green Co., NR petn—U.S. Senate.
Wilcox Co, Allentown. BoU.

ARKANSAS

Johnson Co., Clarksville. BoU. Unspecified. NR petn—U.S. House. BoU.

CALIFORNIA

Sacramento Co., Sacramento. National Reform participation in the Squatters' movement and the later Settlers' League.
Sonoma Co. Squatters' movement, NR petn—U.S. House.

CONNECTICUT

Fairfield Co., Bridgeport. NR activities. Freigemeide. NR petn—U.S. Senate. Norwalk. NR petn—U.S. Senate. Redding. NR petn—U.S. House. Southwick. NR activities. Westport. NR activities, repr. at an I. C.
Hartford Co., Hartford. Ind't Cooperative Store. Commercial Union.
Litchfield Co., Litchfield. NR petn—U.S. Senate. Winchester. NR activities.
New Haven Co., Meriden. P.U. Store. Wallingford. Wallingford Community. Waterbury. P.U. Store.
New London Co., Noank. BoU. New London. NR activities. P.U. Stonington. NEWA.
Tolland Co., Rockville. Some NEWA activities.
Windham Co., Eastford. P.U. Willimantic. NR petn—U.S. Senate.
Unspecified. NR petn—U.S. Senate. Portad[?]. NR petn—U.S. House.

DELAWARE

Kent Co., Dover. BoU.
New Castle Co., Wilmington. NR petns—U.S. House. BoU.

DISTRICT OF COLUMBIA

Washington. NR activities. BoU (6). Pro land reform Workers League. NR petn—U.S. Senate.

FLORIDA

Leon Co., Tallahassee. BoU.

ILLINOIS

NR petns—U.S. Senate and—U.S. House.
Adams Co., Payson. NR activities.
Bureau Co., La Moille. Bureau County Phalanx, or Lamoille Agriculture and Mechanical Association.
Cook Co., Chicago. NR activities. NR petns—U.S. Senate. SRA. BoU. NR press notices of *Chicago Daily News. Chicago Times. Chicago Daily Democrat.*
DeWitt Co., NR petn—U.S. Senate.
Fulton Co., NR petn—U.S. Senate. Bernadotte. BoU. Canton area. Canton Phalanx.

Franklin Co., NR petn—U.S. Senate.
Henderson Co., NR petn—U.S. Senate.
Hancock Co., Nauvoo. Icaria Nauvoo. Pontwosuc. BoU.
Henderson Co., unspec. NR petition. Ouquaka NR petn—U.S. Senate.
Henry Co., Bishop Hill. Bishop Hill Colony.
Jo Daviess Co., Galena. WFVA petition—U.S. House.
Lake Co., NR petn—U.S. Senate.
La Salle Co., Peru. *Junction Beacon.*
Madison Co., Alton. NR activities. Edwardsville. NR petn—U.S. Senate. Upper Alton.
    Upper Alton meeting NR petn—U.S. Senate.
McDonough Co., Macomb. BoU.
McLean Co., NR petn—U.S. Senate. Bloomington. NR petn—U.S. Senate.
Morgan Co., NR petn—U.S. Senate.
Peoria Co., Peoria. NR activities. NR petns—U.S. Senate and—U.S. House. NR press
    Nineteenth Century, eds. David D. Irons, J. R. Watson.
Pike Co., NR petn—U.S. Senate.
Pope Co., NR petn—U.S. Senate.
Randolph Co., NR activities. NR press notices of the *Randolph County Record.* Chester
    and Sparta. NR activities. BoU.
Sangamon Co., Laomi (then Lick Creek). Integral Phalanx absorbing the Sangamon
    Association (see also Ohio).
Scott Co., Lynneville. NR petn—U.S. Senate.
Vermillion Co., Georgetown. BoU.
Will Co., Joliet. NR activities. NR petn—U.S. Senate. Plainfield. NR petn—U.S. Senate. Wilmington. NR petn—U.S. Senate.
Woodford Co., NR petn—U.S. Senate. Bowling Green. NR petn—U.S. Senate.

INDIAN TERRITORY

Choctaw Nation. NR activities.

INDIANA

NR petn—U.S. Senate and—U.S. House.
Dearborn Co., Aurora. NR petn—U.S. Senate.
Elkhart Co., NR petn—U.S. Senate.
Fayette Co., Alquina. NR petn—U.S. House. Everton. NR petn—U.S. Senate.
Fountain Co., Covington area. Site of former community.
Franklin Co., NR petn—U.S. Senate and—U.S. House.
Lagrange Co., Lexington. Congregation of Saints. Mongo (then Mongoquinong) area.
    LaGrange Phalanx.
Marshall Co., Kristeen Community, on the Tippecanoe River.
Parke Co., Rockport. NR petn—U.S. Senate.
Parke Co., West Union. NR petn—U.S. House.
Posey Co., NR petn—U.S. House. New Harmony. Site of former community. NR
    activities.

Randolph Co., Unionsport area. Union Home, on Cabin Creek. Winchester. BoU.
Spencer Co., Centerville. NR petn—U.S. Senate, as Centreville.
St. Joseph Co., NR petn—U.S. Senate. Centre. NR activities. National Reform press
citations of the *Aurora*. South Bend (then Portage). Philadelphia Industrial As-
sociation.
Tippicanoe Co., West Point. BoU.
Vanderburgh Co., Evansville. BoU.
Warren Co., Prairie Township. Grand Prairie Harmonial Institute. Rainsville. Grand
Prairie Community, or Grand Prairie Common Stock Company.
Wayne Co., NR petn—U.S. House. Hagerstown. BoU. Goshen.
Unspecified. Brokeville. NR petn—U.S. Senate Goshen. (Two locations in Elkhart
and Scott Counties) [two petns] NR petn—U.S. Senate. Milifed? [illegible]. NR
petn—U.S. Senate.

IOWA

Clayton Co., Elkader. Communia, south of town.
Davis Co., Bloomfield. BoU.
Dubuque Co., Dubuque. NR petn—U.S. Senate. Arbnd.
Iowa Co., Amana and Homestead. Amana Society, or the Society of True Inspiration.
Jasper. Jaspis Kolonie, or Jasper Colony.
Lee Co., Ft. Madison. BoU.
Linn Co., Marion. Repr. at an I.C.
Mahaska Co., Scott township. Iowa Pioneer Phalanx.
Monona Co., Preparation. Preparation Community.
Polk Co., Ft. Des Moines. BoU.
Unspecified. NR petn—U.S. Senate.

KENTUCKY

Boyle Co., Perryville. BoU.
Christian Co., Pembroke. BoU.
Clarke Co., Oil Mills. BoU.
Jefferson Co., Lexington. *True American*, ed. Cassius Marcellus Clay.
Mason Co., Maysville. BoU. Arbnd. Orangeburgh. BoU.
Wood Co., Louisville. Arbnd.

LOUISIANA

Oreans Parish. New Orleans. Arbnd.

MAINE

Arrostock Co., Houlton. P.U. Store.
Cumberland Co., Freeport. P.U. Naples. P.U. Portland. P.U. (2). Sabbathday Lake,
Town of Gloucester.

Hancock Co., Ellsworth. P.U. BoU. West Gouldsboro. P.U.

Kennebec Co., Albion. P.U. Gardiner. NEWA. citation of David's Sling. South China. P.U. Waterville. P.U. Winthrop. P.U.

Penobscot Co., Bangor. P.U. NR petn—U.S. House. P.U. (2). Ind't Cooperative Store. Mutual Store Co., NR petns to the—U.S. House. Dixmont P.U. East Orrington. BoU. Hamden. P.U. North Newburgh. (laborers) NR petn—U.S. Senate.

Sagadahoc Co., Bath. P.U. Brunswick. P.U.

Somerset Co., Bloomfield. P.U. Norridgewock. P.U. Store. NR activities. St. Albans. P.U. South Norridgewock. NR activities.

Waldo Co., Belfast. Ind't Cooperative Store. Union Mutual Store. Freedom. P.U. Knox. P.U. Unity. P.U. Store.

Washington Co., Addison. P.U. Store. Baring. P.U. Calais. P.U. Columbia Falls. P.U. Store ("Columbia"). Dennysville. P.U. Eastport. P.U. Store. Pembroke. P.U. Robbinston. P.U. Store.

York Co., Biddeford. P.U. Kennebunkport. P.U. Kittery. P.U. Saco., NEWA. Sanford. P.U. South Berwick. P.U.

MARYLAND

Allegany Co., Cumberland. BoU.

Baltimore Co., Baltimore. NR activities. SRA. BoU (5). NR petns—U.S. Senate. Independent Co-op Store. Groceries and Bakery Ass'n. NR press notices of the Arbnd. *Saturday Visitor*, ed. J. E. Snodgrass.

Carroll Co., Union Bridge. BoU.

Cecil Co., NR petn—U.S. Senate.

Frederick Co., NR petn—U.S. Senate. New Market. NR petn—U.S. Senate.

Harford Co., Jarretsville. BoU.

Prince George Co., Laurel Factory. BoU Franklin, No.

MASSACHUSETTS—BOSTON AREA

Essex Co., Amesbury and Salisbury. NR petn—U.S. Senate. Andover. NEWA. P.U. Land reform petns—U.S. Senate and—U.S. House. Andrews [Point]. NEWA with N. Andover. Beverly. P.U. (2). Danvers. NELRL. Haverhill. P.U. Lawrence. P.U. (2). Lynn. NR activities. NEWA. NELRL. P.U. (5). NR press citations of *Pioneer. Awl. Laborer. Free Soil Pickaxe.* Manchester. P.U. Merrimac. Some NEWA activities. Methuen. NEWA. North Andover. NEWA. North Danvers. P.U. Newburyport. P.U. Salem. NEWA. P.U. Salisbury. Ind't Cooperative Store. Salisbury and Amesbury U'n St A. South Andover. NEWA. P.U. South Boston. NEWA. NELRL. P.U. P.U. South Danvers. NELRL. Stoneham. NEWA. P.U. a. Swampscott. P.U. West Amesbury. P.U. Middlesex Co., Cambridge and Cambridgeport. WFVA petition—U.S. House. Cambridgeport,. P.U. Charlestown. NEWA. P.U. (2). Chelmsford. NEWA. P.U. (2). East Cambridge. P.U. Framingham. P.U. b. Lowell. NEWA. NELRL. NR activities, repr. at an I.C.P.U. (8). NR press citation of the *Operative,* the *True Reformer.* Medford. P.U. (2). North Chelmsford. NEWA. NELRL. P.U. a. Pawtucket[ville]. P.U. (2). Reading. NEWA. South Chelmsford. P.U. South Reading. NEWA. P.U. Tyngsboro. P.U. b. Waltham. NEWA. P.U. Watertown. NEWA. NELRL. P.U. Winchester. WFVA petn—U.S. House. P.U. Woburn. NEWA.

Suffolk Co., Boston. NEWA. NELRL. NR activities. P.U. (4). BoU. Ind't Cooperative Store. Work'g'n's Comml Union. P.U. Arbnd. BoU. P.U. Land reform petns—U.S. Senate. Laborer. P.U. NR press citations of *Boston Investigator. Chronotype.* Brook Farm. NEWA. East Boston. P.U. (2). Roxbury. NEWA. NELRL. P.U. (2). NR petn—U.S. Senate. West Chelsea. NR petn—U.S. Senate. West Roxbury. NEWA.

MASSACHUSETTS—BEYOND BOSTON

Barnstable Co., Sandwich. NR activities. P.U. a.

Berkshire Co., Pittsfield. NR petn—U.S. Senate. Hancock. Shaker Village. West Springfield. NEWA.

Bristol Co., Easton. Some NEWA activities. Fairhaven. P.U. Fall River. NEWA. NELRL. NR activities. P.U. (2). Mansfield. P.U. New Bedford. NEWA. P.U. (2). North Easton. NEWA. Taunton. NR activities. NEWA. P.U. b,. P.U.

Dukes Co., Tisbury. P.U.

Franklin Co., Greenfield. P.U. Sunderland. NR petn—U.S. Senate.

Hampden Co., Chicopee. P.U., NR petn—U.S. Senate. Holyoake. NR petn—U.S. Senate. Palmer. NEWA. Springfield. NEWA. P.U. (2). Three Rivers. NEWA. with Palmer. NR petn—U.S. Senate.

Hampshire Co., Florence (then Broughton's Meadows). Northampton Association of Education and Industry. Montague. P.U. Div. Unassigned. Northampton. NR activities. New Eng. Workingmen's Ass'n. P.U.

Nantucket Co., Nantucket. NEWA. P.U.

Norfolk Co., Canton. NEWA. P.U. East Randolph. NEWA. P.U. (2). East Stoughton. NEWA. P.U. Franklin. NR petn—U.S. Senate. Holliston. NELRL. P.U. (2). North Weymouth. P.U. Newton (Lower Falls). P.U. Newton (Upper Falls). NEWA. Land reform petns—U.S. Senate. P.U. Quincy. NEWA. P.U. (2). Randolph. NEWA. P.U. (2). South Braintree. P.U. SouthWeymouth. NEWA. P.U. Stoughton. P.U. West Medway. NEWA. P.U. Weymouth. P.U. (2).

Plymouth Co., Abington. NEWA. P.U. (2). Bridgewater. P.U. East Abington. P.U. East Bridgewater. NEWA. NELRL. East Wareham. P.U. Middleborough. NEWA. North Abington. P.U. South Scituate. P.U. Div. Unassigned.

Worcester Co., Ashburnham. NR petn—U.S. Senate. P.U. Athol. P.U. Blackstone. NEWA. P.U. b. Brookfield. NELRL. P.U. Clinton[ville]. NELRL. P.U. Fitchburg. NEWA. P.U. Grafton. P.U. Harvard. Fruitlands. Hopkinton. NEWA. P.U. a. Hubbardston. NEWA. P.U. Lancaster. NEWA. Leominister. NEWA. Milford. Hopedale. Hopedale Community, or Fraternal Community No. NEWA. Working Men's Movements. Millbury. P.U. North Brookfield. P.U. Northbridge. NEWA. South Ashburnham. P.U. South Gardner. P.U. Uxbridge. Ware. P.U. Warren. P.U. Webster. NEWA. West Brookfield. NEWA. P.U. Winchendon. P.U. Worcester. NELRL. NR activities. P.U. a. P.U. BoU.

Unspecified. Cabotville. NEWA. New Bridge. NEWA.

MICHIGAN

National Reform price citation of the *True Democrat*. Unspecified locality NR petns—
    U.S. Senate and—U.S. House. Grocton(?), NR petn—U.S. Senate.
Alcona Co., Harrisville, NR petn—U.S. Senate.
Allegan Co., NR activities.
Eaton Co., Eaton Rapids. BoU.
Calhoun Co., Albion. MMP. Marshall. MMP.
Hillsdale Co., Hillsdale. MMP. Litchfield. P.U.
Ingham Co., Lansing, NR petn—U.S. Senate.
Jackson Co., Jackson. MMP.
Kalamazoo Co., Galesburg area. Alphadelphia Phalanx. Kalamazoo. NR activities.
Kent Co., Grand Rapids. MMP.
Lapeer Co., Almont. BoU.
Mackinac Co., St. James, Beaver Island. Kingdom of St. James, including Manitou
    and Charlevoix.
Macomb Co., Pontiac. BoU.
Washtenaw Co., Ann Arbor. NR activities.
Wayne Co., Detroit. NR petn—U.S. Senate. Arbnd.

MINNESOTA

Legislature NR petition to the U.S. House to reserve lands for settlers only.
Washington Co., Stillwater. BoU.

MISSISSIPPI

Yalabusha Co., Coffeeville. National Reform press notice of *Dollar Democrat.*

MISSOURI

Adair Co., Connelsville today. Nineveh.
Shelby Co., Bethel. Bethel Community, included Elim, Mamura, and Hebron.
No county [then St. Louis Co.], St. Louis. SRA. Arbnd. NR petns—U.S. Senate.

NEW HAMPSHIRE

Belknap Co., Meredith Bridge. P.U. WFVA petition—U.S. House.
Cheshire Co., East Jaffrey. P.U. Fitzwilliam. P.U.
Hillsborough Co., Manchester. NR activities. National Reform press citation of the
    Democrat. NEWA. P.U. (3). Nashua. P.U. New Ipswish. P.U.
Merrimack Co., Canterbury. Shaker Village. Concord. NEWA. P.U.
Rockingham Co., Chester. P.U. Fremont. P.U. b. Newmarket. P.U. Poplin. P.U. a.
    Portsmouth. P.U.

Strafford Co., Dover. NEWA. P.U. (2). Rochester. P.U. Rolingford [then Salmon Falls].
P.U. Sommersworth [then Great Falls]. P.U. (2).
Sullivan Co., Claremont. P.U.

NEW JERSEY

Industrial Legislature of New Jersey. NR petn—U.S. Senate.
Camden Co., Camden. BoU.
Cape May Co., Middletown. NR activities.
Essex Co., Belleville. NR activities, repr. at an I. C. Newark. NR activities. SRA. NR
petn—U.S. Senate. Independent Co-op Store. P.U. Arbnd. Workers League.
Gloucester Co., Bridgeport. NR activities. BoU Nazarene, No.
Mercer Co., Trenton. Arbnd.
Middlesex Co., New Brunswick. NR activities. BoU.
Monmouth Co., NR activities. NR petn—U.S. House and U.S. Senate. Phalanx, At-
lantic Township. North American Phalanx.
Morris Co., Troy. NR petn—U.S. Senate.
Orange Co., NR petn—U.S. Senate.
Passaic Co., Paterson. Independent Co-op Store. P.U.
Salem Co., Elmer. NR activities. Salem. BoU. Penns Grove. BoU.
Union Co., Plainfield. NR activities, repr. at an I. C.
Warren Co., Allamuchy. NR petn—U.S. Senate.
Unspecified. NR activities. Chanceville. NR activities.

NEW YORK—NEW YORK CITY AREA

Kings Co., Brooklyn. MMP. NR activities. NR petn—U.S. Senate. Williamsburgh. NR
activities. Arbnd. Land reform petns—U.S. Senate. Worcester. NR activities.
New York Co., New York City. MMP (11). NR activities. SRA. Land reform petns—U.S.
House and Senate (including from Mechanics' Mutual Prototection, Ourvrier
Circle BoU, and Veterans of the War). WFVA petition—U.S. House. Independent
Co-op Store. American P.U. Economical Exchange Assoc'n. Arbnd. BoU. Coopera-
tive Labor League. Societe de la Montagne. Workers League.
Queens Co., Jackson [Heights]. NR petn—U.S. Senate,
Suffolk Co., NR petn—U.S. Senate. Brentwood area. Modern Times. Waterville. NR
activities.
Westchester Co., NR activities, repr. at an I. C. Yonkers. BoU.

NEW YORK—BEYOND NEW YORK CITY

Unknown. Mechanics Mutual Protection Association. NR activities. NR petn—U.S.
Senate and—U.S. House.
Albany Co., Albany. MMP (4). NR activities. Independent Co-op Store. Am. U. of
Assn'ts Depot.
Allegany Co., Angelica. NR petn—U.S. Senate.
Broome Co., Binghampton. National Reform press citation of *Iris.*

Bronx Co., Westchester. NR activities.

Broome Co., Triangle. "Triank" NR petn—U.S. Senate.

Cattaraugus Co., Riceville. NR petn—U.S. Senate. Misfiled as New Jersey.

Cayuga Co. NR activities. Auburn. MMP (2). NR activities. NR petn—U.S. Senate.
Day Dawn, ed., T. N. Calkins. BoU. Locke. BoU. Port Byron. MMP.

Chautauqua Co., Busti. NR petition. Misfiled as New Jersey. Dewittville. NR petn—
U.S. Senate. Westfield. MMP.

Chemung Co., Elmira. MMP.

Chenango Co., Bainbridge. WFVA petition—U.S. House. Cohoes. NR activities.

Columbia Co., Mount Lebanon. Shaker Community at Mount Lebanon or New
Lebanon.

Delaware Co., Antirenter stronghold. NR activities. Dewittville. NR petition. (De-
witaller).

Dutchess Co., NR activities. Ebenezer. Ebenezer Society, or the Society of True Inspiration. Poughkeepsie. MMP. Leedsville. NR activities.

Erie Co., Buffalo. MMP (3). Arbnd. BoU. Workers League. Tonawanda. NR petn—
U.S. Senate.

Fulton Co., NR petn—U.S. Senate. See also Herkimer Co.

Genesee Co., NR petn—U.S. Senate. East Pembroke. NR activities. Genesee. MMP.
Pembroke. NR activities.

Greene Co., Coxsackie. Site of former Owenite Community.

Hamilton Co., Piseo. Morehouse Union, in Arietta Township.

Herkimer Co., Land reform petns—U.S. Senate. Frankfort. MMP. Little Falls. MMP.
NR activities.

Jefferson Co., WFVA petition—U.S. House. Dexter. NR petn—U.S. Senate. Ellisburg.
NR petn—U.S. Senate. Theresa. MMP. Watertown. MMP (2). Jefferson County
Industrial Association, Cold Creek. Kiantone Creek or Spiritualist Springs. Har-
monia, Kiantone Community, or the Association of Beneficents.

Livingston Co., Dansville. MMP. North Bloomfield. Bloomfield Union Association,
or North Bloomfield Association, on Honeoye Creek, near juncture of Monroe,
Livingston, and Ontario Counties. Sonyea area. Shaker Community at Groveland,
or Sonyea.

Madison Co., NR petn—U.S. Senate. Kenwood. Oneida Community. Middleport.
MMP. Peterboro. NR activities. Smithfield. NR petn—U.S. Senate.

Monroe Co., Clarkson. NR activities, repr. at an I. C. North Bloomfield. Bloomfield
Union Association, or North Bloomfield Association, on Honeoye Creek, near
juncture of Monroe, Livingston, and Ontario Counties. North Hamlin. Clarkson
Association, or Clarkson Domain (also Port Richmond Phalanx). Rochester. MMP
(2). Land reform petns—U.S. Senate. Arbnd. BoU.

Nassau Co., South Hempstead. NR petn—U.S. House.

Niagra Co., Lockport. MMP (2, one each for "Upper and "Lower"). NR activities.
BoU b.

Oneida Co., Paris. BoU. Rome. MMP. Utica. MMP. Whitesboro. MMP. South Trenton. P.U.

Onondaga Co., NR activities. Jordan. MMP. Mottville. Skaneateles Community, at
Community Place. Skaneateles community. Peru. P.U. Salina. MMP. Skaneateles.
NR activities. Syracuse. MMP.

Ontario Co., Brownsville. MMP. Canandaigua. MMP. Geneva. MMP. NR petns—U.S. Senate. Littleville (then Bates Mills). Ontario Union, or Manchester Union. Manchester. NR petn—U.S. House. North Bloomfield. Bloomfield Union Association, or North Bloomfield Association, on Honeoye Creek, near juncture of Monroe, Livingston, and Ontario Counties. NR activities.

Orleans Co., Medina. MMP.

Oswego Co., Oswego. MMP (2), NR activities. Land reform petns—U.S. Senate.

Otsego Co., WFVA petition—U.S. House. Cherry Valley. BoU. Cooperstown. BoU. Westford. BoU. Worcester. NR activities. NR petn—U.S. Senate. BoU.

Rennselaer Co., NR activities, repr. at an I. C. East Troy. MMP. Lansingburgh. MMP. Troy. MMP (2). NR activities. Independent Co-op Store. Mechanics Mutual Protection. NR petn—U.S. Senate, also filed as New Jersey; only a Troy Hills in Morris County, New Jersey.

Ulster Co., Sholem. Site of former community. South Troy. MMP. West Troy. NR activities.

Richmond Co., Staten Island. NR activities.

Rockland Co., Haverstraw. Site of former Owenite community.

Saratoga Co., Ballston Spa. P.U. Greenfield. P.U. Saratoga Springs. MMP.

Schenectady Co., Duanesburgh. NR petn—U.S. Senate. Schenectady. MMP. BoU.

Schoharie Co., NR activities. National Reform press citation of Guardian of the Soil, ed., William H. Gallup.

Seneca Co., Seneca Falls. BoU. Seneca. NR petn—U.S. Senate. Sherman. NR petn—U.S. Senate.

St. Lawrence Co., Canton. MMP. Clark's Crossing. Site of former community. Massena. NR petn—U.S. Senate. West Potsdam. P.U.

Tioga Co., Owego. Land reform petns—U.S. Senate.

Tompkins Co., NR petn—U.S. Senate. Lansing. NR petn—U.S. Senate. Ithaca. MMP. Wadhams. P.U. (Wadham MIlls).

Warren Co., Hague. NR petn—U.S. Senate. Watervliet. Colonie area. Shaker Community at Niskeyuna or Watervliet. NR petition?

Wayne Co., Newark. MMP. Sodus area. Site of former Shaker community. Sodus Bay Phalanx, later reorganized as the Sodus Phalanx. Weedsport. Independent Co-op Store. Farmer's and Mechanic's Protective Co-op.

Wyoming Co., Covington. NR petn—U.S. Senate.

Yates Co., Jerusalem. Site of former community. Penn Yan. MMP.

Unspecified. Unspecified locality [three petns, one from Watervliet, Albany Co.]. Land reform petns—U.S. Senate. MMP. Connorsville. NR activities. Lagrange. (Dutchess, Orange, and Wyoming Counties) NR petn—U.S. Senate. La Grange. Meadville. NR petn—U.S. Senate, filed New York, possibly PA. Mechiday. NR petn—U.S. Senate. Mixville. Mixville Association (originally called the Genesee Valley Association), Wiscoy, then Mixville Newport. (Four locations in Herkimer, Monroe, Onondaga, Orange counties) NR petn—U.S. Senate. Onosu. NR petn—U.S. Senate. Pekin. (Two locations, Niagra and Oswego counties) BoU.

NORTH CAROLINA

Rowan Co., Salisbury (then Llano). Unspecified. NR petn—U.S. House.

OHIO — CINCINNATI AREA

Butler Co., NR petn—U.S. Senate. Fairfield [two petns] NR petn—U.S. Senate. Middletown area. Integral Phalanx, at Manchester Mills. Preston area. Shaker Community at Whitewater, Dry Forks Creek, border of Butler and Hamilton.

Clermont Co., Bethel. BoU. Milford. NR petn—U.S. Senate. Rural and Utopia. Clermont Phalanx (originally the Cincinnati Phalanx). Utopia. The Brotherhood, or Spiritualist Community. Utopia, or Trialville, both on parts site of the former Clermont Phalanx.

Hamilton Co., Carthage NR petn—U.S. Senate (from Arbnd). Cincinnati. MMP(2). NR activities. SRA. Independent Co-op Store. Provision Store and Workers Hall. NR petns—U.S. House and to the—U.S. Senate. Arbnd. BoU Wayne, No. Local press: *Daily Nonpareil, Herald of Truth. Herald of Progress, Cincinnati Gazette.* Miamitown. MMP. Preston area. Shaker Community at Whitewater, Dry Forks Creek, border of Butler and Hamilton. Westfield. NR petns—U.S. Senate.

OHIO — CLEVELAND AREA

Cuyahoga Co., NR petn—U.S. Senate. Bedford. NR petn—U.S. Senate. Berea. Site of former community. Cleveland. MMP (2), NR activities, repr. at an I. C. Independent Co-op Store. P.U. Store. NR petn—U.S. Senate. Arbnd. BoU. Workers League. Spirit of Freedom, ed., H. E. Calkins. Ohio City (also village in Van Wert Co.). MMP (2), Repr. at an I. C. NR petns—U.S. Senate. Shaker Heights today. Shaker Community at North Union. Westerly NR petn—U.S. Senate.

Lake Co., Kirtland. Site of former community. NR petn—U.S. Senate. BoU. Painesville. MMP.

Lorain Co., Elyria. MMP. Oberlin. Site of former community.

OHIO — BEYOND CINCINNATI AND CLEVELAND AREAS

General. NR activities.

Ashland Co., Ashland. MMP. Jefferson. BoU. Rowsburgh. BoU.

Ashland Co., NR petn—U.S. Senate.

Ashtabula Co., Kelloggsville. Independent Co-op Store. Farmers Union Co.

Auglaize Co., [two petns] NR petn—U.S. Senate.

Belmont Co., Bellaire (then Bell Air). Ohio Phalanx. St. Clairsville. NR activities. BoU.

Carrol Co., NR petn—U.S. House. Carrolton. NR petn—U.S. Senate. BoU.

Clark Co., Green Plain (near South Charleston). NR petn—U.S. Senate. Hennessey. NR petn—U.S. Senate. South Charleston. BoU.

Clinton Co., Oakland. Abram Brooke's Community.

Columbiana Co., NR petns—U.S. House—U.S. Senate. Gilmore. NR petn—U.S. Senate. [New] Lisbon. MMP, NR activities. NR petn—U.S. Senate. Aurora, ed., John Frost. Salem. MMP. National Reform press citation of Friend of Man, and Village Register. NR petn—U.S. Senate. Springfield Township. Site of former community. Wellsville Two petns to the—U.S. Senate.

Coshocton Co., Coshocton. NR petn—U.S. Senate.

Darke Co., Stelvideo. Rising Star Association, five miles northeast of Greenville.

Delaware Co., Troy. Independent Co-op Store. Farmers Company.

Erie Co., Berlin Heights. The Free Lovers at Davis House. Principia, or Personality. New Berlin. NR petn—U.S. Senate.

Franklin Co., NR petn—U.S. Senate. Blendon Township. NR activities. Columbus. BoU Mt. Vernon, No.

Gallia Co., Gallipolis. Ca. BoU.

Geauga Co., Claridon. Independent Co-op Store. Union Company. Munson. Independent Co-op Store. Farmers Company.

Greene Co., Xenia. BoU.

Holmes Co., Berlin. NR petn—U.S. Senate. Independent Co-op Store. Berlin Union Co.

Huron Co., NR petn—U.S. Senate. Ironton. BoU. New Haven (also village of name, Hamilton Co.). BoU. North Fairfield. BoU Washington, No. Norwalk. BoU. Podunk[eville]. NR petn—U.S. Senate.

Jefferson Co., NR petn—U.S. Senate. Jefferson. BoU.

Knox Co., Knox, NR petn—U.S. Senate. Mount Vernon BoU. NR petn—U.S. Senate.

Lawrence Co., NR petn—U.S. Senate. Kelly Mills. BoU. Windsor. Independent Co-op Store. Farmers Company. Community. Zanesfield. Highland Home.

Licking Co., Granville. BoU. Newark. MMP. BoU.

Logan Co., Louisville. BoU. West Liberty area. Prairie Home. Zanesfield. NR petn—U.S. Senate.

Lucas Co., NR petns—U.S. Senate.

Mahoning Co., NR petns—U.S. Senate. Canfield. MMP. Damascus & vicinity. NR petn—U.S. Senate. Marlboro. BoU. Youngstown. MMP.

Medina Co., Litchfield, NR petn—U.S. Senate. Medina. NR petn—U.S. Senate. Wadsworth. BoU.

Mercer Co., Celina. NR petn—U.S. Senate.

Monroe Co., NR petn—U.S. Senate.

Montgomery Co., Dayton. BoU. NR petn—U.S. Senate. WFVA petition—U.S. House. Johnsville. Independent Co-op Store. Farmers Company. Watervliet. Shaker Community southeast of Dayton.

Morgan Co., McConnelsville. NR petn—U.S. Senate.

Morrow Co., Cardington. NR petn—U.S. Senate.

Muskingum & Licking Cos. NR petn—U.S. Senate.

Muskingum Co. Two petitions to the—U.S. Senate and Congress. Zanesville area. Columbian Phalanx or Columbian Association, on the Muskingum River above town.

Noble Co., Sarahsville. NR petn—U.S. Senate.

Perry Co., Oakfield. NR petn—U.S. Senate.

Pickaway Co., Morgan. BoU. Plymouth. BoU.

Portage Co., Aurora. Independent Co-op Store. Farmers Company. Freedom. BoU. Paris. Independence. BoU. Ravenna. NR activities. NR petn—U.S. Senate. Shalersville. BoU.

Richland Co., Ganges. BoU. NR petn—U.S. Senate. Mansfield. MMP. NR petn—U.S. Senate. Rowsburgh. BoU.

Scioto Co., Portsmouth. BoU Rainbow, No.

Senaca Co., Attica. BoU. Shalersville. BoU. Tiffin. MMP.

Shelby Co., Port Jefferson. BoU. Shelby. NR petn—U.S. Senate. Springfield. BoU Nos.

Stark Co., NR petn—U.S. Senate. Alliance area. Marlborough Association or Marlboro Community. Barryville. BoU. Canton. NR activities. Massilon. Site of former community. Navarre. MMP. Independent Co-op Store. Farmers and Mechanics Assoc'n. New Franklin. Ca. BoU.

Summitt Co., Akron. MMP. NR petn—U.S. Senate.

Trumbull Co., Braceville. NR petn—U.S. Senate. Cuyahoga Falls. MMP. Mesopotamia. Independent Co-op Store. Farmers Company. Mosketo. NR petn—U.S. Senate. Warren, MMP. Trumbull Phalanx (eight miles west of Warren at Phalanx Station).

Tuscarawas Co. Site of former community. NR petn—U.S. Senate. Dover. MMP (as "Canal Dover") NR petn—U.S. Senate. New Philadelphia. MMP. Port Washington. NR petn—U.S. Senate. Zoar. Society of Separatists of Zoar.

Vernon Co., Harveysburg. NR petn—U.S. Senate. Vienna Crossroads. BoU. Wadsworth. BoU.

Warren Co., Foster's Crossing. Fruit Hills Community. Lebanon. Shaker Community at Union Village. NR petn—U.S. Senate.

Wayne Co., NR petn—U.S. House and Senate. Wooster. MMP. NR petn—U.S. Senate.

Unspecified location. NR petns—U.S. Senate and House. Caulen[?]. NR petn—U.S. Senate. Portage [Various sites]. NR petn—U.S. Senate. Westville. Two locations (Champaign or Mahoning Cos.). BoU. NR petn—U.S. Senate. Williamstown. Two locations (Defiance or Hancock Cos.). NR petn—U.S. Senate.

PENNSYLVANIA—PHILADELPHIA AREA

Philadelphia Co., BoU, and in the county. Kennett Square. NR activities. Northern Liberties. Commissioners' Hall meeting reform petition to the—U.S. Senate. Philadelphia. MMP. NR activities. SRA. Independent Co-op Store. Economy Exchange Ass'n. Independent Co-op Store. Harmony Division. Quaker City NR. NR petn—U.S. Senate and—U.S. House. Arbnd. BoU. Workers League. NR press citation of the *Dollar Newspaper,* the *White Banner, Jubilee Harbinger.*

PENNSYLVANIA—PITTSBURGH AREA

Allegheny Co., Allegheny City. Independent Co-op Store. P.U. Manchester. Independent Co-op Store. P.U. Pittsburgh. NR activities. Independent Co-op Store. P.U. Land reform petns—U.S. Senate. Arbnd. BoU. NR petition. NR petition. Walker's Mill. NR activities.

Armstrong Co., NR petn—U.S. Senate.

PENNSYLVANIA—BEYOND PHILADELPHIA AND PITTSBURGH AREAS

Beaver Co., Ambridge today. NR activities. Economy. Monaco (then Philipsburg). Site of former community.

Blair Co., Holidaysburg. NR activities.

Bradford Co., Le Raysville. Leraysville Phalanx.

Butler Co., Harmony. Site of former community.

Cameron Co., Brownsville. NR activities.

Chester Co., Marcus Hook. BoU. Valley Forge. Site of former community.

Clarion Co., Brady's Bend. NR activities.

Clinton Co., Lock Haven. BoU.

Columbia Co., Buck Horn. BoU.

Crawford Co., Harts Crossroads. BoU Friendship, No.

Dauphin Co., Harrisburg. BoU Olive Branch, No. NR petn—U.S. Senate.

Delaware Co., Darby Creek. NR activities, repr. at an I.C.

Franklin Co., Snow Hill. Snow Hill Nunnery, or Seventh Day Baptist Church at Snow Hill.

Greene Co., Freeport. NR activities. Land reform petns—U.S. House.

Huntingdon Co. Land reform petns—U.S. Senate. Birmingham. NR activities. Ennisville. BoU Silencia, No. Huntingdon. BoU Friendship, No.

Indiana Co., NR petn—U.S. Senate.

Lackawanna Co., Scranton. NR petn—U.S. Senate.

Lancaster Co., Lancaster. BoU Marion, No.

Lebanon Co., Bloomburg. NR activities. Harrisburg. BoU Olive Branch, No.

Lycoming Co., Williamsport. BoU.

McKean Co., Ginalsburg (near present Smethport). Teutonia, or McKean County Association, or Society of Industry.

Monroe Co. Society of One Mentians, or Promisewell Community Owenite, in the Pocono Mountains. Natchitoches (then Pike Co.). Social Reform Unity, in the Pocono Mountains. Goose Pond area (then Pike Co.). Goose Pond Community Owenite, in the Pocono Mountains.

Northhampton Co., Easton. BoU.

Pike Co., Greeley (then Darlingville, or Darlingsville). Sylvania Association.

Potter Co., Oleona. Ole Bull's Colony, or New Norway, or Oleona, now Ole Bull State Park.

Tioga Co., Tioga. BoU.

Warren Co., Limestone Township. Peace Union, or Friedens Verein. Pittsfield. MMP.

Wayne Co., Prompton. E. E. Guild, Freedom of the Soil. Waymart. NR activities. D. C., Further Signs of Progress,.

Wetherford Co., NR petn—U.S. Senate.

Unspecified. NR petn—U.S. Senate. [illegible] Co., WFVA petition—U.S. House. Charter Creek. NR activities. Franklinville [Three locations in Huntingdon, Montgomery, and Philadelphia counties]. BoU. Holidaysburgh. New Auxiliary at Holidaysburgh, Pa. Williamsburg [Armstrong, Blair, and Clarion Cos.]. NR activities. BoU.

RHODE ISLAND

"Dorr War." NR petn—U.S. Senate.
Bristol Co., Bristol. P.U. and P.U. Store.
Providence Co., Cranston. P.U. Store. Pawtucket. NEWA. BoU Providence. NEWA.
    NR activities. Ind't Cooperative Store. P. Mutual Benefit Society. P.U. (4). Indepen-
    dent Union. BoU. NR press citations of the National Anti Slavery Standard. Slater-
    ville. NEWA. Woonsocket. NR petition. NEWA. P.U. NR petn—U.S. Senate.

TENNESEE

Fayette Co., Macon. BoU.
Maury Co., Columbia. BoU. Williamsport. BoU.

TEXAS

Bexar Co., San Antonio. German socialists.
Dallas Co., Dallas area. Reunion.
Denton Co., Justin area. Icaria, Frenchtown prairie.
Gillespie Co., Castell area, then Llano. Bettina, or Darmstaedter Kolonie. Fredericks-
    burg area. Zodiac Community.
Nacagdoches Co., Nacagdoches. BoU.
Walker Co., Huntsville. BoU.

VERMONT

Addison Co., Bristol. P.U. Store. Ferrisburgh. P.U. Store. Granville. P.U. Hancock.
    P.U. Shoreham. P.U. (2). Vergennes. P.U. Whiting. P.U.
Bennington Co., Arlington. P.U. East Dorset. P.U. Manchester. P.U. N. Bennington.
    P.U.
Caledonia Co., Danville. P.U. Lyndon. P.U. a. Peacham. P.U. South Hardwick. P.U.
    Sutton. P.U. Walden. P.U.
Chittenden Co., Essex. P.U. Hinesburgh. P.U. Huntington. P.U. Jericho. P.U. (2).
    Westford. P.U. (3). Williston. P.U. Winooski Falls. NEWA. P.U.
Franklin Co., Bakersfield. P.U. Berkshire. P.U. Enosburgh. P.U. Fairfax. P.U. Georgia
    Plains. P.U. Georgia. P.U. Store. P.U. Div. Unassigned. Montgomery. P.U. Richford.
    P.U. West Berkshire. P.U.
La Moille Co., Eden. P.U. Store. Elmore. P.U. Johnson. P.U. Morristown. P.U. (2).
    Poss. BoU. Stowe. P.U. Waterville. P.U.
Orange Co., Brookfield. P.U. Chelsea. NEWA. P.U. East Brookfield. P.U. East Orange.
    P.U. Div. Unassigned. Randolph. P.U. South Strafford. P.U. Tunbridge. P.U. (2).
    Washington. P.U. Williamstown. P.U.
Orleans Co., Albany. P.U. (2). Coventry. P.U. Craftsbury. P.U. Derby Center. P.U.
    Glover. P.U. Troy. P.U. Div. Unassigned.
Rutland Co., Benson. P.U. Brandon. Voice of Freedom. Castleton. P.U. Danby. P.U.
    Store. Pawlet. P.U. (3). Pittsford. NR petns—U.S. Senate and—U.S. House. Poult-
    ney. P.U. Rutland. P.U. Wallingford. P.U. Wells. P.U. West Haven. P.U.

Washington Co., Barre. P.U. Cabot. P.U. Calais. P.U. East Montpelier. P.U. Montpelier.
    P.U. North Montpelier. P.U. a. Northfield. P.U. Plainfield. P.U. (2). Roxbury. P.U.
    Waitsfield. P.U. Waterbury. P.U. Worcester. P.U.
Windham Co., Dummerston. P.U. East Dummerston. P.U. Grafton. P.U. (2). Jaimca.
    P.U. Londonderry. P.U. P.U.tney. P.U.tney Society, or P.U.tney Community. South
    Londonderry. P.U. Townshend. P.U. Wardsboro. P.U. (2).
Windsor Co., Barnard. P.U. Bridgewater. NELRL. P.U. East Barnard. P.U. East
    Bethel. P.U. Hartland. P.U. Ludlow. P.U. Store. North Springfield. P.U. Nor-
    wich. P.U. (2). Plymouth. P.U. Pomfret. P.U. Reading. P.U. Store. Rochester.
    P.U. Royalton. P.U. Store. Sharon. P.U. Stockbridge. P.U. West Windsor. P.U.
    Weston. P.U. Windsor. P.U.

VIRGINIA

No county. Alexandria. BoU. Mt. Vernon, No.
Augusta Co., Staunton. BoU.
Dickenson Co., Lebanon. BoU.
Frederick Co., Winchester. BoU.
Henrico Co., Richmond. NR press notices of the Southerner.
Jefferson Co., Middleway. BoU.
Lockbridge Co., Middlebrook. BoU.
Tazewell Co., Jeffersonville. BoU.
Washington Co., Abingdon. BoU.
Wyethe Co., Wyetheville. BoU.

[WEST] VIRGINIA

Fayette Co., Mountain Cove. Mountain Cove Community.
Kanawawka Co., NR petn—U.S. Senate.
Ohio Co., South Wheeling. NR petn—U.S. Senate. Wheeling NR petn—U.S. Sen-
    ate.

WISCONSIN.

Gen. NR petns—U.S. Senate.
Brown Co., Green Bay (then Tanktown). Ephraim at Green Bay.
Crawford Co., Prairie du Chien. Circle of the BoU, apparently formed around the
    time of Lippard's death.
Dane Co., Middleton. NR petn—U.S. Senate.
Dodge Co., Lowell. NR petn—U.S. Senate. Mayville. NR petn—U.S. Senate.
Door Co., Ephraim. Ephraim Community.
Douglas Co., Black River. NR petns—U.S. Senate.
Fond du Lac Co., Ceresco, renamed Ripon. Wisconsin Phalanx. NR activities. NR
    petn—U.S. Senate. Waupun. NR petn—U.S. Senate,.
Grant Co., Hazel Green. BoU.
Green Lake Co., Marquette. NR petn—U.S. Senate.

Iowa Co., Mineral Point. NR activities.

Kenosha Co., Kenosha. NR activities.

Lafayette Co., Shellsburg. Res. BoU member.

Manitowoc Co., St. Nazianz. St. Nazianz Community.

Marquette Co., Parkwackee. NR petn—U.S. Senate.

Milwaukee Co., Milwaukee. NR activities. MMP. SRA. Arbnd. BoU. NR petns—U.S. Senate. Allied press: Wisconsin Free Democrat, Daily Life. North Prairie. Colony of Equality, or Hunt's Colony Owenite.

Racine (also Walworth) Cos., Burlington area. Voree, on the White River prairie. Rochester. MMP. Sheboygan area. Pigeon River Fourier Colony.

Rock Co., NR petn—U.S. Senate.

Sauk Co., Baraboo. NR petn—U.S. Senate.

Sheboygan Co., Mitchell. Spring Farm Phalanx.

Waugh Co., NR petn—U.S. Senate.

Waukesha Co., Mukwonago. NR activities. Utilitarian Association of United Interests Owenite. NR petns—U.S. Senate. BoU. Waukesha. BoU. NR petn—U.S. Senate.

APPENDIX B: THE NATIONAL INDUSTRIAL CONGRESSES

Table 1. Sessions

National Reform Convention	May 5–7, 1845	New York, Croton Hall
Owen's "World Congress"	October 1–5, 1845	New York, Clinton Hall
National Industrial Convention	October 14–16, 1845	New York, unspecified
National Industrial Congresses		
First Session	June 2[?]–8[?], 1846	Boston
Second Session	June 2–9, 1847	New York, Croton Hall and Newberry's Rooms
Third Session	June 7–15, 1848	Philadelphia, Willow Fisk Hall
Fourth Session	June 8?–?, 1849	Cincinnati, Franklin Hall
Fifth Session	June 2–9, 1850	Chicago, Delevan House and Ct. of Appeals
Sixth Session	June 4–10, 1851	Albany, Croton Hall
Seventh Session	June 2–7, 1852	Washington, Temperance Hall
Eighth Session	June 1–3, 1853	Wilmington, Rooms of the Brotherhood of Union
Ninth Session	June 7–9, 1854	Trenton, Temperance Hall
Tenth Session	June 6–7, 1855	Cleveland, Sons of Temperance Hall
Irregular Session	June 4–5, 1856	New York, Worster St. Convention Hall
Irregular Session	November 20–21, 1860	New York, Metropolitan Hotel

Table 2. States Represented at National Industrial Congresses, 1845–60

	'45 (NRA WC NI)	'46	'47	'48	'49	'50	'51	'52	'53	'54	'55	'56	'60
Conn.							X						
Maine													
Mass.	X	X	X	X			X	X	X	X			
N.H.													
R.I.			X				X	X					
Vt.							X						
N.J.			X	X			X	X		X			
N.Y.	X	X	X	X		X	X	X		X		X	X
Pa.	X		X	X	X		X	X	X	X	X	X	
Del.			X	X				X	X	X		X	
D.C.								X					
Ky.			X					X					
Md.			X	X									
Ill.			X			X		X					
Ind.													
Mich.													
Ohio					X	X	X					X	
Wis.						X	X						

APPENDIX C: NEW ENGLAND REGIONAL ASSOCIATIONS

APPENDIX D: NATIONAL REFORM
SONGS AND POEMS

THE AGRARIAN BALL

Tune: *Rosin the Bow,* also Hutchinson's family songs, *The Liberty Ball,*
and *Lincoln and Liberty, Too! Working Man's Advocate,* June 8, 1844.

Come, all you true friends of the Nation,
    Attend to humanity's call,
Come aid in our country's salvation,
    And roll on th' Agrarian Ball.

Ye Democrats come to the rescue,
    And help on the glorious cause.
And millions hereafter will bless you,
    With heart cheering song of applause.

Come, Whigs big adieu to hard cider,
    And boldly step into the ranks,
To spread the broad banner still wider,
    Upset all the rascally banks.

And when we have form'd the blest union,
    We'll firmly march on, one and all,
We'll shout when we meet in communion,
    And roll on th' Agrarian Ball.

The Agrarian army's advancing,
    The Monopoly of Land to destroy.
The glad eye of beauty is dancing,
    Her heart overflowing with joy.

How can you stand halting, while beauty
    Is sweetly appealing to all,
Then come to the standard of duty,
    And roll on th' Agrarian Ball.

THE FREEMAN'S SONG

> This midwestern version of "The Agrarian Ball" hopes not to "upset all
> the rascally banks," but solicits "all the friends of the Banks" to support
> land reform. From John Pickering, *The Working Man's Political Economy*
> (Cincinnati: Stereotyped in [Josiah] Warren's New Patent Method, by
> Thomas Varney, 1847), 194–95.

Come, all ye true friends of the nation,
    Attend to humanity's call;
Come aid in the domain's liberation,
    And roll on the Agrarian Ball.

The Agrarian hosts are advancing;
    The freedom of land they declare;
The down-trodden millions are crying,
    Come, break up our gloom of despair.

Ye Democrats, come to the rescue,
    And aid on the Agrarian cause.
And millions will rise up and bless you,
    With heart-cheering songs of applause.

Let Whiggery forsake its minions,
    And boldly step into our ranks;
We care not for party opinions;
    But invite all the friends of the Banks.

And when we have formed the blest union,
    We'll firmly march on, one and all,
We'll sing when we meet in communion,
    And roll on the Agrarian Ball.

The question of test is now turning,
    And free soil or monopoly must fall;
While hope in the bosom is burning,
    We'll roll on the Agrarian ball.

Ye freemen, attend to your voting;
    Your ballots will answer the call;
While others attend to log-rolling,
    We'll roll on the Agrarian ball.

"WAIT A LITTLE LONGER"

This is a different version of one the best Hutchinson's family songs.
From John Pickering, *The Working Man's Political Economy,* 199–200.

There's a good time coming, boys,
    A good time coming:
We may not live to see the day,
But earth shall glisten in the ray
    Of the good time coming.
Cannon balls may aid the truth,
    But thought's a weapon stronger;
We'll win our battles by its aid;—
    Wait a little longer.

There's a good time coming, boys,
    A good time coming:
The pen shall supercede the sword,
And right, not might, shall be the lord,
    In the good time coming:
Worth, not birth, shall rule mankind,
    And be acknowledged stronger,
The proper impulse has been given;—
    Wait a little longer.

There's a good time coming, boys,
    A good time coming:
War in all men's eyes shall be
A monster of iniquity,
    In the good time coming:
Nations shall not quarrel then,
    To prove which is the stronger;
Nor slaughter men for glory's sake;—
    Wait a little longer.

There's a good time coming, boys,
    A good time coming:
Hateful rivalries of creed
Shall not make their martyrs bleed.
    In the good time coming:
Religion shall be shorn of pride,
    And flourish all the stronger
    And Charity shall trim her lamp;—
    Wait a little longer.

There's a good time coming, boys,
    A good time coming:
And a poor man's family
Shall not be his misery,
    In the good time coming:
Every child shall be a help,
    To make his right arm stronger;
The happier he, the more he has;—
    Wait a little longer.

There's a good time coming, boys,
    A good time coming:
Little children shall not toil,
Under, or above, the soil,
    In the good time coming:
But shall play in healthful fields.
    Till limbs and minds grow stronger;
And every one shall read and write;—
    Wait a little longer.

There's a good time coming, boys,
    A good time coming:
The people shall be temperate,
And shall love, instead of hate,
    In the good time coming:
They shall use, and not abuse,
    And make all virtue stronger.
The reformation has begun;—
    Wait a little longer.

There's a good time coming, boys,
    A good time coming:
Let us aid it all we can,
Every woman, every man,
    The good time coming:
Smallest helps, if rightly given,
    Makes the impulse stronger;
'Twill be strong enough one day;—
    Wait a little longer.

KEEP IT BEFORE THE PEOPLE

From Augustine J. H. Duganne, *Poetical Words*, (Philadelphia: Parry and
McMillan, 1855), 148–49.

Keep it before the People —
 That the earth was made for man!
  That flowers were strown,
  And fruits were grown,
 To bless and never to ban;
  That sun and rain,
  And corn and grain,
 Are yours and mine, my brother!
  Free gifts from heaven,
  And freely given,
 To one as well as another!

Keep it before the People —
 That man is the image of God!
  His limbs or soul
  Ye may not control
 With shackle, or shame, or rod!
  We may not be sold,
  For silver or gold
 Neither you nor I, my brother!
  For Freedom was given,
  By God from heaven,
 To one as well as another!

Keep it before the People —
 That famine, and crime, and woe
  Forever abide,
  Still side by side,
 With luxury's dazzling show;
  That LAZARUS crawls
  From DIVES' halls,
 And starves at his gate, my brother!
  Yet Life was given,
  By GOD from heaven,
 To one as well as another!

Keep it before the People —
 That the laborer claims his meed
  The right of SOIL,
  And the right to toil,

From spur and bridle freed;
    The right to bear,
    And the right to share,
With you and me, my brother!
    Whatever is given,
    By GOD from heaven,
To one as well as another!

FREEDOM'S PIONEERS

Tune: *Auld Lang Syne.* From Lewis Masquerier, "Hymns for the Reconstruction of Society and Property," *Sociology* (New York: By the author, 1877), 173–74.

When slavery reached its greatest crimes,
    Developed yet on earth,
Men's hearts were melted at its woe,
    And brought forth Freedom's birth,
Then Thompson, Garrison and Jay,
    God-fathered the orphan child,
Baptized it in humanity,
    While servile mobs reviles

        Chorus:
        Let sentiments of gratitude,
            Swell every Freeman's breast,
        For those who broke the master's chains
            And unborn millions blest.

Then Adams, Giddings, Tappan, May,
    With Birney, Legget, Wright,
Became its guardians, and against
    Vile slavery braved the fight.
Then Johnson, Douglas, Smith and Brown,
    The weeping child wet-nursed,
As Whittier, Pierpont, and Clark
    Sung while the master cursed,

        Chorus . . .

Then Greeley, Philips, Cheever, Beecher,
    With Sumner and Goodell,
As tutors, taught the growing youth,
    That it could never dwell
In Peace with criminal slavery;
    Which will not legalize;

But tains like sheep-rot all the state,
    And masters demonize!

      Chorus . . .

O may all pioneers still learn,
    When chattel slaves are freed,
That afterwards another form
    Of slavery will succeed.
Unless an equal share of soil
    Is guaranteed to each
The hireling slave when labor gluts,
    Is in starvation's reach.

      Chorus . . .

THE AGRARIAN GATHERING

Tune: *Hunters of Kentucky.* From John Pickering, *The Working Man's Political Economy,* 205.

Hark! With a firm and manly tread
    The Agrarians are coming!
No cap and bells upon the head;
    No fiddling and no drumming:
To clownish antics to excite
    The jest of each derider,
As if they'd sunk their mankind quite
    In puncheons of hard cider.

No banners deck'd with thievish coons.
    Nor mottos foul and scurvy,
With decency, and common sense,
    And truth turned topsy-turvy;
But, marching with unbroken front,
    All resolute and steady,
They come, as they are ever wont,
    For TRUTH's stern battle ready.

A bit of tinsel on a rag,
    With fringe around the border,
Round which to gather, shout and brag,
    Is not the kind of order
For Agrarians to take, when they,
    Like reasoning men, assemble
But at their calm, resolved array
    Their direst foes must tremble.

They come! They come! In phalanx deep,
 Oppression's cohorts braving—,
Unbought, unterrified, they keep
 Their free bold banner waving;
They (as on Bunker's heights were stirred
 The stern sires that began them.)
Impatient wait the onset word
 Agrarians! Up, and at them!

Attune the chords of freedom's lyre,
 To bounding notes of gless:
And swell upon each buirning wire,
 The anthems of the free!
Strike! Strike again the notes of old,
 That swept these hills along!
Where freedom's sons her flag unrolled
 And shouted freedom's song!

Wake! Wake the tones of victory now,
 For freedom's hearts beat high!
And triumph sits on manhood's brow,
 And speaks from woman's eye.
The sun that rose in cloud and gloom,
 Now beams its radiance bright;
And in meridian splendor soon
 Shall blaze with freedom's light.

When slavery's night shall pass away,
 And wide o'er land and sea
Again on every breeze shall play
 The banner of the free!
Then tune the lyre—let music sweep
 Our hills and vales along!
While ocean's wave in gladness leap,
 And dance to freedom's song.

IN MEMORIAM

From Lewis Masquerier, "Miscellaneous Poems," *Sociology*, 195.

"To the memory of Capt. Benjamin Price, who rushed ahead of his
company at Wapping Heights, Va., and who was killed by a sharp-shooter
on July 23, 1863".

With saddened hearts his old free-homestead friends
    Deplore his country's and his mother's loss,
Struck down in manhood's prime by rebel fiends,
    Alas! How dear must freedom ever cost.

His brave, war-worn companion's tearful eyes
    Tell that his genial manners won each heart,
Tell that he never suffered wrath to rise
    And make a brother soldier's bosom smart.

He was one of the honest few who kenned
    That only homesteads guaranteed, can win
The rights of life and labor, and defend
    Mankind from pauperism, crime, and sin.

Rest, dear departed Ben! Thy short life ends,
But victories set free the rebel's slave,
    While wild-wood trees stand round as mourning friends,
And she morn's dew drops on thy lonely grave.

NOTES

ABBREVIATIONS

AF   *American Freeman,* (Mar. 6, 1844–Aug. 23, 1848), continuing the *Milwaukie Democrat,* and continued by the *Wisconsin Freeman* (Aug. 30, 1848–Nov. 29, 1848), and the *Wisconsin Free Democrat* (Dec. 6, 1848–1857?)

NAS   *National Anti-Slavery Standard*

NEI   *New Era of Industry* (June 2, 1848–Aug. 3, 1848), continuing the *Voice of Industry*

NYDyTrib   *New York Daily Tribune* (Aug. 1, 1842–)

PR   *The People's Rights,* published simultaneously with the *Workingman's Advocate* (June 12?–Aug ?, 1844)—v. 1, no. 19 (July 27, 1844), (numbers 18 and 19 are July 24, 27, 1844; a triweekly paper would have had no. 1 at June 12)

SuWmA   *Subterranean united with the Workingman's Advocate* (Oct. 12–Nov. 9, 1844), continuing the *Workingman's Advocate,* and continued by the *Subterranean and Workingman's Advocate*

SWmA   *Subterranean and Workingman's Advocate* (Nov. 15–Dec. 21, 1844), continuing the *Subterranean United with the Workingman's Advocate,* and continued by the *Workingman's Advocate*

VoI   *Voice of Industry* (May 29, 1845–Apr. 14, 1848), continued by the *New Era of Industry*

WF   *Wisconsin Freeman* (Aug. 30, 1848–Nov. 29, 1848), continuing the *American Freeman,* and continued by the *Wisconsin Free Democrat* (Dec. 6, 1848–1857?)

WFD   *Wisconsin Free Democrat* (Dec. 6, 1848–1857?), continuing the *Wisconsin Freeman*

WmA   *Workingman's Advocate* (Mar. 16–July 20, 1844, Aug. 3–Oct. 5, 1844, Dec. 28, 1844–Mar. 22, 1845), continued by the *Subterranean United with the Workingman's Advocate* and by *Young America*

YA   *Young America* (Mar. 29, 1845–1849?), continuing the *Workingman's Advocate*

INTRODUCTION

1. Bovay quoted in Frank A. Flower, *History of the Republican Party* (Springfield, Ill.: Union Publishing Co., 1884), 152. In "Manifesto of the Communist Party," Engels and Marx wrote, "Communists do not form a separate party opposed to other working-class parties," which they specifically identified as "the Chartists in England and the Agrarian Reformers in America." Parts 2 and 4 quoted in *Birth of the Communist Manifesto*, ed. Dirk J. Struik (New York: International Publ., 1971), 103, 124.

2. E. P. Thompson, *The Making of the English Working Class* (New York: Alfred A. Knopf, 1966). See also Martin J. Burke, *The Conundrum of Class: Public Discourse on the Social Order in America* (Chicago: University of Chicago Press, 1995).

3. Anthony Gronowicz, *Race and Class Politics in New York City before the Civil War* (Boston: Northeastern University Press, 1998), 139 and 256n37, taking issue with Sean Wilentz, *Chants Democratic! New York City and the Rise of the American Working Class, 1788–1850* (New York: Oxford University Press, 1984), on the grounds that Wilentz treated National Reformers and their contemporaries as generally an extension of the earlier, radical workers' movements of the 1820s and 1830s. Having blurred a very specific National Reform proposal into the assumed views of the immigrant working-class base of Tammany Hall, Gronowicz found confirmation in his racial approach in Iver Bernstein's *The New York City Draft Riots: The Significance for American Society and Politics in the Age of the Civil War* (New York: Oxford University Press, 1990), which proposed a kind of continuity from the NRA's workers' movement of 1850 to the Democratic Party and into the racist antidraft rioters of 1863.

4. H. H. Van Amringe quoted in *American Freeman*, Mar. 28, 1849.

5. Jamie L. Bronstein, *Land Reform and Working-Class Experience in Britain and the United States, 1800–1862* (Stanford, Calif.: Stanford University Press, 1999), 112–13, 135, which built upon Helene S. Zahler, *Eastern Workingmen and National Land Policy* (New York: Columbia University Press, 1941); see also Reeve Huston, *Land and Freedom: Rural Society, Popular Protest, and Party Politics in Antebellum New York* (New York: Oxford University Press, 2000). Bernard Mandel's *Labor: Free and Slave; Workingmen and the Anti-Slavery Movement in the United States* (New York: Associated Authors, 1954) made excellent points that became oddly unfashionable in the profession. As an early form of *Young America* circulated, many of the sources cited appeared in *Northern Labor and Antislavery: A Documentary History*, ed. Philip S. Foner and Herbert Shapiro (Westport, Conn.: Greenwood, 1994); though many are now digitally available, patient readers may find useful this jumbled compendium, in which Foner seems to have entirely reversed his earlier position.

6. In 1850, 1851, and 1852, the U.S. Congress received hundreds of documents with wording that rarely varied from the standard NRA memorial (including the call for limiting individual land ownership). The representatives of the people referred, ignored, and packed them away to gather dust for nearly a century, before landing in the National Archives. Each petition carried signatures numbering in the handful to the tens of thousands. Without a complete census, no accurate count is possible, but based on the large ones numbering in the thousands, the figure of quarter of a million represents a reasonable estimate.

7. Henry E. Hoagland, "Humanitarianism (1840–1860)," in John R. Commons, David J. Saposs, Helen L. Sumner, E. B. Mittleman, H. E. Hoagland, John B. Andrews,

and Selig Perlman, *History of Labour in the United States*, 4 vols., 2d ed. (New York: Macmillan, 1947), 1: 560n, citing *New York Herald*, July 16, 1850.

8. Evans, "National Reform Association," *WmA*, Mar. 22, 1845.

9. Thomas Ainge Devyr, "American Section" of *The Odd Book of the Nineteenth Century, or, "Chivalry" in Modern Days, a Personal Record of Reform—Chiefly Land Reform, for the Last Fifty Years* (New York: By the author, 1882), 39, 4; the British and American sections of Devyr's book are independently paged, but all references in this work will be to the latter unless otherwise indicated. For George W. Julian, see his *Political Recollections, 1840 to 1870* (Chicago: Jansen, McClurg and Co., 1884), 103, and his "The Spoilation of the Public Lands," *North American Review* 141 (Aug. 1885): 178–79.

CHAPTER 1: NATIONAL REFORM

1. See Walter Hugins, *Jacksonian Democracy and the Working Class: A Study of the New York Workingmen's Movement, 1829–1837* (Stanford, Calif.: Stanford University Press, 1960), 74–75; Wilentz, *Chants Democratic*, 224–25; Lewis Masquerier, *Sociology: or, The Reconstruction of Society, Government, and Property, upon the Principles of the Equality, the Perpetuity, and the Individuality of the Private Ownership of Life, Person, Government, Homestead, and the Whole Product of Labor. . . .* (New York: By the author, 1877), 106, 107; Albert Post, *Popular Freethought in America, 1825–1850* (New York: Columbia University Press, 1943), 20; Devyr, *Odd Book;* Philip Foner, *History of the Labor Movement in the United States: From Colonial Times to the Founding of the American Federation of Labor* (New York: International Publishers, 1947), 567; *A Documentary History of American Industrial Society,* eds. John R. Commons, Ulrich B. Phillips, Eugene A. Gilmore, Helen L. Sumner, and John B. Andrews, with pref. by Richard T. Ely and introd. by John B. Clark, 10 vols., 2d. ed. (Cleveland: A. H. Clark Co., 1910–11; repr., New York: Russell and Russell, 1958), 8: 305, 326 (hereafter cited as *Doc. Hist.*); George A. Stevens, *New York Typographical Union No. 6: Study of a Modern Trade Union* (Albany, N.Y.: State Department of Labor, 1913), 106; F[itzwilliam] Byrdsall, *The History of the Loco-Foco or Equal Rights Party, Its Movements, Conventions and Proceedings, with Short Characteristic Sketches of Its Prominent Men* (New York: Clement and Packard, 1842), 17, 20, 21, 37, 48, 61, 66, 88–89, 105–6, 146, 178, 179, 180–8. For Devyr, see also Gary M. Fink, ed., *Biographical Dictionary of American Labor Leaders* (Westport, Conn.: Greenwood Press, 1974), 78–79.

2. For a recent international and comparative approach, see Hugh McLeon, *Secularisation in Western Europe, 1848–1914* (New York: St. Martin's Press, 2000).

3. Murray N. Rothbard, *The Panic of 1819: Reactions and Policies* (New York: Columbia University Press, 1962), 142. See accounts of Owenism in David Harris, *Socialist Origins in the United States: American Forerunners of Marx, 1817–1837* (Assen, Neth.: Van Gorcum and Co., 1967), 10–19. A. J. G. Perkins and Teresa Wolfson, *Frances Wright: Free Enquirer* (New York: Harper and Bros., 1939); John F. C. Harrison, *Quest for the New Moral World: Robert Owen and the Owenites in Britain and America* (New York: Scribners, 1969). For a neglected predecessor, Ohioan John Cleves Symmes, as "Captain Adam Seaborn," see *Symzonia: Voyage of Discovery* (New York: Printed by J. Seymour for the author, 1820; Gainesville, Fla.: Scholars' Facsimiles and Reprints, 1965). The 1965 reprint has an introduction by J. O. Bailey.

4. Devyr, *Odd Book*, 115. See also "Complimentary Ball" [from *YA*], *VoI*, Mar. 12, 19, 1847; Masquerier, *Sociology*, 99; Byrdsall, *History of the Loco-Foco*, 14–15; Boston *Investigator*, quoted in Zahler, *Eastern Workingmen*, 39n.

5. Although virtually neglected given his importance, Evans has received some attention, including Newman Jeffrey, "The Social Origins of George Henry Evans, Workingman's Advocate" (master's thesis, Wayne State University, Detroit, 1960); Jeffrey J. Piz, "Bread Cast upon the Waters: The Efforts of George Henry Evans to Reform His America" (Ph.D. dissertation, University of Minnesota, 1998); and Jeffrey J. Piz, *The Life, Work, and Times of George Henry Evans, Newspaperman, Activist, and Reformer (1829–1849)* (Lewiston, N.Y.: Edwin Mellen Press, 2001); James S. Bradshaw, "George Henry Evans," in *American Newspaper Journalists, 1690–1872*, ed. Perry J. Ashley, vol. 43 of *Dictionary of Literary Biography* (Detroit: Gale Research Co., 1985), 184–88; and C. K. McFarland and Robert L. Thistlewaite, "20 Years of a Successful Labor Paper: The Working Man's Advocate, 1829–1849," *Journalism Quarterly* 60 (Winter 1983): 35–41; and Masquerier, *Sociology*, 93–99.

6. *WmA*, Jan. 4, 1845. Theophilus Eaton, a member of the New York Typographical Society made his proposal off-handedly in *Review of New-York, or, Rambles through the City* (New York: The author, 1813). For Eaton and the union memberships of Ithaca printers, Ebenezer Mack and Searing, see Mark A. Lause, *Some Degree of Power: From Hired Hand to Union Craftsman in the Preindustrial American Printing Trades, 1778–1815* (Fayetteville: University of Arkansas Press, 1991), 164–68, 187–88.

7. "Dialogue," *Museum and Independent Corrector*, May 14, 1824; "Journeymen Tailors," *Museum and Independent Corrector*, July 16, 1824.

8. Reports on Paine's birthday celebration can be followed through the *Correspondent*. For Evans on his living situation, see "Erratum," *YA*, Sept. 20, 1845.

9. Thomas Skidmore, *The Rights of Man to Property!* (New York: For the author by A. Ming, 1829); Hugins, *Jacksonian Democracy*, 24–25; Edward Pessen, *Most Uncommon Jacksonians: The Radical Leaders of the Early Labor Movement*, 2d ed. (Albany: State University of New York Press, 1970); Wilentz, *Chants Democratic;* Helen Sumner, "Citizenship (1827–1833)" in Commons et al., *History of Labour*, 1: 269–71.

10. Hugins, *Jacksonian Democracy*, 29–30; Pessen, *Most Uncommon Jacksonians*, 95–98; Wilentz, *Chants Democratic*, 292–94; Edward B. Mittelman, "Trade Unionism, (1833–1839)," in Commons et al., *History of Labour*, 1: 461–66. The elected officers of the mass meeting included former Workie Edward J. Webb and John Windt, the freethinker and president of the New York Typographical Association.

11. See the chapter on "The Trades' Union Movement" in Pessen, *Most Uncommon Jacksonians*, 34–51. For various views of Commerford, see *Biographical Dictionary of American Labor Leaders*, 64–65; Hugins, *Jacksonian Democracy*, 62, 72–74; Pessen, *Most Uncommon Jacksonians*, 97–98; Arthur M. Schlesinger Jr., *The Age of Jackson* (Boston: Little, Brown and Co., 1945), 258, 261, 261n, 407; Wilentz, *Chants Democratic*, 219–54, 255–96; Zahler, *Eastern Workingmen*, 103–4, 172n; Sumner, "Citizenship," 263–64; Mittelman, "Trade Unionism," 1: 335–56, 357–80, 381–423, 429, 434; Hoagland, "Humanitarianism," 1: 532; and Philip Foner, *History of the Labor Movement*, 130, 151.

12. For "The Workingmen as Locofocos," see the chapter of that title in Hugins, *Jacksonian Democracy*, 36–47.

13. Hugins, *Jacksonian Democracy*, 105–6, 90–91; Pessen, *Most Uncommon Jackso-*

nians, 95–97, 98; Wilentz, *Chants Democratic,* 292–94; Hoagland, "Humanitarianism," 1: 461–66; Byrdsall, *History of the Loco-Foco,* 99–113.

14. Byrdsall, *History of the Loco-Foco,* 99–113. Van Buren symbolically sealed the reassimilation of the Locofocos, attending the Bowery Theater with Alexander Ming and his wife. Schlesinger, *Age of Jackson,* 259.

15. "To My Old Friends," *The Radical* 1 (Jan. 1841): 15; Byrdsall, *History of the Loco-Foco,* 14–15, the latter including his description of Leggett as "truly the very Jove of editors, and all the fraternity stood in awe of him." On Evans in New Jersey, see "To the Public," *WmA,* Mar. 16, 1844, and "Dr. Jaques on Land Monopoly in 1835," *WmA,* July 20, 1844. On Jan. 22, 1833, Evans bought his farm from Thomas Truax. Deed Book C3, 176–77, Office of Surrogate, Hall of Records, Monmouth County, Freehold, N.J.

16. Hugins, *Jacksonian Democracy,* 95–96; James Grant Wilson and John Fiske, eds., *Appletons' Cyclopaedia of American Biography,* 7 vols. (New York: D. Appleton and Co., 1898–1900), 6: 225; Post, *Popular Freethought,* 157, 159; *The Radical* 1 (Feb. 1841): 32. Philadelphia freethinkers reprinted Dr. James Reynolds, *Equality; or, A History of Litchonia,* 2d ed. (Philadelphia: Liberal Union, 1837; repr., Philadelphia: Prime Press, 1947). See also Post, *Popular Freethought,* 163; George Henry Evans comment on "Sabbath Laws" [from *Brooklyn Star*], *YA,* Feb. 14, 1846. Among the other Moral Philanthropists were veteran freethinkers and reformers Thomas Herttell, Henry Fay, and John Frazee. Sometimes described as originating in 1841, the Mechanics Mutual Protection became public at Buffalo in 1843 and established about 120 affiliates over the next five years. *Doc. Hist.,* 8: 243–62; "Mechanic's Mutual Protections," *Mechanic's Advocate* 2 (May 27, 1848): 182; "Strikes for Wages—Mechanics Association," *Scientific American,* 5 (June 8, 1850): 301.

17. For political antislavery, see Aileen S. Kraditor, *Means and Ends in American Abolitionism: Garrison and His Critics on Strategy and Tactics, 1834–1850,* 2d ed. (New York: Vintage Books, 1969); Lewis Perry, *Radical Abolitionism: Anarchy and the Government of God in Antislavery Thought* (Ithaca, N.Y.: Cornell University Press, 1973); James Brewer Stewart, *Holy Warriors: The Abolitionists and American Slavery* (New York: Hill and Wang, 1976); Richard H. Sewell, *Ballots for Freedom: Antislavery Politics in the United States, 1837–1860* (New York: Oxford University Press, 1976); Vernon L. Volpe, *Forlorn Hope of Freedom: The Liberty Party in the Old Northwest, 1838–1848* (Kent, Ohio: Kent State University Press, 1990); and Ronald G. Walters, *The Antislavery Appeal: American Abolitionists After 1830* (Baltimore: Johns Hopkins University Press, 1976).

18. Carl J. Guarneri, *The Utopian Alternative: Fourierism in Nineteenth-Century America* (Ithaca, N.Y.: Cornell University Press, 1991), 25–32, 57; Albert Fein, "Fourierism in Nineteenth Century America: A Social and Environmental Perspective" in *France and North America: Utopias and Utopians,* ed. Mathe Allain (Lafayette: Center for Louisiana Studies, University of Southwestern Louisiana, 1978), 133–48; Vincent Prieur, "Unsyncretisme utopique: Le cas du Fourierisme Americain (1840–50)" in *1848: Les Utopismes Sociaux,* ed. John Bartier et al. (Paris: SEDES, 1981), 261–72; Robert S. Fogarty, *Dictionary of American Communal and Utopian History* (Westport, Conn.: Greenwood Press, 1980), 183. Among the other prominent Fourierists were Osborne Macdaniel, William Henry Channing, Charles A. Dana, and John Dwight.

19. David Montgomery, *Beyond Equality: Labor and the Radical Republicans,*

1862–1872, 2d ed. (Urbana: University of Illinois Press, 1981), 414; Guarneri, *Utopian Alternative*, 32–56; Francis Wayland Orvis, *A History of the Orvis Family in America* (Hackensack, N.J.: Orvis Co., 1922), 62, 64, 99; "Letter from John Orvis—Infamous Outrage," *Liberator,* Jan. 13, 1843, 8. See also Lawrence B. Goodheart, *Abolitionist, Actuary, Atheist: Elizur Wright and the Reform Impulse* (Kent, Ohio: Kent State University Press, 1990), which regrettably slighted his subject's "Philosophy of Labor" [from *Chronotype*], *AF,* Aug. 13, 25, 1846, and Sept. 1, 1846.

20. George Henry Evans, "To My Old Friends," *The Radical* 1 (Jan. 1841): 15. On Dec. 16, 1839, Evans bought what was known as Middle Island in the Waycake Creek for $20. Deed Book Y3, 293. Note the advertisement for "Vale's Globe and Transparent Celestial Sphere," *YA,* Jan. 10, 1846. For a clear portrait of Evans's life there, see Feb. 19–25, 1856, Inventories, Book U. Assessed at 12 cents per spine, the inventory totaled the value of his books as $51. For Evans as a trustee of the Middleton school, see Deed Book Z3, 340–41, and "Dr. Jaques," *WmA,* July 20, 1844. One room had a power press with inks, various cases of type and galleys, and an adjacent room held a small hand press for proof copies, as well as copperplate engravings of Voltaire, Paine, and freethinker Elihu Palmer.

21. For this and the next paragraph, see Malcolm J. Rohrbough, *The Land Office Business: The Settlement and Administration of American Public Lands, 1789–1837* (New York: Oxford University Press, 1968), and Daniel Feller, *The Public Lands in Jacksonian Politics* (Madison: University of Wisconsin Press, 1984). For a favorable look at the issue from a more elevated social rank, see "Rationale of Land Reform," *The United States Magazine, and Democratic Review* 26 (Feb. 1850): 124–32. For an important, though specialized, category of this discussion, see James Warren Oberly, *Sixty Million Acres: American Veterans and the Public Lands before the Civil War* (Kent, Ohio: Kent State University Press, 1990). Another of Paine's old friends, Albert Gallatin, served as secretary of the treasury during much of this early liberalizing of access to the land. The Pre-emption Act in 1841 gave the squatter an advantage in being able to purchase the land, and the Graduation Act of 1854 allowed for a price reduction of land unsold after thirty years.

22. Masquerier, *Sociology,* 21, 62; "To My Old Friends," *The Radical* 1 (Jan. 1841): 15; "Dr. Jaques," *WmA,* July 20, 1844; "Man's Inalienable Right to Land," *The Radical* 1 (Apr. 1841): 50–52 . W. Whipple's *National Reformer* of Philadelphia, founded in September 1838, was the organ of the American Moral Reform Society. For Evans's reflections on their experience, see his incomplete "History of the Origin and Progress of the Working Men's Party in New York," *The Radical* 2 (Jan., Feb. 1842; Feb., Apr. 1843): 1–16, 17–23, 33–44, 49–60; "To the Public," *WmA,* Mar. 16, 1844; "On the Death of Skidmore," *WmA,* June 29, 1844; "Explanation," *SWmA,* Nov. 16, 1844; and "Rise and Progress of Agrarianism," *YA,* Sept. 20, 1845. See also Bronstein's discussion of the distinctions between Evans and Skidmore, *Land Reform and Working-Class Experience,* 37–45, 120. For the roots of land reform in the Declaration of Independence, see John H. Klippart, *Brotherhood of the Union: Address Delivered at Freedom, Portage County, Ohio. At a Festival of the B.U. (H.F.) C.A. of Circle No. 10. —98.* (Cleveland: Printed by Sanford and Hayward, 1852), 6, 16.

23. "Tyler's Second Veto," *The Radical* 1 (Sept. 1841): 129–30.

24. Nick Salvatore makes this point in a later context in *Eugene V. Debs: Citizen and Socialist* (Urbana: University of Illinois Press, 1982), 19. See also Melvin Yazawa, *From*

Colonies to Commonwealth: Familial Ideology and the Beginnings of the American Republic (Baltimore: Johns Hopkins University Press, 1985).

25. "Working Men's Meeting," *WmA*, Mar. 18, 1844; Hoagland, "Humanitarianism," 1: 531; "Constitution" and "Pledge," *WmA*, Mar. 30, 1844, with a copy of the pledge in *Doc. Hist.*, 8: 312, and *Young America! Principles and Objects of the National Reform Association, or Agrarian League. By a member* (New York: [NRA], [1846?]), 10 (hereafter cited as *Principles*); Zahler, *Eastern Workingmen*, 41n; Masquerier, *Sociology*, 107. For Croton Hall, see I. N. Stokes, *The Iconography of Manhattan Island, 1498–1909*, 6 vols. (New York: Dodd, 1915–1928), 5: 1801; and Bronstein, *Land Reform and Working-Class Experience*, 142, and 15–16, which discussed origins. For later uses, see the "Amended Pledge" in "National Reform Association," *YA*, July 11, 1846. The Norfolk County NRA in Massachusetts adopted the same as an "Industrial Reform Pledge." *VoI*, Mar. 19, 1846. For later examples, see "National Reform Pledge," *YA*, Sept. 23, 1848, and *National Reform Almanac for 1849* (New York: Young America, 1848), 48. A statewide convention of New York Agrarians adopted the same as late as 1850, adding only a requirement to support also other measures "such only as will give strength to the fundamental reform—a Free Soil." "Albany State Industrial Convention," *NYDyTrib* Oct. 8, 1850, 6.

26. On Commerford, see his letter to Andrew Jackson, Apr. 1844, items 24960–24961, Papers of Andrew Jackson, reel 67, microfilm ed., Library of Congress, Washington, D.C., 1913. See also correspondence in the John Tyler Papers, 3 microfilm reels (Washington, D.C.: Library of Congress, 1958), particularly for Mike Walsh. These names reoccur in the reports of meetings reported from *WmA*, Mar. 16, 1844, to *YA*, May 10, 1845, usually under the title, "National Reform Association," but see also Zahler, *Eastern Workingmen*, 57n-58n; Byrdsall, *History of the Loco-Foco*, 37, 55, 178, 188, 111, as well as 109–11, 136–37, 138, 141; Hugins, *Jacksonian Democracy*, 91–92; and *Doc. Hist.*, 5: 228, 230, 261, 267, 270, 271, 274, 281–84, 294, 358, 6: 68, 69, 7: 26.

27. Masquerier, *Sociology*, 73, 97; as phonetic and spelling reformer, see 75, 125, and his "Autobiographical Sketch of the Life of Lewis Masquerier," in *Sociology*, 132–36; Joshua K. Ingalls, *Reminiscences of an Octogenarian in the Field of Industrial and Social Reform* (New York: M. L. Holbrook and Co., 1897), 25; and Stanley J. Kunitz and Howard Haycroft, eds., *American Authors, 1600–1900: A Biographical Dictionary of American Literature* (New York: H. W. Wilson Co., 1938), 513–14. For Masquerier and Barmby, see Carl Wittke, *Utopian Communist: A Biography of Wilhelm Weitling, Nineteenth Century Reformer* (Baton Rouge: Louisiana State University Press, 1950), 291–92. For Barmby and Spence, see Malcolm Chase, *"The Peoples" Farm: English Radical Agrarianism* (New York: Oxford University Press, 1988), 135–36. For Spence's original, see *The Real Rights of Man: A Lecture Delivered at Newcastle-on-Tyne [1775]*, in *The Pioneers of Land Reform: Thomas Spence, William Ogilvie, Thomas Paine*, ed. Max Beer (London: G. Bell and Sons, 1920), 5–34.

28. On Mackenzie, see Devyr, *Odd Book*, 78n. For Beeny, see *Doc. Hist.*, 6: 68, 69. For Bovay, see *The History of Fond du Lac County, Wisconsin* (Chicago: Western Historical Company, 1880), 886 and Zahler, *Eastern Workingmen*, 63n.

29. "Our Cause and Our Paper," *WmA*, Apr. 27, 1844; Bronstein, *Land Reform and Working-Class Experience*, 133–34. On the building, see Masquerier, *Sociology*, 95.

30. Outgoing officers announced an upcoming election in three consecutive general meetings and published notices in at least three newspapers. Appointed wardens then

called meetings in as many wards as possible in the city and Brooklyn and at Williamsburg and Jersey City; any meeting of twenty-four members elsewhere could also elect a delegate. See also "Nomination Meeting," *WmA*, Sept. 9, 1844, and Devyr, *Odd Book*, 41. The later emergence of annual industrial congresses blurred the role of the NRA's leadership bodies.

31. Masquerier, *Sociology*, 95–96. For the "Republican Banner," see "Out Door Meeting," *YA*, June 14, 1845; Zahler, *Eastern Workingmen*, 41–42. For the ladies' auxiliary, see "Eighth and Ninth Out-Door Meetings," *WmA*, July 20, 1844. For Laura Evans, see Masquerier, *Sociology*, 102, 103. For the flag, see "Eighth and Ninth Out-Door Meetings," *WmA*, July 20, 1844. See also the accounts of meetings in *WmA*, Apr. 13 and June 8 through Oct. 15, 1844. Many of these are also cited in Zahler, *Eastern Workingmen*, 58n, 58–59, and Bronstein, *Land Reform and Working-Class Experience*, 142–43, who correctly emphasized this as an early battle over public space. Local Democrats still called themselves "Democratic-Republicans" and even "the Republican Party" as late as 1837. Untitled notice, *SuWmA*, Oct. 19, 1844.

32. "Fourth Out-Door Meeting," *WmA*, June 29, 1844, and July 6, 1844; "National Reform Association," *SWmA*, Nov. 23, 1844; "National Reform Association," *YA*, Jan. 3, 1846.

33. For the Fourth of July report, see *Doc. Hist.*, 7: 293–305; Masquerier, *Sociology*, 95; "Memorial to Congress," *WmA*, Apr. 20, 1844, June 29, 1844, also in *Doc. Hist.*, 7: 317–20.

CHAPTER 2: WORKING-CLASS ANTIMONOPOLY AND
LAND MONOPOLY

1. Evans quoted in "Agrarian League," *WmA*, June 1, 1844; Bovay quoted in "Emigration to Oregon," *WmA*, Dec. 28, 1844.

2. Quoted in Robert Ernst, "The One and Only Mike Walsh," *New York Historical Society Quarterly* 36 (Jan. 1952): 44, 49; see also 43–46. Alexander Saxton, "George Wilkes: The Transformation of a Radical Ideology," *American Quarterly* 33 (Fall 1981): 439; see also 437–38. The Subterranean was the saloon of their friend David Broderick.

3. Ernst, "One and Only Mike Walsh," 46–47; Zahler, *Eastern Workingmen*, 42–43; Hoagland, "Humanitarianism," 1: 538–29.

4. See Marvin E. Gittleman, *The Dorr Rebellion: A Study in American Radicalism, 1833–1849* (New York: Random House, 1973), 18, 19–21, 34, 53; George M. Dennison, *Dorr War: Republicanism on Trial, 1831–1861* (Lexington: University Press of Kentucky, 1976), 43–44; Devyr, *Odd Book*, 98–99; Jacob Frieze, *Facts for the People: Containing Comparisons and Exposition of Votes on Occasions Relating to the Free Suffrage Movements in Rhode Island* (Providence: Printed by Knowles and Vose, 1842); and Charles R. Crowe, "Utopian Socialism in Rhode Island, 1845–1850," *Rhode Island History* 18 (Jan. 1959): 20–26.

5. Dennison, *Dorr War*, 85–86, 107–9.

6. Gittleman, *Dorr Rebellion*, 144n, speculates about the NRA's involvement; see also 168, 168n, 169, 169n, 181–82; "Great Texas Meeting in the Park—Freedom of the Public Lands," *WmA*, Apr. 20, 1844; "Out-Door Meetings," *WmA*, July 6, 1844. See also "Liberation of Gov. Dorr," *PR*, July 27, 1844; Pittsburgh's "Great Meeting,"

WmA, Sept. 21, 1844; "The Rhode Island Question in Missouri," *WmA*, Sept. 28, 1844; "Mr. Treadwell," *WmA*, Oct. 5, 1844; "Gov. Dorr," *SWmA*, Dec. 21, 1844. Dennison, *Dorr War*, focuses on the constitutional questions posed by the "treason" of Dorr and discusses the legal questions, 148–68, 169–92.

7. Huston, *Land and Freedom*, for Devyr, see 138–40, 163–64, and for Boughton, see 100–1, 116, 164; Henry Christman, *Tin Horns and Calico: An Episode in the Emergence of American Democracy*, 2d ed. (New York: Collier Books, 1961), 65–68.

8. "Constitution," *WmA*, Mar. 30, 1844; "Sketches of Speeches at the National Reform Meeting," *WmA*, June 22, 1844; "Cordwainers' Meeting," *WmA*, June 29, 1844; "National Reform Association," *WmA*, Aug. 17, 1844. See also "Circular of the Mechanics of New England" [from *Fall River Mechanic*] in both *WmA*, June 29, 1844, and *PR*, Aug. 10, 1844; "New England Convention," *PR*, July 20, 1844.

9. Zahler, *Eastern Workingmen*, 59–60; Devyr, *Odd Book*, 41.

10. "Speech of Mike Walsh" [from *Boston Bee*] in *SuWmA*, Nov. 2, 1844. Evans quoted in "Trade Associations," *SWmA*, Nov. 23, 1844, and in "The Ten Hour System," *YA*, July 11, 1846. *Investigator* quoted in *SuWmA*, Oct. 26, 1844. For a thoughtful appraisal of the importance of this issue in labor history, see David R. Roediger and Philip S. Foner, *Our Own Time: A History of American Labor and the Working Day* (New York: Verso, 1989).

11. On Pittsburgh, see "National Reform Association," *WmA*, Dec. 7, 1844; untitled letter from John Ferral, *VoI*, Jan. 9, 1846; and Zahler, *Eastern Workingmen*, 44, 56n. For Columbus, see E. O. Randall, "'Land Bill' Allen," *Ohio Archaeological and Historical Publications* 10 (July 1901): 98–101; "Agrarian Candidate for Congress" [from *Columbus Old School Republican*], *WmA*, Aug. 3, 1844; the single manuscript [1884] "~'Land Bill' Allen," George W. Allen Papers, Ohio Historical Society, Columbus; excerpt from *Whig Battering Ram*, *WmA*, Sept. 14, 1844; and "Allen Land Bill Triumphant" with "Second National Reform Victory!!" *YA*, Apr. 19, 1845. Evans used the *Ohio State Tribune* for his stories in *YA* on Columbus: "Mechanics and Laborer's Meeting," July 12, 1845; "Organization at Columbus," July 19, 1845; "Allen's Land Bill Triumphant," Apr. 19, 1845; "Mr. Allen's Address," Apr. 26, 1845; "Land Monopoly," Aug. 2, 1845; and "Free Soil Meeting," Jan. 24, 1846. *Principles*, 13, and *Jubilee* (New York: [NRA], 1845, 13, also quoted from *Ohio State Tribune*. On Columbus NRA by the fall, see *Doc. Hist.*, 8: 26; *Jubilee*, 16; its questioning of candidates and survival into the next year, *YA*, Oct. 4, 1845; and "Ohio Is Coming!" Jan. 3, 1846. For Peoria, see letters in "Illinois," *WmA*, Feb. 1, 1845; "Plain Talk of an Illinois Farmer," *YA*, Apr. 12, 1845; "A Free Soil—Progress of the Cause," *YA*, Apr. 12, 1845, announcing a local NRA; Root letter supporting Antirentism, Nov. 15, 1845, "Reform" [from *Peoria Register*, Apr. 17, 1845]. For further references on the Peoria group, see "H. H. Van Amringe's Mission" in *YA*, Apr. 29, 1848, July 5, 1845, and in *Jubilee*, 16. See also "Public Meeting," *Peoria Democratic Press*, Feb. 12, 1845; Jeriel Root, *Analysis of Theology, Law, Religion and the Rights of Man* (Peoria: Benjamin Foster, 1855), 50–54; and *History of Peoria County*, ed. David McCulloch, vol. 2, *Historical Encyclopedia of Illinois*, eds. Newton Bateman and Paul Selby, (Chicago: Munsell, 1902), 289.

12. "Public Baths—Public Halls—Barbarous Proceedings," *WmA*, July 27, 1844; "Industrial Congress—Its Laws &c." *VoI*, June 19, 1846. See also "City Reform," *WmA*, Mar. 30, 1844, and June 8, 1844; and "Corporation Rascality," *SuWmA*, Nov. 2, 1844. For the NRA demands, see Zahler, *Eastern Workingmen*, 82n.

13. "National Reform Association," *WmA*, Sept. 21, 1844.

14. In addition to "Constitution," *WmA*, Mar. 30, 1844, for memorials, see *WmA*, Apr. 27, 1844, and June 8, 1844; *SWmA*, Nov. 30, 1844, and Dec. 7, 14, 21, 1844; *Principles*, 15–16; and the gold memorial in "Young Men's Ball," *VoI*, Jan. 8, 1847. For a model bill [from *Young America*], see *NYTrib*, Jan. 22, 1847, as well as *National Reform Almanac for 1849*, 31–32. For the questioning of the 1844 candidates, see Zahler, *Eastern Workingmen*, 94, 94n, 95, 95n; "Answers of Presidential Candidates," *WmA*, Aug. 3, 1844; "Mr. Birney's Letter" and "Rejoinder to Gerrit Smith," *PR*, July 27, 1844; "Second Letter from Gerrit Smith," *WmA*, Aug. 10, 1844; Byrdsall to Calhoun, Aug. 2, 1842, Robert L. Meriwether and Clyde N. Wilson, eds., *The Papers of John C. Calhoun*, 20 vols. (Columbia: University of South Carolina Press), 16: 421–22, and Byrdsall's letters of Oct. 11, 1842, 491–92, and Nov. 6, 1842, 530–31. See also the clippings and reports to Calhoun on developments at New York, 397–98, 402–7, 445–46, 468, 560–63 657–50. For Byrdsall, see Hugins, *Jacksonian Democracy*, 90, and for his Southern nativity, see the Federal Census of 1850 for the Eighth Ward, New York City, 124; Devyr, *Odd Book*, 117, 113; Byrdsall to Calhoun, Mar. 18, 1844, Aug. 25, 1844, Dec. 2, 1844, *Papers of John C. Calhoun*, 18: 375–77, 19: 660–61, 20: 441–43. Another veteran of the Locofocos, Daniel A. Robertson, did get his reward, becoming U.S. Marshal for Ohio, a post he held until moving on to the same office at St. Paul, Minnesota Territory.

15. Commerford to Calhoun, June 12, 1844, *Papers of John C. Calhoun*, 19: 22–23. For Evans on Moore's "Calhouniana," see *The Man*, June 26, 1834, 1.

16. Mike Walsh, "Challenge" [from *Subterranean*], "Spartan Band," *WmA*, Sept. 21, 28, 1844; Mike Walsh, "Spartan Doctrine," *SuWma*, Oct. 12, 1844; "Great Meeting of the Spartan Band," *SuWmA*, Nov. 2, 1844. For the involvement of NRA members in Democratic rallies and meetings, see *Daily Plebeian*, Sept. 19, 1844 (Daniel Witter, David Kilmer and Henry Beeny), Oct. 29, 1844 (J. D. Pierson and Edward O'Connor), and Oct. 31, 1844 (Henry Arcularius and Robert Beatty). See also "Protection to American Labor," *Daily Plebeian*, Aug. 23, 1844; "Who Are the Friends of Protection," *Daily Plebeian*, Aug. 27, 1844; Central Committee of the NRA to James Knox Polk, Apr. 20, 1844, Papers of James Knox Polk, microfilm ed. (Washington, D.C.: Library of Congress, 1954), reel 25. The newly elected Central Committee sent another copy of the memorial to Polk on June 1 (reel 26).

17. "Ely Moore," *PR*, July 20, 1844; "The Election—Glorious Victory of the National Reformers," *SuWmA*, Nov. 9, 1844. See also Culver H. Smith, *The Press, Politics, and Patronage: The American Government's Use of Newspapers, 1789–1875* (Athens: University of Georgia Press, 1977); William Gienapp, Thomas B. Alexander, Michael Holt, Stephen Maizlish, and Joel H. Sibley, *Essays on American Antebellum Politics, 1840–1860* (College Station: University of Texas at Arlington, by Texas A&M University Press, 1982); and Howard W. Allen and Kay Warren Allen, "Vote Fraud and Data Validity," in *Analyzing Electoral History: A Guide to the Study of American Voting Behavior*, ed. Jerome M. Clubb, William H. Flanigan and Nancy H. Zingate (Beverly Hills, Calif.: Sage Publications, 1981).

18. With no real explanation, Walsh severed ties to the NRA and extricated his *Subterranean* from the merged paper. Hoagland, "Humanitarianism," 1: 530; Zahler, *Eastern Workingmen*, 37; "The New Administration," *SuWmA*, Nov. 9, 1844. Ernst suggested that his long articles created editorial tensions with experienced newspaper editors like Evans. "One and Only Mike Walsh," 51.

19. "The Central Committee," *WmA*, Jan. 11, 1845; "Circular to the Trades," *WmA*, Mar. 1, 1845; discussions of several meetings in "National Reform Association," *WmA*, Mar. 8, 15, 22, 1845; Commerford discussed in "National Reform Association—Public Meeting," *WmA*, Apr. 13, 1844; "Cordwainers' Meeting," *WmA*, June 29, 1844; "The Tailors," *WmA*, Aug. 3, 1844; "Organization of Segar Makers," *YA*, June 21, 1845. For shoemakers, see *Doc. Hist.*, 7: 307–10. See also the remarks of Pearson, "National Reform Association," *YA*, July 5, 1845.

20. For the "several ladies" in attendance, see "National Reform Association," *WmA*, Aug. 10, 1844; "Constitution of the Industrial Congress," *YA*, Oct. 25, 1845; *George Lippard, Prophet of Protest: Writings of an American Radical*, ed. David Reynolds (New York: P. Lang, 1986), 215–17; "Meeting of the Female Industry Association in the City Hall, Yesterday," "The Working Woman and the Press," *WmA*, Mar. 1, 1845; "To the Working Women of New York," and "Female Industrial Association," *WmA*, Mar. 15, 1845.

21. "Great Public Meeting," *WmA*, Jan. 4, 1845; Christman, *Tin Horns*, 124–28, 131–32, 135–42, 145–47, 164, 166–67. A noteworthy exception, Rev. Hezekiah Pettit, a Baptist minister of "more than forty years," spoke out in Greene County. For mobilization of troops, see 129–31, 133–36. Two additional studies of antirentism have been very significant: Huston, *Land and Freedom,* and Jonathon Halperin Earle, "Undaunted Democracy: Jacksonian Anti-slavery and Free Soil, 1828–1848" (Ph.D. diss., Princeton University, 1996).

22. Christman, *Tin Horns*, 133, 143–44, 147–62, 165–66, 169–70. Only five members of the assembly voted against the resolutions. Devyr, *Odd Book,* 99–100. Devyr built a network of Antirenters sympathetic to the NRA, including Amos Loper, David Sternberg, Van Dusen [also Van Deusen], and Scott; in his visits to Rensalaerville, Livingstonville, Preston Hollow, Coopersburg, and New Scotland, he won John J. Gallup, Maj. Joseph Conner, Valentine Treadwell and other local leaders to the NRA. Jonathan Allaben, John Evans, and Calvin Pepper were associated with NRA activities upstate. Huston found that NRA supporters among the upstate Antirenters tended to be landowners but with smaller holdings than those not supporting the NRA. Huston, *Land and Freedom,* 228.

23. Bovay, "Mr. Bovay's Mission to the Anti-Renters: Letter IV," *YA*, Aug. 30, 1845, also quoted in Christman, *Tin Horns,* 185.

24. Tomlinson quoted "The Land! The Land! The Land!" *YA*, Nov. 22, 1845; Masquerier to the Varneys, a manuscript collection filed in the John A. Lant Papers, Missouri Historical Society, St. Louis (hereafter cited as Lant Papers); Robert Owen, "On the Formation of Rational Communities" [from *New Moral World*], *WmA*, July 20, 1844; "Robert Owen," *WmA*, Sept. 21, 1844; "Mr. Owen's Lectures," *YA*, Mar. 29, 1845. Greeley and Vale noted the publication of the *Memoir of Robert Owen* [from *NYWklyTrib*], *Independent Beacon* 1 (June 1851): 709–14. For Harmon, see "The Homestead" [*Portage Sentinel*], *YA*, Jan. 31, 1846.

25. John R. Smith, "Views of the Socialists," *WmA*, Mar. 1, 1845; "Marlborough Community" [from *Cleveland Plaindealer*], *WmA*, July 27, 1844. For Murray, see "Storm on Lake Erie," *SuWmA*, Nov. 2, 1844, and John O. Wattles's letter on Prairie Home [from *Urbana Citizen*], *SWmA*, Nov. 23, 1844, and Nov. 30, 1844; see also "Letter from John O. Wattles," *VoI*, July 3, 1846; and Wattles's letter, *National Reform Almanac for 1848*, cited in the *National Reform Almanac for 1849,* 47. For activities

in other midwestern communities, see "The Fighting Family," *WmA*, Aug. 31, 1844; Valentine Nicholson, "'Prairie Home' Community" [*Urbana Citizen*], and Miranda B. Randall, "Skaneateles Community," *SWmA*, Nov. 23, 1844; "The Fighting Family, No. 1," *WmA*, Sept. 7, 1844; untitled letter, *WmA*, Dec. 28, 1844; Mary Loomis, "An Appeal" [from *Communitist*], *YA*, Nov. 1, 1845, and on the Alphadelphia Phalanx in Michigan, *YA*, Nov. 8, 1845. Excerpts from Etienne Cabet's *Le Populaire* and stories on his Icarian movements, "The Emmigration of French Communists to the United States" [from *Herald*], *VoI*, Sept. 10, 1847; notice on the Icarians, *Independence Beacon* 1 (Dec., 1850): 543; "Association in Ontario Co., N.Y.," *Harbinger* 1 (Sept. 27, 1845): 247; Fourierists responded to criticisms at Boston meeting at Hall No. 1 and at Marlboro chapel in "Associationists Attend!" *VoI*, Sept. 4, 1846, and Sept. 18, 1846. See Evans on socialists in *WmA*, July 20, 1844, and "Social System" [from *Radical*], *Diamond*, second series, 2 (Dec. 1841): 69. For Evans on Associationists, see *WmA*, July 21, 1844, and Devyr, *Odd Book*, 151; "Robert Owen," *WmA*, Sept. 21, 1844; "Promisewell Community," *WmA*, Dec. 7, 1844; "First National Reform Movement of Newark," *WmA*, Feb. 22, 1845; "Association," *YA*, Apr. 19, 1845. For Jonas Humbert Jr., see Hugins, *Jacksonian Democracy*, 58n, 258.

26. "Skaneateles Community," *SWmA*, Dec. 21, 1844; "Skaneateles Laboring Man's Political Reform Association," *YA*, May 17, 1845; Collins at the conventions discussed, *YA*, Nov. 1, 1845; untitled letter from Richmond, *YA*, Jan. 31, 1846; "P.H.S.," "Symptoms of Progress," *YA*, Feb. 21, 1846; "A. G. S." [from Hopedale], *VoI*, Mar. 26, 1847. For Collins, see John L. Thomas, "Antislavery and Utopia," in *The Antislavery Vanguard: New Essays on the Abolitionists*, ed. Martin Duberman (Princeton, N.J.: Princeton University Press, 1966), 254–59. See also Devyr, *Odd Book*, on the Zoar community, xii; Jaques, "Propositions of Reform—Letter from Dr. Jaques," *YA*, Oct. 11, 1845; *WmA*, July 6, 1844, and Aug. 24, 1844. The author of the first letter may have been S. C. Frey; H. H. Van Amringe, the Pittsburgh Fourierist spokesman; or Elias Longley, the language reformer who had ties to virtually every reform in that part of the Midwest. See also "To the Congress," *SWmA*, Nov. 30, 1844; "A John-the-Baptist Revolution" by "A Revolutionist" [from *Social Reformer*], *WmA*, Jan. 11, 1845; J. M., "Right to Soil—Public Lands" [from *Communitist*], *YA*, Feb. 21, 1846.

27. "German National Reform Meeting," *YA*, Nov. 8, 1845; "Great Social Reform Meeting," *YA*, Jan. 10, 1846; "The Fraternal Democrats" [from *Northern Star*], July 11, 1846; *Doc. Hist.*, 7: 310–12. Bruce Levine provided a long-needed new perspective in *The Spirit of 1848: German Immigrants, Labor Conflicts, and the Coming of the Civil War* (Urbana: University of Illinois Press, 1992), 104–6, 114–16. For an interesting early appearance, see "Molly Maguire," *YA*, Dec. 20, 1845, and "Take Warning" [from *Northern Star*], *YA*, Dec. 27, 1845.

28. Bovay quoted in "The World's Convention," *NYDyTrib*, Oct. 6, 1845; Devyr, *Odd Book*, 99; Brisbane's initial letter, "National Reform Association," [from *NYTrib*, Aug. 22, 1844], *WmA*, Aug. 24, 1844. Commerford quoted in *WmA*, Aug. 31, 1844; "Communities," *WmA*, Aug. 31, 1844; *SWmA*, Nov. 30, 1844; Warden and Gregory mentioned in *SWmA*, Apr. 6, 1844, and in "Association," *Independent Beacon* 1 (Nov. 1849): 129–33, 161–67. When Joshua K. Ingalls later joined the NRA, he met Greeley, George Ripley, Parke Godwin, Brisbane, Warren B. Chase, Benjamin Urner, John G. Drew, D. Munday, and Charles Sears, as well as Stephen Pearl Andrews. Ingalls, *Reminiscences of an Octogenarian*, 52, 53, 54, 153.

29. Edwin C. Rozwenc, *Cooperatives Come to America: The History of the Protective Union Store Movement, 1845–1867*, 2d ed. (Philadelphia: Porcupine Press, 1975), 12–13, 15, 21–23; *Investigator*, Sept. 25, 1844, 19–21, 24; Warren B. Chase, "Protective Unions," *WFD*, May 9, 1849; "Convention of the New England Fourier Society," *Phalanx*, Feb. 8, 1845, 309–17; Zahler, *Eastern Workingmen*, 53f, 72–73, 73n; Bronstein, *Land Reform and Working-Class Experience*, 100–3. See also Sterling F. Delano, *The "Harbinger" and New England Transcendentalism: a Portrait of Associationism in America* (Rutherford, N.J.: Fairleigh Dickinson University Press, 1983), 51–52, 159n53. Among the neglected localized rebellions with Agrarian implications, see Daniel Doan, *Indian Stream Republic: Settling a New England Frontier*, ed. Ruth Doan MacDougall, Introduction and Afterword by Jere R. Daniell (Hanover, N.H.: University Press of New England, 1997).

30. On Godwin, see "Meeting of the National Reform Association," *SWmA*, Nov. 30, 1844; *SWmA*, Nov. 23, 1844, and Jan. 11, 1845. For Ryckman, see *YA*, Dec. 6, 1845, and Bronstein, *Land Reform and Working-Class Experience*, 103; For Ryckman's tour, see *WmA*, Feb. 28, 1845, and Mar. 7, 1845; Zahler, *Eastern Workingmen*, 46n, 54, 61, 61n. For some of Ripley's course, see Joel Myerson, "New Light on George Ripley and the *Harbinger*'s New York Years," *Harvard Library Bulletin*, 33 (Summer 1985): 313–36. Sources do not sustain the inference of factional NRA takeover of the Fourierist movement by the NRA, most clearly posited by Norman Ware, *The Industrial Worker, 1840–1850: the Reaction of American Industrial Society to the Advance of the Industrial Revolution* (Boston: Houghton Mifflin, 1924). Brisbane's course can be traced through the meetings reported in the *WmA* and *YA*, "Mr. Brisbane," Feb. 14, 1846, participation in meetings Dec. 6, 13, 20, 1845, and in "National Reform Association," Feb. 7, 14, 1846. While in the country, Brisbane remained active on the movement's behalf, touring Genessee County in 1846. *YA*, Mar. 7, 1846. "Charter Election" and "Candidate for Mayor," *WmA*, Feb. 22, 1845, and Mar. 22, 1845, and articles from *YA*—"For Mayor," Mar. 29, 1845; "The Mayoralty" and an untitled letter from Ransom Smith, Apr. 6, 1845; "The Election," Apr. 12, 19, 1845; with regular meetings reported under "National Reform Association," Sept. 27, 1845, and Oct. 4, 1845, and Jan. 3, 24, 1846. For his first vote, see "Mr. Brisbane," *YA*, Feb. 14, 1846. See also Stokes, *Iconography of Manhattan Island*, 5: 1789; Edward K. Spann, *The New Metropolis: New York City, 1840–1857* (New York: Columbia University Press, 1981), 429. On the tensions between nonpartisanship and independent political action, see Zahler, *Eastern Workingmen*, 82, 82n, 103–5, and Bronstein, *Land Reform and Working-Class Experience*, 148–49.

31. Quoted in Zahler, *Eastern Workingmen*, 61, 62–63, 63n.

32. "National Reform Association" [from *Awl*], *YA*, May 3, 1845; "National Reform Convention" and "The Convention—An Industrial Congress," *YA*, May 10, 1845; *New York Herald*, May 7, 1845 cited in Zahler, *Eastern Workingmen*, 62, 62n. See also Evans editorial endorsement of the project in *YA*, June 7, 1845.

33. Rozwenc, *Cooperatives Come to America*, 28–29; Lewis Ryckman, "Union of Reformers," *Harbinger* 1 (Aug. 9, 23, 1845; Sept. 27, 1845): 135, 169–70, 245–47; Zahler, *Eastern Workingmen*, 64–65; Jama Lazerow, "Religion and Labor Reform in Antebellum America: The World of William Field Young," *American Quarterly* 38 (Summer 1986): 265–86.

34. "National Reform Association," *SuWmA*, Oct. 26, 1844; Moses Jaques, "Propositions of Reform," *YA*, Oct. 11, 1845.

CHAPTER 3: A JOHN-THE-BAPTIST WORK

1. "National Reform Association," in both *WmA*, Feb. 7, 1845, and *YA*, Dec. 13, 1845. Brisbane's presence also mentioned in "National Reform Association," Dec. 20, 1845; Feb. 7, 14, 1846; and Mar. 7, 1846. Fourteenth Ward NRA met regularly at the Protective Union building. *YA*, Sept. 23, 1848. See also Zahler, *Eastern Workingmen*, 53–54, 61–63.

2. "National Reform Convention," *YA*, May 10, 1845; "Anniversary Week," *Broadway Journal*, 1 (May 10, 1845): 300; "The World's Convention," *NYDyTrib*, Oct. 2, 3, 4, 6, 7, 1845; Zahler, *Eastern Workingmen*, 55. Note this is the same reference as "Principles of Government" advocated at "the World's Convention held in New York in 1846," *National Reform Almanac for 1849*, 37–38. For Bovay and the "Vote Yourself a Farm" leaflet, see *YA*, Oct. 4, 1845, and *Doc. Hist.*, 7: 305–7; Zahler, *Eastern Workingmen*, 45, 55n; *Appletons' Cyclopaedia of American Biography*, 2: 207–8; and "The World's Convention," *NYDyTrib*, Oct. 6, 1845. See also "The World's Convention," *NYDyTrib*, Oct. 2, 3, 4, 5, 6, 7, 1845; Whitman, "Quixotic Labors," *Brooklyn Daily Eagle*, June 6, 1846, in Thomas L. Brasher, *Whitman as Editor of the Brooklyn Daily Eagle* (Detroit: Wayne State University, 1970), 138–39. For NRA reactions to increasingly favorable coverage by Whitman, see "National Reform Association," *WmA*, June 14, 1844, and Jan. 11, 1845.

3. "National Reform in Pennsylvania," *YA*, Sept. 27, 1845. The conference is covered in "Industrial Convention," *YA*, October 18, 1845; "Address of Mr. Wait of Ill." and "Constitution of the Industrial Congress," *YA*, Oct. 25, 1845; Zahler, *Eastern Workingmen*, 65–66, 66n; and *Doc. Hist.*, 8: 26–27. For Wait's earlier activities, see Bateman and Selby, *Historical Encyclopedia of Illinois*, 547, and Jean M. Maire, *History of Bond and Montgomery Counties Illinois*, ed. William Henry Perrin (Chicago: Munsell Pub. Co., 1882), 68, with many of his local activities appearing in the *Springfield State Journal;* Wait quoted in Schlesinger, *Age of Jackson*, 149n. Wait's became "one of the largest apple orchards in the State," and he achieved a net worth of $20,000 by midcentury but remained an active reformer. *Doc. Hist.*, 8: 21, 26, 27. At the time unconvinced of the NRA's merits, Greeley thought land reform had been overemphasized. Zahler, *Eastern Workingmen*, 66, 66n; Bronstein, *Land Reform and Working-Class Experience*, 218–19. However, much of such emphasis came from Greeley's fellow Fourierists as came from National Reformers. Evans to Ferrall in "National Reform in Pennsylvania," *YA*, Sept. 27, 1845, and Ferrall to Young, *VoI*, Jan. 9, 1846, repr. in *YA*, Jan. 17, 1846.

4. "Letter from Mrs. Bagley," *YA*, Jan. 31, 1846. See also Francis H. Early, "A Reappraisal of the New England Labor-Reform Movement of the 1840s: The Lowell Female Labor Reform Association and the New England Workingmen's Association," *Histoire Sociale/Social History*, 13 (May 1980): 33–54.

5. "National Reform Association," *YA*, Aug. 16, 1845; "Reform Movements Originating among the Producing Classes," *Harbinger* 2 (Jan. 24, 1846): 112; *Principles*, 6. See also "Reform Movements Originating among the Producing Classes," 110–12, repr. in *YA*, Feb. 7, 1846.

6. "Industrial Congress—Its Laws, &c.," *VoI*, June 19, 1846, 1; *YA*, Nov. 15, 1845;

VoI, Nov. 21, 1845. "Agrarian Revolution" [from *Social Reformer*] by "A Revolutionist," *SWmA*, Nov. 23, 1844; *Principles*, 13. For *Live Radical*, see *Principles*, 13. For *Laborer*, untitled notice, see *WmA*, June 29, 1844, and *Principles*, 13. For *Investigator*, see *VoI*, Nov. 13, 1846. For *Chronotype*, see *VoI*, Mar. 12, 1846, and Oct. 15, 1847; Wright repr. in *VoI*, Oct. 10, 20, 1846; Zahler, *Eastern Workingmen*, 73.

7. Zahler, *Eastern Workingmen*, 39n; item from the *Laborer* in "Working Men's Movement," *WmA*, Sept. 21, 1844; Bronstein, *Land Reform and Working-Class Experience*, 179–82, noted the petition headed by Clapp 161n, 307, and the role of Fraser, 140n, 306. See also Arthur Bestor's "Fourierism in Northampton: A Critical Note," *New England Quarterly* 13 (Mar. 1940): 110–22.

8. For Douglas in Connecticut, see *Doc. Hist.*, 8: 26–27, 330; Pessen, *Most Uncommon Jacksonians*, 34, 90–91; Ingalls, *Reminiscences of an Octogenarian*, 10; and "Letter from Mr. Douglas," *YA*, Mar. 7, 1846. For Maine, see Marshall P. Hale, "Progress in Maine," *VoI*, Feb. 21, 1846; Hale, "National Reform in Maine," *YA*, Sept. 27, 1845; and Hale, "Old Chelmsford in the Field," *VoI*, Nov. 27, 1846; editorial, *Pleasure Boat*, Apr. 1, 1845; and George E. MacDonald, *Fifty Years of Freethought*, 2 vols. (New York: Truth Seeker Co., 1921, 1929), 2: 113.

9. Van Amringe quoted in "Industrial Congress," *VoI*, June 25, 1847. See also Bronstein, *Land Reform and Working-Class Experience*, 103; Guarneri, *Utopian Alternative*, 230–31; Henry Hamlin Van Amringe, *Association and Christianity* (Pittsburgh: J. W. Cook, 1845); Van Amringe, *Nature and Revelation* (New York: n.p., 1843); and Van Amringe, "H.H. Van Amringe's Mission," *YA*, Apr. 29, 1848. For early socialism in the Midwest, see Arthur Bestor, *Backwoods Utopias: The Sectarian Origins and the Owenite Phase of Communitarian Socialism in America, 1663–1829*, 2d ed. (Philadelphia: University of Pennsylvania Press, 1970); Harrison, *Robert Owen and the Owenites*; Fogarty, *Dictionary of American Communal and Utopian History*.

10. In addition to the general sources cited in note 9, see James M. Morris, "Communes and Cooperatives: Cincinnati's Early Experiments in Social Reform," *Cincinnati Historical Society Bulletin*, 33 (Spring 1975): 57–80, and Cincinnati's *Daily Nonpareil*. See also Hine's series "Association" and "The Land Question," *Quarterly Journal and Review*, 1 (Jan.–Mar. 1846): 70–80, (Apr.–June): 149–59, and (Oct.–Dec. 1846): 289–302; and see Dayton Kelley, "L. A. Hine, Prophet of the Rights of Man" (unpublished manuscript by assistant director of Texas Collections, Baylor University, Waco, copy at Ohio Historical Society, Columbus, ca. 1969), 1–5, 7–11. Hine's publisher, Alcander Longley, covered land reform in his eccentric spelling reform publications such as *Type of the Times* and the *Phonetic Advocate*.

11. Free Land Association Minutes, Dec. 27, 1848, and Jan. 14, 20, 1849. Particularly prominent in the association were Otis Hickley and John C. Wheatcroft of the old Owenite experiment.

12. Fogarty, *Dictionary of American Communal and Utopian History*, 188; *Alphadelphia Tocsin* excerpt in *Jubilee*, 11; *Doc. Hist.*, 8: 26–27. Dr. Samuel Denton quoted in "To National Reformers throughout the United States," *YA*, Apr. 29, 1848; *NYDyTrib*, Aug. 6, 1850; *National Reform Almanac for 1849*, 20; Zahler, *Eastern Workingmen*, 106n-7n. "H.R.S." on "Slavery in the United States" [from *Alphadelphia Tocsin*], *YA*, June 7, 1845. See also N. Gordon Thomas, "The Alphadelphia Experiment," *Michigan History*, 105 (Fall 1971): 205–16; "Homestead Exemption" [from Kalamazoo *Gazette*], *YA*, July 11, 1846; commentary, *YA*, Mar. 6, 1847; notice on Michigan legislation [from

Binghamton Iris], *YA*, Apr. 29, 1848; *National Reform Almanac for 1849*, 46; "Michigan Politics," *NYDyTrib*, July 10,1849.

13. "National Industrial Convention," *YA*, Oct. 18, 1845; "National Reform Association," *YA*, Nov. 15, 1845; "Political Action and the N. York National Reform Association," *VoI*, Nov. 21, 1845.

14. Chrisman, *Tin Horns*, 154, 160–61, 168–72, 176–78, 180, 183–86, and song on 341–43. See also Devyr, *Odd Book*, 46–50, and excerpt from *Freeholder* in *Chester Reveille*, Aug. 19, 1848. Devyr's NRA network included Van Deusen, Scott, Burton Thomas, Rans Coyle, Amos Loper, David Sternberg, John J. Gallup, Maj. Joseph Conner, Valentine Treadwell, Jonathan Allaben, John Evans, and Calvin Pepper. Huston, *Land and Freedom*, 164, 178, 179, 182–87, 228, noting that NRA supporters among the upstate Antirenters tended to be landowners but with smaller holdings than those not supporting the NRA. *Proceedings of the Seventh National Industrial Congress, Held in Washington, D.C., Commencing in Wednesday, June 2d, and ending on Monday, June 7th, 1852* (Washington, D.C.: [National Industrial Congress], [1852]), 13 (hereafter cited as *Proc. of Seventh I.C.*).

15. "To the Democratic Convention," *YA*, June 14, 1845. For Greeley, see "Appeal to the Whigs" in Devyr, *Odd Book*, 105–6; "The Express and the Land Question," *NYDyTrib*, July 31, 1845. *YA*, Sept. 20, 27, 1845, and Oct. 4, 1845. Press discussed in "National Reform Association," *YA*, Aug. 19, 1845, and "Freedom of the Public Lands," *YA*, Nov. 9, 1845; *New York Herald*, Oct. 31, 1845; generally cited in Zahler, *Eastern Workingmen*, 45, 82, 89–90, 96. Masquerier as gubernatorial candidate see *New York Times*, June 6, 1887, 8. For ticket and results, see "National Industrial Convention," *YA*, Oct. 18, 1845. For rallies, Bovay, and poll volunteers, see "National Reform Association," *YA*, Nov. 1, 1845. The assembly ticket also included James, Dennis Lyons, Marston, George Schank, Thomas H. Alliston, B. F. Summerball, Robert Truesdale, Alexander Stott, and Charles R. Burton. For Rowe, see Masquerier, *Sociology*, 125–26, and, for a likely note of his arrival in the United States from Britain only three years before, see Lucy M. Kellogg, "Ship List of the *Orient*, 19 May 1842," *Historical Society for Genealogical Research Magazine*, 26 (Winter 1962): 64, which cited *Passenger Lists*, 3: 1792. "Even John Q. Adams, in a conversation he had with him, said he really could not see that a reform was necessary," reported Brisbane. *YA*, Dec. 20, 1845. Adams's position is less surprising than Brisbane's expectations that it would have been otherwise. "Free Soil—A Whig Doctrine," *YA*, Jan. 31, 1846. For results, see *New York Herald*, Nov. 5, 1845; for organization of adjacent communities, see *YA*, Nov. 15, 1845, and *VoI*, Nov. 21, 1845; and for plans for the city, see *YA*, Dec. 27, 1845.

16. Editorials quoted in Zahler, *Eastern Workingmen*, 43, 44. Commerford discussed in "A Partisan Sentence," *YA*, Mar. 7, 1846; "American Union of Associationists," *VoI*, May 21, 1847. Brisbane discussed in *NYDyTrib*, Apr. 24, 1846. Greeley's depiction of a Brooklyn laborers' strike as the nation's destiny should it not adopt land reform measures in *NYDyTrib*, June 5, 1846; Zahler, *Eastern Workingmen*, 73n; and Devyr, *Odd Book*, 108. Devyr later complained that Greeley had abandoned Fourierism "as soon as the politicians would have nothing to do with him" and waited eighteen months to test the NRA's political viability before declaring his support. "Editorial Notices of the Voice of Industry," *VoI*, Mar. 12, 1847; Greeley's exchange with Levi Slamm's *Globe* in "Land Reform and Banks" [from *NYDyTrib*], *YA*, July 11, 1846; Devyr, *Odd Book*, 99–100. Greeley's endorsement coincided with a major fire that

destroyed the *Tribune* and left the paper scrambling to survive. See "Anecdotes of Horace Greeley," *Printers' Circular,* 4 (May 1869): 84. For the memorials, see *YA,* Dec. 4, 1845; "Industrial Congress," *YA,* June 19, 1846, and "The Public Lands, and Land Limitation," *VoI,* Dec. 18, 1846. For Florida [from *Self-Examiner*], see "Free Soil Documents," *YA,* Apr. 29, 1848; Evans on the "National Reform Settlement," *YA,* Jan. 10, 1846. For Johnson's bill, see Zahler, *Eastern Workingmen,* 133–34; see also "Memorial to the Congress," *NYDyTrib,* June 21, 1848, and "Adjournment of the Fifth National Industrial Congress," *NYDyTrib,* June 17, 1850; and *Proc. of Seventh I.C.,* 3–4. For Bovay, see *YA,* Jan. 3, 1846, and *History of Fond du Lac County,* 886. For Smith's reports and persistence, see "Letter from Washington," *YA,* Feb. 28, 1846, and "National Reform Association," *YA,* Mar. 7, 1846; *YA,* Mar. 21, 1846, and July 11, 1846; *VoI,* July 17, 1846; *NYDyTrib,* Oct. 13, 1850, and Sept. 4, 1851.

17. On the constitutional convention, the NRA formulated a program and discussed running candidates for delegates. "New Constitution Measures," *YA,* Jan. 10, 1846; "National Reform Association," *YA,* Mar. 7, 1846; Zahler, *Eastern Workingmen,* 82n, 83–84; Stokes, *Iconography of Manhattan Island,* 5: 1797, 1798; Spann, *New Metropolis,* 429.

18. Huston, *Land and Freedom,* 158, 159, 170–72; *Report of the Debates and Proceedings of the Convention for the Revision of the Constitution of the State of New York, 1846. Reported by William G. Bishop and William H. Afree* (Albany: Printed at the Office of the Evening Atlas, 1846), 185, 265, 981; Stokes, *Iconography of Manhattan Island,* 5: 1790, 1793, 1797, 1798, 1799, 1800. For the move to rewrite the municipal charter, see 1797, 1799, 1800. The legislature regularly established select committees to address land reform and sometimes made radical recommendations, including, in 1851, the principle of land limitation. Bronstein, *Land Reform and Working-Class Experience,* 233.

19. "National Reform" [from *Regenerator*], *YA,* Mar. 21, 1846; letter in *VoI,* July 3, 1846, repr. in *National Reform Almanac for 1848,* according to the *National Reform Almanac for 1849,* 47; Nicholson in "The Fighting Family," *WmA,* Aug. 31, 1844; A. G. S. in *VoI,* Mar. 26, 1847; Van Deusen quoted in "National Reform Association," *WmA,* Dec. 7, 1844, and "Anti-Suffrage Men," *WmA,* Jan. 4, 1845. NRA defender, J. E. Thompson replied that land reform was "not a 'favor' we ask of Congress . . . but a right of which the people have been robbed for ages past by military despotism or legislative assumption." Thompson's reply, "A.G.S. and National Reform," *VoI,* Apr. 30, 1847, and Thompson again, *VoI,* May 7, 1847. Evans thought those who rejected politics "the most hopeless class of reformers" by leaving the most self-interested individuals to "take charge of political matters, make bad laws" and "*govern too much.*" "Anti-Suffrage Men," *WmA,* Jan. 4, 1845; *YA,* May 10, 1845; "Political Reform and the N. York National Reform Association," *VoI,* Nov. 21, 1845; "Miscellany," *VoI,* Oct. 8, 1847.

20. Clay and *David's Sling* quoted in *Jubilee,* 11. See also William O. Reichert, *Partisans of Freedom: A Study in American Anarchism* (Bowling Green, Ohio: Bowling Green University Popular Press, 1976), 281–83, 285–89, in his chapter "Free Lovers and Free Thinkers: Joseph Dejacque, James A. Clay, and Ezra H. Heywood," 277–300. See esp. "The Land," *David's Sling* 1 (Nov. 25, 1845): 3. For Lyman W. Case, see "All Hail Connecticut Too!" *VoI,* July 16, 1847, and Paul M. Gaston, *Women of Fair Hope* (Athens: University of Georgia Press, 1984), 29–31, which describes Case as a Fouri-

erist. For Andrews, see *Doc. Hist.*, 8: 126. For Ingalls, see *Reminiscences of an Octogenarian*, 5–6, 8–25, 52; Ingalls, "The Stratification of Universalism," *Univercoelum* 1 (Jan. 1, 1848): 75; Ingalls to Labadie, June 2, 1896, Labadie Collection, University of Michigan, Ann Arbor (hereafter cited as Labadie Collection); "National Land Reform" [from *NYDyTrib*], *VoI*, Jan. 22, 1847; and Ingalls, "Uprightness the only Path to Safety, A Sermon Delivered in the Unitarian Church, Southington, Conn., Jan. 7, 1849," *Univercoelum* 2 (Feb. 24, 1849): 193–94. Charles R. Crowe discussed the relationship of antebellum socialism to individualism in terms of the Boston Transcendentalists in a series of articles: "Fourierism and the Founding of Brook Farm," *Boston Public Library Quarterly* 12 (Apr. 1960): 79–88; "This Unnatural Union of Phalansteries and Transcendentalists," *Journal of the History of Ideas* 20 (Oct.–Dec. 1959): 495–502; and "Transcendentalist Support of Brook Farm: A Paradox?" *Historian* 21 (May 1959): 281–95.

21. "Industrial Congress," "Constitution of a Free State," *VoI*, June 18, 25, 1847, and July 2, 1847. See also "Miscellany," *VoI*, Oct. 8, 1847; William West, "Self-Government," *NAS*, Mar. 22, 1849, 171; Masquerier, *Sociology*, 22; West in "National Reform Association," *YA*, Dec. 13, 1845. See also "Revised Constitution," Devyr, *Odd Book*, 252, and "A Model Constitution . . . a New Form of Society and government, and adopted in any State or nation. Addressed to the Property Producers of all Nations," in Masquerier, *Sociology*, 85–90. Regrettably, William West's common name makes his clear identification in records beyond the movement difficult, if not impossible.

22. "Mr. Birney's Letter" and Evans's "Reply to Mr. Birney," in *PR*, July 27, 1844, the latter expessing certainty that Birney's "further consideration of the subject will give you a better opinion" of land reform; "Abolition at Home," *YA*, Apr. 26, 1845; Brisbane in "National Reform Association," *YA*, Dec. 20, 1845; John H. Keyser, *The Next Step of Progress*, 3rd ed. (New York: n.p., [1884?]), 42; and his letter, "Mr. Keyser in Self-Defense," *John Swinton's Paper*, Sept. 20, 1885. Keyser reissued his *Star in the East* ([New York]: For the author, 1871), in a new edition (New York: A. D. F. Randolph and Co. [1880]), then as *The Next Step of Progress*, and finally, as *How Shall the Surplus Labor of the Country to Be Employed?—The Limitation of Wealth and Land the Last Hope of the Republic* (New York: National Limitation Association, 1888).

23. "The New Party," *VoI*, Nov. 19, 1847, oddly disclaimed "agrarians" and "leveller" intent. For calls for national nominations, see "Industrial Congress," *VoI*, July 2, 1847.

24. "Wages and Chattel Slavery," *VoI*, May 7, 1847, 2; "Anti-Slavery Convention," *VoI*, May 8, 1846, 2; "Freedom of the Public Lands" [from *Northhampton Democrat*], *VoI*, Feb. 19, 1847, 4. For Lowell, see *VoI*, Mar. 13, 1846, and Nov. 5, 1847; Ryckman, "Union of All Reformers," *Harbinger* 1 (Aug. 23, Sept. 27, 1845): 169–70, 245–47; Masquerier to Smith, Oct. 5, 1847, Lant Papers; resolutions against slavery by the "New England Convention" [from the *Lynn Pioneer*], *YA*, Jan. 24, 1846. For Massachusetts, see *VoI*, Nov. 6, 13, 1846, and Zahler, *Eastern Workingmen*, 86–87 and 87n. See also "Capital Punishment," *WmA*, Mar. 8, 1845.

25. Hale, "Progress in Maine," *YA*, Feb. 21, 1846; Salmon P. Chase and others, "Correspondence on the Subject of National Reform" [from *Cincinnati Herald*], *Albany Patriot*, Nov. 4, 1846, 205.

26. [Horace Greeley,] Untitled editorial, *NYDyTrib*, July 16, 1858, 4. See also "An Indian Letter of Wisdom," *AF*, Nov. 14, 1844, which later the "Horrible Barbarities"

perpetrated "by this *Christian Nation,* on aboriginal Americans," taking particular pains to ascribe the Seminole war to "that land of *blood hounds, oppression and murder,*" the slave states. *AF,* Feb. 12, 1845. See also "Roman Land Laws," *Herald of Truth* 1 (March 1847): 184–92.

27. Devyr, *Odd Book,* 145, 146; Commerford quoted in "National Reform Association," *YA,* Jan. 17, 1846; Evans, "Civilizing Oregon," *YA,* July 11, 1846; "Railroad to Oregon," *WmA,* Mar. 1, 1845; "Title to Oregon" [*Express*], *YA,* Feb. 21, 1846. This was all part of the process of "keeping the power in the hands of those who governed, and seldom with any view to public happiness." James Reynolds, *Equality,* 100. See also "Great Texas Meeting in the Park," *WmA,* May 3, 1844; "Tax-us," *WmA,* Jan. 18, 1845; "Annexation of Texas," *WmA,* Jan. 25, 1844; "Texas," *WmA,* Feb. 1, 1845; "Annexation of Texas," *WmA,* Feb. 8, 1845; "Texas and Mexico," *WmA,* Mar. 22, 1845. For the views of an abolitionist paper that had already begun to converge with National Reform, see "The Texas Question," *AF,* Apr. 10, 1844; "Annexation of Texas," *AF,* Apr. 17, 1844; "A Letter from Texas," *AF,* Nov. 20, 1844; letter by Albert Gallatin, *AF,* Dec. 4, 1844; and "The Slave Power—Texas," *AF,* Apr. 30, 1845. See also "Mexico," *AF,* Mar. 12, 1845; "Mexican War and the Whitneys," *AF,* Dec. 1, 1846; and "Mexico—What Shall We Do with It" [from *Chronotype*], Sept. 15, 1847. Evans initially offered to support annexation but only with a guarantee to ban slavery (a precursor of David Wilmot's Proviso in the U.S. Congress) and implement land reform measures. "Texas," *WmA,* Apr. 27, 1844. An internal debate resolved opposition to annexation, according to accounts in the regular meetings reported in the *Workingman's Advocate* from Jan. 18 through Feb. 8, 1845.

28. "The Mexican War" and "A Mexican Eden," in the *National Reform Almanac for 1849,* 43, 44. The NRA offered an early organized protest against the North American "filibuster" campaigns that came in the wake of the Mexican War. See Selson Reed, *The Caste War of Yucatan* (Stanford, Calif.: Stanford University Press, 1964), 111, 114; and David I. Folkman Jr., *The Nicaragua Route* (Salt Lake City: University of Utah Press, 1972), 69–97.

29. "Industrial Congress: Second Session—June, 1847," *VoI,* July 2, 1847; "Industrial Congress on War: Address of the Industrial Congress to the Citizens of the United States," *VoI,* June 25, 1847; "Wholesale Robbery of the Peoples' Lands—Sacrifice of the Lacklanders—War for Slavery" [from *Young America*], *VoI,* Nov. 27, 1846; Elizur Wright Jr., "Victory" [from the *Chronotype*], *Harbinger* 4 (Apr. 24, 1847): 326., Pieces from Wright's quoted in "A Catechism of Glory," *AF,* Dec. 15, 1846, and "Shall the Sword Devour Forever!" *VoI,* Jan. 15, 1847.

30. "Modern Dictionary" (which mistakenly capitalized *Democrats*), *AF,* Nov. 8, 1844; "The Old Parties and the War" [from *Green Mountain Freeman*], *AF,* Sept. 29, 1847; "Annexation of Cuba," *Albany Patriot,* Sept. 8, 1847, and its report from the Yucatan, Sept. 15, 1847. See also John H. Schroeder, *Mr. Polk's War: American Opposition and Dissent* (Madison: University of Wisconsin Press, 1973). Among those associated with the NRA who differed with its leadership was Brother of the Union member Charles Goepp, who, with Theodore Poesche, posited a kind of republican expansionism in *The New Rome; or, the United States of the World* (New York: G. P. Putnam, 1853). For filibustering by John McCann and Richardson Hardy of the *Nonpareil,* see the latter's *The History and Adventures of the Cuban Expedition* (Cincinnati: L. Stratton, 1850).

31. "To Young Mechanics," *WmA*, Apr. 6, 1844; "Industrial Convention," *YA*, Oct. 18, 1845; "Industrial Congress," *VoI*, July 2, 1847; "To the Friends of Industry," *VoI*, Dec. 31, 1847; Brisbane quoted in *YA*, Apr. 19, 1845; and Ingalls, "Adjournment of the Fifth National Industrial Congress," *NYDyTrib*, June 17, 1850.

CHAPTER 4: THE SOCIAL CRITIQUE

1. "Meeting of the National Reform Association," *SWmA*, Nov. 30, 1844; address of "Great Rally for Land Reform," *NYDyTrib*, Mar. 2, 1850; Lewis Masquerier, "Declaration of Independence," *WmA*, July 28, 1844; "Our Ticket," *SuWmA*, Nov. 2, 1844; "Our Cause and Our Paper," *WmA*, Apr. 27, 1844; editorial, "Freedom of the Public Lands" [from *Irish Volunteeer*], *YA*, Aug. 23, 1845. Notwithstanding anachronistic standards, the founders of the NRA were what they claimed to be: "workingmen" acting to secure the emancipation of the "the working classes."

2. J. K. Ingalls, R. W. Beebe, and Henry C. Minor, Memorial of Williamsburgh, New York, meeting, SEN32A-H20, tray 141, folder June 3, 1852, U.S. Senate, Ms Records, Legislative Records, National Archives, Washington, D.C. (hereafter cited as U.S. Senate, Legislative Records); "Monopoly of the Soil—Freedom of the Public Lands," *VoI*, Mar. 19, 1847; *WmA*, Aug. 10, 1844; Root's letter, *YA*, Nov. 15, 1845; "Carlisle," *YA*, Dec. 12, 1845; "The Complimentary Ball" [from *YA*], *VoI*, Mar. 12, 1847; *Principles*, 1; *YA*, Sept. 13, 1845, and Dec. 20, 1845; William Young quoted in *Proc. of Seventh I.C.*, 5. For Jefferson, see *WmA*, June 18, 1844, repr. again in the *National Reform Almanac for 1848*, according to *National Reform Almanac for 1849*, 47; "Reminiscences of Jefferson," *Independent Beacon* 1 (Sept., Oct., Nov. 1849; Jan., May 1850): 51–52, 77–78, 108–13, 176–81, 306–7; and "Jefferson upon Homestead Exemption," *Chester Reveille*, Aug. 18, 1850. Among Paine's associations were Alexander Ming, David Bruce, and Charles Christian—artisan radicals in the early American labor movement. Mark Lause, "'The Unwashed Infidelity': Thomas Paine and Early New York City Labor History," *Labor History* 27 (Summer 1986): 385–409; Bronstein, *Land Reform and Working-Class Experience*, 24–25.

3. Treadwell met Thomas Sarle, "an old gentleman of the revolutionary stock" whose home had been "searched for arms, and his family badly treated" by the official repressors of the Dorrites. "Liberation of Gov. Dorr," *WmA*, Aug. 17, 1844. Evans noted revolutionary veterans in a parade for Dorr in *WmA*, Sept. 7, 1844. For upstate veteran Francis Garvey, see Devyr, *Odd Book*, 44, 45, and for the stage, 139. "Spirit of 'Seventy-Six," *WmA*, May 25, 1844; the "patriarch" discussed in "National Reform Association," *YA*, Feb. 7, 1846; Veterans' memorial signed by Col. Nicholas Haight, Capt. Henry Raymond and Privates John Alwaise and Sam Tyler, Feb. 6, 1851, SEN31A-J1-4(tb), tray 106, folder 3/13/50–2/28/51, U.S. Senate, Legislative Records.

4. Devyr, *Odd Book*, 47, 192, 220; "Industrial Congress—Third Session," *NYDyTrib*, June 13, 1848; John Commerford, "To the Editor of the Working Man's Advocate," *WmA*, June 22, 1844; "Address of Mr. Wait of Ill.," *YA*, Oct. 25, 1845. See also Royden Harrison, *Before the Socialists: Studies in Labour and Politics* (London: Routledge and K. Paul, 1965), 212–26. See also Seth Luther, *An Address to the Working-Men of New-England* (Boston: By the author, 1832), 15, 6, and "Seth Luther," *YA*, Apr. 5, 1845; D. M. Ridgeway, "A Call to Land Reformers," in Root, *Analysis of Theology*, 18; and Klippart, *Brotherhood of the Union*, 13. For a look at the egalitarian side of Jefferson,

see Richard K. Matthews, *The Radical Politics of Thomas Jefferson: A Revisionist View* (Lawrence: University Press of Kansas, 1984).

5. "The Complimentary Ball" [from *YA*], *VoI*, Mar. 12, 1847; "Land Reform Meeting," *NYDyTrib*, Aug. 30, 1850; "To the Congress of the United States," *SWmA*, Nov. 30, 1844; "Land Reform Meeting," *NYDyTrib*, Aug. 30, 1850; Root, *Analysis of Theology,* 64, 66; *Jubilee,* 12; "Address of Mr. Wait," *YA,* Oct. 25, 1845. Van Amringe claimed that "the originator of the present movement made their purpose known to General Jackson." "National Reform Banquet" [from *Cincinnati Daily Herald*], *Harbinger,* 7 (June 10, 1848): 46; Commerford to Jackson, Apr. 1844, Papers of Andrew Jackson, reel 67, with supplements, reel 56, and "Jackson on Limitation" [from *Wyoming Democrat*], *Chester Reveille,* Feb. 26, 1848. For a discussion of the manifold complexities of "liberty" in the discourse of the period, see Bruce Levine, *Half Slave and Half Free: The Roots of the Civil War* (New York: Hill and Wang, 1992), 121–44.

6. "Address of Mr. Wait," *YA,* Oct. 25, 1845; Ingalls in *Univercoelum* 4 (Apr. 28, 1849); Caroline [Smith Bovay], "What Is Aristocracy," *YA,* Feb. 14, 1846; "Social Evils" [from *WmA*], *Diamond,* second series, 2 (Oct. 1841): 55. For elite reformers, see Root, *Analysis of Theology,* 72; Devyr, *Odd Book,* 155, 204; Commerford quoted in "The Public Lands," *WmA,* May 11, 1844; Masquerier, *Sociology,* 54, 73; and Klippart, *Brotherhood of the Union,* 14. Mark W. Summers discusses the general fears that haunted contemporaries in *The Plundering Generation: Corruption and the Crisis of the Union, 1849–1861* (New York: Oxford University Press, 1987). National Reformers, however, carried these a step further to ask about the causes of that corruption.

7. Jefferson discussed in *YA,* Oct. 25, 1845; Devyr, *Odd Book,* 150; Sheddon quoted in "National Industrial Congress," *New York Daily Times,* June 9, 1854; "The Homestead" [*Cleveland American*], *VoI,* May 21, 1847. See also Henry George, *Progress and Poverty* (1879; repr., New York: Robert Schalkenbach Foundation, 1962), 535, 540.

8. *Jubilee,* 2; Root, *Analysis of Theology,* 33–34, 40; Klippart, *Brotherhood of the Union,* 14; Ingalls, *Reminiscences of an Octogenarian,* 51; William Heighton, "True and Sham Reformers," *YA,* Nov. 8, 1845; William Heighton, "The Clergy and Free Soil," *YA,* Jan. 31, 1846; William Heighton, "Slavery of Wages," *YA,* Feb. 7, 1846; William Heighton, *Principles of Aristocratic Legislation* (Philadelphia: John Coates Jr., 1828), 5. See also "White Slavery" [from *New York Tribune*], *YA,* Feb. 7, 1846. Devyr, too, spent his last years denouncing the American embrace of "Jay Gould's British Civilization." Devyr, *Odd Book,* 4n, 25, 208, 210–11. Mark W. Summers correctly emphasized the general fears that gripped contemporaries of that generation, *Plundering Generation.*

9. Van Amringe, "National Reform" series, *AF,* Mar. 1, 1848, and Feb. 15, 1848; Yet National Reformers believed, as John H. Klippart said, "[T]he torch on the altar of hope is burning more brightly, and sheds its beautiful light to a far greater distance, than in any previous era or epoch of the worlds history." *Brotherhood of the Union,* 15.

10. Van Amringe, "National Reform" series, *AF,* Feb. 16, 1848, Jan. 19, 1848, Mar. 1, 1848, and Feb. 9, 1848; Kempton quoted in "National Reform Association," *YA,* June 21, 1845; and New Harmony Free Land Association, Ms. Minutes, 1–2, Workingmen's Institute, New Harmony, Indiana.

11. William Heighton, "True and Sham Reformers," *YA,* Nov. 8, 1845, and "Slavery of Wages," *YA,* Feb. 7, 1846; "White Slavery" [from *New York Tribune*], *YA,* Feb. 7, 1846; Klippart, *Brotherhood of the Union,* 14–15.

12. "The World's Convention," *NYDyTrib*, Oct. 6, 1845; "The Movement Party," *YA*, Mar. 29, 1845; "Second Out-Door Meeting," *WmA*, June 15, 1844; "National Reform Association," *YA*, Nov. 22, 1845; Evans quoted in "The Complimentary Ball [from *YA*], *VoI*, Mar. 12, 1847, and in *Jubilee*, 13. John Commerford declared, "[T]he great capital of this county is LAND," coupled to a republican system wherein what was "socially wrong can be politically righted." It remained for the voters "to say whether whole territories shall be thus fastened upon, and that you shall procure the future homes of yourselves and children by paying tribute for them." "Remarks of Mr. Commerford," *WmA*, Mar. 30, 1844; John Commerford, "To the Editor of the Working Man's Advocate," *WmA*, June 22, 1844.

13. James Reynolds, *Equality*, 81, 84, which distinguished Lithconia from "the disjointed countries in Europe and America," 29 (this edition published by the local Liberal Union). For the "Upper Ten," see George Lippard's *Upper Ten and Lower Million* (Cincinnati: H. M. Rulison, 1853), and its use in publications such as Cincinnati's *Western Quarterly Review* 1 (Apr., 1849): 301, and Masquerier, *Sociology*, 31. See also *Proc. of Seventh I.C.*, 12–13, and William Heighton, "Slavery of Wages," *YA*, Feb. 7, 1846. For Pickering, see Hine's report in "Adjournment of the Fifth National Industrial Congress," *NYDyTrib*, June 17, 1850, a digest of John Pickering's *The Working Man's Political Economy, Founded upon the Principle of Immutable Justice and the Inalienable Rights of Man; designed for the Promotion of National Reform* (Cincinnati: T[homas] Varney, 1847), printed using Josiah Warren's stereotyping method. For an overview of how respectable society grappled with this question, see Burke, *Conundrum of Class*.

14. Masquerier, "Declaration of Independence," *WmA*, Sept. 28, 1844; Root, *Analysis of Theology*, 33; Masquerier, *Sociology*, 51.

15. "Prospectus of the People's Rights," *WmA*, May 16, 1844; Van Amringe, "National Reform—No. 7," *AF*, Mar. 8, 1848; "Agrarian Revolution" [from *Social Reformer*] by "A Revolutionist," *SWmA*, Nov. 23, 1844; "First Out-Door Meeting," *WmA*, June 8, 1844; *Proc. of Seventh I.C.*, 5–6; "Rights of Labor," *Waukesha Democrat*, Sept. 4, 1849; "Industrial Congress," *Herald of Progress*, Dec. 22, 1860, 5; Elizur Wright, "Philosophy of Labor" [from *Chronotype*], *AF*, Aug. 13, 1846.

16. Klippart, *Brotherhood of the Union*, 11; George Henry Evans and John Windt, "Prospectus of the People's Rights," *WmA*, Mar. 16, 1844.

17. "Adjournment of the Fifth National Industrial Congress," *NYDyTrib*, June 17, 1850; James Reynolds, *Equality*, 28, 101, 102, 104. For lawyers and farmers, see "Address of Mr. Wait," *YA*, Oct. 25, 1845; "Homestead Exemption," *WFD*, Feb. 7,1849; and Wait in Schlesinger, *Age of Jackson*, 312; "Address of Mr. Wait," *YA*, Oct. 25, 1845; "To the Working Women of New York," *WmA*, Mar. 15, 1845; William Ogilvie, *An Essay on the Right of Property in Land* [1782?] in Beer, *Pioneers of Land Reform*, 60; Masquerier, *Sociology*, 12, 32, 60, 80, 148; Skidmore, *Rights of Man to Property*, 341, 342, 354, 355; "New York Farmers' Club," *YA*, Apr. 19, 1845; "Industrial Congress," *VoI*, July 2, 1847; and "An Address to the Farmers of New York," *VoI*, June 18 (which includes Kouns's letter). Yankee Protective Unions directly mobilized farmers around their common interests with urban labor. George W. Kouns, "a Farmer of Castle County," Kentucky, sent "a long letter" to the 1847 Industrial Congress to discuss his *The Political Guide for Farmers, Mechanics and Laborers in the Choice of Rulers* (Cincinnati: Printed for the author, 1848). Later apologists for the western status quo

would later claim this process to be an expropriation of wealth rightly belonging to capital by virtue of its industry and intelligence, and Marxist critics have also accepted the general terms imposed on this historic debate by the "winners." In contrast, National Reformers discussed the problem from the perspective of the losers—artisans, farmers, and the "middling sort"—who hoped, in part, to defend *their* right to property from an expropriation by capital.

18. Wright, "Philosophy of Labor," *AF*, Sept. 1, 1846; Devyr, *Odd Book*, xiii; Klippart, *Brotherhood of the Union*, 13. Denton quoted in *Michigan Expositor* in "To National Reformers throughout the United States," *YA*, Apr. 29, 1848. Ex-president John Quincy Adams horrified Brisbane by confidently citing unrealistically high wages. When one of Adams's Democratic critics cited a more plausible six shillings a day, Commerford erupted with indignation: "[N]o man with a large family can in this city save money out of *two dollars* a day if he gives his children the food, clothing, and education benefiting the children of freemen." Adams incident recalled by Heighton in "Slavery of Wages," *YA*, Feb. 7, 1846. Commerford in "National Reform Association," *YA*, Sept. 6, 1845, *YA*, Feb. 7, 1846; "Address of Mr. Wait," *YA*, Oct. 25, 1845; Thompson, "Agrarianism" [from *Northampton Democrat*], *VoI*, Apr. 30, 1847; Van Amringe, "National Reform," *AF*, Mar. 22, 1848; and Masquerier, *Sociology*, 63. For proletarians, see the notice of Eugene Sue, *Independent Beacon* 1 (July, 1850): 357; and Devyr, *Odd Book*, 105, 206.

19. "Speech of Mike Walsh" [from *Boston Bee*], *SuWmA*, Nov. 2, 1844; Masquerier, *Sociology*, 32; "Remarks of Mr. Commerford," *WmA*, Apr. 6, 1844; Masquerier's "Declaration of Independence," *WmA*, Sept. 28, 1844; Devyr, *Odd Book*, xiii.

20. Masquerier, *Sociology*, 17–18; Hine quoted in "Conclusion of National Industrial Congress," *NYDyTrib*, June 14, 1851; Van Amringe, "National Reform," *AF*, Feb. 23, 1848, repr. [from *AF*], *VoI*, Mar. 17, 1848; Evans, "Suicide," *YA*, Feb. 7, 1846; Brooks at "Industrial Congress," *VoI*, June 25, 1847; Van Amringe, "National Reform—No. 8," *AF*, Mar. 15, 1848; Remarks of Mr. Commerford," *WmA*, Mar. 30, 1844; "National Reform Association," June 8, 1844. Root, *Analysis of Theology*, 35; See also *SuWmA*, Nov. 9, 1844; Devyr, *Odd Book*, xix; *Mechanics Free Press*, Oct. 11, 1828; *Principles*, 9; *Proc. of Seventh I.C.*, 2, 3, 4; Van Amringe, "National Reform" series, *AF*, Feb. 16, 1848, and Mar. 8, 1848. See also "Education and Crime," *Western Quarterly Review* 1 (Apr. 1849): 284–99. Dr. John H. Griscom wrote *The Sanitary Conditions of the Laboring Classes* in 1845, and there was an 1847 report by the Association for Improvement of the Conditions of the Poor, but the city fathers largely ignored both. Van Amringe, "National Reform" series, *WF*, Feb. 16, 1848, and Mar. 8, 1848. For the impact of mechanization on labor organizations, see "Conclusion of National Industrial Congress," *NYDyTrib*, June 14, 1851; "Surplus of Mechanics," in *Principles*, 8; Skidmore, *Rights of Man to Property*, 388; *WmA*, Sept. 21, 1844.

21. Skidmore, *Rights of Man to Property*, 346, 377–78, 358, 255–56; James Reynolds, *Equality*, 37–43, 111, 112.

22. On the range of reformers advocated, see "Gerrit Smith's Platform," *Jubilee Harbinger for 1854*, 144–45 (hereafter cited as *JH1854*). J. Sidney Jones proposed "the Secret Ballot-Box," appreciating the irony that "labor-saving—time-saving—machinery to degrade and rob labor" might be subdued by the secret ballot. Jaques, "Propositions of Reform," *YA*, Oct. 11, 1845; Masquerier, *Sociology*, 68; J. Sidney Jones in "Great Mass Meeting," *JH1854*, 310–14; *Proc. of Seventh I.C.*, 4; John Commerford

in "National Reform Association," *YA*, Nov. 29, 1845; "Proceedings of the National Industrial Congress [1853]," *JH1854*, 377; William V. Barr in "Conclusion of the National
Industrial Congress," *NYDyTimes*, June 14, 1851; and "National Industrial Congress,"
NYDyTrib, June 9, 10, 11, 1854. Evans in "The World's Convention," *NYDyTrib*, Oct.
6, 1845; and "National Industrial Congress," *NYDyTrib*, June 9, 10, 11, 1854.

23. For these sentiments, see "To the Congress," *SWmA*, Nov. 30, 1844; "National
Reform Association," *YA*, Nov. 29, 1845; Albert Brisbane comment in *Diamond*, second
series 2 (May 1841): 10–11; Masquerier quoted in "Industrial Congress," *VoI*, June 18,
1847; "Pledge of the Candidates," *SuWmA*, Nov. 2, 1844. "If a law can not be enacted
that will defy the tricks of the lawyers," suggested the *Wisconsin Freeman*, "then we
will go for *abolishing the lawyers* that's all." Van Amringe, "National Reform—No. 8,"
AF, Mar. 15, 1848.

24. "Legislators Make Laws in Their Own Favor," *Independent Beacon* 1 (Aug.,
1850): 408–11; "Address of Mr. Wait," *YA*, Oct. 25, 1845; Masquerier, "Declaration of
Independence," *WmA*, Sept. 28, 1844; "Genessee County in the Field," *YA*, Jan. 24,
1846; "Plenty of Work," *WmA*, July 20, 1844; "Large Tracts" [from *Racine Advocate*],
WFD, Mar. 7, 1849.

25. Root, *Analysis of Theology*, 35; Devyr, *Odd Book*, 246, 209, 207, 200; Masquerier, *Sociology*, 12, 67, 22, 72, 81, and his "Declaration of Independence," *WmA*, Sept.
28, 1844.

26. Mungo West in "National Industrial Congress," *New York Times*, June 10,
1854; Masquerier, *Sociology*, 47, and his "Declaration of Independence," *WmA*,
Sept. 28, 1844; Root, *Analysis of Theology*, 31, 65; and Cochrane, "Grand Rally for
Land Reform," *NYDyTrib*, Mar. 2, 1850. Freethinkers had long debated the duties of
"Theophilanthropists" when laws contradicted "the eternal and immutable principles
of justice," when "we ought to refuse our concurrence in the execution of such laws;
and what are the steps reason would dictate to obtain an abrogation of them." *Temple
of Reason*, Dec. 6, 1800.

27. "Priveleges [*sic*] and Duties of Republicanism," *Chester Herald*, Aug. 8, 1853;
"The New Land Law," in Devyr, *Odd Book*, 189; Ingalls to Labadie, Mar. 25, 1889,
Labadie Collection; Masquerier, *Sociology*, 62, 46; and Root, *Analysis of Theology*,
34, which continues that "to establish falsehoods, to make it appear like truth, there
must be a great many men employed, long protracted courts without decisions; the
world filled with stuff called law, with vast expense; even the destruction of every one
that employs them, to much extent. The whole of it is upon this principle, that if you
tell a lie, to hide it, you must tell ten more."

28. Sheddon and Young quoted in *Proc. of Seventh I.C.*, 4, 6; "Adjournment of the
Eighth National Industrial Congress," *NYDyTrib*, June 17, 1850; Sheddon quoted in
"National Industrial Congress," *NYDyTrib*, June 9, 11, 1854; Masquerier, *Sociology*, 53;
"Address of Mr. Wait," *YA*, Oct. 25, 1845; Bovay quoted in "The World's Convention,"
NYDyTrib, Oct. 6, 1845; Root, *Analysis of Theology*, 32, 35; Masquerier, *Sociology*, 22,
and "A Model Constitution," 85–90. Evans in "The World's Convention," *NYDyTrib*,
Oct. 6, 1845; "National Industrial Congress," *NYDyTimes*, June 11, 1854; *Jubilee*, 7;
Devyr, *Odd Book*, 161–62, 24; "The American Movement" [from *Northern State*] and
Evans's reply, *WmA*, Aug. 17, 1844; "Address of Mr. Wait," *YA*, Oct. 25, 1845.

29. Brisbane in "National Reform Association," *WmA*, Feb. 22, 1845; H. H. Van
Amringe, "National Reform" series, *AF*, Mar. 1, 22, 1848.

30. Masquerier, *Sociology,* 20, 30, 67, 54, and his "Declaration of Independence," *WmA,* Sept. 28, 1844.

CHAPTER 5: MEANS AND ENDS

1. Hine, *A Lecture on Garrisonian Politics, before the Western Philosophical Institute, Delivered in Cincinnati, Sunday, April 24th, 1853* (Cincinnati: Printed by A[lcander] Longley for the Western Philosophical Institute, 1853), 13, 16, 21, 22.

2. Gilbert Vale, "Of Governments," *Independent Beacon,* n.d., 1, 8; George F. Gordon "Great Mass Meeting" [May 10, 1852], *JH1854,* 313; *Proc. of Seventh I.C.,* 4; Hine, *Lecture on Garrisonian Politics,* 13.

3. "Miscellany," and "Pure Democracy," *VoI,* Oct. 8, 1847; Allen quoted in "Reform Celebrations of the Fourth at Troy, N.Y.," *Albany Patriot,* July 7, 1847, 139.

4. Elizur Wright, "Land Reform" [from *Chronotype*], *VoI,* Oct. 15, 1847; Devyr, *Odd Book,* 207–08, ix; Masquerier, *Sociology,* 17; Ingalls, "The Wants of the Age," *Univercoelum* 1 (Dec. 25, 1847): 49–51; Joshua Redman's cover statement on petition, May 19, 1852, SEN32-H20, tray 140, folder 5/27–6/3/52, U.S. Senate, Legislative Records; *Principles,* 6. "Williamsburgh," *NYDyTrib,* May 28, 1852 identifies one speaker's surname as "Pink," and the local census for 1850 contains only Caleb Pink. J. M., "Right to the Soil—Public Lands" [from *Communitist*] in *YA,* Feb. 21, 1846; and Van Amringe at the "Industrial Congress," *VoI,* June 25, 1847. "Get first the freedom of the Soil," Greeley told Brisbane who passed it on to the "National Reform Association," *YA,* Aug. 16, 1845. See also Van Amringe, "National Reform—No. 1," *AF,* Jan. 19, 1848. For oversimplifications of Masquerier's views, see Frank T. Carlton, "An American Utopia," *Quarterly Journal of Economics* 24 (1910): 428–33, and L. L. Bernard, "Early Utopian Social Theory in the United States (1840–1860)," *Northwest Missouri State Teachers College Studies* 2 (1938): 90–94. Van Amringe urged "a fair distribution of profits." *AF,* Mar. 8, 1848. Masquerier thought the expanding population could divide land into smaller parcels until it needed "modes for limiting offspring and stripiculture." In this way, said Dr. Douglass, "the older we grow the more democratic we grow." Masquerier, *Sociology,* 19, 49, 14, 57, also 13; Douglass quoted in "National Reform Association," *YA,* Nov. 8, 1845.

5. Masquerier, *Sociology,* 13; Devyr, *Odd Book,* vii, viii, 33, and quoted in "National Reform Association," *WmA,* Feb. 22, 1845; Ingalls, "Relations Existing and Natural between Man and Property," *Herald of Progress,* Nov. 10, 1860, 3.

6. Masquerier, *Sociology,* passim, 13–19, 53, 55, 57, 68, 74, 76, 77, 147, and his *Politicology,* 12, bound with that volume; *National Reform Almanac for 1849,* 36; "Diagram of the Proposed Village," *Principles,* 5, 5n; "Our Principles," *WmA,* Apr. 6, 1844, and June 18, 1844. For Evans's role in formulating this, see "National Reform Settlement, No. II," *YA,* Jan. 17, 1846. Also on Masquerier, see Bronstein, *Land Reform and Working-Class Experience,* 76–77; Huston, *Land and Freedom,* 140; and Roy Rosenzweig and Elizabeth Blackmar, *The Park and the People* (Ithaca, N.Y.: Cornell University Press, 1992), 112, 116. For Etzler, see Howard P. Segal, *Technological Utopianism in American Culture* (Chicago: University of Chicago Press, 1985), 89–91; Etzler's publisher, Peter Eckler, was a freethinker, who also published *To the President of the United States, to each Senator and member of Congress, to the governors of the*

*several states, and to each member of the several state legislatures — greeting: we would
respectfully ask your attention to the importance of a homestead bill . . .* (New York:
Eckler, Printer, [18–]). For overgeneralizations, see Carlton "American Utopia," and
Bernard, "Early Utopian Social Theory."

7. Van Amringe, "National Reform—No. 2," *AF,* Jan. 26, 1848; Masquerier, *Sociology,* 13, 51, 59, 76. Evans suggested that any immediate colonization of eastern city
people to the West would require most to learn farming. See also excerpt [from *New
York Tribune*], *VoI,* June 19, 1846, and "A. G. S." of Hopedale community, *VoI,* Mar.
26, 1847. "Industrial Congress—Its Laws &c." *VoI,* June 19, 1846; "Working Men's
Meeting," *WmA,* March 16, 1844; "Our Principles," *WmA,* Apr. 6, 1844; and Bronstein,
Land Reform and Working-Class Experience, 59–61.

8. Theodore E. Tomplinson at "Grand Rally for Land Reform," *NYDyTrib,* Mar. 2,
1850; Hine, *Lecture on Garrisonian Politics,* 19–20; "National Industrial Congress,"
NYDyTimes, June 10, 1854.

9. Evans discussed in *WmA,* July 20, 1844, and quoted in "The World's Convention,"
NYDyTrib, Oct. 6, 1845.

10. "Land Monopoly" [from *Cleveland True Democrat*], *WFD,* Jan. 10, 1849; Ingalls,
Reminiscences of an Octogenarian, 24; W. H. Whinnery, "Examine Yourselves," *YA,*
Feb. 28, 1846; Root, *Analysis of Theology,* 66; "National Reform Association," *YA,* Nov.
29, 1845; Mechanics' Literary Association of Rochester, "Lecturers Wanted," *YA,* Jan.
3, 1846.

11. Kelley, "L. A. Hine," 9–13, 15–18, with quotes, 12, from an 1881 autobiographical letter. *Hine's Progress Pamphlets* published more speeches from 1850 until August
1852, when they were reissued as the first of two volumes, titled *Political and Social
Economy,* adding to his reform novels and earlier tracts of all sorts. See, too, "Gipsy
Reformers," Oneida *American Socialist* 2 (June 6, 1877): 180–81.

12. "Wendell," and "Our Prospects in New York," *Harbinger* 5 (Oct. 2, 1847): 286;
North Newburgh, Maine petition dated July 6, 1852, SEN32A-H20, tray 142, folder
June 28–July 12, 1852, U.S. Senate, Legislative Records; B. G. Veazie, "Land Monopoly" [from *Boston Investigator*], *YA,* Mar. 21, 1846.

13. For the event and preparations, see "National Reform Ball," *YA,* Dec. 20, 1845;
"First Annual Ball of the National Reformers," *YA,* Jan. 3, 1846; "National Reform
Ball," *YA,* Jan. 10, 1845; "The Ball," *YA,* Jan. 17, 1846; "The Complimentary Ball" [from
Young America], *VoI,* Mar. 12, 1847; and "Land Reform Banquet," *NYDyTrib,* Mar.
23, 1850. See also Bronstein, *Land Reform and Working-Class Experience,* 146–47;
"Give Every Man a Farm," *YA,* Jan. 24, 1846; "New Auxiliary" about Randolph, Mass.,
YA, Feb. 21, 1846; "The Young Men's Ball" [from *Young America*], *VoI,* Jan. 8, 1847.
The best of these was surely "The Agrarian Ball" in *WmA,* June 8, 1844. For A. J.
H. Duganne, see "Who Owneth American Soil," *Chester Reveille* [from *Harbinger*],
Mar. 25, 1848, July 20, 1844, and Aug. 3, 10, 17, 24, 1844; *SuWmA,* Nov. 9, 1844. In
addition to reports of music in the meetings, note Evans's praise of the Hutchinson
family from *YA* in *VoI,* Dec. 11, 1846, with notice in the issue of June 11, 1847. For
artists, see *WmA,* Sept. 21, 1844; *YA,* Dec. 27, 1845, and the letterhead used in the
June 1891 reorganization. Devyr, *Odd Book,* 202–3, 253.

14. "Priveleges [*sic*] and Duties of Republicanism," *Chester Herald,* Aug. 8, 1853;
Van Amringe, "National Reform—No. 8," *AF,* Mar. 15, 1848; "National Reform Association," *WmA,* Apr. 13, 1844; "Working Men's Meeting," *WmA,* June 15, 1844;

"Mike Walsh in Baltimore," *WmA*, Mar. 22, 1845; *An Address, Delivered before the Mechanics and Working Classes Generally* (Philadelphia: Office of the "Mechanics' Gazette," 1828), 11; Evans, "Our Ticket," *SuWmA*, Nov. 2, 1844. J. Sidney Jones at the "Great Mass Meeting at the Chinese Museum," *JH1854*, 309; Root, *Analysis of Theology*, 72; Ryckman, "Poverty a Crime" [*NYTrib*], *VoI*, Jan. 22, 1847; Gilbert Vale's publication of Charles P. Shivas, "The Popular Credo," *Independent Beacon* 1 (Aug. 1850): 399; "Ransom Smith," *VoI*, Mar. 27, 1846; and "Speech of Mike Walsh" [from Boston *Bee*] in *SuWmA*, Nov. 2, 1844. Moses Jaques thought lawyers and officeholders should have "a daily sum equal to the wages of a day laborer or mechanic" with "reasonable expenses." "Propositions of Reform," *YA*, Oct. 11, 1845.

15. "National Reform Association," *WmA*, June 8, 1844; Wright quoted in "Land Reform" [from *Chronotype*], *VoI*, Oct. 15, 1847; "Address of Mr. Wait," *YA*, Oct. 25, 1845; and "Spirit of Gracchus," *YA*, Mar. 6, 1847. See also Theodore Tomlinson's views in "Grand Rally for Land Reform," *NYDyTrib*, Mar. 2, 1850.

16. "National Reform Association," *YA*, Mar. 29, 1845.

17. Devyr, *Odd Book*, 151; Ingalls, "Social Guaranty," *Univercoelum* 1 (Feb. 26, 1848). See also Charles Hosmer, *The Condition of Labor: An Address to the Members of the Labor Reform League of New England, by One of the Members* (Boston: By the author, 1847). For Evans and Pepper, see "National Reform Association," *SWmA*, Dec. 21, 1844, and *YA*, June 14, 1845. And for Commerford, see "National Reform Association," July 26, 1845. The *Spirit of the Age* lasted from July 1849 into April 1850. For Evans on the subject of "Trade Associations," see *SWmA*, Nov. 23, 1844; *YA*, Mar. 29, 1845; "The Workingmen's Protective Union," *Harbinger* 2 (Feb. 13, 1845): 13; "National Reform Convention," *YA*, May 10, 1845. See also "Industrial Congress," *VoI*, June 18, 1847; "Adjournment of the Fifth National Industrial Congress," *NYDyTrib*, June 17, 1850; "Proceedings of National Industrial Congress," in *JH1854*, 378; "Industrial Congress," *Herald of Progress*, Dec. 22, 1860, 5; Ingalls, *Reminiscences of an Octogenarian*, 134; Van Amringe, "National Reform—No. 8," *AF*, Mar. 15, 1848; "National Industrial Congress" and "Adjournment of the Fifth National Industrial Congress," *NYDyTrib*, June 15, 17, 1850; and Charles A. Dana, *Proudhon and his "Bank of the People"* (New York: B. R. Tucker, 1896). See also Hosmer in "Resolutions of the Industrial Congress," *VoI*, June 25, 1847, and Rozwenc, *Cooperatives*, 67, 68–69, 71.

18. "Second Out-Door Meeting," *WmA*, June 15, 1844; "Great and Enthusiastic Gathering of the Working Men in the Eleventh Ward," *WmA*, June 22, 1844; "Circular to the Trades," *WmA*, Mar. 1, 1845; "National Reform Settlement," *YA*, Jan. 10, 1846; "National Reform Settlement, No. II," *YA*, Jan. 17, 1846. Although some of these functioned as a profit-making enterprises, others encouraged workers to pool their resources in a cooperative effort to become homeowners; still others, such as New Bedford's "Reform and Relief Association," went beyond mutual aid functions to build homes for the homeless. See "The Homestead Remedy," *YA*, Jan. 3, 1846; "The Industrial Brotherhood," *YA*, Mar. 7, 1846; and "Dwellings of the Laboring Classes" [from *NYTrib*], *VoI*, Apr. 9, 1847. West wanted agrarians to form their own "Homes for the Friendless," *VoI*, June 25, 1847. See also "Industrial Congress," *VoI*, June 25, 1847. By summer 1852, National Reformers organized the Western Homestead Association with its monthly *Western Homestead Journal* under the presidency of A. G. Levy. "Western Homestead Association," *NYDyTrib*, Aug. 2, 1852; Christopher M. Johnson, "The Rolling Stone Colony: Labor Rhetoric in Practice," *Minnesota History* 49

(Winter 1984): 140–48; *WmA*, July 20, 1844; Price in "Free Homes To All!" *NYDyTrib*, May 28, 1852; Van Amringe, "National Reform—No. 2," *AF*, Jan. 26, 1848.

19. "Resolutions of the Industrial Congress," *VoI*, June 25, 1847; "Industrial Congress," *NYDyTrib*, June 7, 1847; "National Reform Convention," *YA*, May 10, 1845; Devyr, "Free Homes To All!" *NYDyTrib*, May 28, 1852; Ingalls, "Social Guaranty." See also James J. Martin, *Men against the State: The Expositors of Individualist Anarchism in America, 1827–1868* (Colorado Springs, Colo.: Ralph Myles Publisher, 1970) 45, 66.

20. "The Trades' Movement," *YA*, June 14, 1845; "Great Mass Meeting of the Working Classes at National Hall," *YA*, June 14, 1845; "Committee of the Trades," *YA*, June 28, 1845; "General Trades Meeting," *YA*, July 19, 1845. "Sailors' Strike," *WmA*, Apr. 6, 1844; "On Printers' Turn Out," *WmA*, Apr. 13, 1844; "To the Cellar Diggers," *WmA*, May 11, 1844; and Hine in "Conclusion of National Industrial Congress," *NYDyTrib*, June 14, 1851. Evans clearly had long supported trade unionism. See his publication of John H. Bowie's response to an attack on unionism by Jonas Humbert, a former supporter of Thomas Skidmore. "General Trades' Union—To the Public," *The Man*, June 24, 1834, 131. See also Evans's fable of the strike in *YA*, Dec. 20, 1845. Not all papers sympathetic to the Homestead Bill shared the NRA's sympathy with strikes. See "Revolution in Philadelphia" [from *Daily Public Ledger*], *Chester Reveille*, Aug. 19, 1848.

21. "Industrial Convention," *YA*, Oct. 18, 1845; "National Reform Association," *YA*, Dec. 20, 1845. See also "National Reform Association," *YA*, Nov. 15, 1845; "The Homestead Remedy," Jan. 3, 1846; "Give Every Man a Farm," *YA*, Jan. 24, 1846; and "The Industrial Brotherhood," *YA*, Mar. 7, 1846. For Ryckman in the Industrial Guards, see "National Reform Association," *YA*, Nov. 15, 1845. For politics and benefit funds, see "Industrial Congress—Its Laws & c," *VoI*, June 19, 1846. Association with Odd Fellows is noted in Bronstein, *Land Reform and Working-Class Experience*, 217; *YA*, Dec. 20, 1845; and pieces on "The Homestead Remedy" and "The Industrial Brotherhood," "By-laws," and notice of Ohio organization, and accounts of New York meetings in *YA*, Jan. 3, 1846, and Mar. 7, 1846, as well as a notice on the order in "Industrial Congress," *VoI*, June 18, 1847. The order was mentioned as late as 1848 in "Secret Societies," *National Era*, Mar. 9, 1848, 38. Note that the name reappears in the wake of the Civil War.

22. "Free Homes To All!" *NYDyTrib*, May 28, 1852; Devyr, *Odd Book*, 249; Ingalls, "Relations Existing and Natural between Man and Property," *Herald of Progress*, Nov. 10, 1860, 3; Warren Chase, "Association *With* Combination" [from *Boston Investigtor*], *YA*, July 11, 1846.

23. Devyr, *Odd Book*, 248; Collins quoted in "The World's Convention," *NYDyTrib*, Oct. 6, 1845; "Address of Mr. Wait," *YA*, Oct. 25, 1845; Root, *Analysis of Theology*, 31; Wait quoted in "Industrial Congress—Third Session," *NYDyTrib*, June 13, 1848; Devyr, *Odd Book*, 249.

24. "Trade Associations," *SWmA*, Nov. 23, 1844; Zahler, *Eastern Workingmen*, 85n–86n; Ingalls, *Reminiscences of an Octogenarian*, 169; Wright, "Philosophy of Labor" [from *Chronotype*], *AF*, Aug. 13, 1846; Devyr, *Odd Book*, 249.

25. "National Reform Association," *YA*, Dec. 13, 1845. William West signed the 1836 petition against slavery in the District of Columbia. John Jentz, "Artisans, Evangelicals, and the City: A Social History of Abolition and Labor Reform in Jacksonian New York"

(Ph.D. diss., City University of New York, 1977), 378. See also the views of Lippard in David Reynolds, *George Lippard, Prophet of Protest,* 217–22.

26. Evans quoted in "National Reform Association," *YA,* Mar. 29, 1845, and "The World's Convention," *NYDyTrib,* Oct. 6, 1845; Masquerier, *Sociology,* 68; Devyr, *Odd Book,* xi(n), 249. As early as 1800, some radical freethinkers expected such proposals for social reform to be ultimately unacceptable to the elite. "We will be told, perhaps," wrote one, "that to accomplish all this, a general revolution must take place. And in the name of goodness, where is the harm that it should, if for the better? By such a revolution the few would lose, but millions would benefit." *Temple of Reason,* Dec. 6, 1800.

27. "Address of Mr. Wait of Ill.," *YA,* Oct. 25, 1845. Ryckman "hoped ere this to have seen preparations for organizing the Industrial Guards, by the selection of a uniform and organization of Industrial Brotherhoods and Sisterhoods." "The organization of Industrial Guards, in accordance with constitutional rights and duties had not yet been commenced," ran an account of Evans response, "but he hoped would be immediately, by those who felt an interest in the object." "National Reform Association," *YA,* Nov. 15, 1845. Devyr's well-informed tactical advice for a revolutionary rising probably dates from after the Civil War, but see his *Odd Book,* 22, 201, 208, 214, 241, 249, 250.

28. Klippart, *Brotherhood of the Union,* 10; Skidmore, *Rights of Man to Property,* 196.

29. Van Amringe, "National Reform—No. 1," *AF,* Jan. 19, 1848; Hine, *Lecture on Garrisonian Politics,* 18; Masquerier, *Sociology,* 12, 13, 60, 81, 148; Masquerier, "Declaration of Independence," *WmA,* Sept. 28, 1844.

30. Van Amringe, "National Reform—No. 2," *AF,* Jan. 26, 1848; Skidmore, *Rights of Man to Property,* 302, 311. Ryckman's resolutions were unanimously adopted. References were made to "proposed Industrial Government" in "National Reform Convention," *YA,* May 10, 1845; "incipient Legislature" in "Industrial Congress," *VoI,* June 19, 1846; and Evans in "National Reform Association," *YA,* Apr. 12, 1845; "Industrial Congress—Its Laws & c," *VoI,* June 19, 1846; "Appeal to Reformers" in "Adjournment of the Fifth National Industrial Congress," *NYDyTrib,* June 17, 1850. See also Levine, *Spirit of 1848,* 133–35.

31. "Miscellany," and "Pure Democracy," *VoI,* Oct. 8, 1847; "Reform Celebrations of the Fourth at Troy, N.Y.," *Albany Patriot,* July 7, 1847, 139.

32. Masquerier, *Sociology,* 69, 98; "The World's Convention," *NYDyTrib,* Oct. 6, 1845. Evans reprinted a "An Agrarian Revolution," as by "a man after my own heart." *SWmA,* Nov. 23, 1844.

33. "Industrial Congress," "Constitution of a Free State," "Miscellany," and "Pure Democracy," *VoI,* June 18, 25, 1847, and July 2, 1847. See also West, "Self-Government," *NAS,* Mar. 22, 1849, 171; "Miscellany," *VoI,* Oct. 8, 1847; Masquerier, *Sociology,* 22, and "A Model Constitution," 85–90; and West quoted in "National Reform Association," *YA,* Dec. 13, 1845. See also "Revised Constitution," Devyr, *Odd Book,* 252.

34. "A Letter from an Old Reformer," *Freedom* 1 (undated, unpaged No. 5 [1891]); *History of Hamilton County, Ohio,* comp. Henry A. Ford and Mrs. Kate B. Ford (Cleveland: L. A. Williams and Co., 1881), 373. Brown shared with Lucius A. Hine his Connecticut antecedents; a childhood on the Western Reserve; and an avid readership of the *Free Inquirer,* Vale's *Beacon,* the *Investigator,* and other "Infidel" publications,

as well as "several workingmen's papers, two or three Abolition papers." A carpenter, he hovered on the edges of the movement until he bought a farm at nearby Mount Healthy and became a close friend of Frances Wright D'Arusmond.

CHAPTER 6: RACE AND SOLIDARITY

1. Ingalls, *Reminiscences of an Octogenarian*, 35.

2. West quoted in "National Reform Association," *YA*, June 28, 1845; "Rejoinder to Gerrit Smith," *PR*, July 24, 1844; Hine, *Lecture on Garrisonian Politics*, 16.

3. "Industrial Congress—Ninth Session," *New York Times*, June 11, 1854; "Industrial Congress: Second Session,—June, 1847," *VoI*, July 2, 1847, 2; Commerford quoted at an NRA meeting in *WmA*, Jan. 18, 1845; Masquerier, *Sociology*, 48; "Letter of Alvan E. Bovay to the Auburn Convention," *Albany Patriot*, Jan. 26, 1848, 41; Devyr, *Odd Book*, 115, and also his description of Southern "chivalries" who "required a lesson which would teach them man's equality," 111; George Henry Evans, "Slavery," *The Man*, June 9, 1834, 78; Evans, "The Abolitionists," *The Man*, July 19, 1834, 213. See also John R. Wempersten, "Parke Godwin, Utopian Socialism, and the Politics of Antislavery," *New York Historical Society Quarterly* 60 (July–Oct. 1976): 107–26. For some background on Paine and antislavery, see Paine's "African Slavery in America," "A Serious Thought," "Emancipation of Slaves," "To the French Inhabitants of Louisiana," and comments in his letters to Thomas Jefferson (Apr. 10, 1789), to William Short (Nov. 2, 1791) and, again, to Jefferson (Jan. 25, 1805) in *Complete Writings of Thomas Paine*, ed. Philip S. Foner, 2 vols. (New York: Citadel Press [1945]), 2: 15–19, 19–20, 21–22, 963–68, 1288, 1321, and 1462; *An Essay on Common Wealths* (New York: The New-York Society for Promoting Communities, 1822), 24; Lause, *Some Degree of Power*, 91–92; Skidmore, *Rights of Man to Property*, 146, 158–60; and *Daily Sentinel*, July 16, 1830. The antislavery petitions of 1829 and 1839 included the names of Commerford, Hogbin, Pyne, Fellows, West, Gilbert Vale (both Sr. and Jr.), and others. Jentz, "Artisans, Evangelicals, and the City," 322–445.

4. Alan M. Kraut, "The Forgotten Reformers: A Profile of Third Party Abolitionists in Antebellum New York," in *Antislavery Reconsidered: New Perspectives on the Abolitionists*, ed. Lewis Perry and Michael Fellman (Baton Rouge: Louisiana State University Press, 1979), 119–45; Edward Magdol, "A Window on the Abolitionist Constituency: Antislavery Petitions, 1836–1839," in *Crusaders and Compromisers: Essays on the Relationship of the Antislavery Struggle to the Antebellum Party System*, ed. Alan M. Kraut (Westport, Conn.: Greenwood Press, 1983), 45–70, esp. 54–55; Edward Magdol, *The Antislavery Rank and File: A Social Profile of the Abolitionists' Constituency* (Westport, Conn.: Greenwood Press, 1986), 96–97, 110, 137, and, on the presence in the Lowell Female Antislavery Society of two strike leaders from 1833, Martha B. Hawk and Miriam B. Johnson, 37; Kraut, "Forgotten Reformers," 129–33. See also Eric Foner's chapter titled "Abolition and the Labor Movement in Antebellum America," in his *Politics and Ideology in the Age of the Civil War* (New York: Oxford University Press, 1980); and also Philip S. Foner and Shapiro, eds., *Northern Labor and Antislavery*. Although a militant freethinker, Evans refused to accept job advertisements that excluded Catholics, and he later printed the "Letter of Bishop Hughes" on nativism. *Daily Sentinel*, July 2, 1830, and *WmA*, May 25, 1844. For West, see his untitled letter, *Liberator*, Apr. 5, 1839, 56, and "Chardon-Street Convention,"

NAS, Dec. 3, 1841, 196; "Errors Corrected," *NAS*, Dec. 24, 1841, 208; and "J. E. Snodgrass of the Baltimore Visitor," *NAS*, Feb. 26, 1846, 153. Garrison's "Not to Be Trusted" provoked Keyser's "Wages and Chattel Slavery," *Liberator*, Feb. 18, 1848, 26, and Apr. 21, 1848, 63. See also letters by "W.," *Liberator*, Jan. 29. 1831, 19; "To the Editor," *Liberator*, Feb. 5, 1831, 23; "Working Classes," *Liberator*, Feb. 5, 1831, 23; "To the Workingmen of New England," *Liberator*, July 4, 1831, 105; and "Labor and Its Reward," *Liberator*, Sept. 12, 1845, 148.

5. Jonathan A. Glickstein, "'Poverty Is Not Slavery': American Abolitionists and the Competitive Labor Market," in Perry and Fellman, *Antislavery Reconsidered*, 195–218; Ingalls, *Reminiscences of an Octogenarian*, 29–30, 38–40, 167–68. See also the Douglass-Ingalls exchange as reported in Douglass's "Property in Soil and Property in Man," in *The Life and Writings of Frederick Douglass*, 5 vols., 5: *Supplementary Volume, 1844–1860*, ed. Philip S. Foner (New York: International Publishers, 1975), 104–6, and in Ingalls, *Reminiscences of an Octogenarian*, 40–41, 168; Evans, "Dialogue on Free and Slave Labor," *WmA*, June 8, 1844; Evans, "Rejoinder to Gerrit Smith," *PR*, July 24, 1844; Evans, "Second Letter from Gerrit Smith," *WmA*, Aug. 10, 1844; Evans, "Third Letter from Gerrit Smith," *WmA*, Aug. 17, 1844; "Wendell," "Our Prospects in New York," 286; "Wendell Phillips and 'Young America'" [from *YA*], *Liberator*, Sept. 4, 1846, 143; and West on "National Reform," *Liberator*, Aug. 28. 1846, 140; "Chattel and Wages Slavery," *Liberator*, Sept. 25, 1846, 152; and "Wages Slavery and Chattel Slavery," *Liberator*, Apr. 2, 1847, 53. For Hine, see "A Land Reformer," *National Anti-Slavery Standard*, Sept. 30, 1852, 72.

6. "Agrarian League," *WmA*, June 1, 1844; "The American Movement" [from the Chartists' *Northern Star*] and Evans's reply, *WmA*, Aug. 17, 1844; a piece in *WmA*, Feb. 22, 1845; "Slaves in the British Islands" [from the *Guiana Times*], *YA*, May 24, 1845; Captain Kempton quoted in "National Reform Association," *YA*, June 21, 1845, and in *Jubilee*, 13. See also "The Complimentary Ball [from *Young America*], *VoI*, Mar. 12, 1847; the resolutions of the 1848 NIC cited within article; Van Amringe, "National Reform," *AF*, Feb. 23, 1848, repr. *VoI*, Mar. 17, 1848; "Black Slavery and White Slavery Again," and the editorial commentary on "Black and White Slavery" [from the *Northampton Democrat*], *VoI*, Aug. 27, 1847, 2; "White Slavery," [from *Northampton Democrat*], *Chester Reveille*, July 17, 1847; and "Wages Slavery and Chattel Slavery" [from *YA*], *Harbinger* 5 (June 26, 1847): 38. For further discussions of the "different degrees of Slavery here at home," see two pieces entitled "Abolition at Home" discussing the question with the *Albany Patriot*, *YA*, Apr. 26, 1845, and May 17, 1845, and Greeley's "What Is Slavery?" [from *Cincinnati Morning Herald*], *YA*, June 28, 1845; Seth Paine's "Correspondence from Illinois," *Albany Patriot*, June 9, 1847, 123; and "Abolitionists" [from the *Pleasure Boat*], *VoI*, Feb. 26, 1847. It is often asserted that the term *wage slaves* echoed Southern politicians, but the analogy clearly originated with the workers themselves. Lause, *Some Degree of Power*, 202n23.

7. Greeley, "Slavery and Freedom," quoted in Arthur A. Ekrich Jr., *The Idea of Progress in America, 1815–1860* (New York: Columbia University Press, 1944), 246. For feudalism as a better system, see Masquerier, "Declaration of Independence," *WmA*, Sept. 28, 1844; Ingalls, *Reminiscences of an Octogenarian*, 27; and Ryckman quoted in *YA*, Jan. 17, 1846, who thought feudal values made the rulers "compelled to *be* something and to *do* something," whereas Van Amringe used selective medieval wage rates to assert a decline. "National Reform," *AF*, Feb. 23, 26, 1848, repr. *VoI*, Mar. 17,

1848. Clay described "industrial feudalism" as even more oppressive. "A Homestead for Every Man" [from *True American*], *VoI*, Jan. 15, 1847. For Brisbane, see *YA*, Feb. 14, 1846. Historians tend to misread this rhetoric about which form of slavery was the worst as a justification for the militants having assigned priority to wages slavery.

8. "Abolitionists" [from the *Pleasure Boat*], *VoI*, Feb. 26, 1847; "Wages and Chattel Slavery," *VoI*, May 7, 1847; J. E. Thompson, "Black Slavery and White Slavery" [from *Northampton Democrat*], *VoI*, Aug. 13, 1847.

9. Grandin, "Land Reform," *Liberator*, Apr. 21, 1848, 63. For Grandin's support for the labor movement, see also his "Working Men's Protective Unions," *Liberator*, Apr. 23, 1847, 68. Bovay made the same point about Calhoun's favoring free trade in land and human beings. "National Reform Association," *WmA*, Mar. 22, 1845. See also Channing's "Free and Slave Labor" [letter to *Providence Journal*], and "Dignity of Labor" [from *Scientific American*], *AF*, Apr. 16, 1845.

10. Pickering, *Working Man's Political Economy*, 181; Lucius A. Hine, "Social Reform," *Harbinger* 1 (Aug. 23, 1845): 164; Masquerier's "Working Men!" *YA*, Feb. 14, 1846; W. H. Whinery, "Examine Yourselves," *YA*, Feb. 28, 1846; Masquerier, *Sociology*, 23.

11. "Remarks of Mr. Commerford," *WmA*, Apr. 6, 1844; for Cluer, see *Doc. Hist.*, 8: 115, 116, 117–18; pieces from Wright's sermon quoted in "A Catechism of Glory," *AF*, Dec. 15, 1846, and "Shall the Sword Devour Forever!" *VoI*, Jan. 15, 1847. Seth Paine, an Illinois Agrarian, worried that the United States, like all other governments, seemed to be "organized upon the war principle." "Letter from Seth Paine," *Albany Patriot*, July 7, 1847, 138–39. See also "Death of Lieut. Eastman," *VoI*, Dec. 11, 1846. To be one of the "journeymen murderers" in Lithconia was such "a proof of honor" that the reluctant might be sent to prison, flogged, or shot. James Reynolds, *Equality*, 102–3.

12. "Wages and Chattel Slavery," *VoI*, May 7, 1847; "Black and White Slavery" [from the *Northampton Democrat*], *VoI*, Aug. 13, 1847; "The Land Question," *Western Quarterly Review* 1 (Jan. 1849): 29; Root, *Analysis of Theology*, 71; Bovay quoted in "The World's Convention," *NYDyTrib*, Oct. 6, 1845.

13. Van Amringe, "National Reform—No. 9," *AF*, Mar. 22, 1848; "A Slaveholder's Idea of Slavery" [from *Frankfort Commonwealth*], *WmA*, Feb. 1, 1845; Bovay quoted in "National Reform Association," *WmA*, Jan. 17, 1846.

14. "Answers of the Liberty Candidates to the Questions of the National Reformers," *Albany Patriot*, Oct. 21, 1846, 198. See also "The 'Free Soil' Principle," *NYDyTrib*, Oct. 13, 1846; "Antirent Nominations," *Albany Patriot*, Oct. 14, 1846, 194, which also quotes the reaction of *Charter Oak* to *Young America*; *NYDyTrib*, Oct. 12, 1846; Zahler, *Eastern Workingmen*, 96, 96n; "Mike Walsh in Office" and "The Elections" [from *Young America*], *VoI*, Nov. 13, 1846; *The Whig Almanac and United States Register for 1847* (New York: Greeley and McElrath, 1847), 45, and *The Whig Almanac United States Register for 1848* (New York: Greeley and McElrath, 1848), 40, included in *The Tribune Almanac for the Years 1838 to 1868. Inclusive: Comprehending the Political Register with the Whig Almanac . . .* 2 vols. (New York: New York Tribune, 1868). See also "The New Constitution," the critique of the New York convention, and a call for "a *new era* on democratic progress" in *Jubilee*, 1, 2.

15. "To the Friends of Industry and Equal Rights," *YA*, Apr. 29, 1848; "The Liberator on the Question of Labor," *Harbinger* 5 (July 17, 1847): 92–93; George Bradburn to

Gerrit Smith, quoted in Kraditor, *Means and Ends*, 267n35; *Signal of Liberty* cited in Sewell, *Ballots for Freedom*, 115, 116, 117, and Kraditor, *Means and Ends*, 152–53, 173; Green quoted in *AF*, Nov. 24, 1846. For examples of the growing interest of abolitionist papers in land reform, see, for example, article on the NRA press, *Albany Patriot*, June 9, 1847; "The Great Land Reform," *Albany Patriot*, July 21, 1847, 141; "Homestead Exemption," *Albany Patriot*, July 21, 1847, 142; Van Amringe's essay [from *Wisconsin Freeman*] and "Who Owneth American Soil," *Albany Patriot*, Feb. 9, 1848, 152; and "Homestead Exemption in Michigan," *Albany Patriot*, May 3, 1848, 2.

16. "Letter of Gerrit Smith" [from *Young America*], *VoI*, Nov. 20, 1846; Smith, "Poor Man's Party," *AF*, Nov. 24, 1846; Devyr, *Odd Book*, 112, 113; Ingalls, *Reminiscences of an Octogenarian*, 26, which also offers a paraphrase of Smith's argument on the antislavery implications of land reform, 30. The "Poor Man's Party" was the name of the first distinctly "Agrarian" group, founded in 1829–30 by Thomas Skidmore.

17. "Fraud: Indian Lands," *WmA*, May 16, 1835; "The Cherokees," *YA*, Dec. 27, 1845; "Black Hawke's Opinions," with "'Ma-Ka-Tai-Me-She-Kia-Kiak,' or Black Hawk" [from *Family Magazine*, 1834], *WmA*, May 4, 1844; Charles Dewey, "Sketch of the Life of Lewis Henry Morgan, with Personal Reminiscences," *Rochester Historical Society Publications* 2 (1929): 29, and a brief sketch of Grieg, 282–84; "An Indian Town, or Man's Rights in Connection with His Social and Selfish Nature," *PR*, July 27, 1844; Evans, "Which Is the Best, the Life of the Indian Savage, or the White Operative?" *WmA*, Aug. 10, 1844; Mark L. Lause, "'All Rights for All Men': Andrew E. Elmore and the Origins of Wisconsin Agrarianism," *Landmark* 29 (Spring 1986): 3–5. See also "An Indian Letter of Wisdom," *AF*, Nov. 14, 1844, which later discussed the "Horrible Barbarities" perpetrated "by this *Christian Nation*, on aboriginal Americans," taking particular pains to ascribe the Seminole war to "that land of *blood hounds, oppression and murder*," the slave states. *AF*, Feb. 12, 1845. For a short overview, see Lause, "Borderland Visions: Maroons and Outlyers in Early American History," *Monthly Review* 54 (September 2002): 38–44.

18. John Campbell, *Negromania* (Philadelphia: Campbell and Powers, 1851), the second publisher being his Chartist colleague, E. Powers. For his reappearance as a proslavery apologist, see Jonathan Katz, *Resistance at Christiana; The Fugitive Slave Rebellion, Christiana, Pennsylvania, September 11, 1851: A Documentary Account* (New York: Crowell [1974]), 157. "Industrial Congress—1848," *National Reform Almanac for 1849*, 15–20. See also the Chartist controversy in "The American Movement" [from *Northern Star*] and Evans's comments, *WmA*, Aug. 17, 1844. Commerford's admiration for Calhoun's advocacy of "free trade" did not prevent his signing of petitions against slavery in the District of Columbia as early as 1836 or his support of the abolitionist ticket by 1847. Jentz, "Artisans, Evangelicals, and the City," 373. See also Byrdsall, *History of the Loco-Foco*, 51–52, 55, 76, 78–79, 80, 93, and Masquerier, *Sociology*, 102, 125. Marx and Engels, too, praised Southern leaders' demands "for low duties and unfettered trade." "The London Times and Lord Palmerston" [from *NYDyTrib*, Oct. 21, 1861], in *On America and the Civil War*, ed. Saul K. Padover (New York: McGraw-Hill, 1972), 67.

19. "Declaration of Independence, and Expression of Sentiment Unanimously Adopted by the Working Women and Men," *JH 1854*, 102; "Agrarian League," *WmA*, June 1, 1844; Keyser's letter, "Wages Slavery and Chattel Slavery," *Liberator*, Apr. 21, 1848, 63; and Skidmore, *Rights of Man to Property*, 158–59; Hine, *Lecture on*

Garrisonian Politics, 7; Evans quoted in "Rioting," *The Man,* July 14, 1834; "From J. E. Snodgrass," and "From L.A. Hine," *Liberator,* Oct. 22, 1852, 171; "H." letter, *Cincinnati Daily Nonpareil,* June 13, 1851, 1; see also *JH1854,* 145. Beeny quoted in *New York World,* May 11, 1872, 1, col. 6; Hine, *Lecture on Garrisonian Politics,* 6; Van Amringe, "National Reform," *AF,* Mar. 1, 15, 1848; Masquerier, *Sociology,* 53; "Industrial Congress," *VoI,* July 2, 1847; West letter, "Democratic Government," *NAS,* Mar. 1, 1849, 159; *JH1854,* 145; "Declaration of Independence, and Expression of Sentiment Unanimously adopted by the Working Women and Men, in Mass Meeting at the Jubilee Grove, Fifth day of July, 1852," *Monthly Jubilee* 4 (Mar. 1854): 97, having been reprinted regularly in this publication; letter of Martha Hollingsworth, *VoI,* Apr. 14, 1848; Thompson, "Black Slavery and White Slavery," *VoI,* Aug. 27, 1847, 2.

20. Skidmore, *Rights of Man to Property,* 270–71; Evans, "Rejoinder to Gerrit Smith," *PR,* July 24, 1844; Lewis Masquerier, *A Scientific Division and Nomenclature of the Earth, and Particularly the Territories of the United States* (New York: Office of "Young America," 1847), 12, bound into his *Sociology;* West's letter, "National Reform," *Liberator,* Aug. 28, 1846, 140.

21. Van Amringe, "National Reform" series, *WF,* Jan. 19, 26, 1848, and Mar. 22, 1848.

22. "Free Soil," *Western Quarterly Review* 1 (Jan. 1849): 10; "National Reform Banquet" [from the *Cincinnati Daily Herald*], *Harbinger* 7 (June 10, 1848): 45–46.

23. William J. Simmons, *Men of Mark: Eminent, Progressive, and Rising* (Cleveland: G. M. Rewell, 1887), 202, 374–83, esp. 374–75. James M. Morris discusses the relationship of Clark and Haller in "William Haller: 'The Disturbing Element,'" *Cincinnati Historical Society Bulletin* 28 (Winter 1970): 260, 265, 282–83, although he erroneously dates the inception of Haller's involvement as 1861 rather than ten or eleven years earlier. For the Varneys, see the letters in Josiah Warren, *Practical Details in Equitable Commerce* (New York: Fowler and Wells, 1852); Masquerier to the Varneys [undated, ca. 1846], Lant Papers, also published in Pickering, *Working Man' Political Economy,* was printed by Thomas Varney using Warren's stereotyping technique.

24. Hine, *Lecture on Garrisonian Politics,* 10, 11; Skidmore, *Rights of Man to Property,* 158; Masquierer, "Autobiographical Sketch," 132–33; Evans, editorial, *Daily Sentinel,* Sept. 17, 1831, repr. in *Nat Turner,* ed. Eric Foner (Englewood Cliffs: Prentice-Hall, 1971), 76–77. For Collin and Dyer, see Larry Gara, *The Liberty Line* (Lexington: University of Kentucky Press, 1961), 116–17, 174; Dolores T. Saunders, *Illinois Liberty Line* (Farmington, Ill.: n.p., 1982), 124; "H. H. Van Amringe's Mission," *YA,* Apr. 29, 1848. See also Lippard's homage to his fictional freedom fighter, a "Black Sampson," in David Reynolds, *George Lippard, Prophet of Protest,* 124–28.

25. Evans, "Rejoinder to Gerrit Smith," *YA,* Sept. 27, 1845; the earliest mention of the "Indian State" in the "Constitution of the Industrial Congress," *YA,* Oct. 25, 1845; "An Indian State," *YA,* Nov. 15, 1845. Hine most likely penned "Our Coloured Population—A Negro State," *Quarterly Journal and Review* 1 (July, 1846): 193–204.

26. Philip Foner, *American Socialism and Black Americans from the Age of Jackson to World War II* (Westport, Conn.: Greenwood Press, 1977), 10. Foner's assertions of a racially exclusivist NRA ignored his own edition of Frederick Douglass's praising of the movement from *North Star,* Jan. 30, 1851, in *The Frederick Douglass Papers: Series One—Speeches, Debates, and Interviews,* ed. John W. Blassingame et al., 5 vols. (New Haven, Conn.: Yale University Press, 1979–1992), 2: 307. For a marked

departure from this, see Eric Foner, "Abolitionism and the Labor Movement in Antebellum America," 57–76.

27. *JH1854*, 135. Robert E. May, *Manifest Destiny's Underworld: Filibustering in Antebellum America* (Chapel Hill: University of North Carolina Press, 2002), 36–37. Scholarly assumptions about an impermeable color bar in antebellum reform movement are similar to those that deny any black membership in early trade unions. See, for example, Philip S. Foner's *Organized Labor and the Black Worker, 1619–1973*, 2d ed. (New York: International Publishers, 1976), 4–5. Foner applies his general assumption to the specific situations rather than by building the generalizations on an investigation of the specifics, and he transforms a general rule into a self-evident and universally applicable truism. In fact, Alexander P. Niger, "the first man of color to work at printing in Providence," was also a charter member of Local 33 of the National Typographical Union in 1857. Franklin Rosemont, "The Printers of Providence," in *A History of Rhode Island Working People*, ed. Paul Buhle, Scott Molloy, and Gail Sansbury (Providence, R.I.: [Institute for Labor Studies and Research], 1983), 63.

28. Hanes Walton Jr., *The Negro in Third Party Politics* (Philadelphia: Dorrance, 1969), 7, citing Dixon Fox's "The Negro Vote in Old New York," *Political Science Quarterly* 32 (Jan. 1917): 264. For the first notation of black involvement, see "Milford" under "Working Men's Movements," *WmA*, Sept. 21, 1844; Ingalls, *Reminiscences of an Octogenarian*, 35; "Anti-Slavery Convention in the Assembly Buildings," *NAS*, Dec. 28, 1848, 123; "National Reform," in Philip Foner, *Life and Writings of Frederick Douglass*, 5: 111; and Blassingame et al., *Frederick Douglass Papers*, 2: 307.

29. Masquerier, *Sociology*, 172.

30. "Are We Freemen?" *WmA*, July 6, 1844; West quoted in "National Reform Association," *YA*, June 28, 1845; and the workers' resolutions discussed in "Fugitive Slave Law" [from *Boston Protective Union*], *Liberator*, Oct. 25, 1850, 170. For recent misdescriptions from different political directions, see Philip Foner, *American Socialism and Black Americans*, 6; Philip Foner, *Organized Labor and the Black Worker, 1619–1973*, 5, 12; and Anthony Gronowicz, *Race and Class Politics in New York City before the Civil War* (Boston: Northeastern University Press, 1998), 48–50, 69, 126. For the emergence of more balanced views, see David R. Roediger, "Race, Labor, and Gender in the Languages of Antebellum Social Protest" in *Terms of Labor: Slavery, Serfdom, and Free Labor Making of Modern Freedom*, ed. Stanley L. Engerman (Stanford, Calif.: Stanford University Press, 1999), 186–87, and Roediger's *The Wages of Whiteness: Race and the Making of the American Working Class*, rev. ed. (New York: Verso, 1999), 46–48, 71–74, 144–50, as well as the treatment of Gerrit Smith and the NRA in John Stauffer, *The Black Hearts of Men: Radical Abolitionists and the Transformation of Race* (Cambridge, Mass.: Harvard University Press, 2002), 136–44.

31. West quoted in "Reform Celebration of the Fourth in Troy, N.Y.," *Albany Patriot*, July 7, 1847, 139; Hine, *Lecture on Garrisonian Politics*, 20, 12.

CHAPTER 7: FREE LABOR

1. "Mr. Van Amringe," *AF*, Jan. 12, 1848; "The Chicago Industrial Congress," *NyDyTrib*, June 12, 1850; "National Labor Reform Congress," *NyDyTrib*, June 13, 1850; "Labor Movements—National Industrial Congress," *NyDyTrib*, June 15, 1850; "Labor Movements," *NYDyTrib*, June 17, 1850.

2. "Letter of Hon. Moses G. Leonard," *NyDyTrib*, Apr. 13, 1847; "Land Limitation—The Freedom of the Public Lands," *NYDyTrib*, Apr. 15, 1847; two pieces en-
titled "Mayor Brady and Land Reform," *NyDyTrib*, Apr. 14, 16, 1847; "New York for
National Reform," *VoI*, Apr. 23, 1847; Stokes, *Iconography of Manhattan Island*, 5:
1802; Spann, *New Metropolis*, 429; and "Albany County National Reform Convention,"
Albany Mechanic's Advocate, May 20, 1847, 5. For Dennis Lyons, see "National Reform
Association," *YA*, Oct. 11, 1845. Despite some NRA sympathies, Slamm remained a
Tammany loyalist. Zahler, *Eastern Workingmen*, 82, 82n, 83n, 134, 135n. Tammany
referred to National Reformers as "the Nationals," predating by almost thirty years
the use of the term by Greenbackers.

3. "The Industrial Congress," *VoI*, June 11, 1847; "Industrial Congress," *VoI*, June
18, 25, 1847, and July 2, 1847. See also "National Reform" [from *Attica Telegraph*],
and "The Public Lands" [*Binghampton Courier*], *Chester Reveille*, July 17, 1847; Elihu
Burrit's "Universal Brotherhood," *Albany Patriot*, Sept. 30, 1846. For the Louisville
unions, see Ethelbert Stewart, "A Documentary History of Early Organizations of
Printers," *Bulletin of the Bureau of Labor* 11 (November 1905): 908, 921, 933, 937,
944. For Newberry, see George E. McNeil, *The Labor Movement: The Problem of
To-Day* (New York: M. W. Hazen Co., 1887), 102; Roger Wunderlich, *Low Living
and High Thinking at Modern Times, New York* (Syracuse, N.Y.: Syracuse University
Press, 1992), 41–42, 203n45.

4. "Industrial Congress," *VoI*, June 11, 1847; "Industrial Congress on War," *VoI*,
June 25, 1847; "Industrial Congress," *VoI*, June 18, 1847, and July 2, 1847; "Land
Reform," *AF*, May 24, 1848. See also Bruce Laurie, *The Working People of Phila-
delphia, 1800–1850* (Philadelphia: Temple University Press, 1980), 186. Some, like
William Wellington, offered sentiments in one labor meeting that were both patently
anti-Mexican and hostile to slavery such as the "*battered star* on the American flag."
"The Printers of Philadelphia," *Printers' Circular* 3 (May 1868): 7, 8.

5. "Power of a Third Party" [from *YA*], *VoI*, June 19, 1846. See also "The 'Free Soil'
Principle," *NYDyTrib*, Oct. 13, 1846; "Letter of Gerrit Smith" [from *YA*], *VoI*, Nov.
20, 1846; "A Call for a National Nominating Convention" [from *Albany Patriot*], *VoI*,
May 21, 1847; "Proceedings of the Nominating Convention at Macedon Lock, N.Y.,"
VoI, June 2, 1847; and "Gerrit Smith—The Presidency" [from *Albany Patriot*] and
"Resolutions Passed by the Macedon Lock Convention," *VoI*, July 9, 1847. "Industrial
Congress" and "Laws of the Industrial Congress," *VoI*, June 25, 1847; Phillips quote in
Essex Banner, repr. in *VoI*, June 25, 1847; "Industrial Congress," *VoI*, June 18, 1846;
West, "Self-Government," *NAS*, Mar. 22, 1849, 171; "Industrial Congress," *VoI*, June
18, 25, 1847, and July 2, 1847; "Miscellany," *VoI*, Oct. 8, 1847; Masquerier, *Sociology*,
22; West in "National Reform Association," *YA*, Dec. 13, 1845; "Hugh T. Brooks, Esq.,"
and "An Address to the Farmers of New York," *VoI*, Dec. 17, 1847.

6. "National Reform State Convention," *VoI*, Sept. 24, 1847; Fay's untitled letter,
VoI, Oct. 1, 1847.

7. "National Reform Meeting," *VoI*, Oct. 29, 1847.

8. "National Reform Convention," *VoI*, Nov. 5, 1847.

9. "Liberty Ticket," *VoI*, Nov. 5, 1847; "The New Party," *VoI*, Nov. 19, 1847; Zahler,
Eastern Workingmen, 87.

10. "National Reform Vote in New York," *VoI*, Dec. 24, 1847; "State of New York—

Official Canvass," *Albany Patriot,* Dec. 15, 1847, 20; *Whig Almanac for 1848,* 41, 42, in *Tribune Almanac for the Years 1838 to 1868.* Brooks, running independently upstate, eclipsed the Liberty totals, and in cases when the NRA adopted a Liberty candidate such as Lewis Tappan, their combined-vote totals fell to below those of some independent NRA candidates.

11. "Land Reform," *Albany Patriot,* Jan. 26, 1848, 41; "Letter of Alvan E. Bovay to the Auburn Convention," *Albany Patriot,* Jan. 26, 1848, 41; "The Auburn Convention" [from *Albany Patriot*], *AF,* Feb. 16, 1848. S. W. Green and George W. Clarke were also present at the Auburn convention.

12. "Senator Benton and Whitney's Railroad" [from *New York Herald*], *Chester Reveille,* Aug. 19, 1848; "Railroad to Oregon," *WmA,* Mar. 1, 1845; "Whitney's Folly," *YA,* June 28, 1845. See also "'The Great Humbug'" [from the *Randolph County Record*], *YA,* Dec. 6, 1845; "Hurrah for the Railroad," *WmA,* Apr. 13, 1844; Ingalls, *Reminiscences of an Octogenarian,* 27–28; Devyr, *Odd Book,* 157; Ronald E. Seavoy, *The Origins of the American Business Corporation, 1784–1855: Broadening the Concept of Public Service during Industrialization* (Westport, Conn.: Greenwood Press, 1982); John B. Rae, *Development of Railway Land Subsidy Policy in the United States* (Ann Arbor, Mich.: Edwards Brothers, 1938); "Pardoning of the LaSalle Rioters by the Governor," *Chester Herald,* July 28, 1854; *SWmA,* Nov. 30, 1844; and Masquerier, *Sociology,* 17, 64, 65. For the April municipal election of Havermeyer, see Stokes, *Iconography of Manhattan Island,* 5: 1810.

13. Letters in *WmA,* June 29, 1844, and *YA,* Dec. 27, 1845. For radicals in the city, see Laurie, *Working People of Philadelphia,* particularly for Sheddon and the Chartists, 165, 168, 180–81, 192, 193, and for Mullen, 196. For Joseph Jablonski and George Lippard, see *The American Radical,* ed. Mari Jo Buhle, Paul Buhle, and Harvey J. Kaye (New York: Routledge, 1994), and David S. Reynolds, *George Lippard* (Boston: Twayne Publishers, 1982), and his anthology, *George Lippard, Prophet of Protest,* particularly his address to the Industrial Congress, 191–96. Although reformist, New York's *Spirit of the Times* found the play scandalous when it reached that city. George C. D. Odell, *Annals of the New York Stage,* 15 vols. (New York: Columbia University Press, 1927–1949), 5: 115–16. For Germans, see Friedrich A. Sorge, *Labor Movement in the United States: A History of the American Working Class from Colonial Times to 1890,* ed. Philip S. Foner and Brewster Chamberlin, trans., Brewster and Angela Chamberlin (Westport, Conn.: Greenwood Press, 1977), 76, 95.

14. "Industrial Congress—Third Session," *NYDyTrib,* June 13, 1848; "Industrial Congress—Annual Session at Philadelphia," *NYDyTrib,* June 21, 1848. See also "The Industrial Congress of the United States," *Philadelphia Daily Public Ledger,* June 8, 1848; "Industrial Congress," *Philadelphia Daily Public Ledger,* June 9, 10, 12, 1848; "Local Affairs," *Philadelphia Daily Public Ledger,* June 15, 1848; and, *Doc. Hist.,* 8: 27–28. The Industrial Congress deliberated from 8:00 A.M. to noon and from 2:00 A.M. to 6:00 P.M. with evening rallies. "Industrial Congress—Third Session" [from *Young America*], *Harbinger* 7 (July 15, 1848): 82, also printed without title in *NEI,* June 21, 1848, with "Memorial to the Congress of the United States," *NEI,* July 6, 1848, and in *National Reform Almanac for 1849,* 20. That evening, the NRA held a public meeting at the Arch St. Hall. Evans, "Prepare Your Tickets," *YA,* Sept. 23, 1848.

15. West's untitled letters, *NAS,* May 25, 1848, 207, and June 22, 1848, 12. See also

"Self-Government," *NAS*, Mar. 22, 1849, 171. "Fourteenth Annual Meeting of the American Antislavery Society," and untitled letter from West, *NAS*, May 18, 1848, 203; Masquerier, *Sociology*, 69, 98; Ingalls, *Reminiscences of an Octogenarian*, 37.

16. For action on the 1848 presidential election, see Ingalls, *Reminiscences of an Octogenarian*, 26; "Industrial Congress—Annual Session at Philadelphia," *NYDyTrib*, June 21, 1848; "Industrial Congress," *Philadelphia Daily Public Ledger*, June 10, 1848; "Local Affairs," *Daily Public Ledger*, June 15, 1848. See also "Liberty Party Convention" [from *Rochester Advertiser*], *NYDyTrib*, June 20, 1848; *Proceedings of the National Liberty Convention, Held at Buffalo, New York, June 14th and 15th, 1848, including the Resolutions and Addresses adopted by that body, and speeches of Beriah Green and Gerrit Smith on that Occasion* (Utica: S. W. Green, 1848), esp. 9, 25, on land reform; Sewell, *Ballots for Freedom*, 119–20, 121, 136. For Waite, see "Another Candidate Declined," *Niles National Register*, 74 (July 12, 1848): 19. For Foote, see William H. and Jane Pease, *Black Utopia: Negro Communal Experiments in America* (Madison: State Historical Society of Wisconsin, 1963), 115–17, 119. Burritt stimulated interest in his League of Universal Brotherhood. The formation of a branch in Illinois led to interest in forming a similar branch among Wisconsin abolitionists, according to notices in *AF*, Aug. 18, 1847, and Mar. 22, 1848. For Masquerier, 1848 NRA candidate for governor, see "Death of an Eccentric Old Man," *NYDyTrib*, Jan. 8, 1888, 2.

17. David Reynolds, *George Lippard, Prophet of Protest*, 7; *The Papers of Daniel Webster*, ed. Charles M. Wiltse and Harold D. Moser, 3 series (Hanover, N.H.: University Press of New England for Dartmouth College, 1974–1988), series 1: *Correspondence*, vol. 7: *1850–52* (1986): 491; "Necrology, Daniel Webster," *Liberty Bell* [1856], 169–78. For the Democrats, see "Meeting of Factory Operatives," *Daily Public Ledger*, June 14, 2, col. 3, correcting the ascribing of the resolutions to the "Industrial Congress" in the issue of June 9, 1848; Ingalls, *Reminiscences of an Octogenarian*, 25; Laurie, *Working People of Philadelphia*, 12, 165, 168, 192. At the meeting, Robert Wood chaired, with John Perry, Richard B. Young, J. J. Walter and a Mr. Miller among the other speakers. Powers closed the meeting.

18. "Democratic Mass State Convention of Barnburners at Herkimer, N.Y." [from *Charter Oak*], *AF*, Nov. 24, 1847; "Plain Peter," *AF*, Jan 5, 1848; "Free Soil, Free Labor and Free Trade" [from *YA*], *AF*, Jan. 5, 1848. Active in this effort were C. C. Camberling and John Van Buren. For the radicals' critique of the Barnburners, see "A Call for a National Nominating Convention" [from *Albany Patriot*], *VoI*, May 21, 1847; "Proceedings of the Nominating Convention at Macedon Lock, N.Y.," *VoI*, June 2, 1847; "Gerrit Smith—The Presidency" [from *Albany Patriot*] and "Resolutions Passed by the Macedon Lock Convention," *VoI*, July 9, 1847. See also report from *YA* in *AF*, Oct. 27, 1847. In addition to the "Letter of Gerrit Smith," *AF*, Dec. 1, 1846, the course of "broad platform" Liberty Leaguers into the Free Soil Party preoccupied the newspaper: "What Will the Liberty Party Do Now?" *AF*, July 21, 1847; "Liberty National Convention" [from *Boston Emancipator*] and "Position of Liberty Papers" [from *Albany Patriot*], *AF*, July 28, 1847; Elihu Burritt's letter declining the vice-presidential nomination [from *Albany Patriot*], *AF*, Aug. 18, 1847; "Circular of Gerrit Smith" [from *Boston Emancipator*], *AF*, Sept. 22, 1847; "Buffalo Convention," *AF*, Oct. 13, 1847; "Letter from William Goodell" [from *Charter Oak*], *AF*, Nov. 17, 1847; "Gerrit Smith Speech," *AF*, Dec. 8, 1847; "The Response to the Nomination of John P. Hale," *AF*, Dec. 22, 1847; and "Land Reform," *AF*, May 24, 1848; Report from *YA* in

WF, Oct. 27, 1847. For Governor Young, see *NYDyTrib*, Jan. 5, 1848; Zahler, *Eastern Workingmen*, 51, 51n, 96, 96n-97n. Municipal elections were in spring 1848, and William F. Havermayer became the Democrat-elected mayor. Spann, *New Metropolis*, 429; *VoI*, June 15, 19, 1848, and July 6, 27, 1848; *Albany Patriot*, May 3, 1848; "Free Soil Movements," *WF*, Sept. 20, 1848; "Liberty Party Convention" [from *Rochester Advertiser*], *NYDyTrib*, June 20, 1848; *Proc. National Liberty Convention . . . 1848*, 9, 25. See also "C. M. Clay and Gerrit Smith," *WmA*, Oct. 5, 1844; "The Liberty Party," *YA*, Nov. 1, 1845; "Cassius M. Clay," *YA*, Jan. 17, 1846; and Bertram Wyatt-Brown, *Lewis Tappan and the Evangelical War against Slavery* (Cleveland: Press of Case Western Reserve University, 1969), 47, 47n24, 57. Radicals cited as allies in office: John P. Hale of New Hampshire; Henry Wilson and Amasa Walker of Massachusetts; Horace Greeley, Gerrit Smith, William H. Seward, and Ira Harris of New York; David Wilmot of Pennsylvania; Galusha Grow, George W. Julian, and William S. Holman of Indiana; Robert Smith and John Wentworth of Illinois; Benjamin F. Wade, Joshua R. Giddings, Joseph Cable, and Salmon P. Chase of Ohio; Thomas Hart Benton of Missouri; Andrew Johnston of Tennessee; and Isaac P. Walker and Charles Durkee of Wisconsin.

19. "Buffalo Convention," *AF*, Aug. 16, 1848; "Reasons for Sustaining the Nominations of the Buffalo Convention," *AF*, Aug. 23, 1848, which almost included William E. Stevenson. See also Zahler, *Eastern Workingmen*, 97, 97n, and Snodgrass letter in "Buffalo Convention. Reply of Mr. Van Amringe to Dr. Snodgrass," which cited Joshua Leavitt's letter to the *Rochester Daily Advertiser*, *YA*, Sept. 23, 1848. For NRA among Barnburners, see *VoI*, July 27, 1848; Zahler, *Eastern Workingmen*, 97n. Another participant was "Mr. Frisbie," presumably Frisby of the NRA at "Williamsburgh," *NYDyTrib*, May 28, 1852. For Barnburner state position, see *VoI*, July 27, 1848; Zahler, *Eastern Workingmen*, 97n. For Snodgrass's account of building the Free Soil Party in Maryland, see "Another Letter from Baltimore," *National Era*, July 27, 1848, 119.

20. Bovay (with Keyser listed as secretary) to Van Buren, June 24, 1848, and Van Buren to Bovay, July 20, 1848, Papers of Martin Van Buren, microform ed. (Washington, D.C.: Library of Congress, 1960; hereafter cited as Van Buren Papers), along with a clipping from the *New York Evening Post* and *NYDyTrib*, Aug. 3, 1848; and the Utica *Republic* and other newspapers with Van Buren's reply; Evans's comments on D. S. Curtiss's "Real and Sham Free Soil," *YA*, Sept. 23, 1848; Rochester National Reformers to Van Buren, July 28, 1848, and Van Buren to National Reformers, Aug. 22, 24, 1848, Van Buren Papers.

21. "Reform" [from *Peoria Register*], *YA*, Apr. 29, 1848. See also Sewell, *Ballots for Freedom*, 167–69; Ingalls, *Reminiscences of an Octogenarian*, 26, 37; *National Reform Almanac for 1849*, 47; Devyr, *Odd Book*, 312.

22. Letters to *YA* and Evans's comments on letters by D. S. Curtiss, *YA*, Sept. 23, 1848; *Investigator*, Sept. 20, 28, 1848; Zahler, *Eastern Workingmen*, 99n. Curtiss letter on "Real and Sham Free Soil," *YA*, Sept. 23, 1848; *Whig Almanac for 1849*, 49; *Whig Almanac for 1851*, 42, both bound into the *Tribune Almanac for the Years 1838 to 1868* and *National Reform Almanac for 1849*, 47.

23. "A Call for a National Nominating Convention" [from *Albany Patriot*], *VoI*, May 21, 1847; Zahler, *Eastern Workingmen*, 95, 95n; [N.Y. state Liberty Party convention] *Proc. National Liberty Convention . . . 1848*; Ingalls, *Reminiscences of an Octogenarian*, 29–30. For Jackson, see *Doc. Hist.*, 8: 26; Gerald Sorin, *The New York Abolitionists: A*

Case Study of Political Radicalism (Westport, Conn.: Greenwood, 1971); Perry, *Radical Abolitionism*, 178n; Sewell, *Ballots for Freedom*, 69, 76, 117; Ingalls, *Reminiscences of an Octogenarian*, 34; Arnold Buffum in "National Reform Convention," *YA*, May 10, 1845, and *Doc. Hist.*, 8: 26, 27; Madeline B. Stern, *The Pantarch: A Biography of Stephen Pearl Andrews* (Austin: University of Texas Press, 1968), 17–19, 28, 32–33, 35–46, 48–55; "Auxiliary Movements," *YA*, Mar. 21, 1846; editorial, *YA*, Apr. 29, 1848; "Land Reform," *Albany Patriot*, Jan. 26, 1848, 41; "The Auburn Convention" [from *Albany Patriot*], *AF*, Feb. 16, 1848; *Salem (Ohio) Anti-Slavery Bugle*, July 6, 1849; "Anti-Slavery Convention," *VoI*, May 8, 1846. For Rogers, see "An Idea [from *Herald of Freedom*], *WmA*, June 28, 1844. Concord in Merrimack County was the residence of Nathaniel Peabody Rogers and his *Herald of Freedom*. Rogers quoted in *WmA*, Aug. 24, 1844; untitled notice of Roger's death in *VoI*, Oct. 23, 1846; and *Jubilee*, 11, which also quotes the *Concord Freeman*. For "Directory of the W.M.P.U.," see *NEI*, June 2, 1848, and for the nearby community of Shakers at Cantebury, see Fogarty, *Dictionary of American Communal and Utopian History*, 174. The *Aurora* was edited by Beckley and Foster. Ingalls, *Reminiscences of an Octogenarian*, 28, 35. Philip Foner's *American Socialism and Black Americans*, 13, misquoted Charles Lenox Redmond as "out of patience" with the NRA, though the source itself clearly identified the object of his displeasure as antislavery people unwilling to accept the Free Soil Party. For Glenn, see Blassingame et al., *Frederick Douglass Papers*, 2: 202, 202n.

24. Hine, *Lecture on Garrisonian Politics*, 4, 22–23, 14, 15, 16, on disunion, 7–12, and electoral abstention, 16–18.

25. Ingalls, *Reminiscences of an Octogenarian*, 37–38; Masquerier, *Sociology*, 96; Zahler, *Eastern Workingmen*, 88n; "Mr. Van Schaick on Land Reform," *NYDyTrib*, Apr. 14, 1849; "New York City Election—The Defeat of Mr. Van Schaick" [from *New York Evening Post*], *WFD*, May 2, 1849; Spann, *New Metropolis*, 326, 429; Stokes, *Iconography of Manhattan Island*, 5: 1819. In 1849, the state elections reported the Liberty Party with only 1,311 votes, significantly less than the over 8,500 polled two years before, and the Workingmen's Party with only 650 votes, as opposed to over 1,700 two years before. *Whig Almanac for 1850*, 44, in *Tribune Almanac for the Years 1838 to 1868; VoI*, Apr. 14, 1848; Ingalls, *Reminiscences of an Octogenarian*, 35, 37–38; Devyr, *Odd Book*, 50–51, 56–60, 66; Spann, *New Metropolis*, 64, 359, 381. Mayor Daniel F. Tiemann favored leaving lots on the condition they had been improved. Spann, *New Metropolis*, 447n20. For activities across the East River, see Devyr, *Odd Book*, 60, 80, 115.

26. *Spirit of the Age*, Dec. 29, 1849, 410, cited in Martin, *Men against the State*, 117n; Ingalls, *Reminiscences of an Octogenarian*, 47. Seaver quoted Zahler, *Eastern Workingmen*, 39n. Devyr blamed Gerrit Smith for failing to sustain Evans's operation in the city, but the immediate problem was that Congressman Greeley who had earlier loaned Evans $200 had called in his note, which Evans paid by scraping together his reserves, selling $75 worth of his land in New Jersey and getting the balance as a small loan without security or interest from a wealthy benefactor (probably the much-maligned Smith). In the end, Evans had been, in Devyr's words, "literally starved back" to his Granville farm. Devyr, *Odd Book*, 113, 115; Evans's sale of land, Aug. 7, 1849, Deed Book K5, Office of Surrogate, Hall of Records, Monmouth County, Freehold, N.J., 404–6. Evans's wife, Laura, may have become ill as well. She died in 1850, leav-

ing him with a son, George Henry Jr., and two daughters, Edwina, six, and Frances, eight. Evans married his second wife, Mary Emmons, in 1852; she survived until 1876. George Henry Evans Jr. joined the Twenty-sixth and then the Thirty-ninth New Jersey Volunteers during the Civil War. Masquerier, *Sociology*, 99.

27. "Brotherhood of the Union," *NYDyTrib*, Oct. 23, 1851; Zahler, *Eastern Workingmen*, 45n; David Reynolds, *George Lippard, Prophet of Protest*, 203–12; "The White Banner" [from *New York America's Own*, Aug. 3], *NYDyTrib*, Aug. 6, 1850. See, in general, Roger Butterfield, "George Lippard and his Secret Brotherhood," *Pennsylvania Magazine of History and Biography*, 74 (July 1955): 285–309; Zahler, *Eastern Workingmen*, 45, 53n. For 1848–49, see "Independent Order of Liberals," *Independent Beacon* 1 (Aug., Dec. 1849): 8–10, 135–38; Post, *Popular Freethought*, 108–9; Klippart, *Brotherhood of the Union*, 3, 6, 16; *Constitution and By-Laws of Nimisilla Circle of the B.U. [H.F.] C.A., No. 9 of the State of Ohio, and 97 of the C.A.* (Canton, Ohio: A. McGregor, Printer, 1851), 3–4; "The White Banner" [from *New York America's Own*, Aug. 3], *NYDyTrib*, Aug. 6, 1850; and the rites of initiation from the secret ritual book known only as the *B. G. C.* (Philadelphia, [1850?]), 36, 44, 48, 51, 58. Copy in the archives of Brotherhood of the Union, the Brotherhood of America, Historical Society of Pennsylvania, Philadelphia (hereafter cited as Brotherhood of the Union). Moderate land reformer and literati, A. J. H. Dugaanne opted for nativism, and his novel *The Knights of the Seal; or, the Mysteries of the Three Cities; A Romance of Men's Hearts and Habits* (Philadelphia: Colon and Adriance, Arcade, 1845) addressed the dangers of alien conspiracies.

28. Ingalls, *Reminiscences of an Octogenarian*, 34, 43–44.

29. David Reynolds, *George Lippard, Prophet of Protest*, 215–17; untitled letter from Hollingsworth, *YA*, Sept. 23, 1848; *Report of the Woman's Rights Convention, Held at Seneca Falls, N.Y., July 19th and 20th, 1848* (Rochester, N.Y.; John Dick, 1848).

30. "The Secondary, Subsidiary or Auxiliary Principles" in "Fundamental Principles" published in "Adjournment of the Fifth National Industrial Congress," *NYDyTrib*, June 15, 1850.

CHAPTER 8: FREE SOIL AND CHEAP LAND

1. For Van Amringe, see "Mr. Van Amringe's Mission" [from *YA*], *AF*, Dec. 8, 1847; "Mr. Van Amringe," *AF*, Jan. 12,1847; "'Young America'—Mr. Van Amringe's Letters," *AF*, Jan. 24, 1847; "Land Reform," and "National Reform—No. 4," *AF*, Feb. 16, 1848. For his later swing through Illinois back into Ohio, see the notices from the *Chicago Daily Democrat* and the *Chicago Citizen* in the *AF*, Mar. 8, and Apr. 5, 1848; his own letter in *YA*, Apr. 29, 1848; and "National Reform Banquet" [from the *Cincinnati Daily Herald*], *Harbinger* 7 (June 10, 1848): 45–46. See also his untitled Van Amringe letter, *WFD*, Feb. 7, 1849; "Land Reform in Wisconsin," *NYDyTrib*, Apr. 3, 1850; and "National Industrial Congress," *NYDyTrib*, June 15, 1850, 2.

2. For the letter of Daniel E. Curtiss, see "Real and Sham Free Soil," *YA*, Sept. 23, 1848; Joseph L. Norris, "The Land Reform Movement," in "Phases of Chicago History," *Papers in Illinois History and Transactions for 1937* (Springfield: Illinois State Historical Society, 1937), 73–82. See also "Land Reform in the Pulpit," *Chester Reveille*, Aug. 16, 1848.

3. Fogarty, *Dictionary of American Communal and Utopian History*, 22–23, 190. See also Warren B. Chase, *The Life-Line of the Lone One; or, the Autobiography of the World's Child*, 3rd ed. (Boston: Bela Marsh, 1865).

4. William B. McCord, ed., *History of Columbiana County, Ohio* (Chicago: Biographical Pub. Co., 1905), 298. For Camden's vote in Mar. 1848, see Nelson W. Evans, *A History of Scioto County, Ohio*, 2 vols. (Portsmouth, Ohio: N. W. Evans, 1903), 1: 372; Root, *Analysis of Theology*, 64; and *Jubilee*, 12.

5. "Young America" [from *Boston Emancipator*], *AF*, Aug. 11, 1847; untitled letters from Burlington, Wis., *AF*, Mar. 8, 29, 1848; *AF*, Aug. 25, 1846; Elmore's letter in "Land Reform," *AF*, Jan. 12, 1848. Van Amringe's eight lectures, "National Reform," serialized in the *AF*, Dec. 8, 1847, Jan. 19, 26, 1848, Feb. 9, 16, 23, 1848, and Mar. 1, 8, 15, 1848, would be widely republished: his series on "Homestead Exemption," starting in *WFD*, Dec. 7, 1848, and followed by "Land Limitation," *WFD*, Mar. 14 through Apr. 21, 1849. For Booth, see "Macedon Lock Convention—Its Candidates" [from *Charter Oak*], *AF*, Sept. 1, 1847; "Land Reform," *AF*, Oct. 13, 1847; an announcement that "S. M. Booth" would be joining the staff, *AF*, Apr. 5, 1848; its first issue by Olin and Booth, *AF*, May 31, 1848; and also Booth alone, *WF*, Sept. 27, 1848. See also "Land Limitation" [from *NYTrib*], *AF*, July 14, 1847, and "Land Reform" [from *Chicago Democrat*], *AF*, Mar. 8, 1848. For other sources on Wisconsin, see Ms rolls of the Brotherhood of the Union; John G. Gregory, "The Land Limitation Movement: A Wisconsin Episode of 1848–1851," *Parkman Club Publications*, vol. 14 (Milwaukee: Parkman Club, 1897), 89n, 92, 102–4; *Dictionary of Wisconsin Biography* (Madison: State Historical Society of Wisconsin, 1960), 42–43; and Vroman Mason, "The Fugitive Slave Law in Wisconsin, with Reference to Nullification Sentiment," *Proceedings of the State Historical Society of Wisconsin at Its Forty-Third Annual Meeting Held Dec. 12, 1895* (Madison, 1896), 117–44.

6. "Letter from Seth Paine," *Albany Patriot*, July 7, 1847, 138–39. Lovejoy quoted in Magdol, *Owen Lovejoy*, 81; see also 37, 43–45, 60–62, 78–79, 88, 95, 96. See *WF*, July 5, 12, 1848. "H. H. Van Amringe's Mission," *YA*, Apr. 29, 1848; and Larry Gara, *Liberty Line*, 174. For the *Chicago Tribune* support of the Underground Railroad movement by 1854, see 146–47. For the Chicago NRA, see Joseph L. Norris, "Phases of Chicago History II. The Land Reform Movement," in *Papers in Illinois History* (Springfield: Illinois State Historical Library, 1937), 78–79n, 81, 81n.

7. Allan G. Bogue, "The Iowa Claim Clubs: Symbols and Substance," in *The Public Lands: Studies in the History of the Public Domain*, ed. Vernon R. Carstensen (Madison: University of Wisconsin Press, 1963), 47–69. On Lingle, see *The History of Clark County, Ohio* (Chicago: W. H. Beers. and Co., 1881), 260, 606–8, 642, 656, and esp. 962. Among the younger men the Bloomfield circle influenced was James B. Weaver, future presidential candidate of the Greenback-Labor and Populist parties. Lause, "Voting Yourself a Farm in Antebellum Iowa: Towards an Urban Workingclass Prehistory of the Post Civil-War Agrarian Insurgency," *Annals of Iowa*, 49 (Winter/Spring, 1988): 169–86. A. A. Graham, comp., *The History of Fairfield and Perry Counties, Ohio. Their Past and Present* (Chicago: W. H. Beers, 1883), 169–70; and *Lancaster Eagle* excerpts in *Principles*, 13, and *Jubilee*, 13, and read at New York NRA meeting, *WmA*, Sept. 14, 1844. Starting as an English edition of *Der Ohio Adler*, the *Eagle* involved such figures as Owenite John Harmon and Daniel A. Robertson, a veteran of New York's Locofoco movement. For D. A. Robertson, see "Married," *WmA*, June 29, 1844, and

mention of H. B. Dean (of 1831) in *WmA*, Feb. 15, 1845. See also "Reform in Ohio," *YA*, Nov. 8, 1845, and "National Reform in Ohio," *NYDyTrib*, May 15, 1850.

8. Magdol, *Owen Lovejoy*, 95, 118–19. See also Don E. Fehrenbacher's *Chicago Giant, Biography of "Long John" Wentworth* (Madison, Wis.: American History Research Center, 1957), 73, 74, 148, 197. For Charles Dyer's gubernatorial race, see Paul Simon, *Lincoln's Preparation for Greatness: The Illinois Legislative Years* (Norman: University of Oklahoma Press, 1965), 307. Gaston was a thirty-nine-year-old English-born craftsman living with wife and son, according to the 1850 Census, Fourth Ward, Chicago, Cook County, Illinois, printed p. 258; directories *1848–49*, 54; *1851*, 85; *1852–53*, 73. He operated the *Times* from June 12, 1852, to Oct. 18, 1853. Zebrina Eastman, *Newspapers and Periodicals of Illinois, 1814–1879* (Springfield: Illinois State Historical Library, 1910). Gaston's "Columbia Circle" of the *BoU* had a similar diversity, though he died before it was reorganized on Aug. 4, 1854. "Columbia Circle" in the city directory; Roy P. Basler, Introduction to John Lock Scripps, *Life of Abraham Lincoln*, ed. Roy P. Basler, notes by Lloyd A. Dunlap (Bloomington: Indiana University Press, 1961), 17–18; Notice of Gaston's, *Gem of the Prairie* in *AF*, July 19, 1848. See Wittke, *Utopian Communist*, 144, 152, 173; Sorge, *Labor Movement in the United States*, 93, 96, 152.

9. Frances M. Morehouse, *The Life of Jesse W. Fell* (Urbana: University of Illinois Press, 1916), also published as *University of Illinois Studies in the Social Sciences* 5 (June 1916): 265–393. For southern Illinois, see *Combined History of Randolph, Monroe, and Perry Counties, Illinois* (Philadelphia: J. L. McDonough and Co., 1883), 195–96. See *Jubilee*, 14, which cited the *Randolph County Record*, also "Hon. Robert Smith," *YA*, May 24, 1845, and same title Nov. 1, 1845; quote in notice of *Principles*, July 5, 1845; "Progress in Illinois," *YA*, Dec. 6, 1845; "Land Ho! Stop the Sale!" *YA*, Dec. 27, 1845; "Homestead," *YA*, Jan. 3, 1846; and "The Inalienable Homestead, *YA*, Mar. 7, 1846. The *Record* became the *Chester Reveille*. For Steubenville, see James B. Doyle, *The Twentieth Century History of Steubenville and Jefferson County, Ohio and Reprentative Citizens* (Chicago: Richmond-Arnold, 1910): 314, 315. For *American Union*, see *YA*, Nov. 8, 1845; *Principles*, 13; *Jubilee*, 14. For Ohio in general, see *National Reform Almanac for 1849*, 46; "National Reform in Ohio" dealing with preemption bill introduced into the legislature by a Mr. Beaver, *VoI*, Jan. 7, 1848; *NYDyTrib*, May 15, 1850; and "Ohio Land Reform Resolutions," *National Era* 6 (Dec. 16, 1852): 203. Participants in the New Lisbon auxiliary mentioned in *Principles*, 13; "Ohio" [from the *Aurora*], *SWmA*, Dec. 21, 1844; *WmA*, Jan. 4, 18, 1845. They are repeatedly noted in the *History of Columbiana County, Ohio* (Philadelphia: D. W. Ensign, 1879), 32, 33, 36–37, 40, 104–5, 108, 110, 113–15, 117, 120, 170, 229–30, 258, 327. For Carrolton, see *SWmA*, Nov. 30, 1844; *WmA*, Jan. 4, 1845; *NYDyTrib*, May 15, 1850; *Commemorative Biographical Record of Carrol County* (Chicago: J. H. Beers, 1891), 812. See also John Bell Bouton, *Life and Choice Writings of George Lippard* (New York: H. H. Randall, 1855), 92; *WmA*, Jan. 4, 1845; Ms rolls of the Brotherhood of the Union, Brotherhood of America Papers.

10. "Reminiscences of the late Andrew E. Elmore of Green Bay, in an interview with Deborah Beaumont Martin," *Proceedings of the State Historical Society of Wisconsin at its Fifty-eighth Annual Meeting, Held Oct. 20, 1910* (Madison, 1911), 190–92, 195–96; Elmore's 1880 reminiscences in *The History of Waukesha County, Wisconsin* (Chicago, 1880), 358, 369, 371, 420, 491–92, 756, 760, 763. For Chase, see his *Life-Line of the*

Lone One, and his *Forty Years on the Spiritual Rostrum* (Boston: Colby and Rich, 1888). Theodore Clarke Smith, *The Liberty and Free Soil Parties in the Northwest* (New York: Longmans, Green, and Co., 1897), 98, 102, 132, 136, 146, 154–55. For the state convention, see "Democratic Mass State Convention of Barnburners at Herkimer, N.Y." [from *Charter Oak*], AF, Nov. 24, 1847, Jan. 24, 1848.

11. "National Liberty Party at Washington City" [from *Western Citizen*], WF, Oct. 13, 1848; "Charles Durkee and W. P. Lynde on Land Reform," WF, Nov. 1, 1848. For Strong's nomination, see "The Democratic Territorial Convention," AF, July 28, 1847. For Huebschman and Fratney, see WF, Oct. 13, 1848, and Nov. 8, 1848. When a Whig politician spoke against National Reform, Booth commented in WF, Oct. 13, 1848. George Hyer, formerly of the *Rock River Pilot,* announced founding of the *Waukesha Democrat* in AF, May 24, 1848. Henry Barron acquired it, renaming the paper the *Chronotype* after Elizur Wright's press. Barron, like Elmore, sought to reposition the Democratic Party as that of reform. "'Young America'—Mr. Van Amringe's Letters," WFD, Jan. 24, 1849; Van Amringe's letter in response, WFD, Feb. 7, 1849. Van Amringe replied, WFD, Jan. 31, 1849; "Homestead Exemption" [from *Independent Democrat*], WFD, July 24, 1849; discussion of Free Democratic party, WFD, July 31, 1849; "Rights of Labor," WFD, Sept. 4, 1849; excerpt [from *Quaker City*], WFD, Sept. 11, 1849; and account of the election, WFD, Nov. 20, 1849. See also "Letter from Senator Walker" to Elmore, WFD, Jan. 31, 1849; "Letter of I. P. Walker" [from *Waukesha Democrat*], WFD, Mar. 14, 1849; and Smith, *Liberty and Free Soil Parties,* 210–13, 214–15, 215n. For controversy over Senator Walker's response to the Wilmot Proviso, see "Injustice to Senator Walker," WFD, Apr. 18, 1849. For Fratney, born 1815 and died 1855, who was a refugee of 1830, see *Dictionary of Wisconsin Biography,* 135.

12. "Letter of I. P. Walker" [from *Waukesha Democrat*], WFD, Jan. 31, 1849, and Mar. 14, 1849, which also includes a defense of Chase's resolutions in the legislature; Smith, *Liberty and Free Soil Parties,* 210–13, 214–15, 215n. For Clement, see also WF, Feb. 10, 1847.

13. For Worcester, Vermont, and Wright, see Zahler, *Eastern Workingmen,* 88n, 98n.

14. Evans, "Not Quite Right," WmA, Jan. 18, 1845; "Robert Dale Owen," WmA, Mar. 15, 1845; W. Slater, "Robert Dale Owen," WmA, Mar. 15, 1845; "Anti-Rentism in Indiana," YA, Feb. 14, 1846; "Robert Dale Owen's Explanation," YA, Mar. 29, 1845; "Indiana Sold to British Fundmongers," YA, Feb. 7, 1846; Judge Breese and Senator Stephen A. Douglas noted in "National Reform Association," WmA, Jan. 3, 1845.

15. "The Industrial Congress," *Univercoelum* 3 (May 12, 1849): 377; "The Industrial Congress" in both *Cincinnati Gazette* and *Cincinati Daily Commercial,* June 9, 1849; "The Industrial Congress," *Cincinatti Daily Times,* June 8, 9, 1849; "Industrial Congress," *Cincinatti Daily Times,* June 11, 1849, and untitled notices of its activities on June 6, 7, 12, 16, 1849. See also "Homes for All" [from *Philadelphia Dollar Democrat*], *Cist's Weekly Advertiser,* June 13, 1849; *Western Quarterly Review* 1 (Jan. 1849): 103–6; and Van Amringe, "Appeal to Reformers," NYDyTrib, June 15, 1850. Interestingly, when Ohio Agrarians moved toward statewide organization through a Grand Circle of the Brotherhood of the Union, they did so with the moral support of the temperance movement. "Public Lands" [from *Ohio Organ and Sons of Temperance Record*], VoI, Aug. 6, 1847. In addition to Pickering, *Working Man's Political Economy,* see *The Friend of Man; Being the Principles of National or Land Reform:*

Clearly Stated Together with answers to the Various Objections that Have Been Urged against It. (Cincinnati: National Reform Association, 1850).

16. Ingalls, *Reminiscences of an Octogenarian,* 56; "The Chicago National Industrial Congress," *NYDyTrib,* June 12, 1850, 3; "National Labor Reform Congress" (based largely on the *Chicago Democrat* of June 8, 1850), *NYDyTrib,* June 13, 1850, 3; "National Industrial Congress," *NYDyTrib,* June 15, 1850, 2; "Adjournment of the Fifth National Industrial Congress," *NYDyTrib,* June 17, 1850, 3. For Ingalls, see "National Industrial Congress," *NYDyTrib,* June 15, 1850, 2. For Ceresco, see Joseph Schafer, "The Wisconsin Phalanx," *Wisconsin Magazine of History,* 19 (June 1935): 454–74; "The Chicago Industrial Congress," *NYDyTrib,* June 12, 1850, 3; "National Labor Reform Congress," *NYDyTrib,* June 13, 3; "National Industrial Congress," *NYDyTrib,* June 15, 1850, 2; and "Labor Movements," *NYDyTrib,* June 17, 1850.

17. "The Chicago National Industrial Congress," *NYDyTrib,* June 12, 1850, 3; Van Amringe, "Appeal to Reformers," in "Adjournment of the Fifth National Industrial Congress," *NYDyTrib,* June 17, 1850; "Letter of Alvan E. Bovay to the Auburn Convention," *Albany Patriot,* Jan. 26, 1848, 41.

18. *Leaves of History, from the Archives of Boston Typographical Union No. XIII,* comp. by the union (Boston: Boston Typographical Union, 1923), 3–5; Hoagland, "Humanitarianism," 1: 552, 552n; David Reynolds, *George Lippard, Prophet of Protest,* 213–14. This claim for Chicago might be based on a confusion of references to the NIC that met there with a local body, although Cincinnati's "Hamilton Industrial Congress" clearly had delegates from the tristate area and clearly functioned, however briefly. For Philadelphia, see "A Review of the Industrial Union Movement," in *A General Report of the Industrial Union No. 1* (Philadelphia: Published by order of the Union, 1853), 5–21; *Quaker City Weekly,* Feb. [9?], 1850. For Mills, see Bouton, *Life and Choice Writings of George Lippard,* 91, 92; Roll of Members, Circle No. 92, Ms Rolls of the Brotherhood of the Union. James B. Elliott thanked Mills for his assistance in republishing Lippard's *Tom Paine, Author-Soldier of the American Revolution . . . Philadelphia, January 25, 1852* (Philadelphia: n.p., 1894), 16n. The movement helped launch a series of cooperative papers: *Cincinnati Nonpareil; St. Louis Signal; Pittsburgh Union; Allegheny City Enterprise; Auburn Herald; Columbus Fact; Steubenville Messenger; Dayton Item* (?); and an unnamed paper at Louisville. Hoagland, "Humanitarianism," 1: 569.

19. Since the panic of 1837, prices fell continually; there was a brief and limited recovery in 1844–45, and prices began to recover at the close of the decade, encouraging workers to organize for wage increases to keep pace. Wilentz, *Chants Democratic,* 363–64; Zahler, *Eastern Workingmen,* 83, 83n; *New York Herald,* July 16, 1850, quoted in Hoagland, "Humanitarianism," 1: 554, 557n–58n, 562; Ware, *Industrial Worker,* 236, 237; and Levine, *Spirit of 1848,* 117–37. Iver Bernstein largely follows the Bennett thesis as well. Bernstein, *The New York City Draft Riots,* 87–89, 90–91, 92, 93. Independent land reform activities continued only episodically, as in the report on "Land Reform," *Philadelphia Saturday Evening Post,* Sept. 7, 1850, 2. See also Fred A. Shannon, "The Homestead Act and the Labor Surplus," *American Historical Review* 41 (1936): 637–51.

20. Hoagland, "Humanitarianism," 1: 556, 558.

21. The petitions are filed in various manuscript collections of the U.S. House and Senate, particularly those of the Committee on Public Lands or the general folders of

tabled or unfinished business, through the Legislative Research Office, National Archives, Washington, D.C. See also Julian, "Spoilation of the Public Lands," 179–80.

22. Smith, *Liberty and Free Soil Parties*, 215, 234–35. For Paine, see *WF*, Dec. 6, 1848; In general, see Gregory, "Land Limitation Movement," 89–112.

23. Invitation from "Industrial Congress," *VoI*, June 11, 1847. For sympathetic coverage of the 1852 NIC, see the *New York Daily Tribune:* "Industrial Congress," June 6, 1851, 5; "Sixth Session—National Industrial Congress Temporary Organization," June 6, 1851, 6; "National Industrial Congress," June 9, 1851, 5; "National Reform Mass Meeting," June 13, 1851, 6; and "Conclusion of the National Industrial Congress," June 14, 1851, 6. For hostile reports from the Democratic perspective, see the *New York Daily Herald:* "National Industrial Congress," June 8, 1851, 1; "National Industrial Congress—Suicide," June 10, 1851, 8; and "Our Albany Correspondence," June 13, 1851, 3. In addition, Lucius A. Hine, who attended from Ohio, reported on the Congress in "H." letters, *Cincinnati Daily Nonpareil*, June 11, 13, 16, 17, and 20, 1851, on pp. 1 and 2. For Bowers, see Benjamin Quarles, *Black Abolitionists* (New York: Oxford University Press, 1969), 7, 25, 26; Simmons, *Men of Mark*, 202.

24. Hine noted with disgust that "one delegate declared that he would not sit with a colored man, and left the congress." "H." letter, *Cincinnati Daily Nonpareil*, June 11, 1851, 2.

25. "National Industrial Congress—VII Session," *NYDyTrib*, June 3, 1852, 6. At least part of the Philadelphia movement remained aloof from the 1853 NIC, according to Fannie Lee Townsend's "Slices of Wilmington" and her "Proceedings of he National Industrial Congress," *JH1854*, 371–75. See also "Industrial Congress—Ninth Session," *New York Daily Times*, June 11, 1854, 3; "National Industrial Congress," *NYDyTrib*, June 8, 1855, 5; "Industrial Congress," *Cleveland Plain Dealer*, June 4, 1855; untitled item *Cleveland Daily Plain Dealer*, June 6, 1855, 3, which had announced Day's new paper in the issue of June 1. For Day, see Simmons, *Men of Mark*, 978–84; *A Documentary History of the Negro People in the United States*, ed. Herbert Aptheker, 2 vols. (New York: Citadel Press, 1951), 1: 151, 278, 318–19, 320, 342, 411, 499; Boyd S. Stutler's Preface to *Provisional Constitution and Ordinance for the People of the United States by John Brown* (St. Catherine's, Ontario: Printed by William Howard Day, 1858; Weston, Mass.: M and S Press, 1969), 4–5; and Quarles, *Black Abolitionists*, 134, 165, 217, 334–35, 340n5.

26. "Gerrit Smith Donation" [from *YA*], *Independent Beacon* 1 (Nov. 1850): 509–12. When the citywide Industrial Congress sent Day to London in winter 1850–51, it also sent copies of a land reform address by Sen. Isaac P. Walker, who had fast become a hero of the movement. For Day, the address, and a detailed reportage of the citywide body, see, respectively: "Labor Movements," *NYDyTrib*, Dec. 15, 1850, 1; *New York Herald*, Aug. 29, 1850, cited in Hoagland, "Humanitarianism," 1: 558–59; and "Industrial Congress," *NYDyTrib*, Apr. 9, 1851, 7. E. H. Rogers and a delegate of the Typographical Union pressed the case for Walker, supported by J. L. Kinglsey and Edward P. Day of the Brotherhood of the Union. For the Tammany call, see *NYDyTrib*, May 30, 1851, 6. For the Walker "boom," see *NYDyTrib*, Apr. 28, 1851, June 4, 1851, and Aug. 23, 1851. For Hale, see *NYDyTrib*, Aug. 12, 13, 28, 1852, supplemented by accounts in the *New York Herald*, June 4, 1852, and Aug. 11, 12, 18, 19, 1852. See also Hoagland, "Humanitarianism," 1: 560, 560n, 561, which viewed this as the beginning of the end

of the congress. For background, see Amy Bridges, *A City in the Republic: Antebellum New York and the Origins of Machine Politics*, 2d ed. (Ithaca, N.Y.: Cornell University Press, 1987).

27. Julian, "Spoilation of the Public Lands," 180–81. Many came simply from "citizens" who did not even indicate their location, but the usual names came from the NYCIC, the Mechanics' Mutual Protection, Rochester's Emanuel Circle of the Brotherhood of the Union, and the local chapters of Weitling's Arbeiterbund from New York City, Milwaukee, Detroit, and Carthage, just outside of Cincinnati.

28. For *U.S. Journal*, see *Jubilee*, 11–12. Smith's and other letters from Washington are in *YA*, February 28, 1846, and Mar. 7, 21, 1846. Champion attended the National Industrial Congress of 1848 from Philadelphia and was assigned to the Executive Committee of 1848–49 from Pennsylvania. *Doc. Hist.*, 8: 28; *National Reform Almanac for 1849*, 20; *NYDyTrib*, June 13, 1848. See also Bouton, *Life and Choice Writings of George Lippard*, 91, 92; "Washington City," *JH1854*, 379; "National Industrial Congress," *NYDyTrib*, June 5, 12, 1852; "Industrial Congress," *National Era*, June 10, 1852, 94; *Proc. of Seventh N.I.C.*, 1, 14; and memorial of the National Industrial Congress, filed June 8, 1852, SEN32A-H20, box 141, folder 6/7–8/52, U.S. Senate, Legislative Records. For Philadelphia's preparations, see "The Great Mass Meeting at the Chinese Museum," *JH1854*, 309–14.

29. *Proc. of Seventh N.I.C.*, 2. Letters to Pierce from Price, June 7, 1852; Gordon to Pierce, June 14, 1852; Devyr to Pierce, June 18, 23, 1852; A. G. H. Duganne to Pierce, July 2, 1852; Price (with Croly, A. G. Levy, Commerford, and David Marsh) to Pierce, July 5, 1852; E. W. Capron to Pierce, July 27, 1852. Franklin Pierce Papers, microfilm ed. (Washington, D.C.: Library of Congress, 1959). The last of Devyr's letters had several enclosures: a leaflet *To the Land Reform Forces of New York State* dated June 11, 1852; an exchange of letters with Hamilton Fish; and a *Circular to the Friends of a True Republic*, proposing a new reform paper, the *Voice of Truth*. Also Cochrane to Pierce, June 18, 1852, with a cosigned enclosure from Commerford, Franklin Pierce Papers. Cochrane would have surely known that the Mechanics Mutual Protection, by its own account, "began to decline in 1848." "Strikes for Wages—Mechanics Association," *Scientific American* 5 (June 8, 1850): 301.

30. "Meeting of Land Reformers in New York—Important Action" [from *New York Tribune*], *Dollar Weekly Nonpareil*, Aug. 12, 1852; "Another Ticket and Platform," *NYDyTrib*, Aug. 4, 1852; "Meeting of the Independent Democrats at the Chinese Building," *NYDyTrib*, Aug. 7, 1852; "Land Reform," Aug. 11, 1852; "Land Reform Meeting at Military Hall, Bowery," *NYDyTrib*, Aug. 18, 1852, 7.

31. Schuyler Marshall, "The Free Democracy Convention of 1852," *Pennsylvania History* 22 (1955): 146–67; Charles B. Going, *David Wilmot, Free Soiler* (Gloucester: P. Smith, 1966); Joseph G. Rayback, *Free Soil, the Election of 1848* (Lexington: University Press of Kentucky, 1970); John F. Coleman, *The Disruption of the Pennsylvania Democracy, 1848–1860* (Harrisburg: Pennsylvania Historical and Museum Commission, 1975); Joel H. Silbey, *The Shrine of Party: Congressional Voting Behavior, 1841–1852* (Pittsburgh: University of Pittsburgh Press, 1967); "Free Democratic National Convention," *National Era*, Aug. 19, 1852, 2; Thomas H. McKee, *National Conventions and Platforms of All Political Parties, 1789–1900* (Baltimore: Friedenwald Co., 1900), 77; Zahler, *Eastern Workingmen*, 100, 100n. Other NRA associates at the Pennsylvania

state convention included William B. Thomas, William J. Mullen, and probably John Sheddon (given as "John Sheldon" of Philadelphia). "Free Soil State Convention at Pittsburgh" and "The National Free Soil Convention," *NYDyTrib*, Aug. 11, 1852, 5.

32. "Land Reform Meeting at Military Hall, Bowery," *NYDyTrib*, Aug. 18, 1852, 7; "City News," *New York Herald*, Aug. 19, 1852, 2. A subsequent local meeting also sent a memorial to the Senate. Either that of Aug. 12 or of Aug. 16, 1852, both in SEN32A-J2, box 150, folder 8/9/52–2/22/53, U.S. Senate, Ms Records, Legislative Records. The *National Era* offers glimpses of eastern land reformers in the Free Democratic campaign: "Meeting in Philadelphia," *National Era* 6 (July 15, 1852): 114, with Sheddon's spellbinding hour-and-a-half-long address at Chester and Dr. J. E. Snodgrass' tour of the Midwest, reported in "Pennsylvania" and an untitled letter, *National Era* 6 (Oct. 14, 1852): 165, 168.

33. Bovay quoted in Flower, *History of the Republican Party*, 151; Smith, *Liberty and Free Soil Parties*, 256–57. Since Zahler, *Eastern Workingmen*, 96, 96n, 100, 100n, cited sources that predated the meeting at which a final decision was scheduled, I think she was incorrect in stating that the movement formally endorsed Scott. The NRA seems to have played no independent role in the local election in which Jacob A. Westervelt won the mayoralty. Stokes, *Iconography of Manhattan Island*, 5: 1842. To a great extent, midwestern successes established the foundations for the transformation of national politics through what historian Lawrence Goodwyn's classic study of American populism called a "shadow movement." *Democratic Promise: the Populist Moment in America* (New York: Oxford University Press, 1976).

34. Proceedings in Townsend's "Slices of Wilmington," *JH1854*, 371–77; *National Reform Almanac for 1849*, 18; "Industrial Congress—Third Session," *NYDyTrib*, June 29, 1848; untitled publication of resolutions, *NEI*, June 29, 1848.

CHAPTER 9: THE REPUBLICAN REVOLUTION

1. See Commons et al., *History of Labour*, xxx; *Doc. Hist.*, 8: 336–43; Hoaglund, "Humanitarianism," in Commons et al., *History of Labour*, 609–10, 617–18.

2. Ingalls, *Reminiscences of an Octogenarian*, 53; "National Industrial Congress," *NYDyTrib*, June 15, 1850. See also "News from Oregon" [from *Western Expositor*], *SWmA*, Nov. 16, 1844; "From Oregon" [from *Peoria Register*], *YA*, Apr. 12, 1845. See also discussion of Oregon and "Freedom of the Public Land" [from *Seneca Falls Democrat*], *Randolph County Record*, Aug. 12, 1846; Johnson, "Rolling Stone Colony," 143–44. For Henry Waterman, see *Doc. Hist.*, 5: 144; Ms Rolls, Brotherhood of the Union; Bouton, *Life and Choice Writings of George Lippard*, 92; George Lippard, *The White Banner* [1851], 151; and William Rees, "An Agrarian Settlement Proposed," *WmA*, Aug. 10, 1844.

3. For a greater discussion of the context and significance of this development, see Mark A. Lause, "Progress Impoverished: The Origins of Henry George's Single Tax," *Historian* 52 (May 1990): 394–410. For Robinson, see *JH1854*, 134–36; "Charles Robinson, Yankee '49er: His Journey to California," *Kansas Historical Quarterly* 34 (Summer 1968): 179–88; Frank W. Blackmar, *Charles Robinson* (Topeka: Kansas State Historical Society, 1900); and Charles Robinson, *The Kansas Conflict* (New York: Harper and Bros., 1892).

4. On Sutherland, see also Louise Barry, *The Beginning of the West: Annals of the*

Kansas Gateway to the American West, 1540–1854 (Topeka: Kansas State Historical Society, 1972), 1006–7, 1124–25. Budlong letter, *Cincinnati Daily Nonpareil,* June 4, 1851, 1; "Nebraska Emmigration Association," *Cincinnati Daily Nonpareil,* Jan. 30, 1851, 1; "Emmigration to Nebraska," *Cincinnati Daily Nonpareil,* Feb. 1 (p. 2), 6 (p. 1), 17 (p. 2), 1851; Thomas Jefferson Sutherland, "A History of Land Reform in the U.S. Congress," *Cincinnati Daily Nonpareil,* Feb. 18, 1851, 1. Quoted here from "Wrongs of the Backwoodsmen," *Cincinnati Daily Nonpareil,* Feb. 7, 1851, 1, and "Nebraska Association," *Cincinnati Daily Nonpareil,* Mar. 21, 1851, 1; editorial, *Cincinnati Daily Nonpareil,* May 19, 1851, 2; *Cincinnati Daily Nonpareil,* June 25, 1851, 1. H. C. Bazley distributed *Young America* in the Choctaw reserve of the Indian Territory. Untitled notice, *YA,* Jan. 31, 1846. See also "The Missouri Compromise Meeting," *NYDyTrib,* Feb. 1, 1851, 5; "The People's Meeting," *NYDyTrib,* Feb. 18, 1851 4. For its proceedings, see "The Nebraska Fraud," in *NYDyTrib,* Feb. 20, 1854, 4.

5. Smith, *Liberty and Free Soil Parties,* 282, but see also 274, 280, 281. Ceresco, wrote Ingalls, had collapsed when "a craze for land speculation, became contagious in the sacred precincts of the association itself." Ingalls, *Reminiscences of an Octogenarian,* 53. See also Joseph Schafer, "Know-Nothingism in Wisconsin," *Wisconsin Magazine of History* 8 (Sept. 1924): 3–24; Frank L. Byrne, "Maine Law Versus Lager Beer: A Dilemma of Wisconsin's Young Republican Party," *Wisconsin Magazine of History* 52 (Winter 1958–59): 115–20; James L. Sellers, "Republicans and States Rights in Wisconsin," *Mississippi Valley Historical Review* 17 (Sept. 1930): 213–29; Alfons J. Beitzinger, "Federal Law Enforcement and the Booth Cases," *Marquette Law Review* 41 (Summer 1957): 7–32; and Joseph Schafer, "Stormy Days in Court—The Booth Case," *Wisconsin Magazine of History* 20 (Sept. 1936): 89–110.

6. Smith, *Liberty and Free Soil Parties,* 282; see also 274, 280, 281. Bovay quoted in Flower, *History of the Republican Party,* 147–48, 149–153; Hine, *Garrisonian Politics,* 8; See also Allan Nevins, *Ordeal of the Union,* 2 vols. (New York: Scribner's Sons, 1947), 2: 322–23; *NYDyTrib,* June 17, 1856, 4; Eric Foner, *Free Soil, Free Labor, Free Men: The Ideology of the Republican Party before the Civil War* (New York: Oxford University Press, 1970); Eric Foner, "Politics, Ideology, and the Origins of the American Civil War," in *A Nation Divided: Problems and Issues of the Civil War and Reconstruction,* ed. George M. Frederickson (Minneapolis: Burgess Publ., 1975), 15–34; David Brion Davis, *The Slave Power Conspiracy and the Paranoid Style* (Baton Rouge: Louisiana State University Press, 1969); William E. Gienapp, *The Origins of the Republican Party, 1852–1856* (New York: Oxford University Press, 1987); Hendrik Booraem V, *The Formation of the Republican Party in New York: Politics and Conscience in the Antebellum North* (New York: New York University Press, 1983); Roy F. Nichols, *The Disruption of American Democracy* (New York: Macmillan, 1948); Michael Holt, *The Political Crisis of the 1850s* (New York: Wiley, 1978); and Joel H. Silbey, *The Partisan Imperative: The Dynamics of American Politics before the Civil War* (New York: Oxford University Press, 1985).

7. "National Industrial Congress," *New York Daily Times,* June 8, 1854; "Industrial Congress," *New York Daily Times,* June 10, 1854; and article written by "A. W.," *New York Daily Times,* June 11, 1854; See also *Proceedings of the Ninth National Industrial Congress* (Philadelphia: Joseph P. Sailer, 1854).

8. "Fugitive Slave Law" [from *Boston Protective Union*], *Liberator,* Oct. 25, 1850, 170; Albert J. Von Frank, *The Trials of Anthony Burns: Freedom and Slavery in Em-*

erson's Boston (Cambridge, Mass.: Harvard University Press, 1998), 29, on Wright, and 93, 137, 279, 286, 293, on Cluer. See also Mandel, *Labor: Free and Slave,* 118–21, and Philip S. Foner and Shapiro, ed., *Northern Labor and Antislavery.*

9. Ms Rolls, Brotherhood of the Union; Gregory, "Land Limitation Movement," 89n, 92, 102–4; Booth in *Dictionary of Wisconsin Biography,* 42–43; Larry Gara, *Liberty Line,* 103, 113, 135–36; Richard N. Current, *The History of Wisconsin: Vol. II. The Civil War Era, 1848–1873* (Madison: State Historical Society of Wisconsin, 1976), 219, 220-22, 235, 260, 261, 272-73, 276, 277; Henry L. Conard, *History of Milwaukee, from its First Settlement to the Year 1895,* 2 vols. (Chicago: American Biographical Publ., 1895), 1: 89-90, 216–17, 231; and Mason, "Fugitive Slave Law in Wisconsin," 117–44. Wisconsin Public Television produced a short documentary on the rescue and its aftermath, *Stand the Storm,* 1998. While out of prison in 1859, Booth became involved with Caroline Cook, the fourteen-year-old daughter of a workman next door. *The Trial of Sherman M. Booth for Seduction: Evidence and Summing up in Counsel in the Case of the State versus S.M. Booth, for Seducing Caroline N. Cook* (Milwaukee: W. E. Tunis and Co., 1859). On the other hand, the messianic nationalism of the Brotherhood of the Union inspired the Virginian George Washington Leigh Beckley to found an expansionist "Knights of the Golden Circle" to impose "superior Anglo-American civilization" upon more of Mexico, Cuba, and Central America. See also Frank L. Klement, *Dark Lanterns: Secret Political Societies, Conspiracies, and Treason Trials in the Civil War* (Baton Rouge: Louisiana State University Press, 1984), 7–8, 8n, 9–14; and Harvey W. Felter, *History of the Eclectic Medical Institute Cincinnati, Ohio 1845–1902* (Cincinnati: Alumnal Association of the Eclectic Medical Institute, 1902), 41–42.

10. Bret E. Carroll, *Spiritualism in Antebellum America* (Bloomington: Indiana University Press, 1997), contains a solid overview and a good bibliography. The names of people in or around the NRA appear regularly in the *Banner of Light,* and they authored the following titles: Orestes A. Brownson, *The Spirit-Rapper; an Autobiography* (Boston: Little, Brown, 1856), a hostile account by a repentant radical; Isaac Rehn, "Has Spiritualism a Basis," *Banner of Light,* Dec. 16, 1865; Joshua K. Ingalls, "The Idea of Immortality: Its Development and Progress," *Univercoelum* 1 (Jan. 22, 1848): 90–91; Joshua K. Ingalls, "The Divine Gift, Impartial and Immutible," *Univercoelum* 1 (Mar. 4, 1848): 209–12; Eliab W. Capron and Henry D. Barron, *Singular Revelations: Explanation and History of the Mysterious Communion with Spirits . . .* 2d ed. (Auburn: Finn and Rockwell, 1850); Eliab W. Capron, *Modern Spiritualism: Its Facts and Fanaticisms, Its Consistencies and Contradictions . . .* (Boston: B. Marsh, 1855); and William T. Coggeshall, *The Signs of the Times: Comprising a History of the Spirit-Rappings in Cincinnati and Other Places . . .* (Cincinnati: By the author, 1851). Andreas B. Smolnikar sought admission to an Industrial Congress with credentials signed by spirits. Jon Alexander and David Williams, "Andreas Bernardus Smolnikar: American Catholic Apostate and Millennial Prophet," *American Benedictine Review* 35 (March 1984): 50–63.

11. The principal primary source on Modern Times is Wunderlich, *Low Living and High Thinking at Modern Times,* but see also Reichert, *Partisans of Freedom,* 285, 286–87, 289; Ingalls, *Reminiscences of an Octogenarian,* 42–43, 44.

12. "Secret Society, or League," *New York Daily Times,* Aug. 17, 1855, Sept. 8, 1855, and October 10, 17–24, 1855; the first article contained a long and detailed history.

See also Ingalls, *Reminiscences of an Octogenarian*, 153, 156, 157–58, 159; *Free Love in America: A Documentary History*, ed. Taylor Stoehr (New York: AMS Press, 1979), 6, 23, 319–21; Warren Chase, "The Free Love Theory," *NYDyTrib*, Sept. 27, 1855. The police raid of "The Club" netted only its pro tem host, Brisbane, and three others. Henry Clapp defended the right of the group to meet. Their trial ended in acquittal, but the organization collapsed. To some extent, this clash likely fueled the conflict that erupted over the next two years between the Republican state and Democratic city, resulting in a Republican "Metropolitan Police" force functioning alongside the Democratic "Municipal Police."

13. Albert Parry, *Garrets and Pretenders: A History of Bohemianism in America* (New York: Covici, Friede, 1933). For Clapp's earlier arrest in Lynn, see "Land of the Free and Home of the Brave," *VoI*, Apr. 10, 1846.

14. Kenneth Silverman, *Edgar Allen Poe: Mournful and Never-ending Remembrance* (New York: Harper Collins, 1991); Alan Gribben, *Mark Twain's Library: A Reconstruction,* 2 vols. (Boston: G. K. Hall and Co., 1980), 151, 157, 274, 412, 524; Philip S. Foner, *Mark Twain: Social Critic,* 2d ed. (New York: International Publishers, 1966), 155; Ron Powers, *Dangerous Waters: A Biography of the Boy Who Became Mark Twain* (New York: Basic Books, 1993), 193–95. The *Sydney Standard* later published an article in favor of George's Single Tax purportedly by Clemens, reprinted in the United States as *The Story of Archimedes* (New York: Single Tax Publishing Co., [1931]). Roy Morris, *Ambrose Bierce: Alone in Bad Company* (New York: Crown Publishers, 1995); Ambrose Bierce, *Devil's Dictionary,* (New York: World, 1911).

15. Witold Rybczynski, *A Clearing in the Distance: Frederick Law Olmsted and America in the Nineteenth Century* (New York: Scribner, 1999); Rosenzwieg and Blackmar, *People and the Park,* 112, 116.

16. Charles Commerford's obituary notice, *New York Times,* Feb. 7, 1920, 11. The underpaid player drawn into the first major betting scandal to afflict the game was Thomas Devyr, likely the son of the land reformer; the younger Thomas played as a shortstop for the Mutuals of Williamsburg. The census indicates a James and Jeremiah in the state as well as Thomas A. Devyr in Brooklyn; both of the former were upstate. Warren Goldstein, *Playing for Keeps: A History of Early Baseball* (Ithaca, N.Y.: Cornell University Press, 1989), 90–92; Dean A. Sullivan, ed., *Early Innings: A Documentary History of Baseball, 1825–1908* (Lincoln: University of Nebraska Press, 1995), 49–53, 80, 81.

17. Devyr, *Odd Book,* 115; Ingalls, *Reminiscences of an Octogenarian,* 34. See also P5, 425–27, and 427–29; Q5, 49–51, 508–9; Y5, 15–17, 187–88. Minutes of Orphans Court, Book O, 272, Hall of Records, Monmouth County, Freehold, N.J. Debt- ridden, Evans's widow, Mary, his second wife, sold the farm piecemeal. Will Book X6 (Feb. 25, 28, 1858), 250–51, 251–52; Will Book 160 (Sept. 3, 1861), 276–77; Letters of Administration Book B (Feb. 25, 1856), 268, and transactions of April, Sept., and Dec. 1856; April, Sept., and Dec. 1858, and April 1859 in Minutes of Orphans Court, Book O, 142, 199–200, 201, 204, 240, 269–70, 270, 272, 308, and Book P, 140, 148, 177, 219–20. On Evans's death, see the untitled notice, *NYDyTrib,* Feb. 7, 1856, 7; Masquerier, *Sociology,* 99. For movement leadership, see Ingalls, *Reminiscences of an Octogenarian,* 47.

18. "The Saratoga Convention," *NYDyTrib,* Aug. 17, 1854, 4; "Anti-Nebraska Meeting at Saratoga," *NYDyTrib,* Aug. 18, 1854; "Anti-Nebraska Convention at Auburn,"

NYDyTrib, Sept. 27, 1854, 4–5. For the seceding group, see *NYDyTrib,* Sept. 27, 28, 1854. For the Syracuse convention at which Paterson of the Parkville *Industrial Luminary* spoke on the first day, see *NYDyTrib,* Sept. 27, 28, 1855, and editorial, "Republicanism Inaugurated," Sept. 28, 1855. See also "Free-Soil Republican Club," and "Republican Demonstration," *NYDyTrib,* Sept. 14, 1855, 5. For Tobbitt and Freeman Hunt, see "Republican Organization in Brooklyn," *NYDyTrib,* Oct. 5, 1855, 5. For Watson G. Haynes and others associated with land reform, see "Republican Mass Meeting [in Brooklyn]," *NYDyTrib,* Nov. 3, 1855; "Free-Soil Republican Club," *NYDyTrib,* Sept. 14, 1855; "Central Republican Convention," *NYDyTrib,* Oct. 4, 1855; and "Fifth Ward Republicans," *NYDyTrib,* Oct. 9, 1855; the Sumner "Indignation Meeting in New York," *NYDyTrib,* May 31, 1856; and "Free Speech in Brooklyn," *NYDyTrib,* June 2, 1856.

19. Van Amringe, "National Reform—No. 1," *AF,* Jan. 19, 1848; "To the Workingmen of the World," *Friend of the People,* Jan. 18, 1851, 48; "To the World's Industrial Congress," *Friend of the People,* Feb. 15, 1851, 80; "Proposed Industrial Congress: European and American," *Friend of the People,* Apr. 5, 1851, 136; Notices of Day in the New York City Industrial Congress, *NYDyTrib,* Dec. 12, 20, 1850, and Feb. 11, 14, 1851. Also on Day, see *Quaker City Weekly,* Nov. 24, 1849; *Doc. Hist.,* 7: 287, 288, 303; and Day's obituary, *New York Times,* June 9, 1906. Arthur Lehning, "The International Association, 1855–1859," in his *From Buonarroti to Bakunin: Studies in International Socialism* (Leiden: E. J. Brill, 1970), notes the later activities of the European affiliates with regard to their American branches, 198–201, although Americans were most likely involved almost from their origins. See also "Universal Democratic Republicans," *NYDyTrib,* Mar. 7, 1855, 7.

20. "National Industrial Congress," *NYDyTrib,* June 8, 1855, 5; Sorge, *Labor Movement in the United States,* 91, 95, 96; Wittke, *Utopian Communist,* 144, 177, 215. For earlier Shaker and perfectionist Christian presence, see Fogarty, *Dictionary of American Communal and Utopian History,* 178, 182. See also "Young America" [from *Cleveland Universalist*], *YA,* July 5, 1845, and *Jubilee,* 16; "The Homestead" [from *Cleveland American*], *VoI,* May 21, 1847; "National Industrial Congress," *NYDyTrib,* June 8, 1855, 5, col. 1; "National Industrial Congress" and "The Industrial Congress," *New York Daily Times,* June 8, 9, 1855, 1; "Industrial Congress," *Cleveland Daily Plain Dealer,* June 4, 1844; and untitled notice *Cleveland Daily Plain Dealer,* June 6, 1855, 3. The most complete accounts are "National Industrial Congress," *Cleveland Morning Leader,* June 8, 1855, and untitled article, *Cleveland Morning Leader,* June 9, 1855, 3. See also notice in *Cleveland Plain Dealer,* June 1, 1855, 3, col. 4. The short notice in the *Peoria Daily Democratic Press,* June 9, 1855, described the Congress as then adjourning *sine die,* but the *Morning Leader* account says it simply adjourned until 10 A.M. the next day.

21. "Democratic Glorification," *NYDyTrib,* Nov. 11, 1854. See also "Tammany Union and Harmony Demonstration," *NYDyTrib,* Mar. 8, 1855; Bridges, *City in the Republic,* 61n, 116, 117n63, 117n64; *Doc. Hist.,* 8: 27, 287, 288, 301; and "Second Mass Meeting of the American Democracy," *NYDyTrib,* Sept. 18, 1855, 5. For Williamsburg, see Devyr, *Odd Book,* 66–69, 101–2; "A Circular," *NYDyTrib,* Mar. 4, 1856; "Voice of the Radical Democracy of New York," *NYDyTrib,* May 19, 1856; and local reformers A. S. Diven and Benjamin Welch Jr. at Democratic-Republican convention, *NYDyTrib,* July 19, 1856.

22. "To the People of the United States," *NYDyTrib*, June 25, 1856, 5, col. 2; Ingalls, *Reminiscences of an Octogenarian*, 47, and New York City directories. Other signatories were J. C. R. Pooler and T. D. Curtis, the poet. The "National Radical Abolition Convention" preceded that of the Republicans by a day, *NYDyTrib*, May 29, 1856. See also "Radical Abolition State Convention," *NYDyTrib*, Sept. 19, 1856, and "Republican State Convention," *NYDyTrib*, May 29, 1856, involving John Keyser, A. Oakley Hall, John S. Gould, George W. Goff, Samuel P. Allen, Robert Ennis, William Irvine, and George W. Patterson. Keyser, Gould, Goff, Roswell Hart, and Hiram Barry were among the delegates to attend the Republican National Convention, and Thaddeus Hyatt and Porter G. Sherman were among the alternates. "Gerrit Smith, Again," *NYDyTrib*, May 30, 1856; "A Second Letter from Mr. Geritt Smith," *NYDyTrib*, Aug. 17, 1855.

23. "National Land Industrial Congress," *New York Daily Times*, June 7, 1856, 8, col. 1.

24. On Sumner, see "Indignation Meeting in New York." *New York Daily Times*, May 31, 1856. For S. E. Church, see "Free Speech in Brooklyn," *New York Daily Times*, June 2, 1856; Ingalls, *Reminiscences of an Octogenarian*, 34. See also "Great Convention at Pittsburgh," *NYDyTrib*, Sept. 18, 1856, with notices on that campaign through succeeding issues. For Greeley's request, see Devyr, *Odd Book*, 107. California Agrarians found Fremont's declarations of sympathy for the movement less credible.

25. On Vermont, Massachusetts, and Pennsylvania, see Zahler, *Eastern Workingmen*, 83n, 101; James L. Huston, *The Panic of 1857 and the Coming of the Civil War* (Baton Rouge: Louisiana State University, 1987). Wade quoted in William K. Wyant, *Westward in Eden: The Public Lands and the Conservation Movement* (Berkeley: University of California Press, 1982), 60.

26. Ingalls, *Reminiscences of an Octogenarian*, 35. Meetings, including those held in German, were announced in the *Gerrit Smith Banner*, Oct. 18, 1858. For Commerford's 1859 campaign (with references to a Francis "B." Smith), see *NYDyTrib*, Oct. 18, 1859, and Nov. 9, 1859, with notices of "Peoples Union Campaign" in the Seventh, Thirteenth, Fourteenth, and Seventeenth wards, Oct. 26, 1859, the candidacy of E. M. Skidmore in the Seventh Ward mentioned in the same issue and that of Nov. 3, and Duganne's address to local Nativists, Oct. 7, 1859. Commerford to Johnson, Dec. 17, 1859, *The Papers of Andrew Johnson*, eds. LeRoy P. Graf and Ralph W. Haskins, 11 vols. (Knoxville, University of Tennessee Press, 1967–), 3: 356–58; Hine, *Lecture on Garrisonian Politics*, 20, 12.

27. In the local elections of Dec. 6, 1859, Wood defeated both William Havemeyer (Tammany) and George Opdyke (Republican). Stokes, *Iconography of Manhattan Island*, 5: 1882. When Tammany refused to back Wood, Opdyke won the election of Dec. 3, 1861. Stokes, *Iconography of Manhattan Island*, 5: 1900. *NYDyTrib*, Oct. 5 (p. 5), 11 (p. 7), 12 (p. 8), 17 (p. 8), 18 (p. 5), 20 (p. 5), 1860, and Nov. 2 (pp. 4, 8), 6 (p. 4), 1860. For Barr and Kerrigan, see *Biographical Directory of the American Congress, 1774–1971* (Washington, D.C.: Government Printing Office, 1971), 556, 1229; *The Tribune Almanac for 1860* [1859], 19, included in *The Tribune Almanac for the Years 1838 to 1868*. On Breckenridge's Democratic efforts to court Barr, see *NYDyTrib*, Sept. 29, 1860. These accounts described West, Price, Beeny, and John H. Keyser as active Republicans. For Jacobi's Republicanism, see *NYDyTrib*, Oct. 13, 1860. For Garibaldi Wide-Awakes, see *NYDyTrib*, Nov. 3, 1860, with results in *NYDyTrib*, Nov. 6, 1860, 4. On October 22, West opened another meeting in the Fourth Ward, while

Commerford, Price and Dr. Young held another on Pearl Street; a few days later, Commerford spoke to the Fourteenth Ward Republicans. *NYDyTrib*, Oct. 23 (p. 5), 26 (p. 5), 27 (p. 3), 1860. The municipal election of 1860 also led to a second term for Fernando Wood. Spann, *New Metropolis*, 429.

28. Grace Locke Scripps Dyche, "John Locke Scripps, Lincoln's Biographer (Springfield, Ill.: Phillips Brothers, 1925); Basler, Introduction to Scripps, *Life of Abraham Lincoln*, 16–17, 18–19. For a good indication of the complexity of Lincoln's views on land, see Gabor S. Boritt, *Lincoln and the Economics of the American Dream* (Memphis: Memphis State University Press, 1978), 26–28, 83–86, 133–35, 184, 318n4, 327n21, as well as 43, 47, 57–58, 227. When Tammany refused to back Wood, Opdyke won the election of Dec. 3, 1861. Stokes, *Iconography of Manhattan Island*, 5: 1900. Commerford to Johnson, *Papers of Andrew Johnson*, 3: 358. [T. A. Devyr], *The Homestead and the Union by a Land Reformer* (n.p.: 1860, n.p.); *Land for the Landless: the Hon. Galusha A. Grow's Speech, in the House, Feb. 29, 1860* (New York, 1860), which also appeared in German. *A Political Text-Book for 1860*, issued by the *New York Tribune*, included an entire section on "Land for the Landless: Action of Congress on the Public Lands," 182–93. See also Herman Schlueter, *Lincoln, Labor, and Slavery: A Chapter from the Social History of America* (New York: Socialist Literature Co., 1913).

29. The call published for "An Industrial Congress" in both *Herald of Progress*, Oct. 13, 1860, 5, and the *Banner of Light*, Nov. 10, 1860, 7, the former paper noting that it had met and summarizing its resolutions. See three items entitled "Industrial Congress," *Herald of Progress*, Nov. 17 (p.5), Dec. 1 (p. 4), 22 (p. 5), 1860. See also "Industrial Congress," *NYDyTrib*, Nov. 22, 1860, 6.

30. Van Amringe, "National Reform—No. 9," *AF*, Mar. 22, 1848; other expectations quoted in *VoI*, October 16, 1846.

CONCLUSION

1. On Haddock, see "Nomination Meeting," *WmA*, July 13, 1844. Haddock regularly mentioned thereafter in both *WmA* and *YA*, particularly the discussion over the "Circular to the Trades," *WmA*, Mar. 1, 1845, but see also *NYDyTrib*, June 4, 1851; Ingalls, *Reminiscences of an Octogenarian*, 35, 37–38; Masquerier, *Sociology*, 126; Haddock, *A Reminiscence: The Prairies of Iowa and other Notes* (Iowa City, Iowa: Printed for the author, 1901); and *The War of the Rebellion: A Compendium of the Official Records of the Union and Confederate Armies, Published under the Direction of the . . . Secretary of War*, 70 vols. (Washington: Government Printing Office, 1880–1901), series 1, vol. 34, pt. 4, 144 (hereafter cited as *OR*).

2. "Remarks of Mr. Commerford, *WmA*, Apr. 6, 1844.

3. Bovay quoted in "National Reform Association," *WmA*, Mar. 22, 1845; Root, *Analysis of Theology*, 72; Devyr, *Odd Book*, 248; and Prize quoted in "Free Homes for All," *NYDy Trib*, May 28, 1852. Not that long before, the *Tribune* had surveyed the American scene and made a tongue-in-cheek prophesy that the depressed economy would once more require a war. Editorial, *NYDyTrib*, July 16, 1858. Albany County NRA convention "Address," *Albany Patriot*, June 1, 1847, 120. This sense of decline appeared to some later commentators as implying faith in some golden age, starting with William J. Ghent, "The American Workman's 'Golden Age,'" *Forum*, 31 (Aug. 1901): 688–97.

4. [Henry Morford,] *Red-Tape and Pigeon-Hole Generals: As Seen from the Ranks during a Campaign in the Army of the Potomac, by a Citizen-Soldier* (New York: Carleton, 1864), 297.

5. Commerford signed the appeal of the Brotherhood of the Union to Andrew Johnson, July 22, 1861. *The Papers of Andrew Johnson*, 4: 493, 593; *Liberty-Union Songs*, 7th ed. (Brooklyn: Masquerier, 1866); Stephen J. W. Tabor to Masquerier, Lant Papers; Warren B. Chase, *The American Crisis; or, Trial and triumph of Democracy* (Boston: Bela Marsh, 1862); John H. Tobitt, *What I Heard in Europe during the "American Excitement"; Illustrating the difference between Government and People Abroad in Their Hostility and Good Wishes to the Perpetuity of the Great Republic* (New York: H. M. Tobitt, 1865); and Hiram W. Beckwith, *History of Vermillion County, Together with Historic Notes on the Northwest* (Chicago: H. H. Hill and Co., 1879), 361; on his son, see 396–97.

6. For Brown, see Ford and Ford, *History of Hamilton County*, 373; *Official Roster of the Soldiers of the State of Ohio in the War of the Rebellion, 1861–1866*, 10 vols. (Akron: Werner Co., 1886–95), 8: 671; "A Letter from an Old Reformer," *Freedom* 1 ([1891]); and *Remarks of Aaron V. Lane at the Funeral of Joel Brown, Mt. Healthy, Ohio, November 21, 1900* (n.p.: [1900]), 16–17.

7. For quotes in this and the following paragraph, see the Military Service Records of individuals discussed, National Archives, Washington, D.C. For Price, see *OR*, ser. 1, vol. 11, pt. 1, 483, and vol. 27, pt. 1, 192, 564; the petition by Captain Price and others, dated Dec. 30, 1861, in HR37A-G15.3-5, folder HR37AG15.3-G15.5, Records of the U.S. House of Representatives, Legislative Research Office, National Archives, Washington, D.C.; and Masquerier, *Sociology*, 126, and his "In Memoriam" to Price's memory, 165–67, 195; see also 167–75. William West went to Washington to retrieve the body; his letter to Wendell Phillips is noted by Timothy Messer-Kruse, *The Yankee International: Marxism and the American Reform Tradition, 1848–1876* (Chapel Hill: University of North Carolina Press, 1998), 28.

8. Phillip Shaw Paludan, "War Is the Health of the Party," in Robert F. Engs and Randall M. Miller, eds., *The Birth of the Grand Old Party: The Republicans' First Generation* (Philadelphia: University of Pennsylvania Press, 2002), 68–72. Haddock correspondence is in his Combined Military Service Records, National Archives, Washington, D.C.

9. Freda Postle Koch, *Colonel Coggeshall: The Man Who Saved Lincoln* (Columbus, Ohio: PoKo Press, 1985); *Dictionary of American Biography*, 11 vols. (New York: Scribner's, 1974), 4: 272–73. Among Coggeshall's works was *Lincoln Memoria* (Columbus: Ohio State Journal for the Benefit of the Ohio Soldiers' Monument Fund, 1865). For Stevenson, see Mark Lause, *The Civil War's Last Campaign : James B. Weaver, the Greenback-Labor Party and the Politics of Race and Section* (Lanham, Md.: University Press of America, 2001), 99–101. William A. Phillips, *Labor, Land, and Law: A Search for the Missing Wealth of the Working Poor* (New York, C. Scribner's Sons, 1886).

10. Hine, *Garrisonian Politics*, 8; "Land Reform" [from *Southport Telegraph*], *AF*, Apr. 12, 1848; and, Humboldt, "The Universal Brotherhood of Man," repr. *AF*, Apr. 12, June 20, 1848.

11. Masquerier, *Sociology*, 174; Devyr, *Odd Book*, 115.

12. On Barr, see Frank W. Blackmar, *The Life of Charles Robinson: the First State*

Governor of Kansas (Topeka, Ks.: Crane and Co., 1902), 232; Daniel W. Wilder, *Annals of Kansas, 1541–1885* (Topeka, Ks.: T. D. Thatcher, 1886), 214, 215–16, 230, 231, 316, 435–37, 522, 528–29, 530, 531, 532, 533. For the IWA, see Ingalls, *Reminiscences of an Octogenarian,* 47; *Revolution,* Oct. 28, 1859, 261; *New York Daily World,* Dec. 18, 1871, 1; and, generally, Messer-Kruse, *Yankee International.*

13. "Williamsburgh," *NYDyTrib,* May 28, 1852. Their presence is noted in the listings of activities and events on p. 8 of *Irish World,* Aug. 28, 1879; Sept. 3, 10, 18, 1879; Dec. 13, 1879; and May 29, 1880. Pink also wrote *The Angel of the Mental Orient* (London: William Reeves, 1895), discussed in Richard M. Bucke, *Cosmic Consciousness* (Philadelphia: Inness and Sons, 1901), 299–303. His nephew was J. William Lloyd, the anarchist, who wrote *Liberty* 3 (June 20, 1885): 5. See also Morris, "William Haller," 259–92; McDiarmid, *The Organization of Labor, Showing How to Acquire True Independence of Character* (Cincinnati: Times Office, 1863); *Cincinnati Daily Nonpareil,* Oct. 24, 1850, "Hamilton [County] Industrial Congress"; notice of his visit in the *Indianapolis Workingman's Map,* June 17, 1876, and his letter *Indianapolis Workingman's Map,* July 1, 1876; Guarneri, *Utopian Alternative,* 168, 308, 352. Each annual gathering of the ALRL is reported in the *Word.*

14. Solon Buck, *The Granger Movement: A Study of Agricultural Organization and Its Political, Economic, and Social Manifestations, 1870–1880* (Cambridge, Mass.: Harvard University Press, 1913); Charles M. Gardner, *The Grange—Friend of the Farmer* (Washington, 1949); and D. Sven Nordin, *Rich Harvest: A History of the Grange* (Jackson: University Press of Mississippi, 1974). On the Industrial Brotherhood, see "The Industrial Brotherhood" [from *St. Louis Democrat*], and "The Industrial Brotherhood," [Carthage, Mo.] *People's Press,* Feb. 26, 1874, 1, 2, 3. For the claim of Feb. 22 origins, see "Origin, Objects and Plan of the Industrial Brotherhood," July 16, 1874. For Robertson, see *WMA,* June 29, 1844.

15. *A General Report of the Industrial Union: From Its Commencement, Feb. 25, 1850, to the Present Time, April, 1853: With a Statistical Account of the Operations of the Tailoresses' Co-operative Store, under the Management of the Union: Also a Historic Lecture by John Mills* (Philadelphia: Printed by order of the Union, 1853), 11, 18; IWA Records, "Membership Rolls" in Philadelphia Section, International Workingmen's Association, Oct. 9, 1871–Aug. 18, 1873, Box 2, folder C, IWA Papers, which also includes the Sovereigns of Industry, Pioneer Council, No. 1, "List of Members, 1874–1877"; "Isaac Rehn's 'Everlasting' Images," <http://www.spirithistory.com/rehn.html>.

16. Edward N. Kellogg, *Labor and Other Capital* (New York: By the author, 1849), though there were many editions with different titles; Albert Brisbane, "The Modern Currency Problem through a Vista of Fifty Years," *Arena* 46 (Sept. 1893), 467–71; a digest from Redelia Brisbane, *Albert Brisbane: A Mental Biography* (Boston: Arena Publishing Co., 1893). For the 1876 centennial, see Lalla Malloy Brigham, *The Story of Council Grove on the Sante Fe Trail,* 2d. ed. ([Council Grove, Ks.]: Morris County Historical Society, 1921), 59. For the 1884 Greenback Labor convention, see Wilder, *Annals of Kansas,* 1076, and his letter to *John Swinton's Paper,* Oct. 31, 1886. See also Lause, *Civil War's Last Campaign.*

17. Keyser, *Next Step of Human Progress,* 50.

18. See Lause, "Progress Impoverished"; Theodore F. Watts, *The First Labor Day Parade, Tuesday, September 5, 1883* (Silver Springs, Md.: Phoenix Rising, 1983), 8, 71; Samuel Milliken, "Forerunners of Henry George," in *Single Tax Year Book (quin-*

quennial): *The Historical Principles and Application of the Single Tax Philosophy*, ed.
Joseph Dana Mills (New York: Single Tax Review Publishing Co., 1917); Joseph R.
Buchanan, "The Land and the People," *Herald of Truth* 2 (Sept. and October 1847),
169–81, 249–64, repr. as "Nationalization of the Land First Presented," *The Arena*
(Mar. 1891), 401–14; (Apr. 1891), 586–600. Lucius A. Hine regarded the single tax
as an "entirely impracticable" and "supremely absurd" variation on National Reform.
See his letter, "Land Reform—Statistics of Insanity," *Nation*, Dec. 16, 1888, 496–97.
See also William Hanson, *Introduction, Proceedings and Resolutions.submitted to
the Workingmen of the United States for their Thoughtful consideration* (Brooklyn:
189?), and his *The Fallacies in Henry George's "Progress and Poverty" Exposed* (New
York: Fowler and Wells, 1884); Martin, *Men against the State,* 255; "The American
Labor Reform League," *Word* 1 (June 1872), 1; and Hanson's association with the old
National Reformers noted in *Truth Seeker,* Nov. 1, 1874, and May 1, 1875. I could
not find evidence as to whether this was the British-born watchmaker associated with
the anarchists. Paul Avrich, *An American Anarchist: The Life of Voltairine de Cleyre*
(Princeton, N.J.: Princeton University Press, 1978), 97, 107–8. For Barr, see "United
Labor Ticket," *Chicago Daily Tribune,* Feb. 27, 1887, 1, and *Chicago Express,* July
11, 1885, 6. For his participation in the Knights' District Assembly's committee on
land reform, see *Irish World,* May 25, 1885, 7; *The Edwin Burgess Letters on Taxation. First published by "The Racine Advocate" . . . 1859–60* [With an introduction
by Hyland Raymond and William S. Buffham, and a portrait] (Racine, Wis.: W. S.
Buffham, [1912]). Young notes that these letters were reprinted in the *Standard* on
Aug. 5, 1891, and in *The Single Tax Yearbook,* 341–42. T. Thomas Fortune, *Black and
White: Land, Labor, and Politics in the South* (New York: Fords, Howard, and Hul-
bert, 1884); *Denver Labor Enquirer,* Feb. 26, 1887, 4; *Denver Labor Enquirer,* Mar.
9, 1887, 4; Edward B. Mittelman, "Chicago Labor in Politics, 1887–1896," *Journal of
Political Economy* 28 (May 1920), 407–27.

19. Masquerier, *Sociology,* 102. For Thomas Davis, see *NYDyTrib,* Aug. 2, 1852. For
Wood, *see DH,* 6: 43, 99; notice of third annual celebration of George Henry Evans's
birthday. *Truth Seeker,* Apr. 7, 1877, 110, with his later letter in *Liberty* 5 (Dec. 31,
1887): 1. Ira B. Davis's obituaries are in the *New York Daily World,* July 12, 1872, 5,
and the *New York Daily Herald,* July 15, 1872, which forced the adjournment of the
International meeting, IWA clippings. In general, consult Timothy Messer-Kruse's
Yankee International, which discusses the political continuity of land reform into the
emergence of the IWA and the modern political movement for socialism in the United
States. William Bailie, *Josiah Warren: the First American Anarchist* (Boston: Small,
Maynard and Co., 1906). For the death of Rowe, see *Liberty* 4 (July 17, 1886): 1; Mac-
Donald, *Fifty Years of Freethought,* 1: 411–12; Perkins, "Old Guard of Land Reform,"
John Swinton's Paper, Aug. 8, 1886; Smalley's letter in *John Swinton's Paper,* Oct. 31,
1886; Chase discussed in "A Veteran of the Cause," *The Standard,* Mar. 19, 1887, 3; and
Hine, "Land Reform—Statistics of Insanity," *Nation,* Dec. 16, 1888, 496–97. Thomas
Ainge Devyr remained aloof until after the police attack on the unemployed. He edited
the *Irish People* after the close of the Civil War and joined the editorial staff of the *Irish
World* in 1877. He also collected signatures for the National Limitation Association.
Biographical Dictionary of American Labor Leaders, 78–79; Devyr, *Odd Book,* 147–48;
Keyser, *Next Step,* 50. For Masquerier, see "Dedication of His Own Tomb," *New York
Daily Times,* June 6, 1887, 8, and on second anniversary of the initial dedication, "Pe-

culiar Dedication Services," *New York Daily Times,* June 11, 1888, 8; with obituaries in "Death of an Eccentric Old Man," *NYDyTrib,* Jan. 8, 1888, 2, and "Lewis Masquerier," *Truth Seeker* 15 (Jan. 21, 1888): 39. Charles Guinan (also Guinand) represented a tin and sheet iron worker in the New York City Industrial Congress and the State Industrial Legislature. *Doct. Hist.,* 8: 289, 301. Dr. Smith A. Boughton died November 14, 1888, and William Brisbane, who had gone west, died in Minnesota July 25, 1890. Christman, *Tin Horns,* 327. See also Christman, *Tin Horns,* for mentions of the later years of Devyr, 324, and Bovay, 325–26. S. H. Preston wrote Lant from Indianapolis, 1894. Lant Papers. Dr. Weeks clearly became associated with the movement after the war, but I found no reference to him in the earlier accounts; his work became popular among followers of Edward Bellamy and the Nationalist Clubs.

20. Letterhead of the NLRA of 1891, Lant Papers. For Beeny, see MacDonald, *Fifty Years of Freethought,* 2: 74, 75. Kilmer is listed in *Trow's New York City Directory* for 1888–89 and 1892–93, with his widow listed in the 1895–96 directory. See "Dr. Edward Newbery [sic]," *New York Daily Times,* Nov. 8, 1897, 5. Charles Burleigh, *The Genealogy and History of the Ingalls Family in America. Giving the descendants of Edmund Ingalls who settled at Lynn, Mass., in 1629* (Malden, Mass.: G. E. Dunbar, 1903), 149–50. For Hacker, see MacDonald, *Fifty Years of Freethought,* 2: 113. For Orvis, see Orvis, *History of the Orvis Family,* 62, and obituary, *Labor Leader,* May 8, 1897. For Keyser, see "John H. Keyser Dead," *New York Daily Times,* Aug. 23, 1899, 7. For Haddock, see William J. Haddock, *A Reminiscence: The Prairies of Iowa and other Notes* (Iowa City: For the author, 1901), including his essay, "The Passing of the Prairie," 60–69, and a photograph of him in his office. For Booth, see *Dictionary of Wisconsin Biography,* 135. For Hine, see "Veteran Editor and Writer on Economics," *Cincinnati Daily Enquirer,* July 10, 1906, 9. See also Charles Commerford, *Labor and Capital: A Review of the Labor Question,* No. 2 (Waterbury, Conn.: 1874); Joseph Anderson, *The Town and City of Waterbury, Connecticut,* 3 vols. (New Haven: The Price and Lee Co., 1896), 2: 170, 508, 3: 966, 1126, 1160; and "Charles C. Comerford [sic]," *New York Daily Times,* Feb. 7, 1920, 11.

21. Evans in *YA,* Sept. 13, 1845; The bust project discussed in *Truth Seeker,* Oct. 21, 1876, and "Colossal Bust of Thomas Paine, the Author-Hero of the American Revolution" in Masquerier, *Sociology,* 208–211, with names on 211. For Damon Y. Kilgore, see "Carrie Burnham Kilgore" in Dorothy Thomas, *Notable American Women,* 2: 330, which erroneously gives the date as 1878, and Ken Fones-Wolf, *Trade Union Gospel: Christianity and Labor in Industrial Philadelphia, 1865–1915* (Philadelphia: Temple University Press, 1989), 72, which mistakenly overemphasizes Kilgore's Irish name rather than his evangelical Protestant and midwestern background. Other signatories included followers of Charles Fourier supportive of National Reform, such as Albert Brisbane, Parke Godwin, and Warren Chase; prominent freethinkers and spiritualists, such as Ernestine L. Rose, Ella E. Gibson, Horace Seaver, Robert G. Ingersoll, Benjamin F. Underwood, James Lick, D. R. Burt, and D. M. Bennett, as well as Henry Evans, the founder of American positivism; George J. Holyoake, the English cooperationist; Dr. E. P. Miller, the Greenback agitator; and Lucy Stone Blackwell, the abolitionist turned feminist.

22. Evans quoted in "National Reform Association," *SWmA,* Nov. 23, 1844; Masquerier, *Sociology,* 18. See also "Wanton Destruction of Birds," *WmA,* Feb. 1, 1845, and "The Rights of Animals" [from *Herald of Freedom*], *YA,* Nov. 8, 1845.

23. Ray Allen Billington, *Frederick Jackson Turner: Historian, Scholar, Teacher* (New York: Oxford University Press, 1973); Allan G. Bogue, *Frederick Jackson Turner: Strange Roads Going Down* (Norman: University of Oklahoma Press, 1998). For a realistic appraisal of what the Homestead Act did and did not achieve, see Shannon, "The Homestead Act and the Labor Surplus."

24. Elizur Wright, "Land Monopoly" [from *Boston Investigator*], *VoI*, Nov. 13, 1846. *Proc. of Seventh I.C.*, 7.

25. Lant to Labadie, Oct. 2, 1903, Labadie Collection.

26. Lause, *Civil War's Last Campaign*, 61, 77, 81–82, 172.

27. "Workingmen's Party," *Chicago Daily Tribune*, Feb. 17, 1878, 8; "The Wage Workers," *Chicago Daily Tribune*, Aug. 4, 1879, 8; "A 'Long Strike' for Short Hours," *The Socialist*, May 24, 1879, 1; *Arbeiter-Zeitung*, Sept. 16, 1879. Congressional Quarterly Association, *Guide to U.S. Elections* (Washington: Congressional Quarterly, 1974), listed Barr as the GLP candidate in the First Congressional District. See also Everett W. Macnair, *Edward Bellamy and the Nationalist Movement, 1889 to 1894* (Milwaukee: Fitzgerald Co., 1957), 121.

28. Ingalls, "Land Reform in 1848 and 1888," serialized in *Truth Seeker*, Apr. 28, 1888, and May 5, 1888, 258 and 278.

29. Ingalls to Labadie, Mar. 25, 1889, Labadie Collection; Masquerier, *Sociology*, 36. Ingalls remained "unwilling to bet my bottom dollar" any particular group or doctrine. Ingalls to Labadie, June 2, 1896, Labadie Collection.

APPENDIX A

1. *Cooperatives Come to America: The History of Protective Union Store Movement, 1845–1867* (Mount Vernon, Iowa: Hawkeye Record Press, 1941), 125–38. For the Mechanics' Mutual Protection, see the announcements in both *Scientific American* and the *Mechanic's Advocate*.

2. During these peak years, petitions to the U.S. Congress include nineteen lacking any geographic identification. Those to the U.S. Senate include petitions to the 31st Congress, filed Mar. 5, 18, 1850, and June 8, 13, 1850; Jan. 31, 1850, and Feb. 14, 1851; and to the 32nd Congress, May 20, [two] 21, [two] 26, 1852, June [two] 11, 21, 1852, July 29, 1852, and Feb. 2, 1853. NR petitions lacking geographic identification for the U.S. House of Representatives went to the 31st Congress, filed Feb. 4, and 14–17, 1851, and one to the 32nd Congress for the Western Farm and Village Association, May 24, 1852.

3. Fogarty, *Dictionary of American Communal and Utopian History*.

INDEX

MARK A. LAUSE is an associate professor of history at the University of Cincinnati. He is the author of *The Civil War's Last Campaign: James B. Weaver, the National Greenback-Labor Party, and the Politics of Race and Section* and *"Some Degree of Power": From Hired Hand to Union Craftsman in the Preindustrial American Printing Trades, 1778–1815*, as well as articles that have appeared in journals such as *Labor History* and the *Historian*. He is currently working in the Civil War period.

The University of Illinois Press
is a founding member of the
Association of American University Presses.

University of Illinois Press
1325 South Oak Street
Champaign, IL 61820-6903
www.press.uillinois.edu